A Great Grievanc⌐

A Great Grievance

Ecclesiastical Lay Patronage in Scotland until 1750

Laurence A. B. Whitley

WIPF & STOCK · Eugene, Oregon

A GREAT GRIEVANCE
Ecclesiastical Lay Patronage in Scotland until 1750

Wipf & Stock
An Imprint of Wipf and Stock Publishers
199 W. 8th Ave., Suite 3
Eugene, OR 97401
www.wipfandstock.com

ISBN 13: 978-1-61097-990-0
Manufactured in the U.S.A.

To Catherine, Edward and Hilary
who have brought me so much joy.

" . . . patronages, which had their rise in the most corrupt and latter times of Anti Christianism, have always been a great grievance to this Church, as the source and fountain of a corrupt ministry . . . "

To His Grace, His Majesty's High Commissioner and to the right Honourable the Estates of Parliament, the Humble Address of the Presbyterian ministers and Professors of the Church of Scotland. (Edinburgh: 1690)

Contents

Contents

FOREWORD

THIS BOOK, PEPPERED WITH perspicacity, represents a very welcome contribution by an engaged writer to the understanding of what was manifestly a chronic and debilitating problem in Scottish history and its church history of *longue durée*, namely, lay patronage of the Kirk. Underlying this was the basic issue of the Church's funding from medieval times onwards, and thus of the resources to pay its clergy and ministers. While something of a universal problem, this was a particularly contentious issue over those centuries in Scotland when church and state, Christianity and society, faith and nation formed a notional unity or were mutually interdependent as the indigenous expression of "Christendom." The wealthy, notably the aristocracy and landed gentry, and so the ruling classes, usually acted as benefactors and patrons of the Kirk, even if swathes of them were also often its chief plunderers and despoilers. The committed who contributed and who, after the Reformation especially, were well aware that the Church did not just belong to the clergy, naturally expected a considerable "say" in church affairs and ministerial appointments in particular. Yet in a context where there were theological sensitivities about the freedom, autonomy, independence and authority of the Church, be it in the name of hierarchy, presbytery, or Christ, the recipe for tensions and conflicts was endemic and potent. The acuteness of this politicized problem for the infrastructure of Scottish Church, Catholic or Reformed, is well known. It seems to deface much of its history, bearing in mind that economic exigencies in one of Western Europe's poorer nations often exacerbated things.

Laurence Whitley's particular focus in this book is on the religious, political, and church settlements from 1688 to 1712 and their aftermath in the presbyterian Church of Scotland throughout the first half of the eighteenth century. Despite this era's crucial importance for the issue, it has surpisingly not been so intensively studied as many previous and subsequent periods. This enhances the value of this study, which will act as a bridge in treatments of the topic and serve as a reference work for many details of patronage and patrons in that era and before. As one of the diminishing number of contemporary scholar-ministers in the modern Scottish Kirk, and as someone of recognized theological, historical, and literary skills, Dr. Whitley is to be lauded for bringing this research, which embodies some years of arduous academic research, to fruition and to light. The endurance that enabled its completion will have the reward of providing a durable tool and asset for future researchers and others.

W. IAN P. HAZLETT
EMERITUS PROFESSOR OF ECCLESIASTICAL History
UNIVERSITY OF GLASGOW

Preface

Scottish Presbyterianism as a form of church government evolved out of the Reformation of 1560, and was based on a hierarchy of courts. At parish level, the elders met in what was called the kirk session, and their meetings were chaired by the minister, who was termed the court's moderator. Each session in a particular area sent representatives to the superior court, which was known as the presbytery. Superior to the presbytery was the provincial synod, which was in turn answerable to the General Assembly, which met once a year and was the final court of appeal. More on how the system worked in practice will be seen from the book which follows.

In the meantime, the glossary provided below will explain the political and ecclesiastical terms and labels that will occur most.

Advowson—the right of presenting to a benefice, especially in England

Argathelians—members and supporters of the house of Argyll

benefice—an office involving certain duties, for whose discharge revenues are provided

collation—institution to a benefice; the term can be used exclusively to describe institution to a living where the bishop is himself the patron. It is here applied, however, to episcopal institution in general

edict—a legally authoritative public intimation (eg., of a vacancy)

Erastianism—deriving from the Swiss theologian Thomas Erastus (1524–83), the doctrine that the State has the right to legislate in ecclesiastical matters on behalf of its national Church.

extract—a part taken from the minutes of a court by the authorised official

General Assembly Commission—a body specially commissioned at the end of each Assembly to meet (usually four times) and act in its name until the following Assembly. Originally elected without reference to the membership of Assembly, from 1705, presbyteries were to be proportionally represented on it; from 1719, only Assembly commissioners were to be included as members; from 1736, the proportion between ministers and elders was to be the same as for the Assembly. The Commission was properly only empowered to conduct such business as the Assembly had given it authority to handle, but where such a line could be drawn was a subject of intense controversy.

heads of families—the representatives of the ordinary parishioners

heritors—the owners of heritable property in a parish

High Presbyterian—pertaining to the stricter traditions of Covenanting Presbyterianism

horning, letters of—a warrant used to cite a defender to appear or pay a debt

jus devolutum—a right devolved on a party because of its not having been exercised within the appointed time by those having priority

libel—the formal indictment by which a minister or probationer is charged with misconduct or heresy

Lord High Commissioner—the Crown's official representative at meetings of Assembly

Marrowmen—evangelicals, like Thomas Boston, who approved of the English Puritan book, *The Marrow of Modern Divinity,* published by Edward Fisher of Oxford in 1646.

moderate men—pro-establishment, pro-learning and pro-moderation churchmen who eschewed what they regarded as the vulgar and disruptive tendencies of the evangelicals

moderating a call—the Presbytery's representative convenes a meeting of the parish's electors and attempts to guide them into centring harmoniously upon a candidate. If he is successful, a call is signed by the electors. He then attests it and submits it to Presbytery for concurrence

patrimony—the estates belonging to the Church and their revenues

planting a church—filling a vacancy

Popular Party (also, wild, narrow, zealous, warm, hot men)—the mostly evangelical, anti-prelatic, anti-patronage wing of the Church.

Praying Societies—groups of devout evangelicals, originating in the mid-Seventeenth century, which met, usually outside the compass of the Established Church, for prayer and Bible study.

prebends—pensions granted to canons or chapter members

probationer (also, expectant, preacher, entrant)—a candidate for the ministry after receiving his licence.

pro hac vice—for this turn or occasion

qualified according to law—having taken the appropriate Oaths

rabbling—mobbing of a clergyman, either evicting him from his charge or resisting his admission

Reduction—in civil law the annulling of a sentence or deed

serving an edict—proclaiming it in the appointed manner, time and place

simony—the buying or selling of ecclesiastical preferments, benefices or emoluments [see Acts, 8, vv.18–19]

simoniacal paction—where a candidate forms an mercenary agreement with another in order to gain an ecclesiastical preferment

sist—where an appeal to a higher court suspends the operation of the lower court's sentence

spiritualities— the fruits, rents, revenues and offerings of a benefice, as well as the manse and glebe. The *temporality* referred to the land and the profit pertaining to its jurisdiction

Squadrone—known before the Union as the New Party; earned nickname of *Squadrone Volante* through avoidance of permanent alliances. Family ties were strong between the Montrose, Tweeddale, Rothes, Haddington, Hopetoun, Findlater, Dundas, and Roxburghe families. Later associated with English opponents of Walpole, known as the Patriots.

tack—a lease of land or of a benefice

tanquam jure devoluto—as by devolved right

teinds—or tithes: the tenth part of the fruits and profits of a parish, to be paid to its minister

temporality ... the land and the profit pertaining to the jurisdiction of a benefice

Thirds of benefices—an arrangement of 1561 whereby the Crown and the reformed ministry were to share a third of the revenues of all ecclesiastical benefices

transportation (or translation)—the loosing of a minister's relation to one charge and the making up of it to another. The vacant charge prosecutes its call before the Presbytery of the minister it seeks, giving in reasons to show that the move would be for the greater good of the Church. The filled parish is invited to submit answers, and the Presbytery judges accordingly.

trials for licence—after completing his studies, a candidate for the ministry is "tried" by his presbytery, and if deemed suitable, issued with a licence to preach.

trials for ordination—similar to above, and conducted by the Presbytery within whose bounds his future parish lies.

#—when this occurs after a surname, it indicates that a biographical note may be found at Appendix VIII

Acknowledgments

I am most grateful to those who at various times have been of great help and guidance. Most of all, I must thank the late Dr. Eric Stevenson of Edinburgh University, the late Bishop of Portsmouth, Dr. Kenneth Stevenson, Emeritus Professor James Cameron, University of St. Andrews, Dr. Deryck Lovegrove, formerly Lecturer, University of St. Andrews, and Emeritus Professor Ian Hazlett, University of Glasgow.

As well as being indebted to my family for their patience, heartfelt thanks must go to the congregations of Busby, Glasgow, and Montrose Old and St. Andrew's, for their loyalty, affection and kindness. To be their minister was an inexpressible privilege. Although only a short time at Glasgow Cathedral, I would also thank the congregation for their kind welcome.

ABBREVIATIONS

'15	the Jacobite Rising of 1715
'45	The Jacobite Rising of 1745
APS	*Acts of the Parliament of Scotland*
AUP	Aberdeen University Press
BL	British Library
DSCHT	*Dictionary of Scottish History and Theology*
EU	Edinburgh University
EUP	Edinburgh University Press
FES	Fasti Ecclesiae Scoticanae
GA	General Assembly
GAC	General Assembly Commission
GU	Glasgow University
HMC	Historic Manuscripts Commission
LA	Lord Advocate
LHC	Lord High Commissioner
LUP	London University Press
NLS	National Library of Scotland
n.d.	.no date of publication
n.p.	no place of publication
ODNB	*Oxford Dictionary of National Biography*
OUP	Oxford University Press
RSCHS	*Records of the Scottish Church History Society*
SAP	Scottish Academic Press
SAPL	Select Anti-Patronage Library
StAP	St. Andrew Press
SHR	*Scottish Historical Review*
SHS	Scottish History Society

Abbreviations

SRO   Scottish Record Office*

WRH   West Register House

* from 1 April 2011 this became The National Records of Scotland (NRS)

Introduction

ECCLESIASTICAL LAY PATRONAGE IS a system, dating back to the early middle ages, whereby a benefice without an incumbent is supplied with a replacement, a benefice being a church office involving duties for whose discharge, property (sometimes called the temporalities) and income (sometimes called the spiritualities) are provided. Where the patronage system still operates, as in the Church of England, the church's patron, be it a private individual, college, trust, local council, bishop, dean and chapter, or the Crown, has the right, whenever there is a vacancy, to choose who should be the one to fill it. The patron's preferred candidate is intimated to the church authorities, and in England this is the bishop, in the form of a presentation to the charge. If the authorities are satisfied that certain criteria concerning the presentee have been met, he/she is then installed as the legal incumbent.

Although the historic practice remains commonplace within the Church of England, that the right of patronage (*jus patronatus*) continued to exist within the Church of Scotland after the Reformation, especially after the emergence of its presbyterian structure, has sometimes caused surprise. This is despite the fact that lay patronage was the reformed Church of Scotland's official system for filling, or "planting" vacancies, for by far the greater part of its history after 1560, and thus in general continuity with pre-Reformation practice. On occasion, the practice did fall into disuse, and twice it was formally abolished by Parliament, but its absences were never of long duration. Only as recently as 1874 did it disappear for what would seem to be the final time.[1]

---

1. Church Patronage (Scotland) Act 1874, c.82. The key factor in finalising *this* abolition was that (unlike before) patrons were to be bought out whether they wished to sell their right of presenting or not. Even then, all private patrons had to apply for the money (one year's stipend) by 30 June 1875, or lose the right to it forever. Of the 626 private patrons, 242 made claims totalling £59,160. Those, like the crown, who held the other 373 rights of patronage, were not compensated. see Cormack, Alexander A., *Teinds and agriculture, an historical survey.* (Oxford: 1930), 187.

When in 1712 it was restored, after a short suspension, for its last appearance in Scotland, the disruptive effects were deep and prolonged. Quite apart from the changes brought to the character of the Church's courts in their conduct of business, public perception of, and therefore loyalty to, the established church altered. Schism became not only an option, but even desirable for some. By the end of the nineteenth century, there was, as a consequence of the patronage issue, scarcely a community where the parish church did not find itself in competition with at least one other Christian alternative, usually presbyterian. In short, patronage was the cause of some of the bitterest divisions within modern, Scottish society, and as a result, the Patronage Act of 1712 swiftly came to be demonised as one of Scottish history's great deeds of mischief and betrayal. By the middle of the nineteenth century, no language was considered too melodramatic in its condemnation: "Whether the hand of the misguided Sovereign [Queen Anne] shook when affixing the sign manual, has not been recorded; but certainly at that moment, she put her hand to a deed by which her right to reign was virtually rescinded, the Revolution Settlement overturned, and the Treaty of Union repealed."[2]

To read from the Disruption[3] era, some of the indignant speeches, pamphlets and books concerning "This infamous Bill"[4] it might be assumed that in its passing, all the Kirk's enemies had indeed combined to violate "the deep–seated, ineradicable feelings of the people of Scotland"[5] and that those feelings had, by contrast, been triumphantly expressed twenty-two years earlier, when patronage had been abolished. When it is considered that within the short time-span of 1688–1715, Scotland experienced four different sovereigns, the constitutional upheaval of the Revolution Settlement, a parliamentary union, an attempted invasion and a rebellion, then it can be seen that the removal and restoration of patronage took place against a complicated and unsettled religious and political backdrop.

---

2. W. M. Hetherington, *History of the Church of Scotland*, 7th. Edn. (Edinburgh: 1848), 601.

3. The Disruption was the name given to the moment when in 1843, resistance to the principle of lay patronage climaxed, and 474 out of 1203 ministers of the Kirk, while still mostly adhering to the concept of establishment, seceded to form the Free Church of Scotland.

4. G. N. M. Collins, *The Heritage of our Fathers* (Edinburgh: Knox Press, 1974), 40.

5. *Patronage, Presbyterian Union and Home Work of the Church of Scotland: A Chronicle of the General Assembly of 1870* (Edinburgh: W. Blackwood, 1870). Speech by Dr Smith of Leith, 163.

In the following account of how, after the Glorious Revolution of 1688, lay patronage in Scotland was abolished, restored and exercised, five traditionally-held beliefs will be critically re-examined. These are, first, the doctrine that patronage was abolished in 1690 simply because it was the will of the majority of Scottish churchmen; secondly, the much–repeated claim that the 1712 Act was an infringement of the Treaty of Union; thirdly, the tradition that patrons shied away from making presentations within the first twenty years after the Act; fourthly, the assumption that it was possible for a popular franchise to achieve acceptance within the established church, despite the admission of heritors (owners of heritable property) into the process of minister selection in 1690, and lastly, the belief that it is possible to speak of "the Church" making autonomous decisions at its General Assembly, or Assembly Commission, as if such deliberations were free from secular influence and political manipulation.

As will be gathered, the chief intention of what follows is to consider the period between 1690 and 1750, however, by way of introduction, and to demonstrate how lay patronage was historically as much embedded in Scottish life as elsewhere in Europe, the book will begin by giving a brief sketch of the medieval background. It will then follow an approximately chronological pattern, highlighting what might be considered landmarks in the way attitudes towards patronage were affected by the course of Scotland's history.

In each chapter, various key questions will be addressed, as outlined below:

Chapter One

What were the origins of lay patronage?

What, if any, were its Scottish characteristics?

Why was it not abolished at the Reformation?

Chapter Two

How did the early seventeenth century strengthen the place of lay patronage in Scottish society?

Why did the National Covenant revolutionary movement of 1637–9 not sweep it away?

Chapter Three

What conclusions did the Westminster Assembly arrive at regarding presentations?

How did the 1649 abolition of patronage come about?

What system did the Kirk favour as a replacement for presentations?

Chapter Four

How important an issue was patronage in the Restoration period?

How did abolition come about in 1690?

Chapter Five

What was the thinking behind the provisions of the 1690 Act?

What were their defects?

What was meant by a "call"?

Chapter Six

What was the patrons' reaction to the Act?

What contributed to controversy during the 1690–1712 period?

Chapter Seven

Was the 1712 Act a violation of the Treaty of Union?

How did the 1712 Act become law?

Chapter Eight

What were the effects of the Toleration Act?

Did patrons initially hold back from making presentations after the 1712 Act?

Why did the Kirk not resist presentations more strongly?

Chapter Nine

How was the position of the Kirk affected by the `15 Rising?

How and when did the issue of popular election grow to importance?

How was it possible to influence the decisions of the Kirk's superior courts?

Chapter Ten

How did politics affect church settlements?

Did the legislation of 1719 provide a means of nullifying the issue of presentations?

What was it that inflamed so much anger in the 1720s?

Chapter Eleven

What led to the Secession of 1733?

Chapter Twelve

How did the supremely powerful Earl of Ilay and his chief agent, Lord Milton, appear to lose control in 1734–6?

How did they regain it?

How did they then lose office?

What was the English experience of lay patronage?

Chapter Thirteen

How did patronage affect vacancy-filling in disaffected areas like Angus?

Having assumed power, how did the vacancy-filling policy of Scotch Secretary Tweeddale differ from that of Ilay?

Chapter Fourteen

Why was the filling of Edinburgh churches the perennial cause of
controversy?

Chapter Fifteen

After the fall of Tweeddale, did the Argathelian regime continue as before?
Was there a change in the Kirk's response to patronage?

Conclusion

RELIGIOUS ISSUES IN SCOTLAND have frequently been the cause of strong emotions. What is perhaps surprising, however, is that, of all the impassioned controversies since the Reformation, the most enduring concerned something as seemingly unexceptionable as the admission of approved candidates to parish churches. Disturbance, intimidation and even violence repeatedly accompanied this event from early in the eighteenth century until 1843, when the national church experienced its final and most spectacular split as a result of the accumulated bitterness. Clearly then, it was an issue which stirred up intense feelings, yet what prompted them? How could mere concern over the identity of a parochial appointee give rise to so much anger, litigation and expense?

As will be seen, a wide variety of factors played their part. These would include different viewpoints over the relationship between church and state, between church and people, between landowner and people, and between those who held opposing theological or political convictions, to list but a few. Fundamental to countless controversies, however, was one issue: property ownership, or, to be specific, ownership of land, the fruits arising from it and the rights attaching to it. From the moment that the first Christian congregations moved out of makeshift accommodation into purpose-built buildings, these became matters of inescapable importance. This was because virtually all churches had to be built on land that ultimately belonged to someone, and whatever may have been an owner's goodwill at the time of construction, it was always likely that the attitude of his successors might change, particularly if in the selection of an incumbent, the congregation seemed to acquire a disagreeable degree of autonomy. Either way, from the earliest centuries, church and patrons can frequently be found wrestling and bargaining with each other to maximize whatever of income or influence each could claim as theirs.

It is this tension between sacred and secular interests which gives lay patronage its particular fascination as a subject for study. In the selection of an entrant to a territorial ministry, territorially financed, the question remained: which interest, landed or ecclesiastical, should have what privileges, and, no less importantly, who should determine how those privileges should be apportioned, the state or the church? By the eighteenth century in Scotland, church and society had failed to find a satisfactory resolution to this conundrum, and so paid the price in the disputes which followed.

This study will look at the controversies surrounding patronage in Scotland during the first half of the eighteenth century. In order to do so, however, it is necessary to look back to the first appearance of patrons, and from there observe how their role and status evolved.

The Beginning of Lay Patronage

The origins of patronage are not especially clear. However, it would seem that, after the official legalization of Christianity by Emperor Constantine in 313, property–owning Christians came forward to aid the Church's building programme either by giving money to endow a church, by personally erecting it or by donating the ground for one. In so doing, they received the title of that church's *patronus*, that is, its protector, defender or advocate. This general principle endured through the following centuries, summarized in the maxim incorporated in canon law: *Patronum faciunt, dos, aedificatio, fundus* (gift, building, land make the patron).

Naturally, the patron was not always above looking for something in return for his generosity, and this usually took the form of certain privileges. At first, they were in effect, simply marks of respect, as in the *honor processionis* (place of honor in religious processions), the *honor precum* (special place in the prayers), the *honor sedis* (privileged seat) and the *honor sepulturae* (privilege of burial within the church's precincts). However, with the fifth century, an entirely different opportunity presented itself. From this time onwards, the stability of the Roman empire weakened and bishops increasingly found themselves unable to ensure that their congregations were adequately protected and cared for. It became obvious that more reliance upon the protective role of patrons was necessary, and, as an incentive for defending existing foundations and erecting new ones, the right to choose the church's incumbent was allowed. Dating is difficult, but it would seem that, by the close of the sixth century, the practice was well established.[1]

1. It should also be mentioned that, where founding families were perhaps not available to protect religious establishments, the Church also had a policy, during the early Middle Ages, of appointing local magnates as *advocati*, or defenders of churches.

Other honorary rights gradually followed. Having established their right of selection, it was then a short step for landowners to think about their financial privileges. It seemed to them that their position was straightforward: they owned the land on which the church stood, they, or their forebears, had erected the building, its funding came from their produce — even the priest was now theirs to appoint, remove, and generally "use (and abuse) . . . like any other serf serving on their estates."[2] It therefore appeared logical that when the living was vacant, they should receive back the revenues that had been set aside for it. With the Empire continuing to collapse, the Church was not in a position to resist, and a further swing in favor of a patron's privileges unfolded. Indeed, by the eleventh century, there was little to prevent him not only regarding his church as his private property, but, with suitable management, a source of income little different from that of his bake house or mill.

As might be expected, when the early Middle Ages gave way to the comparative stability of the new millennium, the Church began to turn its attention to the task of regaining some of the initiative it had surrendered into lay hands. Probably the most effective counter-measures were achieved under the pontificate of Alexander III (1159–81), who adopted a two-pronged approach to clawing back some of the advantage patrons now held. The first element of his strategy was to introduce a *spiritual* dimension into the right of patronage. Up until then, its basis and character had been entirely temporal - that is to say, a patron's ecclesiastical rights simply derived from his holding of property. Alexander now insisted that these were only legitimate if a patron exercised them along with the Church as part of a joint responsibility for the management of the benefice, and thus designated in the papal decretals as a *jus temporale spirituali annexum* (a temporal right, tacked on to the spiritual). In other words, patronage was now defined as having an identity of which there were two necessary parts, a temporal *and* a spiritual. The effect of the latter's introduction was, naturally, to place the Church in a far stronger position for regulating both

---

Their use faded from the thirteenth century onwards. Although the reward for their protection was originally pecuniary, it is possible their identity, and hence their privileges, often became fused with that of hereditary patrons.

The term advowson, more commonly used in England to describe the right of presenting to a benefice, derives from *advocatio*.

See Alexander Dunlop, *Parochial Law* (Edinburgh: 1841), 187; John M. Duncan, *Treatise on the parochial ecclesiastical law of Scotland*, (Edinburgh: 1869), 77–79; T.B. Scannell, *Addis and Arnold's Catholic Dictionary* (London: 1928), 13.

2. Peter M. Smith, "The advowson: the history and development of a most peculiar property." *Ecclesiastical Law Journal* 26 (2000), 321.

the exercise of the *jus patronatus* (right of patronage) and its passage from one holder to another. Thus, for example, although it could be inherited or bought as part of a property, its spiritual component made its sale as a separate entity theoretically impossible, "both because it was a right the value of which was inestimable, and therefore irreconcilable with the contract of sale, and also because such a transaction was simoniacal."[3]

Alexander's other important achievement was to establish the issue of whose privileges ultimately took precedence, was it the Church's or the patron's? He did this by reaffirming the *jus patronatus* to be a *jus temporale spirituali annexum*, so that the right of patronage becomes explicitly subject to ecclesiastical jurisdiction and assessment. The practical implications of this were that a patron still had the right of selection in a vacancy, but he had to "present" his choice to the bishop for scrutiny and admission. Thus the right of presentation (*jus praesentandi*) meant the right of proposing, not simply a right to nominate or impose a candidate. The patron's role was now auxiliary to the bishop's, so that it was, for example, possible for a bishop to plant a church without a lay presentation,[4] but no presentee could be installed without episcopal collation.[5] With this development, an important landmark had been reached in clergy–laity relations. However much a proprietor might dominate the residents on his estates, the priest was no longer "his" in the way he had been previously. Whoever might initiate the steps to a settlement, in vetting candidates and giving them legal title to their livings, as far as the Church was concerned, its position as ultimate authority was considered to be settled. Theoretically, this reflected the outcome of the Investiture Controversy of the Western Church. In time however, property rights, civil law, and "state building" were to have their effect.

Moreover, as will be seen below in a Scottish context, for the Church to declare an issue settled, was not necessarily to render it non–negotiable for everyone concerned.

3. Duncan, *Treatise*, 81. *simony:* see glossary.

4. The patronage could already belong to the Church (*jus patronatus ecclesiasticum*); alternatively, if a patron did not present within a certain period, the right fell to the bishop. The time allowed could vary. In medieval Europe, including Scotland, the time generally allowed was four months for lay presentations, and six for ecclesiastical ones. For the wealthier benefices belonging to monasteries and cathedrals, Pope Innocent VIII's Indult of 1487 allowed the Crown eight months to make nominations. This was later extended to twelve. In 1567 the period in all cases was fixed at six months. [Acts of the Parliament of Scotland c.7. hereinafter cited as *APS*].

5. Collation can be used exclusively to describe institution to a living where the bishop is himself the patron, thus presentation and institution are the same act. Here it will be applied, however, simply to episcopal institution in general.

Scotland

For the medieval Scottish Church, the marriage of King Malcolm III to the Anglo–Saxon princess, Margaret, in 1069, was a momentous landmark. From then on, the influence and institutions of the Roman Church began increasingly to permeate and dominate the Scottish ecclesiastical landscape. One result was that, early in the twelfth century, a Roman civil parish structure began to emerge, and laymen who had provided churches within their areas of territorial authority, equated themselves with the role of patron of that church and its evolving parish. The foundation of the church at Ednam, in the borders, is an example of how, around 1100, such a relationship developed. The charter describes how a Saxon named Thor Longus, was granted some moor-land near Kelso, by King Edgar (1097-1107). After cultivating the land and erecting a church, dedicated to St Cuthbert, he established the material needs of the foundation by giving the priest a ploughgate of land [c.104 acres] and, afterwards, the tithes of his manor [i.e., the tenth part of its fruits and profits].[6]

By such means,[7] Scots landowners came to have the same proprietorial attitude towards the places wherein they worshipped as their Continental counterparts. Both considered the churches on their land to be "owned", that is, everything about them—the patronage, the building, the income from the glebe, tithes and offerings—was to be as much at their disposal as any other asset. However, as shown above, change was in the air and, in Scotland, the bishops were well aware of the patronage reforms taking place on the continent, having been represented at Pope Alexander's groundbreaking Lateran Council of 1179.[8] They too began to establish the principle of the Church's joint role in vacancy-filling, and reinforced it by making a valid transfer of the spiritualities conditional upon their consent.[9]

6. *Registrum de Kelso*, Bannatyne Club, Edinburgh: 1846, 5; John Cunningham, "Freewill offerings, tithes and other means of supporting religious services, historically considered", in *The Church and the People* (St Giles Lectures) (Edinburgh: 1886), 91; Cormack, *Teinds*, 19.

7. Although Ednam was eventually given over to the monks of Durham.

8. The Scottish representative was Bishop Gregory of Ross, see Cormack, *Teinds*, 57

9. George P. Innes, "Ecclesiastical patronage in Scotland in the 12th. and 13th. Centuries", *Records of the Scottish Church History Society* (cited hereinafter as *RSCHS*), XII, part 1, (1954), 69.

The *spiritualities* of a benefice were its revenues and offerings, as well as the manse and glebe, held or received in return for spiritual services. The *temporality* referred to the land and the profit pertaining to its jurisdiction. Thus, in the case of Ednam, the ploughgate was the temporality, and the tithes the spirituality.

At this point, an important development unfolded which was particularly to affect the history of lay patronage in Scotland. This was that, from the twelfth century, a remarkable proportion of the nation's parish churches came to be appropriated by religious houses as a result of gifts by the Crown and other laymen. The process itself was not new, but rather something which, as Ian Cowan remarks, "had already developed elsewhere and was now to be speeded up in England and Scotland by the advent of the Normans."[10] The commonest motives for such conferments were piety (for the health of one's soul), convenience (divesting liability for upkeep) or generosity (to assist the finances of the monastery). Whatever the reason, however, by the mid-thirteenth century, larger abbeys like Kelso had 37 annexed churches, Holyrood 27, Paisley 29 and Arbroath 33.[11] As time went by, parochial benefices were also annexed to cathedrals and collegiate churches to found or finance prebends [pensions granted to canons or chapter members].[12] All in all, the tide of change was such that, by the eve of the Reformation in 1560, only 14 percent of all parochial benefices remained outwith ecclesiastical control. The magnitude of the trend becomes apparent when compared with England: by this date, 86 percent of Scotland's 1028 parishes had seen their revenues appropriated in some way. In England, the corresponding figure was 37 percent.[13]

Although the Church continued to hold the greater amount of parochial patronage up until the Reformation, this fact does not appear to have been the cause of particular concern among royal or noble circles. Matters

10. Ian B. Cowan, "Some aspects of the appropriation of parish churches in medieval Scotland", *RSCHS*, vol. xiii, (1959), 206. Cowan cites the example of Scoonie and Markinch churches, which were granted, c. 1055, to the Culdees of Loch Leven.

11. J.H.S. Burleigh, *A church history of Scotland*, (London: 1960), 52.

12. Benefactors often appeared to be more concerned about retaining the patronage to prebends, and similar benefices, than to their parish churches. Thus by 1560, only around 80 parish churches out of the total of 1028 remained in the gift of individual lay patrons [see, Ian B. Cowan, "Patronage, provision and reservation, pre-Reformation appointments to Scottish benefices", in Ian B. Cowan, and D. Shaw, (eds), *The Renaissance and Reformation in Scotland*, (Edinburgh: 1983), 90; James Kirk, "The exercise of ecclesiastical patronage by the crown, 1560–1572", in Cowan and Shaw, *Renaissance and Reformation*, 94]. The reason for their interest in prebends was because they provided a means of increasing the income of clerical relatives or friends without transgressing the canon law which disallowed the tenure of more than one office involving the cure of souls.

13. Ian B. Cowan, *The parishes of medieval Scotland*, (Edinburgh: 1967), v; Cowan, "Some aspects of appropriation, etc," 205.

were about to change, however, and the catalyst was the contentious issue of papal provisions.

Papal provisions were instances where the pontiff reserved the right to intervene in a vacancy and appoint an incumbent directly from Rome. Initially, these *special* reservations simply targeted individual benefices which he had earmarked for attention. Beginning with Clement IV in 1265, however, successive popes used *general* reservations to award themselves the right to nominate to an entire category of benefices which had become vacant in particular circumstances. Thus, for example, Rome could intervene in vacancies where the occupant had died at, or near, the Holy See, or where the cleric had resigned to take up a higher appointment, or even where he had died in any month other than March, July, September or December[14]. One way or another, the Holy See increasingly sought to bring appointments within its direct control, desiring both to increase papal income and particularly to make the Church's authority more centralized. The result, according to Innes,[15] was that every year, thousands, possibly tens of thousands, of benefices across Europe were affected.

In Scotland, the business of papal provisions was to sow the seeds of opposition but not, surprisingly, because the pope's nominees threatened to supplant local preferences: the distance between Scotland and Rome was enough to ensure that papal *fiat* without indigenous consent was simply not enough for the pontiff to make his appointments prevail. Rather, it was for two other reasons that provisions engendered annoyance.

The first reason was that they led to a constant stream of litigation by rival claimants for benefices coming before the court at Rome, as well as a procession of hopefuls seeking to purchase pensions and preferments.[16] This inevitably occasioned a steady drain of currency out of the country. To counteract it, James I passed a series of acts in 1424, 1427 and 1428, the last of which specifically condemned "thaim that dois barratry" —barratry being unauthorized dealing at Rome[17]—but the problem would not go away, and James III felt compelled to renew the legislation in 1482 and 1484.[18]

14. Cowan, "Patronage, provision and reservation," 82.

15. George P. Innes, "Ecclesiastical patronage . . . in Scotland in the later middle ages", *RSCHS*, xiii (1957–59), 73.

16. See the series, *Calendar of Scottish supplications to Rome*, published by the Scottish History Society (hereinafter cited as SHS): *1418–1422*, eds. E.R. Lindsay, and Annie I. Cameron, (3rd series, vol. 23, 1934); *1423–1428*, ed. Annie I. Dunlop, (vol. 48, 1956); *1428–1432*, eds. Annie I. Dunlop, and Ian B. Cowan, (4th series, vol. 7, 1970), xx.

17. *APS*. ii, 5; ii, 14; ii, 16.

18. *APS.*, ii, 144; ii, 166.

Secondly, and more importantly, as Rome became increasingly inclined to reserve to itself appointments to the "greater benefices", or bishoprics, successive kings grew deeply uncomfortable. Since their predecessors had been generous founders of monastic houses, they had felt justified in looking upon these with the same proprietorial eye as that with which parochial lay patrons regarded the churches on their estates. Papal interference was unwelcome, and since senior clerics sat in Parliament or council, the king could ill-afford to see these preferments going to men who were unacceptable to him. The result was a battle of wills, from which the Crown eventually emerged the winner. In 1487, Pope Innocent VIII issued an Indult, conceding the right of James III to nominate, within eight months, to such benefices belonging to monasteries and cathedrals, which were worth more than 200 florins, gold of the camera.

This was not the only success to come the Crown's way. Earlier, it had decided that, by long-standing tradition, the monarch had the right, while an episcopal see was vacant, to present to any of the benefices for which the bishop had collation.[19] It was a claim that was to provoke friction between Crown and Pope throughout the fourteenth and fifteenth centuries, and into the sixteenth. However, while the papacy challenged the king's "pretended custom", by various deeds and statements, as in 1323, 1337 and 1440, the Crown was able to hold onto its position, thanks to supportive declarations from the Scottish Church (1450, 1457 and 1459) and Parliament (1462, 1481, 1482 and 1485)[20].

With the 1487 indult, it might have appeared that at last a settled arrangement in Scottish relations with Rome over vacancies had arrived. However, instead of satisfying royal hunger, such concessions merely whetted the appetite. With monasteries and episcopal dioceses now firmly within its sphere of influence, from this point down to the Reformation in 1560, the Crown slowly pushed against limitations as to its power of nomination. A typical example of its mounting assertiveness can be seen in the Act of 1526, which bluntly claimed that the nomination to all vacant bishoprics or abbacies pertained solely to the king, and anyone entering

19. Gordon Donaldson, "The rights of the Scottish crown in episcopal vacancies" *Scottish Historical Review* (cited hereinafter as *SHR*), xlv (1966), 34, where it is argued that *collation*, here, refers only to those livings of which the bishop was actually patron, and not to all ecclesiastical benefices in the diocese. Cowan's point is that, even if this were so, the king lost no time in extending his privilege. The royal expansionism did not, however, go on to include parish churches with known lay patrons. These were left alone. Ibid., 90.

20. Donaldson, "Rights," 34.

such positions by other means "sall incur the cryme of tresone and leise majestie."[21]

So then, thanks to royal resistance, the initiative in the nomination of higher clergy in particular that had been moving in the Church's favor, flowed in the other direction and into royal hands. Thus Cowan suggests that, by the sixteenth century, the Crown may not have made all the gains it might have liked, but, "it possessed a far greater degree of patronage.... than it had ever previously commanded."[22]

As the continuing secularization of church property gained momentum in the century before the Reformation, the Crown was not of course the only interested party. Lay families made sure they did not miss out on what they could gain.[23] However, their primary concern was income, and any right of patronage that was not subsumed into the Crown's growing acquisitions, usually stayed within the Church's hands. It was to be later, when a different ecclesiastical structure was in place, that a desire to consolidate every aspect of their acquisitions prompted a return of lay patrons' attentions to this feature of property ownership.

After the Scottish Reformation of 1560

The dawn of the Reformation brought the opportunity to extend the royal stock of patronages even further. In this, the crucial contribution was the allowance made to the non-conforming clergy of the old faith to remain in their benefices during their lifetime and retain at least two thirds of the parochial teinds or tithes, while the remaining third was earmarked for the reformed ministers. While this situation obtained, it seemed logical to the reformers to allow much of the revenue system of the pre-Reformation Church to remain undismantled. However, this presented the Crown with the golden opportunity to step in and portray itself as the proper heir to the property of the bishoprics and religious institutions. The assets to be gained from such a claim were very considerable, since centuries of appropriation by religious houses and cathedrals had placed by far the greatest number of parish churches in the Church's hands. Accordingly, the Crown wasted no time in asserting its claims, first with the benefices attached to religious houses, then with the bishoprics. Along with them came their presentation rights.

21. *APS.*, ii, 309–10.
22. Cowan, "Patronage, provisions etc," 91.
23. See Gordon Donaldson, *The Scottish Reformation*, (Cambridge: 1960), 36.

All this put the new, reformed Church in a difficult position. As a counter to the clericalism of the old faith, they saw a minister's authority as something that came upwards from the parishioners, as opposed to coming down from a higher source. Thus, in their 1560 blueprint for reform, the (first) *Book of Discipline,* they declared that "election of Ministers in this cursed Papistrie hath altogether bene abused", and, following Luther and Calvin, ordained instead that "It appertaineth to the people and to every severall Congregation to elect their minister."[24] However, although the Acts of the August Parliament of 1560 had swept away the Mass and the authority of the Pope, until its legislation was ratified by the monarch, doubts would always remain as to the legitimacy of the new order, and when Catholic Queen Mary arrived in 1561, she showed no inclination to do so. This obstacle, coupled with the Crown's growing interest in adding to its rights and privileges, did not make it a favorable opportunity for the reformers to insist on their demands regarding patronage.

The situation was made worse by worry over the desperate financial straits of the ministers. Accordingly, on the 24 June 1565, the General Assembly sent Queen Mary a plea to grant legislation on its main claims and desires, prominent among which (Article Two of six) was the request that "sure provision" be made for sustaining the ministry, especially access to the "thirds." The way the reformers saw urgent provision being achieved was by Parliament regularizing the position of the reform clergy already in livings, and by its disponing, one by one, any vacant charges to those approved by the new Church. Presentations are not condemned, yet noticeably, there is no suggestion that either action should be accompanied by one.[25] The queen, however, decided that if she let this wording pass, it would set a precedent which had financial implications. In her reply, she said she considered "it no ways reasonable that she should defraud herself of so great a part of the patrimony of the Crown, as to put the Patronage of Benefices forth of ther own hands; for

24. *The First Book of Discipline,* ed. James K. Cameron, (Edinburgh: 1972), The fourth head: "Concerning ministers and their lawful election," 96 & n.3. The fourth head several times uses the word "present." However, as Cameron points out, 99 n.16, this was designed to mean *either,* a congregation presenting a candidate to the church council of the principal town for examination, *or,* a church council presenting a qualified examinee to a parish for assessment and election. The congregation had the right to reject such a candidate, but not for "unreasonable" causes. In such a way, the attempt was made "to exercise a balance between the rights of the people and the rights of ministers and councils of the Church."

25. *John Knox's History of the Reformation in Scotland* (hereinafter cited as *Knox's history*), ed. William Croft Dickinson, (Edinburgh: 1949), ii, 149.

her own necessity in bearing of her port [living and retinue] and common charges will require the retention thereof."[26]

Accordingly, when the next Assembly met, at Edinburgh, on the 25 December 1565, it had much on its mind. Not only was it unhappy with the queen's answers to its six Articles, but it beheld a ministry now so starved of income, that it was "like to decay and fail."[27] Agreeing it could not be fully satisfied with the former, and having appointed John Row, minister of Perth and former canon lawyer, to draw up answers, it proceeded to approve a supplication to the Crown for an urgent remedy of the stipend problem. It must be guessed whether desperation was responsible for the tone of the entreaty, but it was certainly polite to the point of being conciliatory.

Moreover, a softer note also appeared in Row's responses to the queen's letter, to which the Assembly returned the following day. In the first Article, the Mass was firmly repudiated, but not discourteously. Then, in the second, the *Book of Discipline's* scruples on presentations were discretely ignored: "[our mind is not] that her Majesty or any other patron of this realm should be defrauded of their just patronages. But we mean, whenever her Majesty or any other patron does present any person to a benefice, that the person presented should be tried and examined by the judgement of learned men of the Kirk.....and as the presentation of benefices pertains to the patron, so ought the collation thereof, be law and reason, pertaining to the Kirk."[28] Thus Row, as an ex–canonist, was able to echo the aspirations articulated by Pope Alexander.

Clearly, the Assembly judged it expedient to compromise on the issue of patronage. However, such forced civility was motivated not only by financial considerations. The Assembly's reply reveals yet another cause of alarm to the new Church. Since 1560, it had become obvious that the Crown was increasingly returning to the practice of the early medieval period, namely, the filling up of benefices purely on the authority of the patron's gift, without due deference to the Church's rights of collation.[29] This was not just in respect of abbeys and priories and the lesser benefices

26. Ibid., 152. Knox says the reply was issued on the 21 August 1565; Dickinson suggests it may have been the 29 July. See n.4 there.

27. Ibid., 175.

28. *The booke of the universall kirk of Scotland:* (hereinafter cited as *BUK),* ed., Alexander Peterkin, (Edinburgh: 1839). 36.

29. For examples, see Kirk, "The exercise of ecclesiastical patronage etc." 104; see also memo by Archibald Johnston of Wariston, in *The letters and journals of Robert Baillie, AM, 1637-62,* ed., David Laing, (Edinburgh: 1841), ii, 455.

that went with them, but even parish churches. Moreover, the appointment would often be merely that of a lay titular.[30] For the sake of its authority, this was not something that the Church could ignore, and it is highly likely that it prompted the conclusion that it was better to negotiate a modified system of presentations, than stage an attempt at abolition and subsequently fail on all counts. In addition, if, as would be likely, the new Church's own landowning supporters were lukewarm about dismantling a system that had much to offer them, the Assembly probably felt that, overall, it was no time to be over-ambitious.

In the event, the queen's response to the Assembly was her customary one of delay and prevarication, which left the Assembly's commissioners no option but to return home "waiting upon the good providence of God."[31] Nonetheless, the events of 1566 brought an unexpected change in the Church's bargaining position.

Following the murder, in March, of her secretary, David Riccio, Queen Mary's political strength had started to ebb away, and by the autumn, it obviously occurred to her to use concessions as a means of winning favor from the Church. As a result, the reformers at last won access to the lesser benefices—those worth 300 merks' yearly rental or less—when they became vacant. It was a major breakthrough in securing the new Church's future, but there was a sting in the tail. The benefices would be disponed only to those whom the Church had examined and deemed suitable, but such candidates were then to be "nominat and present to thair Majesteis," whereupon "thair Hienesses sall admit thame, and be thair autoritie caus thame be answerit of the frutis and dewiteis of the saidis benefices."[32] In other words, although only approved candidates would be admitted, the Crown was in effect reserving to itself the right of collation and admission. It was a shift of authority the Church could hardly accept.

Mary continued to make other concessions that were two-edged.[33] However, 1567 brought dramatic developments in the political situation.

30. Donaldson, *Scottish Reformation*, 150.

31. *Knox's History*, 177.

32. *Register of the Privy Council of Scotland* (hereinafter cited as *RPCS.*), P. Hume Brown, (ed.), i, (Edinburgh: 1899), 487–78.

33. One example was that although the impoverished ministers were now to receive assistance, it appeared to the Assembly of 26 December, to have been offered in the form of simply a pension of money and food. This triggered much heart-searching among the members, on the grounds that if they accepted the offer, they might prejudice their continuing claim to *all* of what they considered the Kirk's just patrimony. In the event, material need triumphed over principle, and the funding was accepted.

Darnley, the queen's husband, was murdered in Edinburgh on 9 February, and a mere three months later, Mary married the Earl of Bothwell. The general scandal surrounding both events was enough to make it impossible for the queen to continue in the eyes of some. An armed confrontation took place at Carberry, East Lothian, between rebel lords and Bothwell and Mary. While Bothwell departed eventually into exile, Mary was taken to Edinburgh and then to imprisonment in Loch Leven Castle. On 24–25 July, she signed documents giving the crown to her infant son, James, and naming her half-brother, James Stewart, Earl of Moray, as regent. The following May, Mary escaped and raised an army, only to see it defeated at Langside. She fled south of the border, where she remained in Queen Elizabeth's custody until her execution for treason on 8 February 1587.

Meanwhile, in December 1567, the first Parliament of the new era secured royal assent for the legislation of the Reformation Parliament of 1560, and thereby established the legality of the Reformation and the reformed Church. Thereupon the Scots Confession of Faith (1560) was incorporated into the published Acts of Parliament (but not the *Book of Discipline*).

The December Parliament also went on to legislate on other ecclesiastical matters, including the question of ministerial admission: "It is statute and ordained....that the examination and admission of Ministers, within this Realme, be only in the power of the Kirk, now openlie and publickly professed within the samin. The presentation of laick Patronages alwaies reserved to the Just and auncient Patrones. And that the Patroun present ane qualified persoun, within sex monethes...to the Superintendent of thay partis, quhar the Benefice lyes, or uthers havand commission of the Kirk to that effect; utherwise the Kirk to have power to dispone the samin to ane qualifyed person for that time."[34]

The *Book of Discipline's* aversion to presentations had been ignored. On the other hand, the Kirk would certainly have been relieved to see two vital points established. The first was that only the Church possessed the right to examine and admit candidates, and the second was that, in the event of any dispute, appeals could only be heard by the Kirk's courts, whose decision would be final. On balance, there was justification for the Kirk to consider it had done well out of the 1567 settlement. Indeed, within a few months, Regent Moray was politely writing to the Assembly, enquiring how best to use the King's right of presentation to some chaplaincies, "that ignorantly we doe nothing wherewith the Kirk may justly

34. *APS*, iii, 23.

find fault hereafter."[35] There were, however, other loose ends, which would not be so harmoniously resolved.

The most significant of these concerned the fate of the abbacies and the bishoprics. The Assembly's wish was to have both dissolved, but Parliament balked at the idea. The Crown's lack of enthusiasm was also understandable, since, on account of its traditional claim on the finances and patronage of vacant prelacies, it had most to lose. The Church could not, however, remain passive if the state used the grey area of appointments to greater benefices to flaunt the rights agreed with the Kirk regarding the lesser ones. Thus when, in 1571, the state appointed John Douglas to the archbishopric of St Andrews, John Porterfield to the see of Glasgow, and James Paton to the see of Dunkeld, all without deference to the Kirk's processes of trial and qualification, strenuous protests were made. It became obvious that a meeting was necessary in order to clear the air, and as a result, the Convention of Leith met in January 1572.

The crucial agreement reached at the Leith meeting was over what to do with the bishoprics. The Church agreed to accept the nomination of bishops by the Crown, but on condition that candidates would have to be subject to the approval of their fellow ministers, and after their installation, accept the authority of the Assembly in spiritual matters. As for the priories and abbacies, the Kirk would recognize the Crown's interests in disposing of their patrimony as vacancies arose. Patronage would continue unchallenged. Despite the spirit of compromise evident in the concordat, it did not turn out to be a success. Ignoring the Kirk, James, fourth Earl of Morton, who was Regent between 1572 and 1578, continued to allow the diversion of ecclesiastical property and money into secular hands, while at the same time showing scant sensitivity in his appointment of bishops.

By 1576, a clear note of unease with episcopacy was showing itself in the Assembly registers,[36] coming to a head with the petulant behavior of Patrick Adamson, archbishop of St Andrews, whose defiance of Assembly authority appeared to have Morton's countenance, if not encouragement. Morton's view in reply was that, if the Church could not be happy with the Leith agreement, it should draw up a statement, clearly re-defining its position on all such matters. The Church duly responded and the result was *The heads and conclusions of the policy of the Kirk*, or, the *second Book of Discipline*, which was completed, and accepted by the Assembly, in 1578.

---

35. *BUK*, 103; for a description of how the non-parochial benefices were made available to the new church, see Donaldson, *Scottish Reformation*, 154–55.

36. *BUK*, 154.

In it, patronage is not only disapproved, but replaced a by a mode of election that was now refined into consent by the congregation, after nomination by the eldership.[37] This was a distinct advance on the first book's rather vague axiom of election by the people.[38] It should at once be said, however, that caution should be exercised as to the meaning of "eldership," when used in the book. Rather than meaning individual kirk sessions, the reference here is most likely to groups of neighboring ministers, doctors [i.e., teachers] and elders. Although only three or four parishes might have been involved, these groups were probably (along with the exegetical "exercise" meetings) the prototype for presbyteries, which start to be mentioned in the 1580s. As for the rest of the book, the subject of patronage is raised again, in a section entitled, *Certain special Heids of Reformation quhilk we crave*. What is noteworthy is that, in comparison with the first book's comments on the issue, the language has become markedly more uncompromising:

> 9. The libertie of the election of persons callit to the ecclesiastical functions....we desyre to be restorit and reteinit within this realm. Swa that nane be intrusit upon ony congregation, either be the prince or ony inferior person, without lawfull election and the assent of the people owir quham the person is placit; as the practise of the apostolical and primitive kirk, and gude order craves.

> 10. And because this order, quhilk Gods word craves, cannot stand with patronages and presentation to benefices usit in the Paipes kirk: we desyre all them that trewlie feir God earnestly to consider, that for swa meikle as the names of patronages and benefices, togethir with the effect thairof have flowit fra the Paip and corruption of the canon law only...... And for swa meikle as that manner of proceeding hes na ground in the word of God, but is contrar to the same.....they aucht not now to have place in this licht of reformation.[39]

---

37. see James Kirk, *The Second Book of Discipline* (Edinburgh: 1980), 102.

38. "As to the *mode* of appointment, the practice varied. On some occasions the congregation presented a minister to the superintendent, either chosen by themselves directly, or by commissioners appointed by them; while in others the superintendent and his council suggested or proposed a minister to the congregation": *Report from select committee on church patronage, (Scotland;) with the minutes of evidence, appendix and index. House of Commons, 23 July, 1834* (hereinafter cited as *Patronage report, 1834*), 6.

39. *Second book of discipline*, iii, 4; xii, 9–10.

Burleigh's opinion that the whole book "was in short a demand for a complete reversal of the ecclesiastical policy pursued by Morton since 1572,"[40] certainly seems to be confirmed by the tenor of the passages on patronage. Their tone conveys an anxiety which would have derived not only from unease at the regent's attempts to extend state authority over the Church,[41] but especially from the authors' realizing that the Leith concordat had merely facilitated further secularization of church lands. Yet, for all the defiance of these paragraphs, the upholders of the second *Book of Discipline* well knew that their wishes on patronage would be received with as little enthusiasm as their claims for the old Church's patrimony. In all their deliberations, there would have been an inescapable tension between what they believed ought to happen, and what was realistically possible.

A typical example of the struggle between conscience and political reality can be seen in the writings of one of the book's authors, John Erskine of Dun. During the course of the same year (1571), he writes on one occasion to scorn the fact that, according to human laws, the patron can nominate a pastor to his office even though, "we haif it be the Scriptouris and consuetud of the primitive kirk that the congregatione namit the persone." Against that, however, he writes in another letter: "I mean not the hurt of the King, or others in their patronage, but that they have their privileges of presentation according to the lawes, providing alwise that the examination and admission pertean only to the Kirk, of all benefices having cure of souls."[42]

As for the new king (who had in 1567 succeeded his mother as James VI and whose minority lasted until 1584), the response of his government to the book's passages on patronage, was to act as if they did not exist. Thus, his receipt of a copy of the book in the spring of 1578, did not distract the government from passing an Act a few weeks later, stating that all rights of presentation, previously belonging to abbots, bishops and priors, should now be regarded as the monarch's. A year later, another Act was passed, ratifying all the legislation of 1567, which, of course, included the December Act defending the rights of "the Just and auncient Patrones."

40. Burleigh, *Church history*, 201.

41. Ibid., 197; *Dictionary of Scottish Church History and Theology* (hereinafter cited as *DSCHT*), ed., Cameron, Nigel M. de S., (Edinburgh: 1993), 254.

42. John Erskine of Dun, superintendent of Angus and Mearns, *Miscellany of the Spalding Club.* (Aberdeen: 1849), iv, 99–100; Erskine to Earl of Mar, 10 November 1571, see Violet Jacob, *The lairds of Dun.* (London: 1931), 302.

Again, in 1581, an Act was passed bluntly reaffirming the presentation rights of both the Crown and "the lawit [legal] Patronis."[43]

Given government reaction, which was wholly shared by James on attaining his personal rule, it is unsurprising that the second *Book of Discipline* never received official recognition by the state. This meant that the most status the Assembly could give it was simply a formal recording among its register of Acts, on 24 April 1581.[44] This setback was not without significance, since, as Shaw points out in his work on the first General Assemblies, the second *Book* could not then be considered part of the Church's constitution: "It did, however, represent within the General Assemblies of the period the majority opinion of what the constitution of the church ought to be, but because of the lack of approval by the state, the Assembly did not consider itself competent to go further."[45] As with Erskine's letters, this diffidence led to curious contradictions. Thus, despite the Assembly's approval of the second *Book*, its registers still continued to imply that patronage was as acceptable as before: "[it is ordained] that presentationes of benefices be direct to Commissioners of Countries" (24 October 1578); "That no presentatione of benefice be directit to any persones but sic as beirs commissione" (12 July 1580); "And always the Laik Patronages to remaine haill and unjoynit or provydit, except it be with consent of the patrons' (24 April 1581); "The advyse of the Kirk concerning the direction of Presentations, that they be directit to the presbytries' (24 April 1581).[46]

The situation, then, at the start of the 1580s, was that if the Church had any hopes of relieving itself of the perceived burden of presentations, it knew these would be firmly obstructed by a Crown that now held the vast majority of benefices in its gift. On the other hand, there was still the matter of the nobility and gentry. Although they had been glad to follow the Crown's lead in the plunder of ecclesiastical properties, they had not, as mentioned above, shown the same interest in acquiring the rights of presentation that went with them. It was not inconceivable that they might be sympathetic to the Church's desire.[47] However, if the Church harbored hopes in that direction,

---

43. *APS*, iii, 106; iii, 137; iii, 212.

44. *BUK.*, 219.

45. Duncan Shaw, *The general assemblies of the church of Scotland 1560–1600.* (Edinburgh: 1964), 58.

46. *BUK*, 182; 200; 213; 220.

47. See James Kirk, *Patterns of reform: continuity and change in the Reformation Kirk* (hereinafter cited as Kirk, *Patterns*) (Edinburgh: 1989), 371.

the possibility of their being realized, ebbed away with the measures James was about to take over the medieval Church's temporality.

As an introduction to that crucial legislation, however, it is necessary first to recall in more detail how the Scottish Church came to be funded, and how secular predations left the Crown in the favorable position it eventually found itself.

The Church's Property

It will be remembered that, originally, when a church was founded, it was customary for the patron to ensure its upkeep by a grant both of land and a proportion of all the parochial produce. This proportion, normally a tenth, came to be known as the parish tithes or teinds. Although they began as an act of generosity, by the time of King William the Lion (1165–1214), the state had made them into a compulsory levy.[48]

As already mentioned, there was a continuous process, in the era before the Reformation, of appropriation of parish churches by religious houses, cathedral chapters and bishoprics.[49] This meant that the incumbent no longer received all the teinds directly as the titular parson, or rector. The religious house, chapter or bishop, in effect, became the titular parson, and on their behalf a vicar usually served the church, receiving only a share, or stipend, out of the teinds. Such a charge is called a patrimonial (as opposed to patronate) benefice.[50]

Despite the attempt by the third Lateran Council (1179) to restrict the alienation of tithes, by making it conditional on papal consent, the feuing out of lands and teinds was commonplace in Scotland by the sixteenth century. In this process of secularization, the Crown led the way, and the tactic it employed was to wrest concessions from the Church, and then simply to stretch and expand these as far as possible. Thus, although James II undertook, in 1450, to restrict his claims, in vacant dioceses, to the temporality and patronage of its livings, by 1515, the spirituality

---

48. *APS*, i, 90.

49. According to Cowan, only 148 parishes out of 1028 were unappropriated by 1560. See Cowan, *The parishes of medieval Scotland* , v. 226.

50. A bishop was in an interesting position as a patron. To his patrimonial, or mensal, churches, he simply appointed stipendaries, but where he had actually acquired the patronage of churches within his diocese, his practice could only be to confer and collate the parson, since he could not present to himself. See, James, Viscount of Stair, *Institutions of the law of Scotland*, ii, 487. (Edinburgh: 1981).

was being uplifted by the Crown as well.[51] Again, as seen above, when the Indult of 1487 granted James III privileges regarding certain benefices attached to monasteries as well as cathedrals, the Crown did not hesitate to use this as another avenue for extending its advance into the wealth and patronage of the prelacies.

The monarch could not only garner income during vacancies, but use his power of appointment to provide for friends and their dependents, who could return the favor through a lease on the revenues. In this regard, access to the patrimony of a monastery was frequently gained by appointing a commendator to the abbacy. This would be someone who, not being entitled to the office, held it *in commendam* (in trust) and acted as steward of its resources. By 1560, two thirds of Scottish monasteries had commendators[52]. One particular abuse of religious houses, oft-quoted, took place in 1533, when, exploiting papal anxieties over the Reformation in England, James V asked Clement VII to grant his three illegitimate sons: "any church dignities whatsoever either secular or regular of any order, in title or commend."[53] As a result, they received St Andrews priory, Holyrood, Kelso, Melrose, and Coldingham abbeys. Then, ten years later, the revenues which were surplus to the boys' requirements, were simply annexed by the Crown.[54] As for the thirteen bishoprics, a practice equivalent to that of installing commendators was to make a nomination, while at the same time reserving a generous portion out of the episcopal income.

Turning to the nobility and lairds, these followed the Crown's example in encroaching on the Church's wealth and privileges even to the extent that, for some families, the headship of a particular abbey or priory became their own, private preserve.[55] However, as already mentioned, for all their dilapidation of the religious houses' patrimony, comparatively few laymen by the end of the 1570s had also troubled to take over their right of presentation to parochial charges. In the 1580s, the situation began to change.

---

51. Donaldson, "Crown rights, etc," 33.

52. *DSCHT*, 198; William Forbes, *A treatise of church lands and tithes in two parts* (hereinafter cited as Forbes, *Tithes*. (Edinburgh: 1703).

53. SRO., *Caprington Letter Book*, fo. 6.

54. *APS.*, 11, 424.

55. "Thus Dryburgh tended to be at the disposal of the Erskines, Paisley and Kilwinning of the Hamiltons, Whithorn of the Flemings, Crossraguel of the Kennedys, Culross of the Colvilles and Jedburgh of the Humes." Cf., Donaldson, *Scottish Reformation*, 39.

Temporal Lordships

The lynchpin of the change was James's Act of Annexation of the Temporalities of Benefices to the Crown 1587,[56] and it was certain consequences of this measure that were to have a profound effect on the identity of those who were to hold the majority of patronages throughout the following centuries. Instead of the Crown possessing all but a handful, such was the reversal that, by the time of the Patronage Act of 1712, private rights of presentation outnumbered the Crown's by two to one.

The 1587 Act laid down that all the Roman Church's temporality, that is its lands and their rents, were to be appropriated by the Crown, although various exceptions were made. Manses and glebes were to be exempted, as were the mansions of the bishops, the latter probably being kept by James in preparation for a full restoration of episcopacy later. Teinds were also largely exempted from annexation, which may have provided the Kirk with some small comfort, given that the temporality was now beyond their grasp, but financing the Church through the teinds remained far from satisfactory until the issue was set on a firmer footing by the Revocation scheme of Charles I.

There were other exemptions, and it was these which were to affect the issue of lay patronage thereafter. The first was those church lands already held through lay commendators or erected as temporal lordships.[57] This meant that the noble families to whom this applied now had the security of a heritable right to these assets. Through a judicious beneficence, James continued to create these "lords of erection" to such an extent that, "At James's death in 1625, 21 abbeys, 11 priories, six nunneries and one preceptory, either separately or conjointly, had been erected into temporal lordships. Indeed, of the 54 major ecclesiastical foundations in Scotland, only one—Dunfermline Abbey—had been retained, but not wholly preserved, by the Crown."[58] It was, however, the final exemption within the 1587 Act that was to prove crucial: namely, that all lands and rents of any benefice in the gift of a lay patron were to be excluded as well. Suddenly, the issue of patronage, previously of little particular concern to landed

---

56. *APS*, iii, 433.

57. These lordships simply evolved, thus, for example, the commendator, Robert Keith, who was infeft of the lands of the Abbey of Deer, became Lord Altrie, and Lord Claud Hamilton, infeft of Paisley Abbey, later became Lord Paisley. Cf., Cormack, *Teinds*, 81.

58. Alan I. MacInnes, *Charles I and the Making of the Covenanting Movement, 1625–1641.* (Edinburgh: 1991), 4.

families, was of real significance. As they consolidated their lands as a heritable possession, they also took steps to assert the heritable rights that went with them—of which patronage was one. The newer temporal lords decided it was only wise to follow their example. Some idea of the number of benefices recorded as being in the gift of landed families from this time, can be derived from Kirk's investigations: "The patronage of 29 churches annexed to Paisley, for example, fell to Claud Hamilton by 1592; Kelso with the right to present to more than 40 churches became the heritable property of Francis Stewart in 1588; Kilwinning, with 16 annexed churches, was assigned to William Melville in 1592; Arbroath, with 37 specified churches, was bestowed in 1608 on the Marquis of Hamilton ; and Alexander Lyndsay, created Lord Spynie with the erection of the lordship out of the temporality of the bishopric of Moray, came to possess the patronage of some 40 churches."[59]

The General Assembly's reaction was one of alarm, and the following year, petitioned the king to cease bestowing patronages, since it was "to the evident hurt of the haill Kirk." The plea was repeated in 1591 with equal lack of success.[60] It is possible that these displays of anxiety on the Assembly's part, were not altogether justified by its experiences of patronage from the Reformation up to this time. Indeed, there is little evidence to contradict the impression that presentations had, on the whole, been exercised with sensitivity.[61]

On the other hand, it must be admitted that the Crown had been the main source of presentations before 1587, and, after such consistency, there may have been nervousness that nomination was now in the hands of a heterogeneous collection of "Earles, Lords, Barrones, and uthers."[62] More importantly, the Kirk would hardly have been reassured to witness the ways in which grantees could manipulate the law in order to give themselves a patronal status to which they were not entitled. Thus, instead of simply gifting land and its patronage, the Crown might award someone the right to all the parochial teinds. The result of this was, in effect, to transform the grantee into a benefice holder, and any minister admitted to the charge could therefore only be his vicar, not his presentee. In this instance, as with any of the vicarages which the king chose to erect into benefices, the favored grantee simply awarded himself the title of patron,

59. Kirk, *Patterns of Reform*, 425.

60. *BUK*, 335, 357.

61. See Kirk, *Patterns of Reform*, 416–17.

62. *BUK*, 335.

whether merited or not.[63] Such a practice predictably left the Assembly with a strong sense of unease, and in 1593, they were expressly asking "That his Majestie will consider the great prejudice done to the haill Kirk by erecting of the teynds of diverse prelacies in temporalitie . . . be the quhilks the planting of Kirks is greatly prejudged."[64]

All was not gloom for the Church, however. An historic upturn in fortunes had undoubtedly come the previous year, when Parliament with James's assent passed its famous "Golden Act" which finally recognized and established the presbyterian system of government through kirk sessions, presbyteries, synods and assemblies. The limitation was that the Black Act (1584) asserting the Crown's authority in matters spiritual and temporal was not cancelled; and, crucially, the king retained his right to convene, and to determine the meeting place of General Assemblies. Not unexpectedly, patronage was also retained, but presbytery was unequivocally recognized as the appropriate body to which all presentations were to be directed. If the patron did not present within six months, the *jus devolutum* [devolved right] was to come to the presbytery. If the presbytery did not induct a properly qualified presentee, the patron was allowed to keep all the teinds.[65]

Summary

It is perhaps ironic that the Early Church saw lay patrons as ideal agents for the work of expansion and consolidation: everywhere, patrons would provide, build and endow, then, having done so, exert themselves to protect their investment. The problem for the Church was that succeeding generations inherited the land, but not necessarily their forebears' piety or generous instincts towards the faith. They were prepared to continue a paternal custody over the churches on their property, but increasingly, it took the form of a guardianship that threatened to marginalize ecclesiastical authority, rather than serve it. The Church's ultimate response was Pope Alexander's judicious portrayal of admission to benefices as a joint venture, valid if both church and layman recognized and respected each other's role. For all the merits of such an arrangement, however, the large-scale appropriation of parish churches by religious institutions, and the anxiety of the Crown to defend and expand its rights, were sufficient,

63. Alexander Dunlop, *Parochial law.* (Edinburgh: 1841), 194.
64. *BUK*, 382.
65. *APS*, iii, 541–52.

in Scotland, to upset the balance necessary for this to survive in credible form. The classical question of who, then, should have the greater say in appointments to the nation's ecclesiastical benefices, Crown or papacy, also colored Scottish relations with Rome down to the Reformation. In this, the papal concessions of the Indult of 1487 were crucial in settling who emerged the stronger, although, as can be gleaned from Vatican archives, in reality, the Crown had gained the advantage long before: "on the basis of the supplications . . . it may be concluded that by the reign of James I, if not earlier, there can be little doubt that benefice appointment was effectively controlled in Scotland."[66] Where the king led, individual lay patrons followed. Nobility and royal favorites manipulated the system to advance their confederates and pillage the Church's assets. It was not, however, until the aftermath of the Reformation itself, that laymen came out from the shadow of the Crown and, through the temporal lordships, were able to amass personal collections of patronages. Not surprisingly, James VI later came to regret what he had done to allow such a stockpiling to happen,[67] but by then it was too late. His generosity had more than turned the clock back four centuries, it had laid in place "the untrammelled exercise of a far greater degree of individual lay patronage than had ever been possible in pre-Reformation Scotland."[68]

66. *Calendar of Scottish supplications*, 4th series, vol. 7, xx.

67. In the *Basilikon Doron*, he counselled his son to annul "that vile Act of Annexation," see *A source book of Scottish history*, eds. William Croft Dickinson, and Gordon Donaldson, vol. iii, 51.

68. Cowan, "Patronage, provision, etc.," 92.

CHAPTER TWO

By the time of King James' death in 1625, thirty–nine of Scotland's fifty–four chief religious houses had been erected into temporal lordships. It was a practice which continued to cause deep dismay to the General Assembly and it repeatedly asked the king to stop it.[1] The main cause of their annoyance was almost certainly a fear that such dismemberment would make the task of financing the Church yet more complicated.[2]

However, there was another ground for their concern. This was that, in the relationship between patrons and church, the secularization process was allowing greater license to the former to exploit what they could at the latter's expense. Particularly vexing was that the state appeared ready to support patrons when they overreached themselves. One example was a complaint that surfaced at the 1598 Assembly[3] concerning a loophole which patrons had been exploiting in the law against simony. Although Parliament had, in 1584[4], listed it as a crime, a grey area arose where presentees promised, once installed, to grant the patron a tack of the parochial teinds. Since the tack would invariably be at a rate lower than the teinds' true value, the profits accruing to the patron thereafter could be considerable. The patrons successfully defended themselves against the charge of simony by claiming that the practice could only be considered simoniacal if what was paid to the incumbent did not provide a sufficient stipend. Presbyteries were thus put in a frustrating position. They could

1. 1588, 1592, and 1598.

2. Since the teinds had been specifically excluded from the 1587 Annexation Act, the presumption, in ecclesiastical circles, had been that they were being earmarked for the Church's use. However, it became increasingly obvious that nothing specific was going to materialize: "Sometimes the teinds of the annexed churches were expressly conveyed to the grantee, and erected into benefices with grants of the patronage; at other times there was no mention of the patronage and no erection of the teinds into benefices, but in both cases the Lords of Erection generally assumed to themselves the right of presenting" [*Patronage Report*, #32].

3. Sess. 4, 9 March 1598; *BUK*, 467.

4. *APS.*, iv, 294. The Act does not define simony, but simply lists it, along with the dilapidation of the rents of benefices, as an offence worthy of deprivation.

not but refuse collation to someone who was clearly involved in a disreputable arrangement, yet in the eyes of the law the presentation was still orderly. This meant that if they refused to proceed, the patron was now entitled to uplift the teinds indefinitely,[5]or at least until the presentation was either accepted or withdrawn. To crown all, not only did James ignore the Assembly's complaint about the loophole, but actually gave it legislative validity in 1612.[6]

There were other ways in which patrons were allowed to stretch the law in order to transform an opportunity into a right. One was the anomaly whereby landowners assigned to themselves the rank of patron, when their entitlement was, in fact, spurious. Thus, whereas it was in order for temporal lords to assume presentation rights to *patronate* churches (where solely the patronage belonged to the former prelacy), there was little justification for their taking the title of patron to *patrimonial* churches in their possession. In the latter case, the old religious house, chapter or bishop had been the occupant of the benefice, and, on their behalf, a vicar served the cure, for which he received a stipend out of the tithes. Thus, the new landowner had, in effect, succeeded to the role of titular, and as such, he could hardly be the patron at the same time, since the incumbent was his stipendiary, not his presentee.[7] Nonetheless, the new lords often simply awarded themselves the status of patron, and then were careful to have the fact recorded in any subsequent charters.

Thus it was that with every passing year, the possibility—if it ever existed— of lay patronage being removed from the Scottish parochial landscape grew ever more impracticable. A century that began with a land owning class that was relaxed about ownership of the privilege ended in a very different atmosphere. Nonetheless, such were the twists and turns of the Crown's relations with the Kirk over the ensuing fifty years, suddenly abolition returned, not just as a possibility, but a reality. In order to understand how the change came about, it is important to look briefly at the

---

5. The privilege was affirmed in the Deposition of Ministers Act of 1592 [*APS*, iii, 542, c.9]. On the 23 July 1644, however, Parliament decided that the fruits of a vacant benefice could only be expended on pious uses [*APS*. vi, 128, c.47]. After the Restoration 0f 1660, the 1644 Act was rescinded. Yet, although presentations (abolished in 1649) were then re-established, patrons did not get back their right to the teinds of a vacancy. These were to be applied for pious uses for seven years, then during royal pleasure [*APS*., 1661, vii, 303, c.330].

6. *APS*, iv, 469.

7. Dunlop, *Parochial law*, 193–94.

strategies employed by James and his son Charles as they sought to mould church and state to their liking.

James's Ecclesiastical Policies, 1592–1625

Frustrations over patronage were only part of a wider picture of discomfort experienced by the Kirk, as the king, almost as soon as he had granted its 1592 "Charter of Presbyterianism," devoted the remaining years of his reign to doing what he could to include episcopacy in the Scottish ecclesiastical structure.[8] It was a task that he saw as even more vital on his departure to London after the Union of the Crowns in 1603. Since this ambition raised the question whether the presbytery or the bishop should then vet presentations, and settle vacancies *jure devoluto*, it is necessary to see how events unfolded as the king set about achieving his aims.

James saw parity among ministers as "the mother of confusion," and advised his son, that by "preferment to bishoprics and benefices . . . ye shall not only banish their parity (which I can not agree with a monarchy) but ye shall also re-establish the old institution of three estates in parliament, which can do no otherwise be done."[9] Pursuing the latter aim first, James passed an Act, in 1597, allowing such ministers as he should nominate to bishoprics, abbacies or other prelacies, to have a seat and vote in Parliament.[10] The first appointees were in place by the end of 1600.

He had now to strengthen the bishop's ecclesiastical authority, and having enacted legislation, in 1606, asserting his royal prerogative in all matters[11] and re-establishing the episcopal office, he went on, in 1609, to restore consistorial jurisdiction to bishops and, by now, archbishops. At the Assembly convened at Glasgow in June 1610, the rights and privileges of the episcopate were agreed, laid down as Acts of Assembly, and later confirmed, with modifications, as Acts of Parliament. Among these rights it was stipulated that all presentations were now to be directed to diocesan bishops or archbishops, who could also fill benefices *jure devoluto*. Moreover, the bishop was to make final "trial" of any candidate, and,

---

8. For a discussion of this, see David G. Mullen, *Episcopacy in Scotland: the history of an idea* (Edinburgh: 1986).

9. *Basilikon Doron*, in *Source Book iii*, 51.

10. *APS*, iv, 130.

11. Although an English–style royal supremacy in the Kirk was not constitutionally possible, since unlike England, the Kirk did not issue from the conscious will and pleasure of a monarch.

having found him suitably qualified, ordain him, assisted by such of the ministers as he chose to invite.[12] Up until 1610, presbyteries had become the customary recipient of presentations. Now this practice was swiftly turned around. Indeed, from March onwards, well before the Glasgow Assembly, presentations were, in every case, given exclusively to bishops and archbishops[13]. By an act of 1617,[14] James saw to it that cathedral chapters had their traditional revenues restored, and thus finalized his work on reestablishing episcopacy in the Scottish Church.

Although he was unable to show the same sure-footedness when it came to effecting liturgical changes,[15] as far as his remolding of the Kirk's polity was concerned, James had cause to be satisfied with those ecclesiastical ambitions which had been realized by the time of his death in 1625. His son Charles's diplomatic failings were to do spectacular damage to all James had built up, but it must be admitted that there had been signs that James' authority was not invulnerable. His insistence on pushing the Five Articles of Perth through the Assembly in 1618, and Parliament in 1621, won him little favor. At all levels of Scottish society, the Articles, or at least some of them, bore for many the savor of popery.[16] Again, although James's large financial demands upon Parliament in 1621 were voted through, there is no doubt that these contributed to a souring of attitudes towards him on the part of both merchants and landowners during the final years of his reign. By the time of his death in 1625, there were ample signs that Scotland's quiescence could not be taken for granted: "The convergence of fiscal demands and religious change was an explosive mix, and one that would return to destroy Charles I."[17]

12. *BUK*, 587; *APS*, iv, 469.

13. W. R. Foster, *The church before the Covenants.* (Edinburgh: 1975), 24–25.

14. *APS*, iv, 529.

15. These chiefly concerned a new prayer book and the restoration of certain practices (the celebration of Christian festivals, private baptism, episcopal confirmation, private communion and receipt of the sacrament while kneeling) which came to be known as the Five Articles of Perth. Seeing the hostility both matters engendered, James licensed the former and enacted the latter, but did not press them further.

16. "Fifteen nobles voted [in 1621] against the proposals, amongst them lords of erection who might have been expected to support the King. James had triumphed, but at great cost to the authority of the crown." Ian B. Cowan, "The Five Articles of Perth" in, *Reformation and revolution, essays presented to the Very Rev. Hugh Watt.* (Edinburgh: 1967), 177.

17. Keith Brown, *Kingdom or Province? Scotland and the regal union, 1603–1715.* (Basingstoke: 1992), 97. See also Alan R. MacDonald, *The Jacobean kirk, 1567–1625, sovereignty, polity and liturgy* (Aldershot: 1998).

Charles I (1625–1649)

One important ingredient in the fateful mix was teind reform. Charles would have known that this was an issue of particular sensitivity to patrons, yet it did not prevent his alienating many. The reform was part of the package which came to be known as Charles's Revocation Scheme. The background to the scheme was a principle that had emerged out of the minorities which had plagued the Stewart monarchy in previous centuries. The idea was that a new king, provided he acted before his twenty-fifth birthday, could annul grants of property (and heritable offices and pensions) made during his minority. In a declaration made within four months of his accession, Charles twisted this concession in order to suggest he was entitled to a revocation of all royal grants since 1540. It is probable that the king's basic goal was to make a timely demonstration of his overarching supremacy, and that he had, in fact, no intention of undertaking a wholesale annexation.[18] Be that as it may, the arrogant presentation of the announcement, and Charles's continuing lack of diplomatic *savoir faire*, ensured that a sense of hostility and distrust was ineradicably sown amongst the nobility.

Although a key aim of the project (ratified by Parliament in 1633) was the boosting of crown income, the king's desire was also to redistribute the teinds so as to put the funding of poor relief, schools, colleges and ministers on a sound footing. For both ministers and heritors, this part of the scheme was something of a breakthrough, in that the situation that had evolved under James VI, had often bred confusion over who owned the teinds as well as contention over the amount due to minister or titular. Now, in a way that reiterated the vision of the first *Book of Discipline*, each landowner or heritor would have his own teinds,[19] subject to a proportion going to the parish minister as stipend. Teind redistribution was a slow and complex business, not least because, in every locality, a revaluation to a fixed amount, was first required. However, the machinery for establishing adequate stipends was at least in place, and it is clear that, by the late 1630s, most ministers were receiving a settled and satisfactory maintenance.[20] However, King James had been sufficiently astute to know that

18. See David Stevenson, *The Scottish Revolution, 1637–1644; the triumph of the Covenanters.* (Newton Abbot: 1973), 35–36

19. That is, he was given the right to buy them from the titular or patron at nine-years' purchase.

20. W. R. Foster, "A constant platt achieved: provision for the ministry, 1600–38" in *Reformation and Revolution*, 140.

any implementation of the Reformers' ideal for ministerial funding could only be achieved at a high price in terms of goodwill among the landed interest, which was why, as a compromise, he had established a commission to review and upgrade inadequate stipends.[21] When Charles rejected that piecemeal approach in favor of sweeping reform, he was moving onto dangerous ground.

It should be said that the teind structure *was* in need of revision, and the financing of Church, education and poor relief was, moreover, greatly advantaged by the plan, but the winning of even grudging acceptance for it from those who were most affected, was simply beyond the skills of Charles to achieve. Even the ministers, disappointed at the slow progress of the revaluation, showed scant appreciation.[22] Indeed, notwithstanding their augmented stipends, any enthusiasm by churchmen for the new funding scheme was undermined by the knowledge that acceptance also meant abandonment of their cherished hope of having all the teinds restored to the Church's use.[23]

Another cause of anger among the nobility was what Charles proposed to do about the ownership of former church lands. Many great families had made substantial gains, and, while they were to be allowed to hold on to their acquisitions (at a cost), it was the fate of the properties they had since sold off, which was to give particular affront. The king had seen that the lords continued to exert enormous influence throughout their localities, by the fact that they still remained the feudal superior of any alienated estate. Accordingly, Charles set about "liberating" these feuars, by stripping the nobles of their superiority and vesting it in the Crown instead. The king's ostensible motive was to free the gentry/heritors from the dominance of the aristocracy, however, the latter saw it as a slight on their social position, as well as an attempt to lessen their power.

As for the gentry, if the king had hoped for gratitude in response to his policy, little was forthcoming. Not only did it become obvious to them that the king was more concerned to curtail the nobility than to promote their participation in government,[24] but also it had become clear

21. The first, in 1606, was to see that incumbents of churches in the new erections were properly remunerated. Since the commission's remit was, technically, limited to parishes within former abbey lands, a wider commission was established in 1617 (and renewed in 1621), with the aim of upgrading all inadequate stipends. Being a compromise, the results failed to be comprehensive, but there were significant improvements. See: Foster, "A constant platt achieved," 127–33.

22. Ian B. Cowan, *The Scottish covenanters.* (London: 1976), 19.

23. Stevenson, *Scottish revolution*, 38.

24. Stevenson, *Scottish revolution*, 41.

that the process of buying out their teinds from the titulars was fraught with difficulty and frustration.[25] As a result, many became disenchanted.

The final element in the mix was in the ecclesiastical sphere. Here Charles's actions attracted opprobrium at almost every level, including, yet again, the nobility. When he used his visit to Scotland in 1633 to push forward his wish for greater conformity with Anglican practices and apparel, the resultant petitions showed that a deep dislike for these and the (now reactivated) Five Articles of Perth was not lacking among the higher social ranks[26]. The same men of substance were also experiencing a mounting anger against the episcopate, not only at local level, where patrons complained their candidates were obstructed by the arbitrary imposition of an oath of obedience,[27] but also in national government. There, the king had more and more been using the bishops as a means of imposing his wishes, and in this regard, their dominant role in the Committee of Articles (which controlled all legislation and parliamentary agenda) had been especially useful. Resentment increased when the bishops were perceived to have been instrumental in pushing on an unsupportable prosecution of Lord Balmerino for treason (1634–6). It mounted again when the archbishop of St Andrews, John Spottiswood, was made high chancellor in 1635, and even further when rumors abounded that abbeys and priories were to be retrieved from lay hands and restored to the clergy.[28]

The Revolution of 1637

When, in 1636, Charles published a code of canons for the Kirk to use, not only did it confirm high church practices, but appeared to give scant recognition to the authority of presbyterial courts. It also enjoined the use of a prayer book, which appeared the following year. Even though the book had not been sanctioned by Parliament or General Assembly, its use was insisted upon, purely on the strength of royal prerogative. On

25. See Macinnes, *Charles I*, 67–70.

26. See, ʻThe humble supplication of the lords and commissioners of Parliament undersubscryveingʼ [1633] and "The humble supplication of some lords and others commissioners of the late parliament" 1634], in John Row, *The History of the Kirk of Scotland from the year 1558 to August 1637* Wodrow Society. (Edinburgh: 1842), 364–66; 376–81.

27. Row, *The History*, 351; 360.

28. Row, 381ff.; Macinnes, *Charles I*, 90; John Spalding, *The History of the troubles and memorable transactions in Scotland and England from 1624 to 1645* Bannatyne Club 25 (Edinburgh: 1828), vol. I, 45–47.

the 23 July 1637, the bishop of Edinburgh attempted to read from 'This Popish-Inglish-Scotish-Masse-Service-Booke'[29] in the pulpit of St Giles, whereupon, a riot broke out. In the aftermath of this disturbance, some of the discontent that had been rumbling now began to express itself through protest and petition. Eventually, the widespread opposition united around the momentous National Covenant, which was first signed in Edinburgh on the 28 February 1638. It was principally drafted by the advocate, Archibald Johnston# of Wariston, and the minister of Leuchars, Alexander Henderson#. Both were radical presbyterians, yet the document endeavored to be comprehensive, condemning neither the king nor, expressly, episcopacy, but rather appealing to the religious practices of the Reformation and calling for resistance to "popish" encroachments upon the Kirk's liberty in forms of worship, doctrine and discipline. Patronage was not referred to, yet what was meant by *discipline* was soon to be the subject of earnest debate.

Charles at first determined to face down the protest, but his high commissioner, the Marquis of Hamilton, advised him that such was the universality of its support, concessions would have to be made. Accordingly, Hamilton announced, in September 1638, that the service book, code of canons, court of high commission and the Perth Articles were to be abandoned. Also a General Assembly was convened, at Glasgow, on the first of November. Presbyteries, for the first time, organized a large complement of elders to go up to the Assembly, most of whom were not ready for compromise. The result was that the Assembly's enactments went much further than the terms of the Covenant had suggested: all Assemblies since 1605 were declared null, the service book, code of canons, high commission court and Five Articles were all condemned and episcopacy was abjured.

Since Charles had managed to alienate so many interests, the Covenant attracted support from all over the country, including the Highlands, although the Aberdeen area was a notable exception[30]. In the matter of leadership, the part played by the nobility and gentry was decisive, both in the Assemblies of 1638 and August 1639, and thereafter, in Parliament, which held its first session of the new era on 31 August 1639. Thanks only to their support, could the Covenanting agenda, including the abolition of episcopacy, be ratified by Parliament (June 1640), or at the same time military success be achieved in the "Bishops' Wars," first in the confrontation

---

29. Row, 398.

30. Macinnes, 185; Row, 493ff.

at Berwick (resolved June 1639), then at Newcastle (resolved, at London, August 1641). After the London treaty was ratified by the Scots Parliament, Charles gave it royal assent, thereby ostensibly giving legal recognition to the new regime. As a result, although expressions of dissent from moderates and royalists like the Marquis of Montrose prevented comprehensive unanimity, the Covenanting cause nevertheless ended 1641 in what appeared to be a strong and secure position. This being the case, it might well be wondered what had been happening meanwhile with regard to lay patronage. Was the time now ripe for the Kirk to revive the debate about its place, and perhaps even press for its abolition?

Lay Patronage and the Revolution of 1637–1639

When they reflected upon the revolution, presbyterians knew that the overthrow of episcopacy had been dependent upon the support of the higher social ranks. It was a debt the moderator of the 1638 General Assembly acknowledged in fulsome tones when delivering his closing speech:

> And I must say one word of those Nobles whom Jesus Christ hath nobilitat indeed, and declaired sensiblie to be worthie of that title of nobilitie. Ye know they were lyke the tops of the mountaines that were first discovered in the deludge, which made the little valleyes hope to be delyvered from it also; . . . the Sun of righteousnesse hes beine pleased to shyne first upon these mountaines; and long, long may he shyne upon them, for the comfort of the hilles and refreshing of the valleyes; and the blessing of God be upon them and their families.[31]

The natural result of this obligation was that the presbyterian party were wary of antagonizing the aristocracy by declaring patronage a grievance much in need of reform. On the other hand, as will be seen, it was not an issue that was about to go away, and it is illuminating to note how some of the leading figures in the Kirk struggled to reconcile the demands of diplomacy with the desire of the *Second Book of Discipline* to terminate patrons' presentation rights.

The most valuable insights into contemporary attitudes to patronage are found in the papers of Robert Baillie# (1599–1662), who was minister of Kilwinning (Irvine presbytery) until his appointment to the chair

---

31. Alexander Peterkin, *Records of the Kirk of Scotland, containing the acts and proceedings of the General Assemblies from the year 1638 downwards*, (Edinburgh: 1843), 191.

of divinity at Glasgow university in 1642. Baillie was a man of moderate principles, and appears as someone who was happiest "straddling to some degree the divide between presbyterian and Episcopalian."[32] This stemmed more from open–mindedness than the desire to trim, and made him willing, on issues like royal authority and episcopacy itself, to modify his views according to the merits of the situation. His opinions on the subject of patronage, however, remained consistent during the period of the revolution, and these were that, although it might be good to give the topic of reform a public airing, the time was "not seasonable," and to do so would only stir up difficulties, especially with the king, as largest patron.[33]

Despite its boldness in other matters, the Glasgow Assembly of 1638 shared Baillie's circumspection. According to Johnston of Wariston, the Assembly avoided making subscription to the *Second Book of Discipline* compulsory, purely in order to avoid raising "scrouples anent teynds and patronages."[34] Instead, while avoiding any objection to presentations, it simply required that "there be a respect had to the congregation, and that no person be intruded . . . contrare to the will of the congregation."[35] The issue of patronage would not, however, lie down, but instead surfaced for debate at the Assembly of 1639. Alarmed at the damage any prolonged confrontation on the matter would do to the presbyterian cause generally among the landed interest, Johnston hurriedly intervened to emphasize that no harm was intended against the rights of patrons, and he prevailed upon the Assembly not only to affirm that this was their view, but also to express their gladness that parliament had recently ratified "the Act of Parliament 1592, quhairin Laick Patronages ar expreslie reserved."[36]

Interestingly, Johnston's intervention failed to reassure the king's commissioner to the Assembly, John Stewart, first Earl of Traquair, who felt sufficiently worried to enter a minute in the registers of the Privy Council, disassociating himself from any hurt which might yet occur to the king's patronal rights, and reserving the Crown's right thereafter to

32. David Stevenson, *King or Covenant? Voices from the civil war.* (East Linton: 1996), 21.

33. *The letters and journals of Robert Baillie, AM, principal of the university of Glasgow, 1637–62* ed. Laing, David, 3 vols, (Edinburgh: 1841), i, "To William Spang" (his cousin and minister of the Scots church, Veere, Netherlands), 12 February 1639, 114.

34. Baillie, *Letters*, ii, "Letter from Archibald Johnston of Warristone to Mr Robert Baillie, 25 December 1639," 451.

35. Pitcairn, *Acts*, 26.

36. Baillie, *Letters*, ii, 459.

seek redress.[37] Almost certainly, Traquair saw that a popular, reforming movement like the one he was witnessing, would be difficult to control, and that the Covenanting leaders had put themselves in a particularly precarious position on the matter of presentations. On the one hand, they had been rousing the people to assert their spiritual liberty, while at the same time, they were asking them to refrain from challenging the continuation of a privilege like patronage, purely on the expedient that it was "maist convenient for the Kirk at this tyme to silence these questions, and tolerat many thingis (quhairof they wald faine haiff redres) for the setling of the substantiall Governement of this Kirk."[38] Traquair would have seen it as inevitable that those less able to discern the diplomatic niceties of the situation would, eventually, break ranks. In the event, he was correct.

What became the focus of contention was whether or not the Covenant's reference to the "discipline" of the Church, should be directly equated with what was laid out in the *Second Book of Discipline*. If so, it was a serious matter, for members of a congregation would therefore be in breach of their sworn allegiance to the Covenant, if they accepted a presentee who had not been elected by them. This was precisely the argument put forward by the people of Glassford (Hamilton presbytery), when they took an aversion to the patron's choice for the vacancy there, and such was the anxiety it aroused in Baillie, he wrote, in 1639, for help to Johnston, who was legal adviser to the Assembly. On hearing that a similar scenario was unfolding in another parish, Johnston considered the situation serious enough for him to leave his sick-bed to make, as he saw it, a definitive statement of the Kirk's position on presentations, before things got out of hand.[39]

Johnston of Wariston's Statement

Johnston's paper is lengthy, but it provides a remarkable insight into what the leading figure in the Church at the time was thinking, and is worthy of attention. Its salient points can be summarized:

37. 30 August 1639. *RPCS.*, vii, 132. On the 31 August 1641, Parliament ordered the protest to be deleted.

38. Baillie, *Letters*, 459.

39. "Letter from Archibald Johnston of Warriston, to Mr Robert Baillie. 25 December 1639." Baillie, 450–60. Johnston does not reveal the location of the other place where the issue was in contention. The background to the Glassford dispute is ably described in W. Makey, *The church of the Covenant 1637–1651*, (Edinburgh: 1979), 174–75.

(i). only fanatics could think of raising, unnecessarily, questions of national significance at a time when the Church is trying to settle after the recent upheavals;

(ii). swearing to maintain the Kirk's discipline is not the same as maintaining the *Book of Discipline*; there has been no specific instruction for the book to be subscribed by congregations, and in any case, there are also other guides to doctrine and discipline contained in past Acts of Assembly, which the Kirk could equally refer to—indeed, where an Act and the book conflict, the Act is to be preferred; whatever the *Books of Discipline* might say, the clear thread of parliamentary legislation since 1560 has been to uphold the rights of patrons, moreover, the Assembly itself has virtually done the same; even the Assembly of 1581, which entered the text of the second *Book* in its registers, contradicted it soon afterwards, by recording a requirement for all presentations to be directed to presbyteries; repeatedly, in subsequent Assemblies, the language of the minutes seem to suggest that presentations are an accepted fact of life; in summation, it is obvious from observation and from Acts of Parliament and Assembly, that the practice suggested by the *Book* "hes never come in practise, is obsolet, and the contrarie thairof continuallie tolerated."[40]

(iii). the complainers are mistaken about the form of the book; only the first ten chapters contain directives, and none of these expressly condemns patronage; in chapter eleven, abuses are complained of, and in chapter twelve, supplication is made to have matters like patronage reformed; however, the abandonment of presentations was only *sought*, not enacted; this means the Covenant oath can hardly apply to something that *ought* to be done, but only to matters which are actually enjoined;

(iv). the complainers are also mistaken about the book's use of the word presentation; in present usage, a presentation is separate from collation and institution; in earlier times however, it is clear, from Acts of Parliament and Assembly, that a settlement by presentation meant it took place without any collation, admission or examination by the Church at all; this habit of patrons planting benefices *pleno jure* [with full authority], was an issue of great

---

40. Baillie, 454.

annoyance to the Church, as may be seen from the resolutions of Assembly from 1563 onwards; yet patronage *per se* was not condemned, indeed, surely someone whose presentation is directed to the presbytery, who is then tried before the congregation and admitted by the presbytery, cannot be said to be intruded upon that people; be that as it may, Johnston personally thinks that a presbytery should resist implementing a presentation where the people are unanimously averse to the candidate, and that, on the face of it, the congregation has a right of negation (which should not nullify a patron's right of patronage any more than the presbytery's limited power of veto does, since, after all, he can continue to present other candidates); on the other hand, if a parish's opposition is obviously "of will, and not of witt,"[41] then presbytery should regulate its obstinacy; in summation, he does not think patronage is incompatible with election— it is like a parent or guardian initiating a marriage for his ward; in such a situation, it does not matter who is the proposer of the match, as long as it proceeds on the basis of consent;

(v). if the complainers wish to invoke the Covenant, let them remember that by it they swore to eschew the type of dangerous and divisive conduct they are now pursuing, "quhairof treulie I know none so great as this war to putt the Nobilitie, Gentrie, and Ministrie, be the eares togider [i.e., at variance];"[42] further, the Covenant binds them to seek, by all means lawful, to recover the purity and liberty of the gospel as was practiced before the recent novations, however, they should remember, (a), settlements without presentations were not established as a part of that liberty before now, and indeed, the opposite custom has been tolerated; "All that can be said, that it [abolition] was wishit for and supplicated for; and so aucht we to doe, even as much as they did, to compleine of the abuse, and supplicat superior poweris,"[43] (b), it is for the Assembly or parliament to declare whether or not something is a corruption, before it can be said that the Covenant implies it should be abjured, (c), on such a national issue as this, it is not for individuals

41. Ibid., 458.
42. Ibid., 459.
43. Ibid.

to question what the Assembly expressly allows, and they should properly be censured for it, and (d), for all their fervor, they are in fact only binding themselves "to recover that quhilk was never had, and so was never lost."[44]

In conclusion, he hopes his statement will be used, not to defend patronage—for he will labor, by all lawful means, to free the Church from it—but only for removing the objections that the complainers have to it.

Critique of Johnston's Arguments

Taken as a whole, Johnston's statement is coherent and persuasive, except for his fourth point, much of which is confused, if not questionable. It is important to consider this in detail, since some of the matters it covers reappear in later controversies.

The first part of his argument appears to be that the Church has never been opposed to presentations as such, only the particular way in which presentations were understood to operate in earlier times, that is, as a process by which a vacancy could be filled without deference to ecclesiastical examination and admission. He substantiates this claim by referring to the frequency with which the Assembly, from the beginning, called for its collation rights to be upheld, yet, by contrast, was silent on the subject of patronage's abolition. To this it must be answered, however, that there is little indication that the early Reformers collectively entertained a different definition of the word *presentation* from that used by the next generation. It is certainly difficult to derive such an impression from the text of either *Book of Discipline*, and Gordon Donaldson makes no allowance for it: "Between 1560 and 1567 . . . while the crown showed a certain hesitation about making presentations and usually preferred to dispone benefices by simple gift, other patrons in general adhered to the traditional procedure of presentation followed by episcopal collation."[45]

As for the existence of actual dialectic about the issue of lay patronage during the early Reformation period, Johnston is right when he alludes to its paucity. Nonetheless, it is still justifiable to conclude that the early Reformers' ideal vision of "lawful election" did not include presentations (of any kind) by lay patrons.[46] That there was not more attention paid to

44. Ibid., 460.
45. Donaldson, *Scottish Reformation*, 73.
46. Unless it is considered that an oblique reference was made to them in the 1562

a campaign for actual abolition, was due to a pragmatism which obliged them to stifle such ambitions until a more favorable climate showed itself. In this respect, for example, a particular inducement to tread warily seems to have taken place in 1565, when the Queen took the opportunity of warning the Assembly that the Crown was not prepared to make compromises on the patronage issue. Since the Church was in need of the queen's assistance in trying to resolve its increasingly desperate financial crisis (see chapter 1), the incentive would have been overwhelming for the Assembly to soften its position on presentations, and, instead, focus on the vital, but less confrontational issue of collation rights.

Johnston's next argument is that patronage and the Kirk's freedom of election need not be incompatible, since the crucial issue is always whether or not a forced intrusion takes place. In his view, such intrusions should not happen so long as presentations are channeled through presbyteries, where the candidate can again[47] be examined and then admitted. He forms this conclusion on the grounds that, "the Presbyterie, whilk being composed of some delegatis from the Kirk-Session of every pareoch, importis in thair Actis the consent of the haill."[48] It must be allowed that Johnston's claim has validity when applied to those settlements where the presbytery was, from the start, the prime mover in the vacancy process, perhaps sending a leet of candidates to the parish and thereafter canvassing opinion upon it. In such instances, it might actually seek a presentation from the patron as its final step before admission. As A.I. Dunlop has pointed out in his article on the polity of the Kirk between 1600 and 1637, this was not uncommon.[49] Indeed, as was the case in the planting of Calder (Edinburgh) in 1617, and St. Andrews (St. Andrews) in 1639, the presentation might even be made weeks, or even years, after the admission had taken place.[50] Clearly, in such situations, a congregation's sentiments would have been reflected in the presbytery's actions. However, Johnston is noticeably uncertain on the matter of what the presbytery was to do when

---

Assembly Act: "That inhibition shall be made to all . . . that hes not been presented be the people, or ane part thereof, to the Superintendant." *BUK*, 12.

47. A presentee would already have been examined and "licensed" as a probationer or expectant. The Church's intention was that he would always be re-examined before admission to his first charge.

48. Ibid., 457,

49. A. I. Dunlop, "The polity of the Scottish church, 1600–1637," *RSCHS*, xii, (1955–6), 177.

50. Hardy Bertram McCall, *The history and antiquities of the parish of Mid-Calder.* (Edinburgh: 1894), 223; *Patronage report, 1834*, 402.

(as became more common) the patron took the initiative and issued a presentation first. Having said that there should not be an intrusion problem if the presbytery's privileges are observed, he then, in effect, contradicts himself by conceding that determined, parochial opposition can indeed happen. In such a case, his solution is that the presbytery should not admit the presentee. He then goes a step further, by adding: "And to tell yow my thochtis, as they ay come into my head….I think the pareoch hes *quandam speciem vocis negativae* [something akin to a negative voice] at the leist, quhilk yit takis no wayes away the patrones right of patronage."[51] He does not, however, provide any references to confirm his view, which itself is complicated by his additional opinion that congregational refusals should be overruled if redolent of obstinacy. Even this statement fits awkwardly with the succeeding argument, which likens the patron's role to that of a matchmaker: "quhither any freind to the partie, or the partie to thair freindis, be the first proponer of the match, I think thair is no so essentiall a difference...gif the match be maid with consent of parties."[52] The difficulty, of course, with the analogy was that, in the ecclesiastical domain, consent was not unrestricted, nor was there guidance for presbyteries as to what constituted unreasonable refusal.

To be fair to Johnston, however, the whole issue of consent, that is to say, *how* it could be incorporated into a presentations system and *by how much*, had been unresolved since the legislation of 1567, as Donaldson mentions: "How, if at all, the patron's presentation and the superintendent's collation were reconciled with any right of congregations to choose their ministers is by no means clear . . . and the indications are that the wishes of the parishioners, if not wholly ignored, could be influential only by being made known informally to the patron."[53]

To sum up, the flaw of Johnston's main argument is that he accepts that patronage is a "thraldome" which the Kirk would be better without, yet, instead of simply saying that it is something which must be endured for reasons of expedience, he also attempts to convey that it is not a burden at all, if properly exercised. This contradiction is one indication that the statement's author is not entirely confident that he has a sufficient answer to all the issues raised by the Glassford complaint. His declared ill-health and the necessity for haste would possibly have had a bearing on this, but, almost certainly, there were other contributory factors.

51. Ibid., 457–48

52. Baillie, *Letters*, 458.

53. Donaldson, *Scottish Reformation*, 154.

In the first place, Johnston's major difficulty was that he could not bear to think, given the importance of the Kirk's quickly consolidating the gains of the revolution, that parishes and presbyteries could actually allow themselves to become embroiled in disputes over what were, to him, largely matters of opinion and preference—and this at a time, when, above all, the pressing need was simply to fill vacancies.[54] Indeed, he knew there were areas where long vacancies would have been especially damaging. These were centers of influence, like Edinburgh, or parishes where the local magnates were Roman Catholic or episcopal in sympathy. This was why the 1638 Assembly, seeing the urgent necessity to advance to such places men able to "stop the mouthes of the adversaries," had revived an Assembly Act of 1596, ordering presbyteries to take particular care that this be done.[55]

Secondly, it would have occurred to Johnston that Glassford's challenge to the Kirk's working relationship with the patrons might well be repeated in other parishes. Glassford's patronage was in private hands, but the worrying thought was that, since many parishes still had the king as patron, these too might now be emboldened to complain about the level of attention paid to their preferences, thereby creating the possibility of much damage to the Covenant's professions of respect for the Crown.

These two concerns would have fuelled Johnston's anxiety to produce a rebuttal which was both swift and assertive. In the immediate term, he was probably successful, but, as will be seen in the next section, the issues which had risen to the surface at Glassford were not to disappear. If anything, Johnston's treatise served to stimulate debate about patronage rather than dissipate it. Nonetheless, what is significant about his essay is that it provides not only a revealing insight into the thinking of the Covenanters' leading legal adviser, but also emerges as the Kirk's first serious discussion of the tensions involved in attempting to reconcile the ideal of congregational consultation with the interests of a landowning elite, jealous of their rights.

54. A 1640 parliamentary Act *For planting of kirks unprovided with ministers through the patron's default* complains of the large number of continuing vacancies. *APS.*, v, 299.

55. Pitcairn, *Acts*, 22–24.

Attitudes to Lay Patronage in the 1640s

For all his attempts to quash the complaints raised at Glassford, it is clear that Johnston also knew the Church could not afford to ignore them. Having now been voiced publicly, they were not likely simply to go away. That the Kirk was well aware it could not forget about the issue can be glimpsed in the wording of some of the Assembly legislation ratified by Parliament in 1640. Although the rights of patrons were upheld, the *Act for planting of kirks unprovided with ministers through the patron's default* reminded presbyteries to use every opportunity to fill vacancies, but at the same time to obtain the consent of the parishioners.[56] Again, the *Act anent admission of ministers to kirks which belonged to bishoprics* reassured patrons of their status, yet took the opportunity of pointedly asserting that presentations had not always been necessary to establish right to a stipend.[57]

An indication of how matters were now rapidly developing can be seen the following year in a book, *The Government and Order of the Church of Scotland*, by the prominent Covenanter, Alexander Henderson.[58] In the section on the admission of ministers, Henderson (who writes in the guise of a detached observer) suggests by his tone that the principle of popular consent should be regarded as settled in Scotland, and that presentations are, by contrast, merely endured for diplomatic reasons: "liberty of election is in part prejudged and hindered by patronages and presentations which are still in use there, not by the rules of their discipline, but by toleration of that which they cannot amend; in the meantime procuring, that in the case of presentations by patrons, the examination and tryall by the presbytery is still the same. The congregation, where he is presented to serve, is called, if they have aught to object against his doctrine or life, after they have heard him, or [if they have not] that their consent may be had."[59]

---

56. *APS.*, v, 299.

57. *APS*, v, 299–300. By this Act, the Kirk claimed the right to settle charges that had been put into the hands of bishops, by virtue of the Act of 1606 restoring their estate.

58. Alexander Henderson (1583–1646) was originally a supporter of episcopacy, and had been given the charge of Leuchars (St Andrews) against the wishes of the parish; he subsequently changed his opinions and spoke against episcopacy, the Five Articles and Laud's liturgy; he was the chief draughtsman of both Covenants, and after his election as moderator of the Glasgow Assembly, was a towering figure in church affairs; called to Edinburgh in 1638.

59. Alexander Henderson, *The government and order of the church of Scotland*, (Edinburgh: 1641), section ii, quoted in *Patronage Report*, 475. For a summary of the section on calling of ministers, see Appendix I.

By 1642, it is clear that the *status quo* was becoming less and less attractive. At that year's Assembly, an attempt at reform appeared in the guise of the *Act anent the order for making lists to his majestie, and other patrons, for presentations; the order of tryall of expectants, and for trying the quality of Kirks*.[60] The main feature of this was the revelation that an arrangement had been negotiated with the king, so that, if a vacancy were to arise within the gift of either the Crown or anyone to whom he had disponed the patronage after 3 January 1642, then the presentation would only be given to a candidate selected from leets provided by the Church. On the occurrence of each vacancy, the presbytery would send the patron a blank presentation and a list of six persons who were both acceptable to the majority of the congregation, and willing to take the charge.[61] To the parliamentary commissioners who had arranged the agreement, it may well have seemed a suitable compromise, but Baillie saw no future in it: "The overture . . . was of no use to us; for it was hard for us to find one person to a vacant kirk; bot to send up six . . . "[62]

Baillie felt the same lack of enthusiasm for another compromise, this time put before the Assembly by the Marquis of Argyll.[63] Hoping to persuade his fellow patrons to join him, Argyll offered a bargain whereby, "they would give free libertie to presbyteries and people to name whom they would to vacant places, on condition the Assemblie would obleidge intrants to rest content with modified stipends."[64] Baillie's view was that it was foolish to tie the Church's hands, but further debate on the matter was aborted when it became obvious that some landed patrons were outraged that any such arrangement was being discussed at all. Accordingly, it was thought wise to drop the subject of patronage for the remainder of the court's sitting.

When the 1643 Assembly came around, it was obvious the patronage debate was still very much alive. The fact was, Johnston's optimism that patrons and parishes should not find it difficult to work in harmony, was

60. Act Sess. 7, 3 August 1642, Pitcairn, 54–55.

61. A candidate could already be in a parish, but if an expectant, he was not eligible for the leet unless he had been tried and admitted to the "exercise" for at least six months.

62. *Letters*, ii, 47.

63. Archibald Campbell, 1607–61, was eighth earl of Argyll and became a marquis in 1641. At this time he was probably the Covenanters' leading figure, and a dominant force, nationally.

64. Ibid., From 1617, the Commisssioners of Teinds had the power to "modify" or decide a level of stipend.

starting to be contradicted by a succession of tiresome altercations. Since 1641, lengthy disputes had arisen between the preferences of patron and people, as at Dundee and at Inverness second charge; between patron and presbytery, as at Kilrenny [St. Andrews]; and between patron against presbytery and people, as at Campsie [Glasgow] and Largo [St. Andrews].[65] It was perhaps not unexpected, therefore, that some should have considered the time had come for a full airing of the subject, as Baillie was to report: "We are like to be troubled with the question of Patronage. William Rigg [Sir William Rigg of Ethernie, who sat in Parliament for Fife] had procured a sharpe petition to us from the whole Commissioners of shyres and burghes against the intrusion of ministers on parishes against their minde; diverse noblemen, patrons, took this evill. We knew not how to guide it; at last, because of the time, as [with] all other things of great difficultie, we got it suppressed."[66]

Clearly, however, stifling the debate could only act as a temporary expedient. When the Assembly returned to the issue a few days later in a resolution to reduce, through scarcity of candidates, the leets submitted to the king from six to three, the Marquis of Argyll used the opportunity to make a suggestion that "pleased all." This was that a start should be made in drawing up a code of practice for other patrons beside the king. To this end, he moved that presbyteries be asked to consider the best way of admitting ministers to charges, and send their opinions to the following meeting. The Assembly, thinking it "very necessary that some general course were set down . . . whereby all occasions of contests and differences among patrons, presbyteries and paroches may be removed,"[67] gratefully accepted the suggestion.

Given the weakness of the Crown at the time, it is possible that the Argyll proposal might well have thrashed out a system which preserved patronage in a form acceptable to most interests and opinions. Whether it would have survived and thereby spared the Kirk the anguish of the next two centuries, is hard to guess. In the event, however, Argyll's initiative petered out as developments south of the border rose to occupy the main focus of national attention.

65. Peterkin, 306–7; Baillie, *Letters*, i, 369–73; ii, 93.

66. Baillie, *Letters*, ii, 94.

67. Sess. ult., 19 August 1643, *The Assembly's humble desires to his majestie anent the lists for presentations, with a recommendation to presbyteries*, Pitcairn, 86–87.

Summary

The 1587 Act of Annexation heightened landowners' awareness of, and concern for, the heritable rights which applied to their property, of which patronage was one. Although the Kirk would have been alarmed by the powers vested in the episcopate to receive and expedite presentations, by the end of James's reign, it looked as though the system he set in place for filling vacancies had a good chance of reaching a settled state. Charles's misfortune was that although his intentions for teind reform had merit, the handling of so sensitive an issue required skills that he did not possess. This, along with mounting disquiet at his ecclesiastical policy, led to the revolution of 1637–8, the success of which would have been impossible without the support of the landed interest. Out of the ensuing turmoil came a renewal of the debate within the Church as to the acceptability of presentations. This in turn was intensified when attentions turned to the civil war that was brewing south of the border. As dialogue opened with the English Parliamentarians, the question arose, how far could both nations work together, or moreover, form a common ecclesiastical polity? If the latter were possible, what place would presentations have in the new regime?

Such questions were to occupy much attention north and south of the border as both nations groped towards a possible consensus at what came to be known as the Westminster Assembly of Divines.

CHAPTER THREE

The Westminster Assembly (1643–1649)

BY AUGUST 1642, CHARLES and the English Parliament were embroiled in civil war. Both sides appealed to the Scots for support. This, in turn, started to polarize opinion within Scotland, between moderate royalists who felt the revolution had progressed as far as it decently should, and those who believed security lay, not in trusting Charles, but in closer union with England—a union in which Scotland would be an equal partner, and whose constitution would limit royal power.[1] Whereas it is probable that most of the nobility favored the former stance, the great majority of the lesser ranks sided with the General Assembly's conviction that the Covenanting movement would best be served by opening negotiations with the English Parliament. Accordingly, since Charles refused to call a Scottish Parliament, the Privy Council voted, on the 12 May 1643, to summon a convention of estates for the 22 June.[2] Meanwhile, Charles, looking for reinforcements, had opened negotiations in Ireland with a view to recalling English soldiers from there. By the time the information reached Scotland, it was believed that the troops were in fact Irish Catholics bent on destroying the protestant cause. Thus, when the convention assembled, the credibility of the king's supporters was undermined and they were unable to stop negotiations commencing with the English representatives on the 7 August.[3]

The ultimate result was the Solemn League and Covenant, a treaty whose principal points were that each country would endeavor, (i), to

1. See David Stevenson, "The early Covenanters and the federal union of Britain" in *Union, Revolution and Religion in 17th-century Scotland.* (Aldershot: 1997), 163–81.

2. *RPCS* , vii, 427.

3 Godfrey Davies, *The Early Stuarts 1603–1660.* Matrix: The Oxford History of England, 2nd. Edn. (OUP: 1959), 135–36.

preserve the reformed religion in Scotland, and continue the reformation of religion in England and Ireland according to "the example of the best reformed churches" (in other words, presbyterianism), (ii), to extirpate popery and prelacy, (iii), to preserve the rights and privileges of both parliaments and the authority of the king, (iv), to deal with any "incendiaries, malignants, or evil instruments" who oppose the Covenant, (v), to promote peace and union between the two countries, and (vi), to assist the other partner in maintaining adherence to the Covenant.[4]

Although the document bears the hallmarks of a proposed religious settlement, the English parliamentarians' overriding concern was the winning of Scottish military assistance. They were prepared to accept the Covenant as a price to be paid, but the fact remained, "the more they saw of Presbyterianism, the less the parliamentarians liked it, and the more they labored to keep it out of sight."[5] Nevertheless, The English Long Parliament showed interest in the Scottish alternative to episcopacy, and had, in June, already commissioned an assembly of divines to meet at Westminster and consider what form of government might "be most agreeable to God's Holy Word, and . . . nearer agreement with the Church of Scotland."[6] The divines met on the 1 July, and invited the Kirk to send representatives. On the 19 August, the General Assembly appointed a pool of eight commissioners, from whom a minimum of three would be constantly present at the assembly. This initial pool of Scots representatives was composed of some of the Kirk's leading figures. From the ministry, there was Samuel Rutherford (St. Andrews), Robert Baillie (Glasgow), Alexander Henderson, Robert Douglas and George Gillespie (Edinburgh), and from the elders, John, Earl of Cassillis, John, Lord Maitland and Johnston of Wariston.[7] The first three Scots commissioners were formally welcomed at the Westminster Assembly on the 15 September 1643.

4. *APS.*, vi, 41. The Solemn League and Covenant was approved by the convention of estates on the 17 August 1643, and in London on the 25 September.

5. J. P. Kenyon, *The Stuart constitution, 1603–1688.* (Cambridge 1966), 252.

6. *An ordinance for the calling of an assembly of learned and Godly divines, to be consulted with by the Parliament, for the settling of the government of the Church* [12 June 1643]; the assembly was to consist of 121 clergymen, 10 lords and 20 MPs. Kenyon, 261 & 255.

7. George Gillespie (1613–48): former chaplain to the earl of Wemyss, ordained to Wemyss, without episcopal collation, in 1638; translated to Edinburgh in 1642; a resolute opponent of episcopacy.
Robert Douglas (1594–1674) admitted to Kirkcaldy 2nd. charge in 1628, called to Edinburgh in 1639; elected moderator in 1642, 1645, 1647, 1649 and 1651; probably the Kirk's leading figure after the death of Henderson; although a commissioner, did

Business moved slowly in the early months, however the pace began to quicken when, on the 2 January 1644, the agenda turned to the theory and practice of election and ordination. Although the gathering approved the proposition that the apostles had power to ordain officers in all churches and to appoint evangelists to ordain, the Scots, through Gillepsie, challenged the translation of one of the proof texts, which read: "And when they had ordained them elders in every church" (Acts, xiv, 23).[8] Gillepsie claimed that the Greek word which "Episcopal translators" had deliberately rendered as *ordaining*, was "truelie *choyseing*, importing the peoples suffrages in electing their officers."[9] This sparked off much debate until Henderson contrived a compromise which added the provision that the meeting was referring to the verse as a whole, and that it did not intend thereby "to prejudge any argument which in due time might be alleadged out of this place, either for popular election, or against it."[10] It was a liberty which the Kirk was glad to remember and put on record the following year, when it ratified the articles on ordination.[11]

Shortly after this, detailed discussion on the issue of ordination was halted until March. Meanwhile, discussion began on whether or not

---

not actually attend at Westminster.

Samuel Rutherford (1600–61) became minister at Anwoth (Kirkcudbright) in 1627; denounced and eventually exiled to Aberdeen for his resistance to the Five Articles and episcopal arminianism; appointed Professor of divinity at St Andrews in 1639; published books defending presbyterianism and setting limits on the authority of the secular power; highly regarded internationally as a Reformed Church theologian; deprived and indicted for treason after the Restoration.

John Maitland (1616–82) 2nd Earl and 1st Duke of Lauderdale; a Covenanter, but remained a royalist, and was prominent in arranging the Engagement of 1647; captured at Worcester and imprisoned until Restoration, when he was appointed Secretary of State; notorious for his policy regarding presbyterians after episcopacy restored.

For Baillie, Henderson and Wariston, see above. John Kennedy, 6th Earl of Cassillis, did not attend at Westminster.

8. *The whole works of the Rev John Lightfoot, D.D., minister of Catharine Hall, Cambridge*, ed., John Rogers, (London: 1824), vol. xiii, "The journal of the proceedings of the assembly of divines, from January 1st, 1643 to December 31, 1644," 98.

9. Baillie, 129. It was a moot point, in that the literal meaning of the Greek verb *cheirotoneo*, was "to stretch out one's hand." In classical Greek, this was used in connection with signifying one's vote, but the early Church also used the word to mean "lay hands on."

10. Ibid.

11. February 10, 1645, *Act of the General Assembly of the kirk of Scotland, approving the propositions concerning kirk government and ordination of ministers*, Pitcairn, 121.

presbyterian church government was scriptural.[12] Although little was conclusively settled, the Scots did well out of the debate which led to the validity and standing of presbyterianism being viewed in a more respectful light than previously.[13] However, as the reopening of the discussions on ordination was to demonstrate, any endorsement of presbyterianism was not to be equated with a wholehearted acceptance of popular control of the Church.

On the 21 March, the Westminster Assembly turned its attention to the proposition that a congregation should accept a minister recommended to them by the superior church authority, unless they could show "just cause of exception against him."[14] The Scots had two difficulties with this. First, having already had experience of parochial intransigence, they felt obliged to press for a more detailed definition of what the qualification allowed, Gillespie asking, "But if they cannot shew just cause against him, what then is to be done?"[15] There was also the matter of what Henderson called "the people's interest, in point of election"[16] He wanted to know how much preliminary consultation would there be? In seeking to resolve these scruples, the Scottish commissioners found themselves sandwiched between two opposing positions.

On the one hand, there were the moderate English Puritans, who considered that the proposed concession already bestowed a privilege upon a congregation that was more than adequate. On the other side, there were the Independents, who argued that the proposition's approach was the wrong way round, and that any recommending should be by the people to the presbytery. In their view, what had been suggested came "not up to the privilege of the people."[17]

For their part, the Scots were in the difficult position of being unable to speak with one voice, since their own church was at the time engaged in the process of internal debate upon congregational rights in vacancies. There were those, like Rutherford, who unequivocally adhered to the belief

12. "Notes of debates and proceedings of the Assembly of divines and other commissioners at Westminster, February 1644 to January 1645, by George Gillespie, minister at Edinburgh, from unpublished manuscripts," ed, David Meek, in *The presbyterian's armoury: the works of Mr George Gillespie in two volumes*. Edinburgh: 1846, 9. [hereinafter cited as Gillespie, "Notes"].

13. See Robert S. Paul, *The Assembly of the Lord*, (Edinburgh: 1985), 314.

14. Lightfoot, *Journal*, 230.

15. Ibid., 232

16. Ibid.

17. Ibid., 231.

that, "The Scriptures constantly give the choice of the pastor to the people. The act of electing is in the people; and the regulating and correcting of their choice is in the presbytery."[18] Set against that, there were those like the historian and presbyterian apologist, David Calderwood (1575–1650), who wrote from Scotland censuring the Scots commissioners for allowing the power and status of kirk sessions, and thereby congregations, to be elevated to a point that, as Baillie ruefully reported, "we put ourselfe in hazard to be forced to give excommunication, and so entire government, to congregations, which is a great stepp to Independencie. Mr H[enderson] acknowledges this; and we are in a pecke of troubles with it."[19]

Gillepie's solution was to make obtrusion the central issue. If the Westminster Assembly could be persuaded specifically to outlaw settlements *renitente et contradicente ecclesia* [the church being in opposition], then he felt it would be a suitable compromise: "for the prelates are for obtrusion, the Separation [separatists] for a popular voting: *ergo* let us go in a medium."[20] When it came to the vote on the 22 March, however, the motion which finally passed still withheld an unrestricted veto: "No man shall be ordained a minister for a particular congregation, if they can shew (any) just cause of exception against him."[21] Despite the rearrangement of words, the Scots had, in the end, made little impact on the original proposition. According to Robert Paul, the reason for this was that the basic instinct of the conservative majority in the Westminster Assembly was to see the authority and status of presbyteries as being equivalent to that of the earlier bishops. Far from seeking popular empowerment, it was instead clear that for these men, "new Presbyter certainly was but 'old Priest writ large.'"[22] Nevertheless, thanks to discretionary powers which allowed the Kirk freedom to revise the details of the section on calling of ministers, the propositions on ordination were approved, despite their shortcomings, by the General Assembly on the 10 February 1645.

Before finishing with the Westminster Assembly, however, two questions remain to be asked, namely, did all the arguments surrounding election presuppose that presentations by patrons were to be repudiated and, secondly, if the Scots had been granted a free hand to regulate the admission of ministers to vacancies, what would their preference have been?

18. Ibid., 231.

19. Baillie, *Letters*, ii, 182.

20. Lightfoot, 232.

21. Ibid., 233; "any" appears in Lightfoot's record of the day's vote, but it is absent from the minutes.

22. Paul, *Assembly of the Lord*, 322.

The answer to the first question is that, although patrons and presentations are very rarely mentioned in the minutes,[23] or in the notes of observers like Gillespie or John Lightfoot, master of Catharine Hall, Cambridge, there is no indication that all discussion was to be founded upon the principle that they were unacceptable. An example can be seen in the unexceptionable tone with which patrons are mentioned in a debate on the 21 March: "*Mr Vines:* The recommending by the presbytery heals all, for do either the patron or the people choose, yet is he to be recommended by the presbytery."[24] Again, all minutes appear carefully worded so that nothing obstructs the possibility of a presbytery receiving presentations. Thus, the procedure for the admission of ministers, approved on the 18 April, simply says: "He that is to be ordained must address himself to the presbytery, with a testimony . . . especially of his life: and then the presbytery to examine him: being approved, to be sent to the church where he is to be, and preach three days; and, on the last, notice to be given, that some of the congregation go to the presbytery to see him admitted or excepted."[25] Furthermore, it is recorded for the day before, that the meeting considered what legal action might befall a presbytery should "they stop a man presented, if they find him unworthy."[26] The word *presented* need not necessarily infer the use of a patron's presentation, yet it is clear that the possibility is not discounted.

As for the question of Scottish preferences on election, a prevailing viewpoint is not immediately obvious. That the Kirk was itself unable to make up its mind is evidenced by the great debate which arose on the issue when the Westminster Directory came up for discussion at the 1645 General Assembly.[27] Encouraged by a recent Act of the Convention of Estates, which virtually handed all crown presentations to presbyteries,[28] Calderwood's inclination was to stay with the traditional view that a presbytery's authority was central and that the initiative in all vacancies should remain in its hands. By way of concession, however, he was prepared to allow a congregation its choice, provided the selection was from a list provided by the presbytery. On the other side of the argument, there were those,

23. See, *Minutes of the sessions of the Westminster Assembly of divines*, Alexander F. Mitchell, & John Struthers, (eds.) (Edinburgh: 1874).

24. Lightfoot, *Journal*, 231.

25. Ibid., 250.

26. Ibid., 253.

27. 7 February 1645. Gillespie, *Notes*, 120.

28. 6 January 1644; *Act anent presentation of ministers, APS*, 66.

like Rutherford, who saw no reason why the people's freedom to choose should be restricted at all. It therefore comes as no surprise to find that even five years later, opinion on the matter was as divided as ever:

> ... some ascrybeis this power [of election] to the multitude of professouris promiscuouslie within the flock or congregatione; some to the particulaire eldershipe within the congregatione quhairunto thei require att least a tacite or prerogative conseil of the wholl people; some ascrybe it unto the most eminent for light and lyf of religione in the congregatione, neglecting otheris altho never so eminent in other respectis and concerned in that place; some ascrybe it to the presbyterie onlie without any concurrence of the people; some ascrybe this power to the presbyterie and people joyntlie, everyone acting their owne part distinctly - whose judgement seems to approach nearest unto divine truth.[29]

Out of the confusion, it was a version of the system espoused by George Gillespie which won approval after the Scotish Parliament ultimately abolished patronage in 1649. This placed the power of election with the kirk session rather than the congregation and it is possible that it would have been the compromise choice of the Scots representatives at Westminster. However, before considering Gillespie's preferences further, it is important to move on from the Westminster Assembly to look at the circumstances which led to the abolition of patronage and then return to how the Kirk coped with the far from straightforward task of agreeing upon an alternative.

The Abolition of Lay Patronage in 1649

The Political Background

The Scottish decision to provide military support for the Parliamentarians against the king in 1644, provoked deep divisions north of the border. A Scottish pro-royalist party emerged, although not all of its adherents were prepared to go to the violent lengths of the Marquis of Montrose, whose military campaign on the king's behalf got underway in August 1644. Despite the defeat of Charles at Naseby in June, and Montrose at

---

29. *Wodrow mss* [NLS Wod.Fol.xxviii, 28], "Concerning the people's interest in calling them pastoris": notes on calling of ministers addressed to Rev William Tweedie [of Slamanan, Linlithgow presbytery]. Anon. c.1650.

Philiphaugh in September 1645, support for the king deepened and spread when, in the following year, he surrendered to the Scots forces, only to be handed over to the English Parliament on 8 January 1647. The fact was, most presbyterians had no liking for the churchmanship of the Independents, now gaining ascendancy in England, and when, in addition, the king was seized by the army during June 1647, there was general alarm for his safety. As a result, a group of nobles were emboldened to enter into an "Engagement" with Charles, whereby they would endeavor to restore his authority in return for concessions which included his (qualified) support for the Solemn League and Covenant and presbyterianism. Although the Estates came out in favor of the Engagement, the General Assembly remained suspicious of royal intentions, and resolved to oppose it. In the event, the Estates sent an army south, only to see it heavily defeated by Oliver Cromwell at Preston, in August 1648.

In the tide of recrimination which followed the debacle at Preston, an anti-Engager grouping, led in particular by Archibald, eighth Earl and first Marquis of Argyll, came to power. Encouraged by the Church, it immediately set about purging all public offices of "malignants," as those tainted by any association with Montrose or the Engagement were styled. Since the nobility's presence in the Estates was thus drastically reduced, it seemed that the opportunity had at last arrived for the hardline remnant within the Kirk to do something about the burden of patronage.

Ecclesiastical Influence upon the Scottish Parliament

If, as Walter Makey has suggested, the purged Parliament was now obedient[30] to the ministers, then the realization of cherished goals like the abolition of presentations would indeed have become all but inevitable. However, it would be mistaken to conclude that the political situation had simply been transformed into a sacerdotal dictatorship. The work of John R. Young has shown that although the executive bodies of both church and state shared a proportion of their membership, yet neither operated as if one were the captive of the other.[31] Young stresses that at this juncture, as

30. Makey, *Church of the Covenant*, 78.

31. Young, John R., "Scottish covenanting radicalism, the commission of the kirk and the establishment of the parliamentary radical regime of 1648–1649." *RSCHS*, xxv, (1995), 355. Young uses attendance figures to show, for example, that "Nine of the 16 nobles (56%), 11 of the 46 gentry (24%), and seven of the 51 burgesses (14%) recorded in the parliamentary rolls of 4 January 1649 were also members of the commission of the kirk established on 11 August 1648. Yet only a small minority of these lay elders

throughout the 1640s, the way ecclesiastical influence was most exerted upon Parliament was in the form of lobbying, and that this was effected through a body created by the General Assembly for such a purpose, called the Assembly Commission.

General Assembly Commission

According to Young, the Kirk's need for an executive arm, with powers between Assemblies to negotiate on its behalf at the highest diplomatic levels, arose previously out of the post-1638 political turmoils. Thus he traces its first, formal appointment to 5 August 1642,[32] but there are strong indications, however, that the Commission in fact had earlier antecedents. These emerge particularly in Alan R. MacDonald's book, *The Jacobean Kirk, 1567–1625*. Although Assembly commissioners, sent out to perform specific remits, are mentioned frequently in the early 1590s, MacDonald notes that from 1596 their function appeared to broaden out into what was, in effect, a standing commission with the capacity to act in a wide range of matters:

> They sent delegations to the king and Privy Council, demanding action against Huntly, Errol, their wives and Lady Livingstone, Errol's daughter and an openly practicing Catholic. Alexander Seton, president of the Court of Session . . . was referred to the commissioners by the synod of Lothian and Tweeddale for dealings with the Catholic earls. They even found time to deal with a dispute over a benefice in the presbytery of Glasgow. The commissioners were acting, and were seen by the rest of the Kirk, as a privy council for the Kirk, wielding the power of the General Assembly between its meetings.[33]

It was the king himself who then added impetus to this development, since he realized that to enhance the status of such a body was to provide himself with a vehicle on which he could to carry through his plans to restore episcopacy: "King James rewarded those who had loyally served as commissioners of the Assembly by making them bishops. What better way of providing the episcopate with powers which did not require ratification by Parliament or General Assembly? Episcopacy with teeth was

---

were in semi-regular attendance according to the 44 recorded sederunts of the commission of the kirk between 12 August 1648 and 4 January 1649." Ibid., 353–54.

32. Ibid., 345.

33. MacDonald, *The Jacobean Kirk*, 65.

thus not reintroduced at a stroke; it was drip-fed into the system via the commission of the General Assembly and ecclesiastical representation in Parliament."[34]

The role and powers of the Commission were to be the source of much controversy in the following century, as the number of controverted settlements threatened to overwhelm the Assembly. Returning, however, to the situation of the late 1640s, the Commission's function of "prosecuting the desires of the Assembly"[35] became especially relevant as it utilized the Church's strengthened position in the aftermath of Preston to press for a programme of reforms which ranged from incest to care of the poor. Also within the agenda was the question of patronages.

The Approach to Abolition

The Commission's lobbying campaign began on 30 January 1649 with a petition to Parliament. Calling it an old grievance, the petition based its appeal for removal on the grounds that it was a). unconstitutional, b). contrary to Scripture, c). prejudicial to free election and calling of ministers, d). a popish institution and e). condemned by the *Books of discipline* and the Acts of former General Assemblies. It considered its presence to be an item of unfinished business left over from the Reformation, and asked for its removal—or repeal, if any Act could be found to validate it as a law instead of merely a "corrupt custome."[36]

To assist the Estates in their deliberations, the Commission resolved, two weeks later, to have a petition and memorandum drawn up which would demonstrate in detail why patronage was unlawful. The task was entrusted to the much-respected Samuel Rutherford (1600–61), now Principal at St. Mary's College, St. Andrews, and James Wood (d.1664) third Master of the college. Their finished work was approved on the 28 February and at once sent up to Parliament.

The memorandum's introduction[37] commences with the tactful submission that as the ministers sought no benefit for themselves but only the removal of that which was unlawful and sinful, so they hoped that

34. MacDonald, *Jacobean Kirk*, 119.

35. Peterkin, *Records of the Kirk*, 330.

36. *The records of the commissions of the general assemblies of the church of Scotland holden in Edinburgh the years 1648 and 1649*, A.F. Mitchell, and J. Christie, (eds), Scottish History Society, vol. xxv, II, (1896), 184.

37. Ibid., 205–11.

"your Lordships, in the integrity of your hearts, without any byas or eye to self-interest" would do the same. It then suggests that in doing so, their lordships might thereby free some parochial income, which could be diverted into caring for the poor—a ploy likely to incur no small popularity at a time of widespread want.

There then follows seven reasons justifying the church's aversion to patronage. First, it is contrary to God's law. The practice of a great man choosing the minister is as much a usurpation as his choosing the elders and deacons would be. Scripture grants to no one the right, unilaterally, to nominate any officer in the house of God; the New Testament reveals that this is given to the people and presbytery.[38] Secondly, it is contrary to the received doctrine of the Kirk. Patronage is a violation of the *Books of Discipline* and many Acts of the General Assembly, of which last, two examples may be cited, the Acts of 1562 (session 3) and 1570 (session 2), where both imply a rejection of the practice.[39] Thirdly, the office of patron is superfluous to the exercise of ministry and therefore unworthy of preservation. Moreover, since he cannot make the laborer worthy of his wages, he can hardly give him right to those wages. As for defending the minister in his maintenance, it is the magistrate's job to do so. Fourthly, a patron should have no right to meddle in the remuneration of a properly qualified, called and admitted minister, yet as things stand, if the incumbent has not a presentation, the patron may withhold his maintenance. Any other profession would regard such interference as most unjust. Fifthly, to be lawful, patronage has to be either a spiritual, ecclesiastical or civil right. It is none of those. Sixthly, any office that can tempt either its holder or another party into corrupt agreements such as simony, ought to be banned. Seventh, patronage is both unnecessary and a complying with the practice of papists and idolaters.

The contrast with Johnston of Wariston's treatise of just a few years earlier is interesting, in that the cautious tone is gone. The former is pragmatic, the latter is about principle. For the former, what is important is to seek a *modus operandi*, for the other, the issue is one of boundaries. Most

---

38. Ibid., 207. The proof-texts cited are, Acts 1, v. 26; Acts 6, vv. 3 & 5; Acts 14, v2; I Timothy 8, v. 22, and Titus 1, v. 5 (Acts 14 and I Timothy 8 are clearly mistaken. In view of their prominence in the ordination debates at the Westminster Assembly, it is very likely that the intended references are Acts 13, v2 and I Timothy 5, v. 22).

39. The text of the Acts in fact reads: 29 December 1562: "[inhibition shall be made to all] that hes not been presented be the people, or ane part thereof, to the Superintendent." 5 March 1570: "[it pertains to the jurisdiction of the Kirk to have] Electione, examinatione and admissione of them that are admittit to the ministrie." *BUK*, 12 and 124.

of all, the latter envisages a remarkable arrangement whereby the secular arm is to protect, preserve and uphold the Church, yet deny itself any interference in its life and work. It was a proposition that did eventually receive the state's explicit agreement in legislative form, but it was not to come until 272 years later.[40]

Just over a week after receiving the memorandum, Parliament debated the issue, passing the *Act Abolishing the patronages of Kirks* [see Appendix II] on the 9 March. The preamble repeated, in much the same language, the justifications contained in the petition and memorandum. However, once again, it should not be assumed that this was a confirmation that the legislature was merely the puppet of the ministers. The Act was part of a programme that the Kirk envisaged for national improvement, but it was also symptomatic of a flexing of muscle by the middle ranks of Scottish society. What made it possible was the dramatic reduction in the presence of the nobility in the Estates after the Preston fiasco. John R. Young's statistics show how the nobles' attendance dropped from 56 in the 1648 Parliament to 16 in the one beginning 4 January 1649.[41] It was this crucial circumstance that freed the laird class to go on and promote measures characterized by their potential to erode the feudal hegemony of the nobility and large landowners.

Thus it was, in the same parliamentary session, power was given to presbyteries and kirk sessions to pressurize landowners into shouldering concern for the poor in their locality. Again, on the 8 March, the *Act in favours of the Vassals of Kirk-lands* revived one of the contentious aims [see above, Chapter Two] of King Charles in his legislation of 1633. Charles had tried to "liberate" the vassals of the Lords of Erection by stripping the latter of their superiority and vesting it in the Crown. To the frustration of the former, this had not happened. Now, this Act attempted to make good the deficiency and the lords were obliged "to accept the same sums from the vassals themselves whilk they are liable and bound to accept from His Majesty for redemption thereof." Another example was the legislation of 29 June, which sought to enhance the status of others beside

---

40. *An Act to declare the lawfulness of certain Articles declaratory of the Constitution of the Church of Scotland in matters spiritual prepared with the authority of the General Assembly of the Church.* Acts of the British Parliament, 1921, c.29.

41. John R. Young, *The Scottish parliament 1639–1661, a political and constitutional analysis*, (Edinburgh: 1996). The remaining membership was composed of gentry (46 minimum to 52 maximum) and burgesses (51 min. to 58 max.).

the aristocracy in the shires and burghs, by encouraging the revival of the office of Justice of the Peace.[42]

By such means, Parliament attempted to free the lesser landowners from the dominance of the magnates and allow them greater freedom to contribute to the life of their localities. Accordingly, when the Act abolishing patronage appears, it is as a part of this context. As a motivation, there was indeed the principle that it was a burden under which the Church "groaned," but there was also the underlying reality that the great man with the block of patronages was no longer to have the same sway in parochial matters. This realization was undoubtedly in the mind of those like the Earl of Buccleuch (who had seven churches in his gift) when, in protest, he and others walked out of the chamber during the debate. The contemporary writer, Sir James Balfour, describes the scene: "The Parliament past a most strange [i.e., foreign, alien] Acte this monthe, abolishing the patronages of kirkes, which pertained to laymen since ever Christianity was planted in Scotland. Francis, Earl of Buccleuch, and some others, protested against this acte as vrangous [wrongous] and all togider derogatory to the just rights of the nobility and gentrey of the kingdom of Scotland, and so departed the Parl: House."[43]

The objectors had Balfour's sympathy, especially as two other facets to the debate caused him annoyance. The first stemmed from his conviction that the leading role played by Argyll, the Lord Chancellor (John Campbell, first Earl of Loudoun) and Johnston of Wariston in favor of the Act, was entirely driven by their fear of losing the Kirk's favor. The second was that the phraseology of the Act gave the implication that the people were about to be given the liberty to choose their own ministers. He considered this to be hypocrisy, since such an outcome was never likely. Whereas there was probably truth in his first point, Balfour's claim that the people had been duped in their expectations was exaggerated, since it is clear that the wording, "suit and calling of the congregation," is open to a variety of interpretations. Indeed, the framers recognized as much in the Act itself.[44]

---

42. 1 March 1649, *Act anent the Poore*, APS, vi, 389; 8 March 1649, *Act in favours of the vassals of Kirk-lands*, APS, vi, 408; 29 June 1649, *Act anent JPs and their Constables*, APS, vi, 470.

43. Sir James Balfour, *The historical works of Sir James Balfour of Denmylne and Kinnaird, Kt. and Bt.; Lord Lyon, king of Arms to Charles I and Charles II*, ed., J. Haig, (Edinburgh: 1824), iii, 391.

44. Doubtless aware of this, the framers added the qualification: "because it is needful that the just and proper interest of congregations and presbyteries . . . be clearly determined by the General Assembly, and what is to be accounted the congregation

Balfour was, however, correct about the disunity and confusion which surfaced at the Assembly four months later over what selection system should replace patronage. On the other hand, some clash of opinion should not have been unexpected. For reasons of tact and expediency, the Kirk had perennially shied away from plenary debates about patronage, so there had never been a regular opportunity for differing opinions to be aired and agreement reached on an alternative system. Differing opinions were to be expected: what did take observers, like Baillie, by surprise was the intensity with which they were expressed.

The directory for the election of ministers [see Appendix III]

The 1649 Act remitted it to the July meeting of the Assembly to draw up a directory which would determine in what way the congregation's interest could be fittingly expressed when a vacancy is filled, and to form that into a standing rule. When the debate began, the starting point for most members' thinking was the views previously expressed by George Gillespie. Despite his death on the 17 December the previous year, he had been held in the highest regard,[45] and so when, shortly after, Gillespie's brother Patrick published a series of articles by him, including one on congregational consent in vacancies, it was given widespread attention.

Although the work was concerned with proving, from scripture and the practice of the early Church, that the approval of the people is essential for a valid ministry, it was equally emphatic in rejecting any separatist notion of giving the people a *juridical* power, that is to say, one in which their judgement was legally binding. That would be to place "the whole essentality of a calling in election, accounting ordination to be no more but the solemnization of the calling."[46] In Gillespie's view, the most sensible course was for the eldership of a vacant church, with the advice of the "ablest and wisest men of the congregation, especially . . . magistrates," to elect a

having that interest, therefore it is seriously recommended unto the next General Assembly clearly to determine the same, and to condescend upon a certain standing way for being a settled rule therein." *APS* , vi, 412.

45. see letter to him from the Assembly Commission, 23 September 1648. Also, his family was awarded a pension by parliament on his death "as an acknowledgement for his faithfulness," see "The works of Mr George Gillespie, minister of Edinburgh," ed., W.M. Hetherington, i, xxx, in *The presbyterian's armoury in three volumes.* (Edinburgh: 1846).

46. *The presbyterian's armoury*, ii, pt.2, George Gillespie, "A treatise of miscellany questions," ii, "Of the election of pastors with the congregation's consent," 11.

candidate, and then seek the congregation's consent for their choice. This consent was not, in Gillespie's eyes, to be considered a suffrage. The eldership had already decided the issue: their secondary task was to strive to carry with them at least the majority of the congregation.

The problem with Gillespie's plan was that it contained too much room for uncertainty, especially over the issues of advice and dissent—a difficulty remarked upon by one contemporary commentator, who felt he would "not contend to understand all the particulaires mentioned."[47] For men like Rutherford and Wood, however, there was no need for such confusion. Whereas Gillespie's concern was not to promote the franchise of the untutored many over the privileged few, but rather to keep what he saw as a spiritual act (vacancy–filling) in the hands of the church's spiritually-commissioned officers, in Rutherford and Wood's eyes, the issue was otherwise. The question for them was straightforward: the power of election resided "in the body of the people, contradistinct from their eldership."[48] It was a premise they promoted with some passion.

The most bitter resistance to Gillespie's views, however, came from David Calderwood. His revulsion against congregationalism, expressed at the time of the Westminster Assembly (see above), led him to feel that any arrangement which did not make presbytery unequivocally the electors (although the people could dissent), was a betrayal of presbyterianism. Baillie records that the sharpness of his protestations were such that he was fortunate to escape censure, although the court did afford him the honor of commissioning a written response to his objections.

The paper reveals how the main constituent of Calderwood's argument was that the Assembly's inclinations were a departure from the *Second Book of Discipline*, which had stated: "Election is the choosing out of a person or persons, most able for the office that vaikes, by the judgement of the eldership [i.e., presbytery] and consent of the congregation."[49] In reply to this, it was argued that church and society had moved on since that era. Since the *Book* did not "determine every particular belonging to the practice of election," and that nothing in the new version was contrary to God's word, men were surely free to alter the doctrines of men. Then, moving their reasoning onto less certain ground, the authors claim that the *Book* did not give the power of choosing to the presbytery only "as if the consent of the people were not an essential ingredient and part of

47. "Concerning the Presbytery's interest, etc."
48. Baillie, *Letters*, iii, 94.
49. Kirk, *Second book of discipline*, 102.

election," but to both jointly. Accordingly, the kirk session is not given "complete and free" election, but only a nomination by vote, which the people must acquiesce with.[50]

The respondents' answers underline the difficulties encountered by the Church when it sought to make the second *Book* its guide on the planting of parishes. Baillie watched the interpretations ebb and flow and considered Calderwood had the better of the argument, nevertheless his own inclinations remained with the majority who favored a version of Gillespie's ideas. The general sticking-point for the Assembly, however, remained the matter of how the candidate(s) for nomination were to be brought to the attention of the session—was presbytery to be the sole source? In the event, a compromise was reached whereby the presbytery would send candidates to be heard, but if the session petitioned them to allow, in addition, a hearing of someone else, then they would endeavor to facilitate it.

In reality, since malignant congregations (or their sessions) were to be denied participation in the vacancy process, the directory's final form ended up giving most advantage to the presbyteries. Baillie, however, still disliked the plan, believing there was a danger presbyteries might decide to hold back altogether from becoming involved, and thereby leave the field clear for trouble-makers to promote the cause of virtually anyone.[51] In the event, the ensuing political upheavals brought about a situation even worse than he imagined.

The Period of Cromwell

The beheading of Charles I on the 30 January 1649 caused a pro-royalist reaction north of the border. Partly because of this and partly through annoyance that the execution had been done without any consultation, the Scots Parliament proclaimed the Prince of Wales as the new king on the 5 February. Two days later, it passed further legislation, clarifying the limitations to be put upon his authority and making presbyterianism and the Covenants a central fixture to any subsequent negotiations with him. Commissioners were sent to Charles in Holland but because of his re-luctance to agree to any of the key conditions, nothing was settled until a year had passed. By May 1650, Charles realized he was running out of

50. *Wodrow mss*, NLS. Wod.Fol.xxix, 22. 'Answer to the paper of Mr Calderwood against the directory for election of ministers presented to the General Assembly.' nd.

51. *Letters*, iii, 95.

options for regaining his throne and accordingly came to terms at Breda, although it was not until actually arriving at Speymouth that he finally, on the 23 June, subscribed the Covenants. News of Charles's return stimulated Cromwell into action and he crossed the Tweed with an army on the 22 July. The Scots army, although larger, was weakened by purging of its supposed malignant elements, and was routed at the battle of Dunbar on the 3 September.

The Dunbar disaster damaged the Kirk's credibility and coherence. The Covenanting hardliners in the south and west (especially Lanarkshire, Renfrewshire, Ayrshire and Galloway) banded together[52] and issued, on 17 October, a Remonstrance in which they detached themselves from supporting the king's cause unless he showed real repentance for his sins and repudiated the company of malignants. During November, both the Committee of Estates and the Assembly Commission conducted angry and divisive debates on the "Western Remonstrance" before deciding to reject it. Polarization of opinion increased when, in response to further success by the English forces at Hamilton (1 December), Parliament decided to approach the Church with a plan to bolster both national unity and military effectiveness by relaxing the ban on Engagers and royalists. The Commission's reaction was to agree that the crisis warranted such a move, and gave it their approval on the 14 December. However, Parliament's determination to rally mixed support and the Commission's continued adherence to the policy, set the Kirk on the path to schism.

On the one side, moderates or "Resolutioners," still hoped that Charles would live up to the trust placed in him, and they gave their blessing to his coronation at Scone on the 1 January 1651. In addition, on the second and third of June, they agreed to the repeal of the *Act of Classes* of 1649, which had discriminated against malignants, and also approved the *Act against the Western Remonstrance*, which demanded that it be formally renounced by its adherents.[53] On the other side, the Remonstrant party, led especially by James Guthrie (Stirling first charge) and Patrick Gillespie (Outer High kirk, Glasgow), clamored with mounting disgust against what it saw as the Church's defections. Matters climaxed over the General Assemblies held, because of the advance of Cromwell's army, at St. Andrews and Dundee in July and August. A clumsy attempt to prevent opponents

---

52. They had previously done so in the aftermath of the battle of Preston in 1648, when they marched on Edinburgh and helped establish the anti-Engager regime. The incident was called the Whiggamore Raid.

53. A similar Act of 1646 was also repealed. *APS*, vi, 676–7, 683–84.

of the Resolutioners from attending resulted in angry scenes and a protest being lodged by Rutherford, after which over twenty colleagues joined him in walking out. From this point, a bitter breach opened up between the Resolutioners and the Remonstrants (or Protesters), who thereafter refused to countenance the validity of the Assemblies. Unfortunately for the former, their backing for Charles's invasion of England and subsequent defeat at Worcester on the 3 September, meant that as Cromwell now took control of Scotland, his administration throughout the 1650s would give its favor to their numerically inferior rivals.[54]

The Settlement of Vacancies

Although the 1649 directory was in place at the start of the period of the Protectorate, any assessment of how it worked is immediately complicated by the partisan split within the Kirk and the readiness of the state to interfere. This began on the 4 June 1652, when Cromwell's commissioners announced that they were intending to purge the Kirk of all unsatisfactory ministers and replace them with those they considered suitable. In practice, their role tended to be that of arbiter in settlement disputes, and, in such circumstances, the Protester interest was, not unexpectedly, the one which received their repeated favor. Thus encouraged, the latter pursued a policy of placing like-minded candidates in vacancies, even if that involved splitting church courts and establishing rival ministries, as at Douglas (Lanark presbytery) in 1654, where the settlement of their nominee had to be enforced by English dragoons.

Armed force was not the only advantage the Protesters could draw upon. It was open to them to obtain an order ensuring only their candidate received the stipend, even though the other might be supported by virtually all the congregation. As Baillie ruefully noted: "Our churches are in great confusion: no intrant getts any stipend til he have petitioned and subscribed some acknowledgement to the English. When a very few of the Remonstrators or Independent partie will call a man, he gets a kirk and the stipend; but whom the Presbyterie, and well near the whole congregation calls and admitts, he must preach in the fields, or in a barne, without stipend. So a sectarie is planted in Kilbryde, ane other in Leinzie."[55] Having powerful backing meant that the Protester version of a presbytery

54. The areas where the Protesters had a strong interest were the west, south-west, Lanarkshire and Fife.

55. *Letters*, iii, 244, 248.

could even avoid having to wait for vacancies to appear but instead could create them through depositions. Then, if the congregation still held to the former incumbent, it could be claimed that, by adhering to a deposed minister, they had showed themselves malignant. This then opened the door for the right of planting to fall into the presbytery's hands.[56]

In terms of parochial placements, potentially the most significant threat for the Resolutioners stemmed from a development which came to be known as "Gillespie's Charter." Although there was a wing of the Protesters, led by Johnston of Wariston and Guthrie, which remained wary of too close a relationship with the English administration, this was not a concern shared by Patrick Gillespie, who, through his rapport with the regime, had received the principalship of Glasgow University in February 1653. In August 1654, he persuaded the authorities to set up an examining body, the majority of whom would be Protesters or Independents, which would vet all candidates for vacancies. The ordinance at once provoked much alarm and protest on the grounds that it appeared to turn ministerial fitness into a matter of state concern. The Resolutioners also knew that, at a stroke, it removed any advantage accruing to them from their numerical superiority in the church courts. Fortunately for them, however, the Guthrie/Wariston alignment feared the scheme might act as an encouragement of Independency, and so ruled out any participation. Since Gillespie's own interest was not big enough to make it workable, the Charter remained an unfulfilled threat.[57] Finally, in August 1656, the Resolutioners came to a compromise with the president of the governing Scottish Council whereby church courts would retain their disciplinary authority, provided they submitted returns certifying that entrants were "able and fitt to preach the Gospel," and that those who had been inducted made supplication to the Council, pledging to live "peaceably and inoffensively" under the government and to behave "as becometh a minister."[58] This arrangement remained in place down to the Restoration of the monarchy in 1660.[59]

---

56. Ibid. 257.

57. see F. D. Dow, *Cromwellian Scotland 1651–1660*, (Edinburgh: 1979), 101, 197–98.

58. *Register of the consultations of the ministers of Edinburgh and some other brethren of the ministry*, Scottish History Society, 3rd. series, (Edinburgh: 1921), i, 202.

59. Dow, *Cromwellian Scotland*, 207.

The Application of the 1649 Rules

In looking at how the directory guidelines were applied in the 1650s, it quickly becomes clear, once obvious examples of Resolutioner/Protester manipulation of procedures have been discounted, that customs varied widely. The directory decreed that the power of electing was placed in the hands of the session, who would then intimate their choice to the presbytery, the congregation having given concurrence. The act of election was to be moderated [that is, guided, supervised] by a minister from the presbytery.

To begin with, there was variation in the ways a word like "call" was used. Some presbyteries (in common with the directory) did not speak of a call at all, but only of election. Others, like Cupar presbytery, used the term to describe the choice that had taken place and which was now being intimated to the presbytery.[60] If any documentation was produced, it would frequently be in the form of a petition to the court, signed by some prominent parishioners (not necessarily elders), requesting it to proceed to the next stage in filling the charge.[61] Some presbyteries spoke of a "call and invitation"[62] as if they were two separate activities. In Paisley presbytery, a call is a signed document to be lodged with the court, specifying the person sought to be minister.[63] By contrast, the word call could be used in courts like the synod of Aberdeen or the presbytery of Strathbogie, simply to mean a request for an expectant to come and be heard.[64] How use of the word "call" came to develop will be considered later.

There was also the matter of an election's moderation by a member of presbytery. Although the directory specified that this should be done, little attention appears to have been given to the regulation. Usually, presbytery minutes record only that a session had met and made choice. Repeatedly, as in the case of South Leith, the elders seem to have been left to organize such elections by themselves. Again, at Paisley presbytery on the 27 February 1655, when a call from Houston was suddenly refused by the

---

60. Cupar presbytery minutes, 10 May 1655.

61. Ibid, 12 March 1657.

62. 26 May 1657, see W. A. Stark, *The book of Kirkpatrick Durham*, (Castle Douglas: 1903).

63. Paisley presbytery minutes, 27 February 1655.

64. Synod of Aberdeen minutes, 21 April 1652, in *Selections from the records of the kirk session, presbytery, and synod of Aberdeen*. Spalding Club, (Aberdeen: 1846), 216–7; *Extracts from the presbytery book of Strathbogie, 1631–54*, 11 June 1651, Spalding Club, (Aberdeen: 1843), 195–96.

candidate named, some parishioners immediately appeared with another call to someone else. Presbytery proceeded on the basis of the second call, although neither it nor the first one had been moderated.

Mention of the Houston parishioners raises the question of whether or not the session were indeed the sole electors in every instance. Once again, it is clear that the practice varied. In general, sessions were not especially concerned to protect the exclusivity of their privilege. Similarly, if it meant vacant charges could be filled more quickly, the church courts were not inclined to be fastidious about the details of the directory's injunctions, as at Kemback (St Andrews presbytery) in 1653, where the session, heritors and heads of families were invited jointly to elect.[65] Flexibility could not, however, be allowed to drift into irresponsibility, and Aberdeen synod were shocked to discover, in April 1660, that the elders of Innernochtie (Alford presbytery) had meekly handed over their right of choice to the Earl of Mar. They were immediately instructed to elect a minister for themselves and thereby "preserve their owne liberty of nomination as iff ther hade never been done any thing theranent."[66]

Some sessions were to find, however, that they had never possessed their right in the first place. In June 1654, the session of three congregations that made up the High Kirk of Aberdeen (St Nicholas) discovered that the magistrates had, without any consultation, elected and called the minister of Ellon, John Paterson, to fill the third charge. Their protestations sparked off a period of strained relations between the two bodies, which was not ameliorated when, in December 1658, the city Council nominated Paterson again, and demanded the session's concurrence. When the controversy climaxed before the synod of Aberdeen on the 20 April 1659, the Council produced a charter from 1638 which showed that election had been given to the provost, bailies and the people of the city. Accordingly, since the Act of 1649 had taken away the right of patronage in order to give it to the people, "thie act of Parliament doth nowayes concerne us, becaus our nomination was still befor in thie people's hands, and could not fall under that act as bieing taken away." The session's response, that the directory had been commissioned in order to provide a uniform system for the whole country, failed to impress the synod and the Council won its case.

---

65. 23 March 1653, *Selections from the minutes of the presbyteries of St Andrews and Cupar 1641–98* Abbotsford Club. (Edinburgh: 1837), 66. The laird of Kemback nonetheless challenged the prebytery's method of election.

66. 19 April 1660, *Selections*, Spalding club, 260.

The subject of magistrates' rights in planting churches in Scotland's major burghs became a matter of national debate in the mid–eighteenth century, and will be discussed in a later chapter. However, it will be noted that the Aberdeen controversy is of interest in that it exposed a question that would certainly have arisen again, had the Restoration not occurred: were council members truly interchangeable with elders as representatives of the people in church affairs? If not, then, logically, they belonged in the category of patrons. In 1690, when a system for vacancy filling without patronage was next considered for legislation, the regulations recognized this was a delicate area, and so were careful to bring urban councils into the camp of the former by *pairing* them with kirk sessions. However, after the return of presentations in 1712, they acted on their own and often in the same manner as Aberdeen. By way of contrast, kirk sessions in the 1650s tended to follow the opposite pattern. Although there was no formal requirement upon them to consult with other bodies, it was usually accepted that if there were powerful interests connected with the parish, then these could not easily be ignored. In most towns, the kirk session were happy to respect the sentiments of those magistrates who were not already elders, and as at Cupar in 1657,[67] the line between consultation and effectual joint election was commonly blurred. Another, but parallel, situation applied at South Leith, second charge, in 1657, when the election was by the session and the Four Incorporated Trades.

In the more remote areas, consultation was not just a matter of courtesy but necessity. At Birnie (Elgin presbytery) in 1658, for example, when the session decided to assert their independence over the choice of minister, the presbytery and synod hastily stepped in and suppressed the call, stating as one of their reasons that it had been "without the consent of the heritors."[68] Since neither the directory nor Act makes any reference to heritors, the statement is extraordinary, and yet it gives an indication of the niche heritors had been establishing for themselves within the election process. As lesser landlords grew in status and importance through the rest of the century, it became obvious that when next the identity of ministerial electors came to be debated, the role of the heritor could not be ignored.

67. Cupar presbytery minutes, 19 October 1654.

68. "Proceedings in the presbytery of Elgin, in the settlement of a minister at Birnie, 1658," *Report on Church Patronage*, app. ii, 144. The earl's candidate was settled on the 22 June 1659.

Summary

The Westminster assembly did not close finally until the 25 March 1652. The original vision of ecclesiastical uniformity between the two nations, based on a presbyterian system, withered away, especially after 1645, when the military importance of the Scots diminished. In the end, its enduring significance for the Scottish Church lay in its fostering of a confession of faith, larger and shorter catechism, directory for public worship and psalter, all of which were adopted by the Kirk and retained through the ensuing centuries.

When in 1644, the agenda turned to the subject of election and ordination, the floodgates opened within the Kirk to a debate that was to continue to the end of the decade. The discussions focused upon how, in filling a vacancy, the roles of presbytery, eldership and congregation should be apportioned. The majority view was that the people should be given a voice, but the question was, how loud a voice should it be? In the end, it was felt that it could safely be no more than a dissenting voice, but the weight accorded that disagreement was the vexed issue.

Although the matter continued to stimulate debate within the Church, the Westminster Assembly did not formally condemn patronage nor was the Kirk in a position to bully the Scottish Parliament into removing it. However, the Engagement and subsequent defeat at Preston in 1648 altered the political landscape sufficiently for the 1649 abolition to take place. The procedure for vacancy–filling now had to be decided. George Gillespie's view that an intransigent congregation could be worked upon until brought round was rejected as being impractical. As a result, the 1649 Act of abolition stated baldly that no one should be obtruded against the will of the congregation. The directory, however, inserted a qualification: for the process to be halted, the majority of the congregation had to dissent and their reasons judged by the presbytery. If these were grounded on "causeless prejudices," then the settlement was to go ahead.

By drawing a line, the directory showed that the Church had turned its back on congregationalism. However, the intensity of the debate about the people's role had ensured that the genie of popular rights was out of the bottle. The vicissitudes of the Restoration era were to ensure that issue was not going to go away, but rather reappear in the subsequent generation with renewed vigor.

CHAPTER FOUR

The Restoration

OLIVER CROMWELL DIED ON 3 September 1658, and the power–base he had built up began slowly to crumble. With disorder mounting in the south, General Monck[1] decided at the end of the following year to remove his army from Scotland and march to London. Arriving early in 1660, he restored Parliament to its full membership which then dissolved itself in order to elect a Convention Parliament. Since the latter was dominated by those in favor of the monarchy, the way had now cleared for its restoration. Charles was duly affirmed as king on 8 May 1660, and he returned from exile two weeks later.

Since 1654, the cause of the Resolutioners had been promoted at London by the minister of Crail (St Andrews presbytery), James Sharp#. He continued this role through the change from commonwealth into royal rule, and after initially reporting that Charles was resolved to be coy about ecclesiastical arrangements for Scotland, eventually returned north bearing a letter from the king for circulation to the presbyteries. Dated 10 August 1660, the letter promised to protect and preserve the government of the Kirk as settled by law, recognized the Assemblies of 1651 (a signal to the Protesters of royal disfavor) and gave notice that another would be called as soon as possible.[2] It was to be a false assurance.

When the Scottish Parliament re-convened on the 1 January 1661, a programme of legislation ensued which began to dismantle most of what the Covenanters had gained since 1638. Its initial enactment was to

1. George Monck (1609–1670), English soldier. In 1650 he went to Scotland as lieutenant general under Oliver Cromwell, and in 1651, when Cromwell returned to England, he stayed on as commander in chief. After the Restoration, Monck was created Duke of Albemarle.

2. Baillie, *Letters*, iii, 410; *Register of the consultations of the ministers of Edinburgh and some other brethren of the ministry*, ii, 1657–1660, Scottish History Society, third series. (Edinburgh: 1930), xlvii.

approve an Oath of Allegiance which bound the subscriber to acknowledge the king as supreme governor "in all causes."[3] On 9 February, the passage of the *Act approving the Engagement 1648 and annulling the parliament and committees 1649*[4] meant that patronage was no longer abolished. Then on 28 March, the *Act Rescissory* annulled the "pretendit" parliaments of 1640, 1641, 1644, 1645, 1646, 1647 and 1648.[5] On the 18 June, the *Act anent presentation of ministers* not only warned patrons to be careful about whom they presented, but specified that entrants must take the oath of allegiance or the presentation became void.[6]

Meanwhile, progress towards the restoration of episcopacy continued, and Sharp himself and three others were consecrated in London on the 15 December. At the new Scottish Parliament in May 1662, bishops and archbishops were formally restored, after which an Act was approved which condemned the Covenants.[7] The measure which acted as a watershed, however, came on the 11 June, with the *Act concerning such benefices and stipends as have been possest without presentations from the lawful patron.*[8] Under its terms, if anyone had been settled since 1649, they had no right to the stipend, manse or glebe and their charge was to be regarded as vacant. However, any minister who applied to his patron, received a presentation (which the patron was bound to bestow) and received collation from the bishop before 20 September,[9] could enjoy his position as before. Failure to comply gave the patron the right to present another by 20 March, otherwise the presentation fell to the bishop, *jure devoluto*.

To be fair to Charles, his original instructions to his commissioner to Parliament, John, Earl of Middleton, did not include the requirement for episcopal collation and it is possible that it was added simply out of malice by the fiercely anti-presbyterian Earl.[10] Either way, if the original intention of the Act had been—apart from reinforcing the principle of patronage—to rid the Church of a few Protester radicals, Middleton's addition, together

3. *APS*, vii, 6–7.

4. *APS*, vii, 31–32.

5. *APS*, vii, 86–87.

6. *APS*, vii, 272.

7. *APS*, vii, 372–74; 377–78.

8. *APS*, vii, 376.

9. This was extended twice, to 1 November 1662 and then 1 February 1663. The term "collation" here should be taken to mean "approval." It was not intended that the incumbent be ordained or inducted over again.

10. Julia Buckroyd, *Church and state in Scotland 1660–81*. (Edinburgh: 1980), 46.

with the severity with which he prosecuted recalcitrants, triggered a large-scale exodus of ministers from their parishes. Instead of isolating and dispersing those whom Middleton saw as extremists, the policy united them and drew in support from Resolutioners as well. Over the next five years, between a quarter and a third of the country's approximately 952 ministers were deprived of their livings,[11] mostly south of the Tay. Their places were often filled with candidates imported from elsewhere, particularly the more conservative and conformist north-east.[12] The new presentees were widely known by the derogatory term of "king's curates," and it is noticeable, in areas like Dumfries and Galloway where feelings ran highest against them, that the lay patrons opted to deflect popular opprobrium away from themselves by eschewing their right to present and leaving the bishops to inherit the *jus devolutum*.[13]

The outed ministers, meanwhile sought sustenance where they could, many taking part in "exercises" or theological colloquies, out of which field meetings or conventicles were to evolve. As increasingly punitive attempts were made to suppress these irregular services in the *Act against conventicles* and *An act against separation and disobedience to ecclesiastical authority*,[14] attitudes hardened on both sides.

Through the following twenty-five years, the government attempted to resolve the fact that it had helped to create what was, in effect, a schismatic church, by alternating between repression and conciliation.[15] Although some ministers took advantage of the indulgences of June 1669, September 1672 and June 1679, such defections simply reinforced the determination of the remnant who endured. For them, the true Church of Scotland had been driven into the wilderness by a corrupt establishment, which was now in the pocket of a sovereign whose rule they could no longer accept. Thus the root cause of their dismay was not so much the

11. c. 270 is the figure suggested by Colin Kidd, "Religious realignment between the restoration and union," in *A union for empire, political thought and the British union of 1707*, ed, John Robertson, (Cambridge: 1995), 147; see also Cowan, *Covenanters*, 53.

12. James Kirkton, *A history of the church of Scotland 1660–79*, ed., Ralph Stewart, (Lampeter: 1992), 93; [written c. 1693, first pub., 1817, as *The secret and true history of the church of Scotland from 1660 to 1678*.]; Gilbert Burnet, *History of his own time*. (London: 1883), 103.

13. *Fasti*, ii, 258ff.; Cowan, *Covenanters*, 56; Kirkton, *History*, 94.

14. *APS*, vii, 377–78; vii, 455.

15. For a full and detailed account of the controversy between episcopalians and presbyterians during this period, see Alasdair Raffe, *The Culture of Controversy: Religious Arguments in Scotland, 1660–1714*, Studies in Modern British Religious History, vol. 28, (Woodbridge: 2012).

actual existence of bishops, but the Erastian implications which their appointment and presence brought to the nature of the Church.[16] More will be said below about how elements of this understanding of the condition of the Church surfaced after the Revolution and in the patronage disputes of the following century. First, however, it is important to consider how prominent a part, if any, patronage played in the philosophical war of words that was also conducted in the period subsequent to the return of presentations.

The Patronage Issue After the Restoration

Whereas patronage had its place (albeit a small one) in the tide of polemical literature of the 1660s, it was to become marginalized as other issues, such as the permissibility of resistance to tyrants, moved to the centre of attention. The notable works that did pay attention to the question of lay presentations were that of John Brown#, who was minister of Wamphray (Lochmaben presbytery) until he was exiled to Holland in 1663, James (later Sir James) Stewart of Goodtrees#, James Stirling#, minister of Paisley second charge (deprived 1662) and Andrew Honyman#, bishop of Orkney.

In 1665, Brown published *An apologetical relation of the particular sufferings of the faithful ministers and professors of the church of Scotland since August 1660*. As its twenty-three sections were a comprehensive repudiation of the conduct of the Restoration regime since 1660, Sharp unsurprisingly labeled it "a damnable book,"[17] and blamed it for turning mere grievance into defiance of the Crown. In section nine, Brown sets out the reasons why ministers refused to seek presentations under the 1662 Act, and these afford an insight into whether the basic arguments against patronage had altered greatly since their expression in the preamble to the 1649 Act. These had been that it was unscriptural, popish, contrary to the second *Book*, prejudicial to the liberty of the people and restricted freedom of choice.

Brown opens by rehearsing the familiar argument that presentations were supported neither by Scripture nor the best Reformed tradition. Similarly, he claims that the 1649 Parliament had simply completed the

16. Alasdair Raffe, "Presbyterians and Episcopalians: the formation of confessional cultures in Scotland 1660–1715." *English Historical Review* 53. (2010) 574.

17. J.D. Douglas, *Light in the north, the story of the Scottish covenanters*. (Exeter: 1964), 108.

work of reformation, by restoring the Church's original rights. To seek a presentation, therefore, would be to approve what the state had done in removing those rights. He next points out that receiving a presentation now meant taking the Oath of Allegiance as well, which right–thinking ministers could not do.

At this point, he attempts to answer two counter–arguments that had been leveled against the outed ministers. The first one challenged them to agree that since ministers admitted before 1649 were not elected, they must surely be classed as intruders. Brown's curious reply is to say that although patronage was sinful, this was "not so fully seen and perceived before" and, in any case, "there was no other way of entry . . . practicable by law." No doubt sensing that he has just weakened his own case,[18] he thereupon goes on the offensive by claiming that any fault on the pre-1649 entrants' part was small compared with that of those who have seen the evil reformed, yet "now again lick up that vomit."[19]

Secondly, he deals with the point that since post-1649 entrants have already had a call from the people, then they cannot become intruders by now accepting a presentation. Brown this time has a more convincing answer. He suggests that for an incumbent now to accept a presentation would be to imply that he was not properly called on the first occasion. Moreover, the criticism itself is fatally flawed in that it suggests that election and presentations can be complementary to one another when in fact they are mutually exclusive: "the patron's presentation is not *cumulative* unto, but *privative* and destructive of the people's liberty of free election, because where patrons do present, the people's suffrages are never asked, and, where people have power to elect, patrons have no place to present."[20]

A similar reflection is made two years later by Stewart and Stirling in their *Naphtali, or the wrestlings of the church of Scotland for the kingdom of Christ, contained in a true and short deduction thereof, from the beginning of the reformation of religion until the year 1667*, the popularity of which

18. Opponents could point out that, a), anti-patronage campaigners maintained that the Church had *always* regarded it as a sinful burden, and b), if it had been unacceptable for ministers to defy the law previously, this surely remained the case. Later, in section xv, n. 9, Brown returns to the issue and gives a more detailed and coherent argument, comparing reformation with the ascent of a hill, where it is wholly acceptable to advance by degrees. It would, by contrast, be reprehensible for present generations to "return backward because their forefathers could not advance further" (146).

19. John Brown, *An apologetical relation of the particular sufferings of the faithful ministers and professors of the church of Scotland since August 1660* (n.p. 1665), in *The presbyterian's armoury*, iii, 62–63.

20. Ibid, 63

caused it to be burnt and banned in December 1667, and a fine of £10,000 Scots imposed for its possession. Its two references to presentations do not hesitate to condemn them as an abuse, and the traditional arguments are cited as a justification. However, like Brown, the authors considered the real evil of the restoration of patronage to have been in its use as a snare, whereby "the ministry of this Church were reduced to this sore dilemma, either to take that oath of supremacy . . . and, by accepting of collation, to acknowledge these perfidious and usurping prelates, or to lose, and be cast out of, the ministry."[21] Whereas patronage was still an issue for those dissatisfied with the state's wishes on settling vacant churches, there was greater revulsion at the fact that to accept a presentation meant registering it with a bishop.

For the other side of the debate on presentations, Bishop Honyman did not miss the opportunity to alight upon what he saw were weaknesses in the arguments against patronage which appeared in the *Apologetical Relation* and *Napthali*. In 1668, he published *A survey of the insolent and infamous libel entitled Naphtali, etc.*, which contained a mixture of historical, utilitarian and philosophical rebuttals. From the historical aspect, he asserts, patronage has a thousand years of tradition behind it, and moreover, since it was so entrenched in the practice of the Church, it was still in place when the Covenants were composed and subscribed, which thereby means that to engage oneself, by means of the Covenants, to uphold the order of the Kirk, is to uphold patronage. It is also significant that the Westminster Assembly chose not to abolish it. Turning to the practical disadvantages of popular election, he suggests that nobles and gentlemen would be discouraged from building churches, especially in areas of need like the Highlands, if they thought that their own tenants would overrule them in the selection of a minister. It is a suggestion he virtually cancels out, however, by adding that the experience of popular election in the 1650s meant it was of little consequence anyway, since one or two leading men in the parish normally worked on the parishioners to follow their inclinations.

Honyman's final reasonings possess a greater cogency. Moving into the field of biblical exegesis, he challenges the anti-patronage lobby 's frequent assertion of scriptural warrant for their view. To this end, he argues a), that in Acts i, the use of lots in the selection of Matthias cannot

---

21. James Stewart, and James Stirling, *Naphtali, or the wrestlings of the church of Scotland for the kingdom of Christ, contained in a true and short deduction thereof, from the beginning of the reformation of religion until the year 1667.* n.p. 1667, ed., Henry Duncan, (Kirkcudbright: 1845), 132–33, 162–33.

be construed as an election by any human agency; b), in reference to the popular election of deacons in Acts vi, it is illogical to insist that other ecclesiastical offices must therefore be filled in the same fashion (especially since the apostles, unlike presbyteries, made no claim to vet the qualities of the person presented); c), the Greek word in Acts xiv, which they allege means voting by raising of hands, is plainly used here in its other sense of stretching out in ordination, and d), their appeal to early Greek writers in fact undermines their case, since the latter knew of no distinction between electing and admitting. To imitate their practice therefore, would be to place the whole validity of a ministry in the act of election, which thereby removed the function of presbyteries and amounted to Independency.[22]

That Honyman had the best of the arguments seems to be confirmed by the fact that Stewart was to make a general response to *A survey, etc.* in his *Ius populi vindicatum* of 1669, but had nothing to say in answer to its points on patronage. It is also worth noting that Honyman was even willing to concede that abuses of patronage and presentations did go on, and that there was a case for more regulation.[23] He does not define what these were, but some malpractice had certainly been taking place from the start of the 1660s, as with the case of simony at Monquitter (Turriff presbytery) in 1662.[24] In the following decade, simony was exposed at Maryculter (Aberdeen presbytery) in 1678,[25] Other abuses included an attempt to present successive incumbents on one presentation, as at Caputh (Dunkeld presbytery) in 1677[26], and even a minister buying the patronage and presenting himself, as at Maryculter, again, in 1679.[27]

In contrast to such abuses, it should be noted, however, that it was not uncommon for the role of patron also to be fulfilled fairly and sensitively. This was particularly the case when the right belonged to the bishop, and W. Roland Foster has noted several instances where presentations were exercised with genuine solicitation for the views of the parish, as at Straiton (Ayr presbytery) in 1662, Kilmodan (Dunoon presbytery) in 1682,

---

22. Andrew Honyman, *A survey of the insolent and infamous libel entitled Naphtali, etc.* (Edinburgh: 1668), 248.

23. Ibid., 248–49.

24. see Duncan, *Parochial law*, 118.

25. Synod of Aberdeen minutes, 19 March 1679, in 'Selections from the records etc', 330.

26. 24 January 1677, see W.M. Morison, *Decisions of the court of session.* (Edinburgh: 1805), 9899.

27. *Fasti*, vi, 61. This violated not only the medieval church's canon law but also the law of Scotland, see Duncan, *Parochial law*, 110.

Alyth (Meigle presbytery) in 1686, and Moy and Dalarossie (Inverness presbytery) in 1680.[28] Moreover, it is illuminating to observe that when the patronage debate re–ignited towards the end of the 1680s, having gone cold during the 1670s, reference to specific abuses featured little in the substantial corpus of anti-patronage literature.

The Glorious Revolution

Returning to the troubled times following Charles's Restoration settlement, the murder of Archbishop Sharp in 1679 acted as the flash-point for further unrest in the western counties. In retaliation for the murder, but also in fear of general insurrection, the authorities sent John Graham of Claverhouse into Ayrshire. At Drumclog, he attacked a conventicle only to discover he had underestimated the strength of the participants, and his troops were routed. The success caused more sympathizers to rally to the conventiclers' cause, but the increased numbers made unanimity difficult between those who could be classed as moderates and those who were more radical. The former were unwilling to condemn outright the king's Indulgences of 1669 and 1672 and those who accepted their terms, and while they opposed the excesses of the civil power, they would not renounce all allegiance to it. The latter on the other hand, preferred separation from the indulged and abhorred any compromise with what they saw as Erastianism. Such disagreements weakened the military vitality of their ranks, with the result that, when they engaged with the Duke of Monmouth's vastly superior force at Bothwell Bridge in Lanarkshire, he easily won the field.

One result of the violence was the fall of the king's Commissioner, John Maitland, Earl of Lauderdale. He was replaced by the king's Catholic brother, James, Duke of York, who set about using his authority with Parliament to facilitate both his succession to the throne and eventual toleration for all catholics. To this end, he was able to bring about, in August 1681, the *Act acknowledging and asserting the right of succession to the imperial crown of Scotland,* and the *Act anent religion and the test.*[29] The second was to be the cause of particular anxiety to churchmen of tender conscience, since it prescribed an oath requiring all subscribers, among other matters, to acknowledge the monarch as supreme governor in ecclesiastical causes.

28. W. R. Foster, *Bishop and presbytery, the church of Scotland 1661–88.* (London: 1958); 52–53; 100–1.

29. *APS*, viii, 238; 243.

The succession would, of course, eventually place James in such a position. This added fuel to the fire of resistance by the remaining followers of field–preachers, otherwise known as Society People or Cameronians (so named after Richard Cameron who was leader until his death in 1680) and a one-sided open war, the "Killing Times," continued between them and government forces down to 1688.

Finally, Charles II died on 5 February 1685, and James became king. Despite renewed persecution of conventiclers, general loyalty to him remained steady. His campaign to promote his faith, however, increasingly raised alarm and antipathy. When the 1686 parliament balked at granting further relief for catholics, he had it dissolved and began replacing senior figures of state with his co-religionists. Finally, in February and June 1687, he issued a partial then complete toleration, allowing all "to meet and serve God after their own way."[30] The Indulgence was a major undermining of James's cause in Scotland, in that it appalled the episcopalian establishment and at the same time allowed mainstream presbyterianism to re-group and be invigorated by exiles returning from the continent.

It was, however, James's attack on the privileges of the Church of England with his English Declaration of Indulgence that precipitated his final undoing. The anger and alienation provoked by the action thereafter turned to alarm when, on the 10 June 1688, the queen produced a son, James (the "Old Pretender"). Until then, the heir apparent had been his daughter Mary, who had married the Protestant Prince William of Orange. Fearing the establishment of a catholic dynasty, seven leading members of the political and ecclesiastical establishment sent word to William inviting him to intervene in the situation. He duly arrived at Torbay on 5 November 1688. After a period of indecision, James eventually realized his situation was hopeless, and, on 22 December, availed himself of the opportunity to escape to France.

The Patronage Debate Re-opened

Even before William set sail for England, he had become the target for what was to become a tide of addresses, supplications and propaganda leaflets. The imminence of constitutional and, possibly, ecclesiastical change meant that those with a particular interest in either now strove to advance their cause in the estimation of both the prince and public opinion. An address subscribed, according to the historian Robert Wodrow#,

---

30. *Source book of Scottish history*, iii, 197.

by "many thousands of Presbyterians" was quickly drawn up. As well as recounting the many afflictions they had endured in the previous decades, it also made twelve petitions, of which the sixth was: "that laical patronages be discharged as was done in the Parliament 1649 and the people restored to their right and privilege of election, according to the warrant of God's word."[31] In the event, it would seem that the document was never sent. The probable reason, in Wodrow's opinion, was that William landed at Torbay before it could be completed, but, given that patronage was a largely uncontested fact of life in William's Dutch Reformed Church, it is also possible that it was held back so that something less controversial could be composed. Certainly, the official address that was sent, early in 1689, to William from the presbyterian grouping was much more general and contained no reference at all to patronage.[32]

However, one event later in 1689, ensured that the issue of patronage was not about to disappear. This was the publication of a book by Robert Park, son of the minister of Kilmaurs (Irvine presbytery), entitled *The rights and liberties of the church asserted and vindicated against the pretended right and usurpation of patronage*. There had not before been a similar study of the subject and it was an opportune time for one to be published, as Park himself realized: "the subject of these papers is but little treated of by any, especially in this way, therefore the publication may be as necessary as seasonable."[33] Park was an advocate by profession (he was also town clerk of Glasgow and clerk to the Assembly after the Revolution), and he brings his legal mind to bear, in particular, on the medieval antecedents of the practice. The book has its faults in that it is somewhat rambling and makes no concession to views other than the author's, nonetheless, the range of its scholarship ensured its continuation as something of a standard reference work until well into the next century.

If Park saw his treatise as a rallying cry to the anti–patronage lobby not to miss the present "golden opportunity so wonderfully and

---

31. Robert Wodrow, *The history of the sufferings of the Church of Scotland from the Restoration to the Revolution* ed., R. Burns, (Glasgow: 1828), iv, 477.

32. It is quoted, in full, along with a commentary by George MacKenzie, Earl of Cromarty, and Sir George MacKenzie, Lord Advocate, in *A memorial for His Highness the prince of Orange, in relation to the affairs of Scotland together with the address of the presbyterian party in that kingdom to His Highness and some observations on that address by two persons of quality.* (London: 1689).

33. Robert Park, *The rights and liberties of the church asserted and vindicated against the pretended right and usurpating of patronage.* (Edinburgh: 1689), i.

unexpectedly brought to their hand,"[34], it did not fall on deaf ears. When, in anticipation of the first session of the 1690 Parliament, the presbyterian grouping sent a petition to the Parliamentary commissioner setting out their legislative requests, they did not omit to ask for the removal of patronage, describing it in uncompromising terms, as "a great grievance to this church, as the source and fountain of a corrupt ministry."[35] This was certainly a change from the early Covenanting period, when reluctance to offend the large landowners ensured patronage remained discreetly off the political agenda. The factors which made such boldness possible will be discussed below.

In the interim, it should be emphasized that the forthright demeanor of those who upheld presbyterian principles like patronage abolition or the *ius divinum* [divine right or authority] of presbytery, did not mean that they were entirely disdainful of the views and ideals of their opponents. It was realized that the Kirk had to be careful of how it was perceived within the ruling establishment. Accordingly, there was a group of apologists - identified by Colin Kidd as churchmen like Gilbert Rule (?1629–1701), who became principal of Edinburgh University in 1690, Thomas Forrester (?1635–1706), who became principal of St Andrews in 1698, William Carstares# (1649–1715), who became principal at Edinburgh in 1703, George Meldrum (?1635–1709) who became a minister of Edinburgh in 1692 and the lawyer and future Lord of Session, Francis Grant# (c.1660–1726) — all of whose writings displayed a moderation that attempted to disassociate presbyterianism from the taint of extremism and obduracy.[36] Thus when Rule, in a pamphlet published on the eve of the church settlement of 1690, addressed the subject of patronage, he showed he was not insensitive to some of the doubts and fears patrons were harboring. He makes clear his opinion that popular election "is not to be left to the management of the confused rabble." For him, it is to be handled by the elders, among whom heritors and men of interest will surely be willing to serve, thereby having a share in the process. As for consulting the people, he envisages that the "heady and schismatic" would be excluded, and more recognition given to fixed members than those who are not. In any case, he is confident that great men can usually influence those under them,

---

34. Ibid.

35. *To his grace, his majesty's high commissioner and the right honourable, the estates of parliament, the humble address of the presbyterian ministers and professors of the church of Scotland.* (Edinburgh: n.d., prob. early 1690).

36. Colin Kidd, 'Religious realignment', 158–61.

just as in the 1640s, when it was the constant practice of the church to give deference to men of interest so that they were generally satisfied with the results: "and they may still be persuaded that it will be the care of Elderships and Presbyteries to do nothing that they can justly complain of."[37]

When, however, Parliament did decide to settle the patronage question, in July 1690, it was not achieved because such reassurances had been accepted or because an argument had been won, but through simple miscalculation.

The 1690 Abolition of Patronage

On the 7 January 1689, William met, at London, with around thirty Scots nobles and approximately eighty of the Scottish gentry. When he invited their advice as to what should be done for securing the Protestant religion and the country's laws and liberties, they responded by going into council, with William Douglas, third Duke of Hamilton acting as their president. Returning two days later, they suggested the Prince administer Scottish affairs until a Convention of Estates could be elected and then summoned for 14 March.[38] William agreed. The Convention duly met and on 4 April decided that James had forfeited his crown. In the ensuing weeks, the Claim of Right and the Articles of Grievances were adopted, the former condemning prelacy (patronage is not mentioned) and, in effect, declaring William and Mary to be king and queen. On accepting the joint throne, William and Mary also agreed to turn the Convention into a parliament. Superficially at least, the new era had begun fairly smoothly.

Almost at once, however, the new king found his authority in difficulty. One major cause was the Convention's refusal to continue the Committee of Articles. Theoretically, this body was designed, in liaison with the sovereign, to prepare legislation and steer it through Parliament, but, during the Restoration period, it had become discredited and was widely regarded as an instrument of dictatorship. Although the Articles were not formally abolished until 8 May 1690, nonetheless William

37. [Gilbert Rule] *A true representation of presbyterian government wherein a short and clear account is given of the principles of them that owne it, the common objections against it answered and some other things opened that concern it in the present circumstances, by a friend of that interest.* Edinburgh: 1690.

38. *His highness the prince of Orange, his speech to the Scots lords and gentlemen, with their address, and his highness, his answer. With a true account of what passed at their meeting, in the council chamber at Whitehall 7 January 1689* (n.p. 1689–90) [NLS.1.22].

quickly discovered that his ability to influence the Convention/Parliament through the crucial months of 1689–90 was worryingly deficient.

William's position was further troubled by anger on the part of some at his initial appointments to office. Many felt deeply disappointed at being overlooked and jealous of those who had been favored, while others considered that the advancement of men like Sir John Dalrymple# (who became Lord Advocate) showed that no real care was being taken to omit those tainted by the old regime.[39] This envy and frustrated ambition crystallized into an effective opposition group which came to be known as "The Club."[40] It has been described as "a quite exceptionally turbulent, factious opposition party . . . formed out of an unexpected alliance of crypto-Jacobites and extreme Presbyterians,"[41] yet it was out of the activities of this unlikely body that lay patronage came to be abolished in the following year. It remains one of the curiosities of history that a grouping like the Club, whose presbyterian presence was neither especially strong nor influential,[42] should have been responsible for so radical a measure as the 1690 Act of abolition. Since religious principles had little or no bearing upon its public maneuvers,[43] it must be wondered how it was that the legislation came about.

As far as conduct was concerned, the Club's overarching strategy was straightforward, and has been succinctly summarized by Lionel Glassey: "The Club was . . . prepared to go to almost any lengths to prevent those to whom William had entrusted Scottish government from actually exercising it."[44] In other words, they believed that by maintaining pressure upon the administration, they could create a climate in which favors could be wrought as a means of buying them off. Better still, if their activities caused a government minister to fall from office, they could look forward to even greater possibilities for scavenging some advantage. Consequently, when

39. "Opinion, supposed by Sir James Stewart, Lord Advocate. 24 May 1689", *Leven and Melville Papers*, Bannatyne Club. lxxvii. (Edinburgh: 1843), 23; see also E. J. G. MacKay,*Memoir of Sir James Dalrymple, 1st Viscount Stair*, (Edinburgh: 1873), 218.

40. *Melville Papers*, Dalrymple to Melville, 25 June 1689, 81–85.

41. Lionel Glassey, "William II and the Settlement of Religion in Scotland, 1688–1690," *RSCHS*, xxiii, 3, (1989), 326.

42. see P. W. J. Riley, *King William and the Scottish politicians*. (Edinburgh: 1979), 31–32 for discussion of its diminutive size.

43. James Halliday, "The Club and the Revolution in Scotland 1689–90," *SHR*, xlv, 154: "it has to be realised that political requirements not presbyterian zeal dictated the handling of the religious issue by the Club leaders."

44. Glassey, 326.

the first session of the now officially-named Parliament convened on 5 June 1689, Hamilton, as king's commissioner, found himself so restricted by opposition that he was barely able to advance any of William's desires, least of all any which related to the Committee of Articles.

When, eventually, attention turned towards a settlement for the Church, once again the Club detected an opportunity for harassment. The proposed legislation which came before the Parliament was almost certainly drawn up by William Carstares. Son of the minister of Cathcart (Glasgow presbytery), Carstares came from a Covenanting background and had suffered for his allegiance. While in exile in Holland, he became chaplain to William, and remained his close confidant and adviser on Scottish church affairs until William's death in 1702. For his part, the king awarded him the revenues of the Chapel Royal and permanent accommodation at Kensington palace. Knowing William's desire to see a settlement that was characterized by moderation and restraint, Carstares proposed that it be based upon the one of 1592—which would, of course, have meant the retention of patronage. As the biography of him[45] in Joseph McCormick's *State papers and letters addressed to William Carstares* suggests, this was no oversight on Carstares' part, since there were several reasons for his not wanting to press for abolition. The first was that this would be asking too much of William, who had originally been told only of the Kirk's complaint against prelacy, not patronage; secondly, William would not allow the 1649 Act to be recognized as legal, since the 1662 Parliament had abolished it and thirdly, it might result in putting too much power into the hands of those embittered by the troubles of the previous thirty years.

Whatever underlay Carstares' thoughts, his proposal for a 1592 settlement came to nothing as the radical or "high" presbyterians saw in the package dire consequences for their cause. Their parliamentary leader, the Earl of Crawford, later wrote fearfully to the Earl of Melville# that if first the Church were not purged, "then the conform clergy will be six to one, and would readily depose them of the presbyterian way," moreover, with patronage remaining, "though those that daily pray for the late King were laid aside, many in this nation would present to churches such as were not of our partie."[46] Accordingly, Crawford's group set about organizing opposition.

---

45. *State papers and letters addressed to William Carstares*, ed. Joseph McCormick, (Edinburgh: 1774), 47–51.

46. *Melville Papers*, 172. 16 July 1689.

The assault on the Act[47] was led by Henry Erskine#, third Lord Cardross, who, having suffered in the Conventiclers' cause during the 1670s, was also on the advanced wing of the presbyterian party. His desire to have both episcopacy and patronage abolished found ready support among the Club, who pressed ahead with these and other radical demands—demands which, nonetheless, only a minority of those supporting him would seriously have wished to see fulfilled. For some eye witnesses, it was not an edifying sight. Sir John Dalrymple commented scornfully: "you may consider...whether there be more that pretend to be presbyterians than these who [are] truly des[ir]ing it,"[48] while for Lord Belhaven it was simply depressing: "In one word, for what I can see, and to my sad regret, I see self-interest is heavier in the balance than the interest of either religion or country."[49]

If Hamilton, the king's Commissioner to Parliament, been more astute, he could have surprised and divided the Club at this point by challenging their bluff and granting royal assent to at least some of their proposals, in particular the repeal of the 1669 Act of Supremacy. Hamilton was fearful, however, of damaging his career prospects by going beyond William's wishes and so decided to stall for time. On the 22 July 1689, he approved the abolition of episcopacy and then, without putting anything in its place, adjourned Parliament on the 2nd August. Admittedly, William had refrained from defining in detail what the church settlement should be, but Hamilton's hedging pleased no one and he was replaced in February 1690 by the Earl of Melville.

The change in king's commissioner only served to encourage opposition, and as the Club set its sights on unseating Melville, it was joined in the chase by Queensberry and Atholl, along with their respective interests. Even though the latter were episcopalian, they were happy to help promote a high presbyterian agenda when Parliament convened again on the 25 April 1690. The assumption of course was that it would be unthinkable for Melville to give it any approval. However, anxiety was growing in London over news of disturbances at parish level between hard-line presbyterians and those ministers whom, as episcopalians or conformists, they regarded as usurpers. Melville therefore knew that he had to start

47. In Scotland the word "Act" was used to describe proposed legislation as well as that which had been passed by parliament and sovereign - see Riley, *King William*, 10, n. 23.

48. *Melville Papers*, Sir John Dalrymple to Melville, 25 June 1689, 84.

49. *Melville Papers*, 20 June 1689, 70.

moving towards some church settlement as quickly as possible. His first act was to give the royal assent both to the repeal of the *Act of Supremacy* and to an Act restoring the clergy who had been outed in 1661.[50] Shaken by the development, and already weakened by recruitments to the court interest,[51] the Club began to fragment. This did not mean, however, that Melville's numerous opponents were no longer eager or able to undermine his position, especially as they would know William was uncomfortable with what his commissioner had done. While the pressure on him continued, Melville for his part saw that, if he was to continue in power, his best hope lay in playing the high presbyterian card. Not only would he thereby garner support among the radicals, but at the same time he would be leaving his remaining opponents bereft of their customary means of harassing him.

The commissioner was, however, embarking on a hazardous course. Admittedly, the king had declared himself resigned to a presbyterian settlement in private instructions on the 25th February, 1690.[52] Indeed, in what must have been a singular encouragement to Melville, the instructions even permitted him to go as far as abolishing patronage "if the Parliament shall desire the same." However, William had since had second thoughts. Two months later, the solicitor-general, Sir William Lockhart, wrote from London to say, "The King, as to the settlement of Presbyterie, seems only to stick at the Patronadges; he says it's the interest of the crown, and the taking of men's propertie."[53] Nor did William like the wording of the proposed *Act for Settling Church Government*, where it sought to make absence of congregational consent a justification for declaring vacant those parishes which had outed their minister at the Revolution. As far as he was concerned, the Act was suggesting that the entire concept of patronage as a system was irregular. He would have none of that.[54]

Chance, however, suddenly turned the situation in Melville's favor. In June and July, an ongoing conspiracy to restore King James percolated to the surface. It concerned those who had felt themselves cheated of advancement under the current regime, chief among whom was Sir James Montgomerie of Skelmorlie. This, along with the news of a French fleet's

50. *APS*, ix, 111.

51. see Halliday, "The Club", 157.

52. *Melville Papers*, 414.

53. *Melville Papers*, 29 April 1690, 430.

54. Ibid., 438; "His Majesty's Remarques upon the settling of Church Government in Scotland," 22 May 1690.

approach to the English coast,[55] and the king's absence in Ireland, gave Melville an ideal opportunity to seize the advantage in Parliament. He knew that in the climate of fear created by a plot uncovered, opposition would become muted. At the same time, the Court could hardly complain if its commissioner acted decisively to undermine antagonists and promote the cause of loyalists. Accordingly, Melville wrote to the queen:

> I doubt not but your majestie is convinced how difficult a province I have, considering the unsettled condition of this nation, and a multitude of disguised enemies, who only wait an opportunity to show themselves; all which oblige me to go a greater length than otherwise I would have done in satisfying those here who are only to be relied on, without which I could not anywise answer for the safety of the country; and I must humbly beg that your majesty will be pleased to put a favourable construction upon my actions; for I doubt not but that I shall be able to make it appear, whatever be the issue, that I have taken the methods that were most proper, in present circumstances, for preserving and advancing your majesties interest in this kingdom.[56]

Having, as he hoped, covered his back, two weeks later, on the 19th July, he passed the Act abolishing patronage.

It was a disastrous moment for the Club: not only had they collapsed as a coherent force, but in the process had been instrumental in bringing about a measure which only a minority had desired.[57] Melville, unsurprisingly, became a casualty as well. From 1689, the Scottish episcopalians had already been pressurizing William from south of the border by lobbying their Church of England counterparts about their ill-treatment.[58] Now with the July church settlement pushed through, a new cycle of complaints came up to Court, prompting William from December 1690 to make a show of responding to at least some presbyterian excesses.[59] In January 1691 he neutralized Melville's influence by appointing Sir John Dalrymple,

---

55. The battle off Beachyhead was on the 30th June 1690 (and was won by the French).

56. Earl of Melville to the Queen, 2 July 1690. *Melville Papers*, 456.

57. Riley, *King William*, 42

58. Melville [London] to Crawford, 1st December 1689: "I hear the Convocation here flies high; their pretence is the rigour used against those of their persuasion in Scotland, which they say, if not redressed, they will show the less favour to the Nonconformists here." *Melville Papers*, 336.

59. Tristram Clarke, "The Williamite episcopalians and the Glorious Revolution in Scotland," *RSCHS*, xxiv (1990), 46–47.

who was pro-episcopalian and a rival, as his joint Secretary of State. By the end of the year, Melville had been appointed to the comparatively insignificant office[60] of Keeper of the Privy Seal. Despite plaintively protesting to William that he had only granted the abolition of patronage for the soundest of political reasons,[61] his influence was largely over.

The Act, however, remained in place.

Summary

Since lay patronage was a property right, it is to be considered remarkable that a parliament strongly influenced by property owners should have abolished it at all in the seventeenth century, let alone twice in forty-one years. However, as has been seen, the Acts of 1649 and 1690 took place in extraordinary circumstances. In the earlier case, the purge of Engagers after the battle of Preston created an unprecedented situation out of which abolition became possible. Similarly, in 1690, amidst the turmoils engendered by the birth of a new constitutional settlement, there was always the likelihood that some unexpected results would ensue. However, later commentators, especially in the nineteenth century, would regularly make the understandable assumption that the heroes of the resistance to King Charles were bound to insist on their rights being recognized in the Revolution settlement, and thus the demise of patronage became all but inevitable. This was not the case. Whereas the drive for popular election did gain momentum during the troubled times after 1660, it was overshadowed by other concerns such as the Erastian encroachments of royal authority. It is also noteworthy that Melville's 1690 Act did not award any more electoral rights to the congregational rank and file than had been allowed in 1649. Most of all, it is clear that, far from abolition coming about by the force of an irresistible popular will, chance, political miscalculation and the desire of a king's minister to buy parliamentary peace for the Court at a critical juncture remain the true story.

60. See *Melville Papers*. xxvii.

61. "As to the taking away of Patronages, tho it was frequently and earnestly desired of me by the Presbyterians, yet I did still forbear to do anything in that matter, till the French fleet was upon the english coast, and a dangerous conspiracy against your majesty's government was discovered, and I having reason to think that affairs in England were in a dangerous posture . . . did conceive it was for your Majesty's service to dismiss the Parliament of Scotland with as little discontent as might be, and to gratify the Presbyterians in the business of patronage, in the way that might be the least offensive." Melville to King William, prob. 1691. *Melville Papers*, xxiv.

Chapter Five

THE BULK OF THE 1690 *Act concerning patronages* [see Appendix IV] was drafted by Sir James Stewart of Goodtrees (1635–1713), and introduced into Parliament by his brother Thomas, the MP for North Berwick.[1] During the Restoration period James Stewart had been a supporter of the Covenanting cause, not only using his writing skills to good effect, as with *Naphtali* and *Ius populi vindicatum*, but also in his capacity as a lawyer, when so needed. On his death, the historian Robert Wodrow described him as "a great Christian, an able statesman, one of the greatest lawyers ever Scotland bred."[2] Whereas it is doubtful that Stewart's character merited so uncritical an assessment as Wodrow's,[3] nevertheless, in view of his professed loyalties, it might be expected that his work on the 1690 Act would have resulted in at least a comprehensive eradication of lay patronage and, possibly, the establishment of popular elections. In the event, Stewart, whose advisers included the conciliatory Gilbert Rule,[4] chose to exercise a restraint which bordered on generosity.

According to the Act, those ministers already settled by presentation were to be left alone, a patron's right to apply vacant stipend on "pious uses" was to continue (Catholic patrons to do so on advice of presbytery) and—a particular beneficence—all patrons were now to have ownership of the parish's teinds (unless already heritably disponed) once stipend and other ministerial burdens had been deducted. This was not all. Although

1. G. W. T. Omond, *The Lord Advocates of Scotland*, i, (Edinburgh: 1883), 256.

2. Robert Wodrow, *Analecta*, Maitland Club, lx, ii., (Edinburgh: 1842), 205; Omond, 243; *The Coltness Collections*, 1608–1840, (Glasgow: 1842), 90ff.

3. Earlier, in 1687, he forsook exile in Holland and returned to London for rapprochement with King James—an incident which certainly left a cloud over his reputation for a time.[see, *The Coltness Collections*, 365]. He is described by P. W. J. Riley as, "an able lawyer with a dubious past and a well-founded reputation for venality." [*King William*, 83] See also, E. Calvin Beisner, "His Majesty's Advocate: Sir James Stewart of Goodtrees (1635–1713) and Covenanter resistance theory under the Restoration monarchy," PhD diss. St Andrews: 2003.

4. His main advisers were reputedly Gabriel Cunningham, Hugh Kennedy and Gilbert Rule. *Coltness Collections*, 94; Wodrow, *Analecta*, i, 275.

congregations were to have the right of appeal to presbytery against a nominee for their parish, there was to be no suggestion of choice by popular elections. Instead, not only was it awarded to kirk sessions (as was the 1649 practice) but, in an unprecedented move, it was also given to the local heritors (or, in the burghs, the magistrates) on a shared basis.

More will shortly be said about the latter decision, but first it should be remembered that Stewart and his colleagues probably had little option but to keep the franchise away from the congregational rank and file. One unwelcome consequence of their unrestricted choice would have been the inevitable election, in the Covenanting regions, of the most hardline ministerial candidates—hardly a desirable outcome for presbyterians hoping to convey an image of moderation to the new administration. Again, in the rest of Scotland, there was no shortage of places where a presbyterian candidate would be embarrassingly unwelcome to the local community.[5] Clearly, the Act recognized that there were problems and sought to counter them by turning again to the kirk session. It may not have been immediately obvious to everyone [see below], but magnifying the role of the session in disaffected areas was, in reality, to strengthen the influence of the presbytery. In a way similar to the 1649 arrangements, this came about because, in the many vacancies where the kirk session was in disarray or non-existent, the standard procedure was for presbytery to summon the heads of families with a view to their nominating candidates. However, if these refused or failed to appear, the presbytery could select its own candidate. Similarly, even where there was a session, if the elders failed to agree on their choice (a not unlikely event), it fell to the presbytery to intervene and choose as it saw fit. Finally, if there was an eldership, but presbytery decided its members were part of a "prelatic" session, then it could resolve it should be disowned and replaced or simply ignored, as happened at Musselburgh, Tranent and Burntisland.[6] It was only later that these advan-

5. John Sage cites as examples, Perth, Stirling, Burntisland, Musselburgh, Cupar as well as the regions north of the Tay. See, *An account of the present persecution of the church in Scotland in several letters*, iii. (London: 1690). [John Sage (1652–1711) was nominated to a chair at St. Andrews University before the Revolution, but on adhering to episcopacy, went to serve a meeting house in Edinburgh. He was made a Bishop in 1705.]

6. Walter Steuart of Pardovan, "Collections and Observations Methodized, Concerning the Worship, Discipline and Government of the Church of Scotland". [c. 1709]. Title VII, "Of Ruling Elders," 2, in *A Copious and Comprehensive Summary of the Laws and Regulations of the Church of Scotland from 1560–1850*, (Aberdeen: 1850), 209; J. Cunningham, *Church History of Scotland*, ii, (Edinburgh: 1859), 288n; [Alexander Munro], *An apology for the clergy of Scotland chiefly opposed to the censures, calumnies*

tages became clear to observers like the episcopalian propagandist, John Sage: "it surprised me at first that the Presbyterian preachers were so easily pleased with this [the 1690 electoral arrangement], after their so warm and frequent protestations for the Jus Divinum of popular elections: But this surprize was soon over when I found that this method in the result brought the whole power as effectually into their hands."[7]

Turning from the issue of a congregation's power of election back to the issue of those who did receive the privilege, Stewart's giving a formal share in the choosing process to local heritors and magistrates, regardless of whether they even supported the 1690 presbyterian settlement (the only requirement was that they should be Protestant), was a bold innovation. Almost certainly, it reflected a desire to win goodwill among the local gentry (and modify William's annoyance), yet, given the diversity of political and religious loyalties, the initiative was in fact a gamble of some magnitude. There were probably two considerations which made the Act's framers decide the risk was one worth taking.

First, there was the example of Holland. It should be remembered that men like Stewart had been in exile there before the Revolution, and had been able to acquire a knowledge of the workings of its reformed church. There, magistrates and patrons did have a locus in the selection process, but an accommodation between lay and ecclesiastical interests had been reached to the extent that friction between the two was kept to a minimum. Thus, although the magistrates in the municipalities had the power of veto over the choice of a consistory [session], they rarely provoked its ire by doing so. In the rural areas, patronage did operate, but it was accepted that a local consistory could, if antipathetic to the nominee, appeal to the Provincial States and get a presentation overturned. Having observed the Dutch experience, and how public opinion seemed to hold strife and unreasonable behavior in check, Stewart and his advisers may well have felt that a similar spirit of co-operation could well evolve, in time, under their system.[8]

---

and accusations of a late presbyterian vindicator in a letter to a friend wherein his vanity, partiality and sophistry are modestly reproved (London: 1692), 17; SRO. PC2/24, Privy Council Decrees, 22 March 1692.

7. [John Sage], *An account of the late establishment of presbyterian government by the parliament of Scotland, anno 1690, together with the methods by which it was settled . . .'* [London: 1693], 78.

8. Andrew L. Drummond, *The kirk and the continent* (Edinburgh: 1956), 107; *Edinburgh Christian Instructor*, xxvii (1828). Like Scotland, European Reformed churches such as those of France, French Switzerland, Rhineland Palatinate, East Frisia,

Secondly, the socio-political changes which had been taking place since 1649 had so raised the status of what might be termed the heritor class, that the argument in favor of including them in the Act's provisions was probably ineluctable. Accordingly, it is important to look at these changes before continuing.

Heritors in the Seventeenth Century

What had been happening throughout the seventeenth century was the emergence of a new social presence, a laird class, whose position was founded not on feudal superiority, but on property. The watershed for the transition had been Charles I's teind legislation of 1633. It will be remembered that its achievement was to allow what were formerly vassals to carve out for themselves an independence through property ownership, enhanced by the rights and privileges which such purchase brought. As the century progressed, further influence came to them in such roles as Commissioners of Supply and JPs.[9] Thus, by 1690, they were, in effect, a land-owning, Scottish middle–class, relentlessly pushing for greater influence in justice, in commerce, in civil administration and, inevitably, in the affairs of the Church.

It would have been hard enough to exclude them from parochial settlements for the reasons just stated, but, as had happened so often in the past, financial issues were also present, for heritors now had a key role in the matter of teinds. This went back to the legislation of 1633 whereby teinds, having been valued and commuted to a fixed sum, could be bought outright by the proprietor. The problem which then arose for the Church was that since the valuation had been fixed, the stipend to be appropriated from it became fixed as well, and by the end of the 1640s prices had risen sharply. Augmentations of stipend did occur, but as Roland Foster has pointed out

---

Holland, and Hungary, all claimed exclusive control over ministerial appointments for theological reasons. However, for one reason or another, especially the ever–present threat of a resurgent Catholicism, each had to reach a *modus vivendi* that might be less than they wished. The relative harmony over patronage within the Dutch Reformed Church was partly for this reason and partly because, unlike Scotland, it had managed to inherit much more of the old Church's patrimony.

9. The office of JP had been established in Scotland by James VI in 1609. Its impact upon the community was not great, although attempts were made to enhance it after the Union [see below]. JPs' main responsibilities were criminal law, maintaining highways and care of the poor; see, A.E. Whetstone, *Scottish County Government in the 18th. and 19th. Centuries* (Edinburgh: 1981), 27ff.

in his work on the Constant Platt ("common plan" for ministerial support), it did not mean that a minister would receive any augmentation as a matter of course.[10] By the 1690s, with the problem of finances still acute, the Church could hardly expect favorable terms from the heritor while resolutely refusing to award him a fitting place in the new settlement. As it was, the Act's inclusive approach did help to create some goodwill.

However, there still remained those locations where there was a determination to resist presbyterian settlements, and it was there that finance became a useful weapon. The allowance granted by the Act whereby all non-heritably disponable teinds left over after deduction of stipend went to patrons, was to act as a trojan horse for a further concession in 1693.[11] The *Act anent parsonages* turned the advantage further towards the patron by giving him the whole tithes to start with, on the understanding that stipend would then be deducted. Naturally, this served to increase the patron's sense of ownership. He might not have the right of parochial presentation, but without his co-operation an incumbent would have the enervating task of pursuing him for income. A particular example of this occurred at Rathven (presbytery of Fordyce) where, even as late as 1720, "the lapsed stipends were still unpaid. Mr. Gordon, the minister, had got no decreet of locality, and was still gathering his stipend so far as he could, according to use and wont."[12] Similarly, when a charge became vacant, it became even harder for the patron to resist treating the stipend money as his own, although technically he was obliged to discharge it for "pious uses"[13] within the parish. Occasionally, disgruntled co-heritors did challenge their patron's tight-fistedness, as with the case of Roxburgh manse in 1706. Faced with the cost of repairing its dilapidated condition, the heritors, led by George Rutherford of Harrington, brought a Bill of Suspension against the Earl of Roxburghe over the fate of the vacant stipend between 1700 and 1702. Such processes, however, were not easy to pursue and few equalled the success of the heritors of Kirkbane (or Kirkbean, presbytery of Dumfries) who managed to prove in 1699 that the Laird of Cairnmont had misappropriated the stipend money and so had forfeited his right to administer it.[14]

---

10. W. Roland Foster, "A Constant Platt Achieved: Provision for the Ministry, 1600–1638" in, *Reformation and Revolution: Essays presented to the Very Rev Hugh Watt.* ed. Duncan Shaw, (Edinburgh: 1967), 135.

11. *APS*, Act anent parsonages, 1693, c. 25.

12. Cormack, *Teinds*, 119.

13. For a definition of these, see J.M. Duncan, *Parochial Law*, 326 ff.

14. Cairnmont v. Heritors of Kirkbane, 1699, (*Morison's Dictionary of Decisions*, 9947).

The Acts of 1690 and 1693 were by no means the only legislation by which Parliament advanced or consolidated the influence of heritors within their local communities. Through the 1690s, there was a crucial series of measures concerning the poor, schooling, teinds and the care of churches, manses and churchyards. To take the administration and disposal of the poor's provision, for example, this had been placed by the statutes of 1597, c.272, and 1600, c.19, entirely in the hands of the kirk session, working under the supervision of the presbytery. However, by the acts of Parliament of 1695, 1696 and 1698, jurisdiction was now conferred jointly upon heritors and kirk session, with no supervisory power of control granted to any court. Indeed, provided the meeting was properly constituted, there was no need for the kirk session to be represented at all.[15]

Heritors were advantaged by other legislative landmarks in the 1690s, especially involving agricultural reform. Two Acts in particular stand out. The first was the 1695, cap.23, *Act anent Lands lying Run-rig*. This allowed landowners to apply to have their property re-divided "according to their respective interests," and in a way "as shall be most commodious to their respective Mansion houses." The other was the Act 1695, cap. 38, *Concerning the Dividing of Commonties*. This permitted heritors to petition the Court of Session for a dividing up in their favor of any commonty land (except that belonging to the Crown or a royal burgh) which lay adjacent to their property. Not unexpectedly, as interest in estate improvement increased, so also did alarm and resentment among those affected cottars and small tenants who viewed these, and similar Acts, as encroachments upon their traditional rights. Such were the disturbances in the South West, for example, that in 1724 the presbytery of Kirkcudbright had a paper read from its pulpits criticizing both levellers and enclosers, and calling for an end to the trouble that had broken out.[16] That such feelings found a means of retaliatory expression in popular opposition to a patron's presentation of a minister was therefore unsurprising. One patron who encountered repeated resistance to his presentees, most notably at Morebattle in Kelso presbytery (1723),[17] and Bowden in Selkirk presbytery (1739), was the first Duke of Roxburghe, and it is indicative to find among the Roxburghe muniments a petition, dated 1729, from disgruntled tenants of Roxburgh

15. Dunlop, *Parochial Law*, 445ff.

16. Wodrow: *Correspondence*, 3 vols., ed Thos. McCrie, Wodrow Society, (Edinburgh: 1843), iii, 125. 16 May 1724.

17. McCrie, editor of Wodrow's *Correspondence*, claims this was the year when enclosing began in earnest. [iii, 125].

parish (Kelso presbytery), complaining bitterly of the grievous harm done to them by the Duke's enclosure of the local Muir.[18]

Having looked at the thinking behind the terms of the 1690 Act, it must now be considered whether it did in practice fulfill the framers' hopes of establishing, for all time, a settlement system broadly acceptable to the majority.

The Act's Deficiencies

The major problem of the Act was that it lacked practical guidelines which would have smoothed its operation. To begin with, the formal combination of heritors and elders in ministerial elections was a new and untried procedure, yet there was no provision for the precise way in which the Kirk Session and heritors were to meet and determine. As seen above with the measures concerning the parish's provision for the poor, co-operation between the two bodies could be minimal. Indeed, a prime example of perplexity over the equality in status of each type of elector arose in Paisley presbytery in 1709, when it considered the call from Inchinnan parish to Matthew Crawford, probationer. The sticking point was that of the eleven votes cast in favor of his call at the moderation, only two were elders, while nine were heritors. Meanwhile, of the ten cast against him, seven were elders and three were heritors. The presbytery were deeply uncomfortable with the way the vote had divided, yet, buckling under extreme pressure from the chief heritor, the Duke of Montrose, they eventually declared the vote valid on the 28 November 1709.

The presbytery's discomfort over Inchinnan would have been aggravated by the Duke being episcopalian, but like most others of the nobility, his "peremptoryness"[19] was more to do with distaste at having to share his ministerial preferences with inferiors, than a desire to make life difficult for a presbytery. Thus, it made no difference that the Earl of Marchmont was presbyterian when a vacancy occurred at Channelkirk, in the presbytery of Earlston (later Lauder) in 1697. As chief heritor, his determination

18. Roxburghe Muniments. TD87/9/1277 SRO. 'Petition of the Tenants of Nether Roxburgh to His Grace the Duke.' 1729. Interestingly, there was no obvious resistance to the next incumbent there, on his presentation in 1735, although this was reputedly due to the irenic qualities of the previous minister, John Pollock. The next rebellion against the Duke was among his fellow heritors in 1739, over his refusal to allow them to draw divots from the muir for the church roof. See memo in TD87/9/1277, 4 Oct. 1739.

19. Wodrow, *Analecta*. i, 213.

that only his choice, and not the kirk session's, could be allowed to prevail ensured a strife-torn continuation of the vacancy for five years.[20]

Another uncertainty was whether or not heritors and elders should be allowed to vote by proxy. In the absence of a directive, each presbytery was left to follow its own inclinations, thus generating a constant potential for argument. There was also the old issue of how a presbytery was to judge a congregation's objections to the candidate elected by the heritors and elders. The 1690 Act simply empowered a presbytery to "cognosce" the reasons given, but laid down no criteria for so doing. The framers would almost certainly have assumed that, even though its accompanying parliamentary Act had been rescinded, the practice of the 1649 Assembly's directory[21] would automatically be the model for conduct. Indeed, Pardovan's notes on vacancy procedures, published c. 1711, frequently cites it. Unaccountably, however, the Act did not think it valuable either to refer to it specifically or, as in 1649, order the Assembly to publish recommendations. Once more, each presbytery was left in the difficult position of having to act as it saw fit, and then defend its position in the absence of statutory reinforcement. In 1705, the Assembly tried to help by decreeing that, "though a plurality of heritors and elders will always be thought to be the voice of the meeting . . . yet it is most desirable to have the universal consent of the heads of families, and this ought to be endeavored."[22] However, since it was again left to individual presbyteries to follow their own judgment in their interpretation of how diligently, if at all, they were to pursue something that might be desirable yet often fraught with difficulty, it was impossible for the Church's higher courts to impose consistency.

As the 1690s progressed, yet further divergence of opinion emerged over what precisely constituted a congregation's *call* to a minister. As was seen in chapter three, application of the word call had previously been wide-ranging and not consistently restricted to any particular action. By the end of the Restoration period, however, a tighter definition appears to have emerged, so that when both the 1690 Act and the later *Act*

20. A. Allan, *History of Channelkirk* (Edinburgh: 1900), passim. Sir Patrick Hume (1641–1724) was made Lord Polwarth in 1689, became Lord Chancellor in 1696 and was created Earl of Marchmont in 1697. The Earl's candidate was his former chaplain, Charles Lindsay.

21. If a majority of the congregation objected, and it was not for reasons based on pure prejudice, then a new election had to be called. If a minority objected, the settlement was to continue unless the dissenters' objections were relevant and verifiable.

22. *Acts of the General Assembly*, 351, "Of the proceedings and methods in presbyteries" (1705), Sect. iii, *Of vacant congregations and planting thereof*, para 13.

Against Intrusion (1695) use phrases such as "calling and entry," "calling and choice," and "an orderly call," it seems clear that they are referring to a conjunct act: the heritors and elders' choosing and the congregation's concurring. The tangible expression of this call emerged as a document addressed to the candidate, inviting him to take the charge and offering the congregation's respect, encouragement and obedience in return [see Appendix VI]. It was signed by the heritors and elders, who, according to the text, did so with the advice and consent of the parishioners. The parishioners (that is, the heads of families) could then, if they wished, add their names.

As time went by, acceptance of the principle that the conjunct activities constituted a call began to wane among an increasing number of the congregational rank and file. Originally, as Wodrow later noted, when the heads of families subscribed their names, it was understood simply as a confirmation, for the entrant's benefit, of their approval of him. They were not the callers.[23] However, times had changed. For those who had experienced the era of conventicles and field preachers, with its dangers and test of personal loyalties, such an arrangement was no longer satisfactory. To them, the bond between a people and their spiritual leader had to be forged on something more substantial than what was merely, in effect, the record of their accepting a choice made by others.

Accordingly, the principle grew that a "popular" (or "gospel" or "evangelical") call from the people themselves was necessary to give a true validity to any settlement, even though it could not be regarded as having a legal existence independent of the electors' voting. Despite this lack of legal endorsement, nonetheless, the *idea* of a separate, popular call was now to grow in stature to the extent that when a settlement took place, the focus of attention centered on the question, was the appointment accompanied by a popular call? [24] This question, indeed, became the nub around which many of the arguments concerning vacancy-filling were now to revolve for the next 150 years. Given the high regard with which calls had come

23. Wodrow *Correspondence*, ii, to Col Erskine, 28 Sept 1717, 321.

24. This is not to suggest that the concept of a minister being called from God by the people to minister among them was anything new. Indeed, it went back to the Reformation. As early as 1587, Robert Bruce was summoned, by what appeared to be popular acclaim, to minister in the 1st. charge at St Giles', Edinburgh. [see, Elizabeth Y. Whitley, *The two kingdoms* (Edinburgh: 1977), 14 and 38]. What was now being regularized as The Call, was the formal, popularly subscribed document addressed directly to the recipient. In his *Parochial Law*, Dunlop cites a call from the parish of Gullane to Andrew MacGhee, dated 1597, but like many others, it is addressed to the presbytery (280).

to be held by 1712, it is significant that, early on after the restoration of patronage, care was taken by concerned patrons to underline the fact that, whatever might be believed, calls had no legal impact upon a settlement's validity. Thus when, in 1713, William Livingstone, Lord Kilsyth, presented James Robe, or Robb, for the vacancy at Kilsyth church (Glasgow presbytery), he actually forbade his tenants to sign any call. When none did, presbytery nevertheless felt it had no choice but to install Robe[25] in the charge. Being episcopalian, Kilsyth had a further reason for seeking to undermine the value of a call, in that a rumor was circulating at the time that Parliament might be about to allow presentations to parish churches of those episcopalian clergy who had sworn allegiance to the Crown.[26] In the event, the rumor was to prove groundless.

There was yet another way in which the 1690 Act opened a door to contention. This was in its inattention to the matter of a heritor or elder's eligibility to vote. According to Stewart of Goodtrees,[27] when heritors were mentioned in the section dealing with the payment of compensation to patrons [see below], it was considered logical that it should be paid by such as were on the cess-roll[28], but it was never anticipated that the cess-roll might also be taken as the definition of a heritor's voter status in the nomination of a minister. Stewart's oversight, however, ensured that the potential for weighting elections by the artificial creation of heritors then became obvious. This was indeed what happened when a protracted dispute at Cramond came to a head in 1710. One side simply started to create new heritors until it had won the battle—although not, in this case, the war [see next chapter].

On the other hand, kirk sessions were not above attempting an equivalent maneuver, as in the above mentioned clash at Channelkirk, when they threatened to resolve that five-year dispute by flooding the session with new elders.[29] There was a similar instance of the ploy at Haddington, first charge, in 1702, although on that occasion it was the episcopal elders who tried to swell their numbers in order to obtain their choice.[30] In 1712,

25. James Robe (1688–1753): an evangelical who was to be a leading figure in the revivals at Cambuslang and Kilsyth in 1742.

26. Wodrow, *Correspondence*, i, Rev John Hart's letter to Wodrow, 7 Feb. 1713, 404, n.

27. see Wodrow, *Analecta*. i, 275–76.

28. For the purposes of taxation, this was a record of the names of the owners of heritable property and its value.

29. Allan, *History of Channelkirk*, passim.

30. HMC Portland MSS, x, memo by the General Assembly to the Government, (c.1714), 261.

attempts were made to get the Assembly to address both these problems through passing Acts which would have banned the creation of elders during a vacancy, and empowered presbyteries to disregard heritors who had not been infeft. However, overshadowed by the impending passage of the Patronage Act, the moves came to nothing.[31]

Finally, one of the most glaring flaws in the 1690 Act was its failure to prevent any later restoration of patrons' rights. The attempt it did make took the form of an late amendment by the member for Queensferry, William Hamilton of Whitelaw, which sought finally to denude patrons of their presentation privilege by awarding the local heritors and liferenters the right to purchase it from them for 600 merks (£400 Scots; £33 6/8d sterling). The clause, however, contained two major weaknesses. The first was that although the legislation ordained that the heritors and liferenters were to pay the money, there was no obligation upon the patron to seek it, nor were the heritors threatened with any sanction should they fail to proffer it.

Secondly, if the intention of the clause was to fortify abolition, it in practice had the opposite result. The addendum meant that, technically, patronage was not abolished: it was *conditionally* abolished, that is, it disappeared for all time provided the local heritors and life–renters paid the fixed sum of 600 merks.[32] If the patron did not receive the money, it might seem reasonable for him to consider that, effectively, his right was merely in suspense, in which case, there was the obvious incentive to wait and see how national affairs unfolded, while in the interim ensuring his fellow heritors made no attempt to buy him out. That this was almost certainly why very few parishes secured their freedom from patronage through the Act's provision, is reinforced by an Advocate's Opinion for government use, dated 7 July 1710: "Scarce any subject patron that I know has thought fit to insist on the 600 merks lest the taking payment of that sum may prejudge them if they should seek redress in Parliament of the Act [1690]."[33]

31. See Wodrow, *Correspondence*, i, 12 May 1712, 293.

32. J. S. More, *Lectures on the Law of Scotland*, (Edinburgh: 1864), Vol.II, section XVII, p 78, 'No mistake can be greater than the popular opinion, that by this statute patronage was abolished; it was only conditionally transferred to the heritors and elders.'

33. HMC. Portland MSS, x, "Advocate's Opinion concerning the Patronage Acts," 7 July 1710. 220. The Opinion is signed by David Dalrymple. Again, Dalrymple, in his pamphlet on patronage of 1711, repeats that the tiny response was by design rather than default: "if this execution [ie. the compensation] has not been made use of by the patrons, 'tis their own fault." [Sir David Dalrymple, *An Account of Lay Patronages in Scotland, and of the Fatal Differences they have occasioned Betwixt the Church and*

Again, decades later it is taken for granted that, "[the patrons] prudently concluded that it was more eligible to lie in wait for a proper opportunity of procuring the revival of the old statutes."[34]

The crowning indication of the Hamilton amendment's failure was that only four patronages were actually purchased and even then, two of the sales were later deemed invalid. Of the four, three: Cadder, or Calder,[35] (Glasgow presbytery) and Old and New Monkland (Hamilton presbytery), belonged to the College of Glasgow.[36] It is likely that lack of money was the motivation for the sale. By the turn of the century, the college was down to a handful of staff, some of whom received no salary, and was burdened with debts of over £2000 sterling. In such desperate circumstances, funding from any source would have been thankfully received, especially as 600 merks was the annual salary of staff like the professor of mathematics, who by 1701 was receiving no income at all.[37]

In the case of Cadder, a problem later arose in that, although the 600 merks was paid before the deadline of the 1712 Act restoring patronage, the formal renunciation was not given until 1725. Eventually, as a result of litigation before the Court of Session, it was decided in 1840[38] that it was necessary for both the payment and the renunciation to be completed before the required date, and so the sale was invalidated.

A very different problem appeared with regard to the fourth affected parish, that of Strathblane, in the presbytery of Dumbarton. The situation arose when, some years before, the liferentrix, the Duchess of Lennox appointed one of her entourage, Cunningham of Enterkin, to the provostry of the collegiate church of Dumbarton. Included in the privileges of the office was a life interest in the patronage of Strathblane. Spying an opportunity for financial gain, in 1692 he successfully, but illegally, charged

---

lay patrons; with observations on the arguments for Restoring them in 1711. in *Select Anti-Patronage Library*, (Edinburgh: 1842), 10].

34. British Library, *Tracts Concerning Patronage by Some Eminent Hands*, [1354 e.1], (Edinburgh: 1770): "A Candid Enquiry into the Constitution of the Church of Scotland in Relation to the Settlement of Ministers", 51, n.

35. Not to be confused with Calder, in Midlothian.

36. Laing MSS in Edinburgh University Library: LA II.620.29. Wallace Papers, 10. The University was also patron of Govan. It is not clear why the patronage was not sold, although this may be connected to the fact that, from 1621, it had the right of presentation only, and lost access to the teinds (see *Fasti* iii, 409), or it may simply have been related to the importance of the charge and its proximity to the University.

37. NLS., Saltoun MSS 17603, 17–33; J. Coutts, *History of Glasgow University*, (Glasgow: 1909), 169, 174–75.

38. Cullen v. Sprott, 17 November 1840, 3 D. 70.

the heritors, who included the Marquis of Montrose, for the 600 merks in exchange for the patronage. Unhappy with what had happened, Montrose eventually took action by buying out the patronage privileges of the provostry (which had now passed to Queen Anne), then, having obtained a legal reduction of Enterkin's renunciation, had himself declared the only valid patron.[39] The parish was now subject to a patron once more.

It is not recorded whether Enterkin ever returned the 600 merks.

Summary

As will have been seen, the 1690 Act was seriously flawed. Above all, it failed to achieve what was intended to be a permanent relief from patronage. Sir James Stewart tried to argue to Wodrow twenty years later that his Act had indeed abolished it,[40] and that something different—nomination and proposal to the congregation—had been put in its place, but while that may have been his intention, so long as the payment and renunciation remained outstanding, the validity of such a claim had to be questionable. Indeed, even without the Hamilton amendment, it was not obvious that the Act had truly done away with patronage in the first place. As Stewart admitted in the same conversation with Wodrow, there were those, even among senior churchmen, who believed that the right had not been removed, but only *transferred* to the heritors and elders. There is a logic behind the view. If the Acts of 1649 and 1690 wished to eradicate patronage, then realistically, it was necessary to abolish patrons. As it was, however, the latter continued as before in name, status, and privileges, only without the right of presentation. The framers of the Acts were certainly constrained in what they could dismantle lest they irrevocably alienated the landowning interest, yet it is a measure of how little, for example, the 1690

39. SRO, Montrose MSS GD220/5/31, 12 April 1702; Duncan, *Parochial and Ecclesiastical Law*, 91–92; Dunlop, *Parochial Law*, 203, n; Elchies, 'Patronage', no. 2. The third marquis became a Duke in 1707. When the charge became vacant in 1743, the heritors tried to claim that Enterkin's renunciation had been valid. However, Montrose went back to court and had his right to present confirmed in 1747; see, John Guthrie Smith, *The parish of Strathblane* [Glasgow: 1886], 217–20.

40. Wodrow, *Analecta*, i, 275. Another perspective was adopted by Sir Francis Grant, afterwards the Court of Justiciary Judge, Lord Cullen, in a pamphlet published in 1703. His highly individualist view was that the right of presentation had always been a public right, and therefore incapable of possession by private individuals. Thus the 1690 Act did not in reality 'abolish' any right so much as restore it. (See Sir Francis Grant, 'Reasons in Defence of the Standing Laws about the Right of Presentation in Patronages' [1703], in *Select Anti-Patronage Library*.

Act damaged the structure of patronage, that the 1712 Act felt it necessary to repeal no more of it than what specifically related to "the presentation of ministers by heritors and others mentioned therein."[41]

Secondly, the legislation did not give sufficient attention to the details of how it was to work. The resulting confusions presented the 1712 restoration with the opportunity to justify itself on the grounds that, following the 1690 Act, "that way of calling ministers has proved inconvenient, and has . . . occasioned great heats and divisions among those who . . . were entitled and authorized to call ministers."[42] However, this particular claim, that the Act only served to ferment passion and strife, became a matter of intense debate over the following 150 years, with anti-patronage campaigners complaining that the amount of settlement controversy was exaggerated. Accordingly, it would be useful to look at the post–1690 era and see if it were possible to gain an idea whether the Act indeed contained the seeds of its own destruction, or if, in the words of Thomas Chalmers, the preamble of the 1712 legislation was simply "lying."[43]

41. *An act to restore the patrons to their ancient rights of presenting ministers to the churches vacant in that part of Great Britain called Scotland,* 10 Anne, c.12, 1712 [see Appendix V] Unsurprisingly, the Act never suggests that patronage was ever abolished, but rather says, "presentation was taken from the patrons, and given to the heritors and elders."

42. Act Q. Anne c 12.

43. Letter to Lord Aberdeen, cited in John Warrick, *The Moderators of the Church of Scotland, 1690–1740,* (Edinburgh 1913) 11.

CHAPTER SIX

The 1690 Act in Practice

THE QUESTION OF JUST how many settlements prompted dispute during the 1690–1712 period has been a matter of strong contention and estimates vary. At the time, proponents of the return of patronage were adamant that, as the 1712 Act said, the previous system occasioned great heats and divisions. On the other side, apologists like Wodrow claimed that only four or five cases inflamed passions, and that this was due to in-fighting among the heritors.[1] Later, the Disruption leader Thomas Chalmers decided, after making his enquiries, that the Act had been responsible for fourteen disputed cases.[2] In fact, any accurate assessment is obstructed by the difficulty of distinguishing between controversies that could be ascribed directly to the 1690 Act and those that might well have arisen anyway, due to other circumstances.

For example, if it were considered that a reference or appeal concerning a vacancy from a presbytery to a higher church court constituted a controverted settlement, then it is probably fair to say that around 130 such cases appeared during the 1690–1712 period.[3] On the other hand, of these cases at least 100 involved transportations (the transfer of a minister already installed in one parish to another), with the remainder made up of competing calls. Transportations were certainly the cause of long and intense disagreements, and as early as 1694, the Assembly was complaining that transportations had become "too common . . . and very

1. *Letters*, ii, 11 February 1717. 233.

2. Warrick, 11.

3. Although a full study remains to be done, it would seem that this figure, estimated by the Rev George Cook, in his evidence to the Parliamentary Commission on Patronage in 1834, is reasonably accurate. see *Patronage Report*, para 2219.

troublesome."[4] The procedure in such cases was that once a settled minister had been called, it was then open to his parish to present reasons
against his removal to the presbytery. The callers and respondents would
then fight it out before the Church courts until a resolution was reached.
However, the existence or otherwise of a presentation was irrelevant.

The core problem was that such was the shortage of candidates to fill
the large number of vacancies that existed through the 1690s, the incentive
to attempt the poaching of another parish's incumbent remained strong.
Sometimes the approach was not always supported by the highest motives:
if a congregation in a disaffected area wished to obstruct the installation
of a presbyterian minister by the presbytery's use of the *jus devolutum*, it
could extend the vacancy by continually seeking to call holders of presti-
gious charges whose transportation would be considered absurd. It should
be noted, however, that the same ploy was used after presentations were
restored. Only when parliament made it compulsory to accompany the
lodging of a presentation with a letter of acceptance, did the practice abate.

Given the vacancy problem, and the fact that as far back as the 1640s,
there had been complaints about the "misorder of transportations,"[5] there
is a case for removing transportations from the list of controversies directly related to the 1690 regulations. If that were done, the number of
disputes would fall to around thirty.

The Political Dimension

There is another factor that complicates the enumeration of what conflicts
were attributable to the 1690 regulations during the period to 1712. This
was the contribution of political rivalry.

By way of introduction, it should be explained that, in the early
Revolution period, political groupings were fluid, that is to say allegiances
frequently fluctuated, usually according to the possibility of personal
advancement. Nonetheless, it can be said that there were basically three
interests, the Court party, who were those currently in favor with the
monarch, the Country party, who were a broad association loosely equivalent to an opposition, and the Cavaliers, who were episcopalian nobles and
lairds, many of whom tended to remain on the outer circles of a political/

---

4. "Act for the better regulating transportations of ministers, and appeals thereanent." *Assembly Acts*, 1694, vi, sess. 5, 4 April 1694.

5. Baillie called them: "packed businesses, little for the credit either for the trans-
porters or the transported." Peterkin, 529.

religious settlement they disliked. By 1712, the political landscape still contained three main interests, but with a greater similarity than before to political parties. These were the Tories, who were episcopalian and tinged with Jacobite sympathies and two broadly "whig" groupings, namely, the followers of the Duke of Argyll, and the New Party or *Squadrone Volante* (flying squadron). The latter had emerged out of the Country party by 1702,[6] and was an association in which most of the leading families were related to one another. Prominent among the nobility involved were Marchmont, Tweeddale, Roxburghe, Rothes and Montrose. There had also been a fourth interest centered upon the Duke of Queensberry, but when he died in 1711, the majority of his supporters joined the *Squadrone*.

Particularly in the scramble for influence after the union of 1707 and the uncertainty left behind by the removal of government to London, it became imperative for the groupings just mentioned to signal to a wider audience that they were a force in which confidence could be placed and that their influence north of the border was ubiquitous. Since church affairs could not be ignored, it thus became important to advance supporters to leading positions such as a moderator or professor's chair, or to important charges, especially those in and around Edinburgh. One such charge was that of Cramond, which is why it became the most prominent *cause célèbre* of the 1690–1712 period.

The Cramond case of 1710, already referred to above, was fuelled entirely by political maneuvering. The patron was the Earl of Ruglen, who wanted to please his friend Sir Gilbert Elliot of Minto by having his chaplain and nephew, Robert Lithgow, settled in the charge. Elliot was Whig in tendency, eventually ending up in the Argyll interest. In opposition to the projected call to Lithgow was Charles Kerr, second son of the Marquis of Lothian, who, along with Adam Cockburn of Ormiston, the Lord Justice Clerk, promoted the cause of the Rev James Smith# of Morham (Haddington presbytery). Smith had been tutor to Robert Dundas# of Arniston, who was related to Cockburn's wife. Both Susanna Cockburn and the Dundases were of the *Squadrone* interest. As passions mounted, Ruglen's supporters were accused of bribery, intimidation and of turning feuars into heritors three days before the moderating of the call. After two days passionate argument, the Assembly ordered Edinburgh presbytery to begin again and a third choice was made of Robert Mutter, probationer.

6. NRA (S). Atholl Papers, 234, box 45; Rev R. Wylie, Hamilton to Tullibardine, 16 October 1702: "a third party seems to be getting up among ourselves, different from the notions we have hitherto had of Court and Country, and which I know not what to call unless it be a ` *Squadrone Volante*.'"

However, since it was such a strategic charge, the battle continued, and it would appear Mutter was pressurized into giving up the call. This left the field clear for Smith to triumph and he was settled on 16 January 1712, after a vacancy of two years and three months.[7]

If transportations were to be included, it is difficult to say how many of the approximately 130 settlement disputes of the 1690–1712 period were politically colored, since few were from the start so obviously affected as Cramond. On the other hand, as Scottish political life became more affected by party allegiances after the emergence of the *Squadrone*, any controversy, even one that originated on the humdrum grounds of the patron's personal dislike of the candidate, then the tendency was for it to become a political *casus belli* as soon as it reached the higher courts of the Church. The situation had arrived, as Wodrow remarked in the aftermath of Cramond, where it no longer seemed to matter for heritors whether they were electing ministers or members of Parliament.[8]

The most famous cases that became politicized as they advanced up the hierarchy of ecclesiastical courts were Duddingston, (Edinburgh presbytery 1704), Crawfordjohn (Lanark presbytery 1709) and Closeburn (Penpont presbytery 1710)—the latter provoking, in Wodrow's eyes, the worst chicanery he had ever seen.[9] To add a further dimension to these controversies, intermingled with party politics was also the politics of social distinction. When, for example, the Crawfordjohn dispute came up to the Assembly, the visiting English observer, Dr Edmund Calamy,# was shocked that the commissioners ignored his advice not to "disgust their nobility" and rescind the settlement. He learned that the younger members of the Assembly believed that, "it was evident (whatever might be pretended) they had no power at all, if a nobleman was at liberty to control them at his pleasure. I told them, I thought they might easily strain that string until it cracked; but there was no moving them."[10] There was

7. SRO, Edinburgh Presbytery Minutes, CH2/121/8, 7 September 1709–1706 August 1711; NLS, MSS 3517, Lee Papers, Notebook on settlements, anon; Warrick, *Moderators*, 273; Smith (1680–1736) changed, in the late 1720s, to the Argyll interest. Under their patronage he became principal of Edinburgh university in 1733 and one of the Church's dominant figures (see my article in the *ODNB*.)

8. *Analecta* i, 260.

9. Wodrow, *Correspondence*, 21 May 1711, i, 234–35. The call was ultimately defeated, but largely through the reluctance of future colleagues in the presbytery to have him in their midst. See Wodrow, *Analecta*, ii, 91. The charge was filled in 1718 by John Lawson.

10. Edmund Calamy, *An Historical Account of my own Life*, Vol. I, (London: 1829), 154.

substance to Calamy's fears, in that, as already observed with Montrose and Marchmont, many former patrons found the very idea of any block to their wishes deeply distasteful. Moreover, there was potential embarrassment for those of high social rank in seeing their vote placed on equal standing with that of elders who were their inferiors. These feelings were to be articulated soon after the re–introduction of presentations when several nobles were approached to support a repeal of the 1712 Act. In their view, a return to the *status quo ante* would be giving the Church an excessive power "which she had not well used in setting elders against their masters."[11]

There is no doubt that the aforementioned confrontations left behind a residue of deep resentment among noble patrons which left them even more disinclined to make the 1690 Act work. To add to the Kirk's difficulties, such affronts to noble feelings were made most of by the Kirk's enemies in London circles during the last years before 1712 (of which more below). Its diplomatic efforts there were singularly unsuccessful in countering doubtful but damaging stories, as with the planting of St. Martins (Perth presbytery), about which it was reported that the presbytery had opposed the candidate merely out of prejudice against his promoter, Viscount Stormont.[12] It was also unable to publicize how the Church for its part also suffered assaults on its dignity and integrity, as when the dowager Duchess of Argyll drew up her own, bowdlerized version of a call to the candidate for Duddingston, forbade the subscription of any other, and then, through her son, bullied the presbytery until it gave in and accepted it.[13]

---

11. *Diary of the Rev. William Mitchell, Minister at Edinburgh, 1717*, in Miscellany of the Spalding Club, i, (Aberdeen:. 1841) 228. Mitchell had been sent to London in 1717 by the Commission to lobby for a redress of the Kirk's grievances. The conversation took place when he dined on 18 February with Roxburghe, Montrose, Rothes and Jerviswood.

12. Wodrow *Letters*, i. 8 May 1712. 286. David Murray, 5th. Viscount Stormont, his family was episcopalian with strong jacobite associations.

13. The Duke wrote to presbytery saying he had no wish to fall out with them, but since his mother insisted upon her call, he hoped they would not put the Argyll family "in the balance with any that now appears against it." The Duchess's draft omitted the phrases which promised subjection to the incumbent's ministry, as well as all due encouragement and maintenance. SRO, Edinburgh Presbytery minutes, CH2/121/5, 11 August 1704. (The dispute became politicized when the *Squadrone*, through Marchmont, organized a protest against the call.)

The Act in Disaffected Areas

Meanwhile, away from the lowland areas, it was north of the Tay that the Kirk experienced the most consistent difficulty in making the 1690 Act workable, and coping with the reluctance of probationers and ministers to be sent to northern charges was a regular and embarrassing drain on the time of the Assembly Commission. Aware of the hostile reception often awaiting them, many simply refused to go, or ostensibly went, but never arrived, as the presbytery of Moray complained.[14] Disaffected heritors and former patrons regularly expressed their distaste by locking an unwelcome incumbent out, depriving him of income, or simple intimidation. An effort to curtail the worst excesses was made by parliament in July 1698, with an *Act for preventing of disorders in the supplying and planting of vacant churches*[15]. The aim was to hold the heritors and liferenters responsible for any disorders and obstructing of the lawful minister, by fining them £100 Scots. A similar fine was to be imposed upon magistrates who did not see to it that presbyteries gained access, on demand, to any church locked against them. Unfortunately for presbyteries, since complaints under the Act were to be pursued through the Privy Council, the abolition of the latter in 1708 was a major blow to an effective use of the legislation.

On the other hand, parliament's compensatory extension in the same year of the authority of Scotland's Justices of the Peace, did contain some assistance. Indeed, in the case of Fetteresso (Fordoun presbytery), the veteran intruder Gideon Guthrie, who had already seen off one attempt to replace him in 1705,[16] was finally dislodged by virtue of the JPs' intervention in 1709. Again, when a major riot greeted presbytery's attempt, in 1711, to settle John Gordon in Old Deer, Aberdeenshire, the fact that a JP and his officers were attacked with them, made much easier the legal proceedings which eventually brought the desired result. Despite these successes, however, before long it became obvious that significant assistance for presbyteries from JPs was not going to materialize, especially as there appeared, in some areas, no shortage of those whose loyalties lay elsewhere.

14. SRO. Register of Assembly Commission, 1701–1706, CH1/3/6. 6 June 1701.

15. *APS.*, 19 July 1698, cap. 2.

16. See Minutes of the Presbytery of Brechin, SRO CH2/40/5, 6 July 1709. The case is cited in respect of Aberlemno, where the heritors followed Guthrie's example by claiming that the presbytery could not settle anyone in a charge by their *jus devolutum* until the intruding clergyman had been deprived by the Lords of Justiciary. The Assembly rejected the plea.

In September 1710 there was a general election in which the Tories made substantial gains. As presbyterian spirits ebbed, episcopal partisans became emboldened by the ineffectiveness and/or unwillingness of local functionaries to enforce the law, and resistance to presbyterial settlements in sensitive areas stiffened. The most notorious incident occurred when, on the 6th. December, the presbytery of Fordoun decided to use the *jus devolutum* to settle an incumbent on the charge of Benholm. The JP Hercules Scott of Brotherton and John Burnett of Monboddo galvanized their retainers into offering such sanguinary resistance (they were heard swearing "if any ministers came they would cut their throats and . . . make minched meat of them"[17]), the ordination had to take place in the Laird of Benholm's house.[18] Meanwhile, the minister of Birsay and several of his colleagues found themselves enduring such "hellish malice" from the disaffected JPs of Orkney, that the neighboring Presbytery of Caithness felt impelled to beg the Assembly on their behalf to help them.[19]

It was particularly difficult in Angus. In 1712, for example, on a fast–day appointed by the synod, three JPs (including the Provost and the former MP) publicly burnt the synod's edict at the mercat cross of Montrose. They furthermore prevailed upon the rest of the Angus Justices to resolve to do the same at the door of every church which observed the fast, and charge its minister with sedition. The Kirk was outraged but could do nothing.[20] As the magistrates of burghs like Brechin and Montrose did everything in their power to frustrate a presbyterian ministry, as late as 1716 the presbytery was complaining that, notwithstanding the failure of the 1715 Rebellion, not only were many county magistrates and JPs still disaffected, but so also were the Sheriff Depute, the Sheriff Clerk and the "whole town of Forfar."[21]

---

17. NLS., Lee MSS., 3430, #164; Rev. David Archer, Fordoun presbytery, to the General Assembly, 7 December 1710.

18. The *Fasti* mistakenly says it was in the Old Tower of Brechin [Cathedral].

19. HMC Portland MSS, x, Presbytery of Caithness to the General Assembly, 19 September 1710, 344.

20. HMC. Portland MSS., x, Carstares to _____, 23 August 1712, 278; Sir James Stuart to the Earl of Oxford, 26 August 1712, 280. The JPs were James Scott of Logie, Colonel Stratoun and Provost Milne of Montrose.

21. Minutes of Presbytery of Brechin, SRO. CH2\40\6, 25 April 1716. By the time of the rebellion, the president of the Court of Session was writing off Scottish JPs as "altogether ineffectual." (SRO., SP 54/7/29, Hew Dalrymple to Duke of Montrose, 13 August, 1715.) For an assessment of the effectiveness of Scottish JPs, see, Ann E. Whetstone, *Scottish County Government*, Chapter 2.

Elsewhere, there were large areas like the Earl of Breadalbane's estates, where not one presbyterian clergyman was permitted a foothold.[22] As for the number of candidates available for charges, in 1713 the presbyteries of Meigle, Arbroath, Fordoun, Alford, Garioch, Aberlour, Abernethy, Elgin, Shetland, Dunoon and Skye all had to admit that they had not one probationer under their supervision.[23]

Such were the difficulties, yet it would be mistaken to suppose that all opposition to the 1690 church settlement derived from those patrons and heritors who were episcopalian (or catholic[24]) and therefore Jacobite. Although he was ostensibly pro-Hanoverian, the first Duke of Atholl, resolutely protected his episcopal incumbents, regardless of whether or not they even took the Oaths.[25] Again, although the patron of Fraserburgh, William Fraser, 11th. Lord Saltoun and Philorth, was a dedicated Hanoverian, he led the local episcopal/jacobite resistance to Deer presbytery's attempts to settle the charge with any other than their (episcopalian) candidate. The bitter and litigious struggle began in 1703 and continued well beyond 1707, when the admission of the presbytery's candidate was achieved.[26]

Since each area was susceptible to its own particular set of influences or circumstances, how any of the parties involved in the filling of a vacancy—heritors, elders, patron or congregation—might respond to a projected candidate was far from certain. Thus although Argyll, Moray and Ross were north of the highland line, the lingering threads there of

22. Jean Gassion [alias Ogilvie] to Robert Harley, 16 September, 1707. HMC., Portland MSS., 15th Report, Appendix, iv, [1897], 447.

23. GRH., Miscellaneous MSS, CH8\195.

24. At around 5400, the Catholic population was, however, small and concentrated in a "narrow strip of country stretching from the Duke of Gordon's lands in the east to the southern Hebrides." John MacInnes, *The evangelical movement in the highlands of Scotland 1688–1800*, (Aberdeen: 1951), 11.

25. "I have . . . thought it just and reasonable to preserve the Episcopal ministers who are good men in the Churches they possess." Mar and Kellie Papers, SRO., GD124\15\410, Atholl to the Earl of Mar, 31 May 1706. The Duke and his second son, James, stayed out of the '15, while the eldest, William, Marquis of Tullibardine along with Lord George, Lord Charles and their uncle, Lord Nairne joined. The Duchess was a committed presbyterian and used her influence with the Duke to promote presbyterian ministries where she could. See also Leah Leneman, *Living in Atholl, 1685–1785*, (Edinburgh 1986), 4 & 89.

26. *The Scottish Chronicle*, series of articles entitled "A Ten Years' Conflict", 15 June 1906 - 16 November 1906; John Cranna, *Fraserburgh: Past and Present*, (Aberdeen: 1914), 95–97.

Covenanting traditions ensured one parish's response to a presbyterian settlement could be very different from another. To take a cross-section of the charges in the presbytery of Dingwall, for example, the parishioners of Alness sought ministers of impeccable presbyterian pedigree, while in Dingwall, presbyterian candidates were violently resisted; in Kiltearn the choice of ministers was dominated by the staunchly presbyterian Munro of Fowlis family, while in Kilmorack, the presbyterian candidate was comprehensively resisted by a parish two thirds of whom were catholic, the rest episcopalian.[27]

The Praying Societies

Mention of the Covenanting legacy prompts reference to the remaining major contribution to controversy during the period after 1690, namely the influence of the praying societies. It will be remembered that these were devotional groups that took root after the Restoration during the times of persecution, especially in the south-west. Although they naturally welcomed the overthrow of the Stewarts, they remained disappointed and suspicious of the Erastian tendencies of the Church then established.[28] It was a frustration which intensified as Scotland moved towards Parliamentary union with a neighbor whose Church was not only prelatic but thoroughly tied into the machinery of the state.

As to the settlement of vacancies, it is not obvious that the presence of society people in a parish led directly to disagreement over candidates, however, their desire to have men of proven rectitude did mean they were regular instigators of transportation processes, many of which had little chance of succeeding and therefore occupied much time through the Church courts. Since their ministerial leaders, Alexander Shields, William Boyd and Thomas Linning, had gone into the national Church at the Revolution, they tended thereafter to make their presence felt mostly as the conscience of their local parishes, monitoring incumbents for any sign of defection from covenanting principles. It was not until the rise to

27. J. Noble, *Religious life in Ross,* (Edinburgh:1909), 41–88; *Fasti*, vii, 25–51.

28. As the Revolution period proceeded, their dissatisfaction centered on five complaints: The Church had not, a). vindicated the presbyterians who stood fast during the persecution, b). approved the Reformation achieved between 1638 and 1649, c). continued loyal to the National Covenants, d). prevented persecuting curates from re-entering pulpits without evidence of repentance and e). prevented state encroachment on the Church through its calling/dissolving Assemblies, appointing fasts, imposing oaths etc.

prominence of John MacMillan (1669–1753) and John Hepburn (c.1649–1723) that the evolution of their criticism into defiance and (in MacMillan's case[29]) secession, was to come about.

Summary

Whether the cause was politics or personalities, there was much to trouble the process of vacancy-filling in the aftermath of 1690. However, with regard to antipathy between presbyterians and episcopalians, there were instances where the church was shared, with both ministries operating side by side, as at Haddington, Dunfermline and Inverness.[30] Indeed, it is important to remember that, at the time of the Revolution settlement, there was often little difference in worship between the episcopal and presbyterian liturgies: in places like Brechin (Angus), most of those who counted themselves presbyterians were happy to attend episcopal worship and eucharist in the parish churches.[31] It was only later, when it was considered politically more advantageous to identify with the English high church tendency, that Scottish episcopal practice drew away from its former, more plain character.

Despite the difficulties presented by political rivalry, issues of social standing and the flaws in the terms of the 1690 Act, the system it laid out was not, however, intrinsically unworkable. The fact was, patrons simply wanted their privileges restored at the earliest opportunity. When William died on the 8 March 1702, it looked for a time, as if the moment had come.

29. After his deposition in 1703 from the parish of Balmaghie (Kirkcudbrightshire) MacMillan went on to minister to those Society People repelled by the apostasy of the National Church. In 1743, along with Thomas Nairn, he formed the Reformed Presbyterian Church. Hepburn of Urr was repeatedly disciplined for his denunciations of authority and government; anti-Union; his followers were called Hebronites.

30. J. Cunningham, *The church history of Scotland*, (Edinburgh:1882), ii, 196. NLS. 1.108, *Pamphlets*, iv, n.d.

31. Webb D. Pomeroy, "John Willison of Dundee 1680–1750," PhD thesis, Edinburgh, 1953, 17; for a discussion of the differences and similarities, see Raffe, "Presbyterians and Episcopalians", 576, 581–82, 594; also see Raffe, *Culture of Controversy*, 134–48.

CHAPTER SEVEN

The Approach to 1712

Union with England

QUEEN MARY HAD DIED in 1694, and since she and William were child-less, the Crown was given to her sister, Anne, the last Stewart sovereign of the British Isles. It was not an auspicious development for presbyterians, and they and their episcopalian counterparts knew it. Not only was Anne a Stewart, but a staunch admirer of the Church of England and she did not hesitate to promote members of the Church Party (alias English Tories) to positions of favor. In Scotland, affection for the Revolution and William's administration had been damaged during the 1690s by the Glencoe atroc-ity, the failure of the Darien scheme to colonize central America and even the food shortages of the closing four years of the century—all of which had tarnished the king in public consciousness. Change was in the air, and an election was eventually called for November 1702.

The Duke of Queensberry remained the dominant force in the Scottish Parliament, yet he knew he had to look to ways of maintain-ing his influence, particularly in the face of a challenge from George Mackenzie, Viscount Tarbat (later Earl of Cromartie), who became a Secretary of State and had the backing of the Earl of Nottingham, an ad-viser to the Queen on Scottish affairs. One course Queensberry decided to take was to lose from his administration some of those especially as-sociated with Revolution/presbyterian principles, and bring in men of a different hue, like the Marquis of Tullibardine (he succeeded his father as Marquis in May 1703). Since Tullibardine, Tarbat and Nottingham were all committed to promoting a toleration for Scottish episcopalians, alarm grew within presbyterian ranks, especially as the Queen seemed to be paying some attention to the petitions and addresses she had been receiving on behalf of the toleration cause.[1]

The Kirk's dismay increased even further when it then became obvious that the Court Party, in looking for allies in Parliament, were set on turning their blandishments upon the Cavaliers, whose presence had increased since Anne's accession—many non-jurors now believing the time was ripe for them to qualify and take an active political role. According to the memoirs of George Lockhart of Carnwath, they were promised a share in government, an episcopal toleration and that nothing would be required of them nor even passed in Parliament "that did in the least ratify what had passed since the year 1689."[2]

Although it was not officially spelt out, by early 1703 it was obvious that the gathering momentum in favor of relief for episcopalians was bound to carry with it a return to ecclesiastical lay patronage. Hoping at least to slow the juggernaut, the Kirk countered with admonitory sermons before Parliament, condemnation of the idea by the Assembly Commission and various printed pamphlets.[3] Political ineptness on the part of Queensberry, however, was to save the Kirk, for the time being, from its worst fears. When the time came for him to deliver on the pledges the Court had made in his name to the Cavaliers, he failed to do so. In fact, it was an affirmation of presbyterian government and discipline which was passed, and the proposal for a toleration was shelved.[4] An angry backlash and a series of Acts, guaranteed to cause alarm and

1. A typical list of complaints can be found in *Instructions given by undersubscribing noblemen to their commissioner [to lay before the Queen]* (n.d.; c. 1702), SRO. CH8/184. The Queen responded to the lobbying by writing to the Privy Council on 4 February 1703, commending Scottish episcopalians to their care and protection. The letter was a significant boost to episcopalian hopes. See, P. W. J. Riley, "The formation of the Scottish ministry of 1703," 129.

2. *Scotland's Ruine, Lockhart of Carnwath's memoirs of the Union*, ed., Daniel Szechi, (Aberdeen: 1995), 27. George Lockhart (1681–1732) was an MP in both the Scottish and English parliaments and, in adult life, a staunch jacobite.

3. William Law Mathieson, *Scotland and the union, a history of Scotland from 1695 to 1747*, (Glasgow: 1905), 204; *Registers of the General Assembly Commission*, SRO. CH1/3/6, 20 May 1703; Wodrow, *Correspondence*, ii, 326; Sir Francis Grant, *Reasons in defence of the standing laws about the right of presentation in patronages* (Edinburgh: 1703), *A letter from a friend in the city to a MP anent patronages* (Edinburgh: 1703). The latter was answered by, Anon., *Sound and solid reason against the presbyterian prints anent patronages whereby the pretended divine right of the popular election of pastors is perpetually barred* (np. 1703).

4. Lockhart, *Scotland's ruine*, 46, n.31.

offence in London were passed: the *Act anent peace and war* [disallow-
ing declarations or alliances without the consent of the Scottish par-
liament]; the *Wine Act* [contravening the English trade embargo with
France] and the *Act of security* [asserting that the Scottish crown would
not go to England's choice of successor without certain conditions].[5]
Queensberry withheld royal assent for the *Act of security*, but the damage to his prestige had been done, and he ultimately fell from power in
May 1704. His successor was a leader of the Country party, the Marquis
of Tweeddale, who along with his friends formed a ministry out of the
alliance which was known as the New Party or *Squadrone Volante* [see
above].

With his country heavily involved in the War of the Spanish Succession against France (1702–7), the English Lord Treasurer, Godolphin, put pressure on Tweeddale to moderate the terms of the *Act of
security*. The tide of Scottish opinion was, however, running against co-
operation with the southern neighbor and the Act still went through in
much of its original form. Godolphin's reaction was to step up calls for
a Parliamentary union of the kingdoms, which he reinforced with the
passage, in February 1705, of the *Alien Act*, which threatened to close
the border to Scottish exports of black cattle, wool and linen, as well
as declare English-domiciled Scots to be aliens, unless commissioners
for union were in place by Christmas. The Act threw the *Squadrone*
into disarray, leaving John Campbell, second Duke of Argyll to present
himself as the one able—along with Queensberry, who was, at Argyll's
insistence, allowed back into office—to manage Parliament on behalf
of the Court. It was not to be an easy task, as resistance to union, at
least without major concessions, remained strong. However, on the
first of September, any possibility of the Scots driving a hard bargain at
the negotiating table evaporated, when the Duke of Hamilton pushed
through a motion giving the queen the power to nominate the Scots
commissioners.[6] Not surprisingly, when both nations' representatives
met on 16 April 1706, the Scots' side contained only one known opponent of union, Lockhart of Carnwath.[7]

As the commissioners set about working through the articles
of a treaty for an incorporating union, the religious issue raised two

5. *APS*, xi, 74ff.
6. *APS*, xi,237.
7. W. Ferguson, *Scotland: 1689 to the present*, (Edinburgh: 1968), 47.

awkward questions. First, if one treaty establishing two Churches were presented to each legislature, would an English Parliament be willing to establish a presbyterian one, and would a Scottish Parliament happily approve the establishment of a prelatic one? Resistance to the idea of reciprocal approval was not confined to north of the border, as some English Tory peers actively opposed union on the grounds that they had no wish to suggest that presbyterianism might be on a par with Anglicanism.[8] Moreover, it should be remembered that some of the outed episcopal clergy had moved to London during the 1690s, and had been publishing a stream of anti-presbyterian pamphlets.[9] The second difficult question was whether a situation could realistically be expected to last whereby one Parliament presided over two national churches?

The first was met by the expedient of keeping the Church question separate from the articles themselves, the idea being that each Parliament would frame its own Act securing its national Church and then insert it into the Articles prior to their final passage. The second question was more difficult to answer, and provided additional fuel for the pamphlet war over the union that had been raging for most of the decade. At its heart was the concern expressed by one poetic propagandist:

> and when our church depends
> on English votes, will they not make amends
> to prelates here in Scotland and redress
> their present troubles[?] How can we express
> our fears and doubts when we are left a prey
> to British Parliament's discretion[?][10]

As Wodrow reflected, the assurance of a Scottish Act securing religion was effectively no assurance at all in a British Parliament: "It is vain to talk of preliminaries, for there being no power superior to that

---

8. R. Paley and P. Seaward. *Honour, interest and power: an illustrated history of the House of Lords, 1660-1715.* (Boydell Press: 2010) 286.

9. These were especially: James Canaries (ex-Selkirk), Alexander Monro (ex-St Giles and the Town College), and John Cockburn (ex-Ormiston). John Sage stayed in Scotland. See Raffe, Alasdair, "Episcopalian polemic, the London printing press and Anglo-Scottish divergence in the 1690s", *Journal of Scottish Historical Studies*, 26 (2006), 24–26.

10. Anon., *A voice from the north or an answer to the voice from the south, written by the presbyterians of Scotland, to the dissenters in England - a poem,* (Edinburgh:1707).

of a Parliament of Great Britain, they can break the preliminaries at pleasure; and those that oppose them shall be treated as rebels."[11]

According to John Robertson's article on the union debates of 1698–1707, it was the argument put forward by Daniel Defoe, who had been sent from London to promote the unionist case, which did most to answer the anxiety summarized by Wodrow, especially after Defoe secured the backing of the lawyer, Sir Francis Grant (later Lord Cullen).[12] Their case was that the Articles of union were matters of fundamental law and therefore formed what was in effect a constitution for the united Parliament. The problem was that neither Defoe nor Grant put forward any legal justification for their claim—they simply declared that what they argued was so. As a result, the issue has been the focus of intermittent debate ever since, and is still unresolved. From the standpoint of the patronage issue, however, it remains the key question to which so much debate on the subject ultimately returns, namely, was the Patronage Act a violation of the Treaty of Union?

The Patronage Act and the Treaty of Union

Since 1957, a work of enduring value on the constitutional implications of the Union has been a paper given to the International Law Association (Scottish branch) by the Professor of Scots Law at Aberdeen, T.B. Smith, entitled *The union of 1707 as fundamental law*. Drawing upon a test case of 1953, whereby the Lord Advocate had been challenged over the validity of the new queen's title of Elizabeth the second (only England had known an Elizabeth the first), Smith concurs with one of the findings of the presiding judge, Lord Cooper. In Smith's view Lord Cooper was correct to decide that the various Articles of Union came into three categories: those whose later alteration was allowed for, those which were unalterable and those whose permanence was unspecified. The unalterable or fundamental provisions made up what Smith considered to be a constitution for Great Britain, about which he famously stated: "Every schoolboy knows

11. Robert Wodrow to George Ridpath, 21 June 1706, *Abbotsford Club Miscellany*, i, (Edinburgh: 1837), 395.

12. John Robertson, "An elusive sovereignty. The course of the Union debate in Scotland 1698–1707," in *A union for empire; political thought and the British union of 1707*, ed., John Robertson (Cambridge: 1995), 223–24.

that the British Constitution has no fundamental written basis; but in my view every schoolboy has been misinformed."[13]

If Smith's reasoning were to be accepted—and, clearly, the presence of fundamental laws provides the best ground for arguing that the Patronage Act was a violation of the union and not simply a legitimate alteration in keeping with changing circumstances—then the crucial question is whether or not patronage possessed the character of a fundamental provision. Although Smith does not expressly say so, by his criteria the religious settlement, as a whole, was within the latter category.[14]

As for the actual issue of patronage, however, the picture suddenly becomes blurred. The reason for this is that the *Act for securing the protestant religion and presbyterian church government* (3 October 1706) based itself on the Church settlement as contained in the Act 1690 c.5,[15] which itself was based on the 1592 Church establishment, which allowed patronage. The1690 Act did qualify the revival of the 1592 legislation by excepting "that part of it relating to patronages, which is hereafter to be taken into consideration." That "consideration" eventually materialized as the Act of abolition entitled *APS* 1690 c.23. The crucial point, however, was that the 1706 Act did not specifically mention the twenty-third Act, only the *fifth* one. In the aftermath to the 1712 restoration of patronage, the Kirk was therefore left to base its arguments against it wholly on the clause in the 1706 Act which stated that the 1690 fifth Act was confirmed, "with the hail other Acts of Parliament relating thereto."[16] This phraseology obviously implied, the Assembly Commission insisted, that "the said Act abolishing patronages must be understood to be part of our Presbyterian constitution,

---

13. T. B. Smith, "The union of 1707 as fundamental law," reprinted from *Public Law*, Summer 1957, 109. See also *The Laws of Scotland, Stair Memorial Encyclopedia*, v, paras 338–58.

14. That it was is affirmed in the UK Parliament's Regency Act of 1937.

15. Its full title was, *Act ratifying the Confession of Faith and settling Presbyterian church government.*

16. Twenty-five years later, the Kirk was still claiming that this clause "appears evidently to comprehend the said 23rd. Act 1690." - see the "Resolution of the General Assembly of the Church of Scotland, upon the report of their commissioners sent to London, to endeavour the repeal of the Act 10, Anne, reimposing patronages," 22 May 1736. (quoted in Select Anti-patronage Library, *A Collection of Important Acts etc.*, (Edinburgh: 1842), 30.

secured to us by the Treaty of Union for ever."[17] The Kirk was obliged to stand by this contention thereafter; nonetheless, there was no escaping that its case was weakened by the way the legislation had evolved.

The major problem with the Commission's case was that, arguably, the Scottish Parliament had already defined the Kirk's constitutional position in relation to the fifth Act back in 1702, when Queen Anne came to the throne, and in doing so had left little room for the claim it was now making. There, the *Act for securing the true protestant religion and presbyterian government*, having described what it meant by presbyterian government and discipline ("the government of the Church by kirk sessions, presbyteries, synods and General Assemblies"), then confirmed the Act 1690 c.5 "in the hail heads, clauses and articles thereof as if at length herein set down."[18] Crucially, patronage was nowhere mentioned, and although it was still just possible to claim that it was included by implication, to do so was truly to stretch the argument to its limits.[19]

The clause in the later 1706 Act did provide more substance upon which to build a case, but the significant question must be whether its vagueness could ever establish unassailably the abolition of patronage as part of the Scottish Church's constitution. If Smith's view were to be followed, it certainly did not: such measures might be against the spirit of the Union, yet, as he says, "Measures politically in conflict with the spirit of the Union agreement may, nevertheless, be legally unassailable."[20]

What then can be made of the enduring allegation that the 1712 Act was a violation of the Union? It would seem that, at best, only two things can be said with certainty. The first is that the case for the Act being a great injustice is severely wounded by the absence of any specific mention of patronage in the Union Treaty. Secondly, in *practical* terms,

17. "To the queen's most excellent majesty. The humble address and representation of the commission of the late general assembly of the church of Scotland." 13 May 1712. *Collection of Important Acts etc.*, 25.

18. *APS.*, xi, 16.

19. There was a claim that since kirk sessions had been constitutionally established, then to remove one of a session's rights (the joint election of the minister) was to violate its constitutional integrity. See, Gilbert Burnet, *History of his own time*, 882. The argument was weakened by the fact that although it was a right, it was not an exclusive right, since it was shared by others who might not even be of the same communion.

20. Smith, 112.

the reality is that it was of no consequence whether the 1712 Act was legal or not. This point comes to the fore in a newspaper article written in 1996 during the Scottish devolution debate of the time, by Professor Robert Rennie of Glasgow University's Centre for Research into Law Reform. Discussing whether or not a British parliament can establish a permanent law at all, he considers a sentence from Lord Cooper's 1953 summing up to be determining: "it is of little avail to ask whether the Parliament of Great Britain can do this thing or that without going on to enquire who can stop them if they do?"[21] In other words, even if it were accepted that the Treaty of Union represented a British, written constitution, its glaring omission was that it neglected to establish a constitutional Supreme Court to adjudicate upon and enforce its provisions. Admittedly, T.B. Smith's response to this point is that the functions of such a court could already be exercised by Scotland's law lords if they so chose.[22] However, they have consistently elected not to do so.

The inescapable reality remains that twice in the decade and a half which followed the Revolution, the Kirk had the opportunity to do away, in express terms, with presentations forever, and it failed. That it had failed was something the Kirk found hard to live with when patronage was restored five years later, and outrage was concentrated upon those who had brought it about. Nonetheless, had the Church shown more prescience and determination before 1712, then, at the least, the weight of their arguments against it could have been heavier in the years that followed.

To be fair, in 1706, presbyterians were under strong pressure not to be fastidious about what safeguards were on offer in the *Act for securing the protestant religion and presbyterian church government*. Not only were they curtly told to be thankful for the concessions it gave them, but the warning was circulated that if they dragged their feet and held up the progress of the Union, the Court would withdraw its offer and set about establishing episcopacy in Scotland in their stead.[23] By such means, those who well understood the Act's vulnerabilities were

21. *MacCormick v. Lord Advocate*, 1953 S.C. 396. R. Rennie, "The key is Westminster: how could a Scottish Parliament ensure it would not be swept away by a future UK government?" *The Herald*, 9 September 1996.

22. see T. B. Smith, *British Justice: The Scottish Contribution*, (London: 1961), 209–12.

23. WRH. Atholl papers, NRA (S) 234, box 45; James Murray to Atholl, 4 September 1706.

able to fend off presbyterian attempts to strengthen it. As Wodrow later recalled: "we applied again and again for a solid security against a toleration, patronages, and the English service; but in vain. Our friends in the house were enraged with us, because we could not get our light brought up to believe their act for security was fully sufficient, and not a clause in it would they alter"[24]

After the Union, the episcopalian Earl of Stair, whose brother was later to frame the Patronage Act, wrote to Robert Harley[25] to express his satisfaction at the outcome. That he and his associates had their eye on the possibility of future changes is all too evident: "This day we have finished our Act for the security of our church, without making any alterations for [i.e., as a result of] the Address from the Commission of the Kirk to which they were ill advised, though that doth give them full assurance of the continuance of their government after the Union, yet there is no insinuation of Divine right to check the Church of England, nor is there direct exemption from the power of the Parliament of Britain in which we found you very nice?"[26]

After the Union

When the Union formally took effect on the 1 May 1707, it became obvious that no clear plan had been set for the administration of Scotland. For convenience's sake, it was considered expedient to invite the two Scottish secretaries, the Earls of Loudoun and Mar, to continue to operate the machinery of state for a time. Loudoun did so until 1708, Mar until 1709, when it was decided to abolish their offices. Instead, there were now to be three Principal Secretaries of State for Great Britain (previously there were two): Sunderland, Boyle and the Duke of Queensberry. Although all three were intended to share equally the business of British domestic affairs, in practice, Scottish business was handled almost exclusively by Queensberry. When the Duke died in July 1711, this Secretaryship was abolished. Henry St. John (he became Viscount Bolingbroke in 1712) then

24. *Correspondence*, i, 249. Wodrow to Rev Hugh Maxwell, 26 October 1711.

25. Robert Harley (1661–1724), MP for New Radnor Boroughs 1690–1711, was Chancellor of the Exchequer 1710–11 and Lord Treasurer 1711–14. He used Defoe as both informant and propagandist and was responsible for pushing through the Peace of Utrecht in 1713; created Earl of Oxford and Earl Mortimer in May, 1711.

26. HMC. Portland MSS. xv, pt. 4, 348. Earl of Stair, Edinburgh, to Robert Harley, 12 November 1706. *Nice* could mean either precise or, possibly, coy

became the man nominally responsible for the administration of Scotland, although John Scrope, an English baron of the exchequer based north of the border, was one on whom Harley probably placed most reliance for advice and assistance.

Meanwhile, the Kirk looked on nervously as the new Parliament showed it was not reluctant to alter Scottish institutions. In 1708, the Privy Council was abolished and, in the wake of an invasion scare, the English law of treason along with the English procedure for its prosecution was imposed upon the Scottish legal system.[27] Although Godolphin wrote to the Assembly Commission to reassure them that the queen had no plans to impose any "innovations" upon the Scottish Church,[28] presbyterians well knew that the signs of the times were not good. In places like Angus, intruders were still flouting the orders of the courts with apparent impunity, while in the Crathie\Braemar area, nothing was being done to check a strong resurgence of Roman Catholicism.[29]

While this was going on, an unrelenting propaganda war against the Kirk at Westminster took place,[30] aggravated by the fact that many episcopalians, by adopting the English liturgy, were seeking to present themselves as persecuted Anglicans. The latter was a powerful card to play, and when in 1709 Edinburgh Town Council (supported by a judgment from the Court of Session) cracked down upon James Greenshields for using the English prayer book, Greenshields took the case to the House of Lords as an advertisement of the ill-treatment accorded to those wishing to use the Anglican form in Scotland. The affair arose at a bad time for the Kirk's image, since public opinion in London was already incensed by the prosecution of forty episcopal clergymen earlier in the year, and indeed, such was the fear of what retaliatory action might be taken in Parliament— "We are daily threatened with attempts to restore patronages"[31]— several actions against episcopal clergy were

---

27. *AP*, Treason Act, 1708, c. 21.

28. *Registers of the General Assembly Commission*, SRO. CH1/3/11, 4 January 1709.

29. *Assembly Commission Registers*, SRO., CH1/3/11, 4 January 1709; Jane B. Fagg, '"Complaints and clamours": the ministry ofAdam Fergusson, 1700–1754', *RSCHS*, 1994, xxv, part 2, 294–95.

30. E.g., the open letter, c. 1708, sent by the bishops of Scotland to the bishops of England claiming hundreds of their clergy had been turned out and were in a 'deplorable' condition. *State Papers*, SRO. RH2/4/299.

31. *Correspondence*, 23 November 1709, Wodrow to Hugh Maxwell. i, 84,

quietly dropped.[32] It was, however, to no avail, as the general election of 1710 was to show.

In the election, the Cavaliers, who became the Scots equivalent of the English Tories, did well and quadrupled their representation in the Commons to sixteen of the forty-five Scottish seats. Meanwhile south of the border, Robert Harley (later Earl of Oxford) had come to power, and when Queensberry died he turned for support to the Scots Tories. Since these were committed to seeking relief for the Scottish episcopalians, some kind of toleration—and more—became increasingly likely.

Momentum gathered pace in March 1711, when the House of Lords, after much lobbying by the Tory/Jacobite interest, issued its judgment in the Greenshields case, finding in his favor and reversing the Court of Session's verdict. Immediately, the Scots Tories were exultant, with their leader in the Lords, Lord Balmerino, declaring: "We have it in our hand to get presently a Tolleration, or the Act against Baptising rescinded, or patronages restored."[33] Harley, however, was not yet ready to be pushed into such legislation, his administration being in too unstable a state to risk alienating a large tranche of Scottish opinion. Accordingly, he moved quickly to head off the trouble. Those hungry for advancement, like the Earl of Mar, were persuaded to hang fire: "A great many of our commoners here, with some of our lords, have had meetings where it was proposed to restore the patronage in Scotland. I must acknowledge that I think it is very reasonable that they were restored but I cannot think this is a seasonable time for doing it, therefore I have done all I cou'd to divert it at this time."[34]

Meanwhile, the Queen was prevailed upon personally to intercede with the leading Scots agitators, Balmerino, George Lockhart of Carnwath and Sir Alexander Erskine of Cambo, the Lord Lyon king-at-arms. She succeeded in persuading them to desist from pursuing their intentions regarding patronage at least until the next Parliamentary session, however at the same time she committed the government to

32. HMC., Mar and Kellie MSS., [London 1904]. 482: "Papers relating to the prosecution of 40 of the Episcopal clergy before the Judges of the Northern Circuit in May 1709." Also, 12 March 1709, Earl of Mar to Lord Grange, 481. WRH., Atholl papers, 234, Box 45, 15 October 1709.

33. Dalhousie MSS 14/352. 8 March 1711. [cited in W. Ferguson, Scotland, 1689 to the Present, (Edinburgh: 1968), 59].

34. 15 March 1711. Mar, at London, to his brother, the Justice Clerk. HMC., Mar and Kellie MSS. 489.

giving its assistance, should they choose to go ahead with the project after that. The commitment was probably one Harley could have done without, but it had bought him valuable time, and cover enough to allow him to write unblushingly to Principal Carstares with assurances that: "there will be no attention given to any proposals which may justly alarme your friends, and particularly as to that affair of patronages. It was never entertaind and was really an invention suggested to two rash persons with a design to create jealousies, but it never was movd nor in the least countenanced or entertaind."[35] At the same time, his Scotch Secretary, Queensberry, had written on the same subject to Edinburgh presbytery with equal blandness: "I can inform you that there is good reason to believe that no such thing will be attempted in either of the Houses of Parliament."[36]

When Carstares passed Harley's letter on to his colleagues in Edinburgh, they wrote back to the Treasurer that they were much comforted.[37] The Scots were not so myopic, however, that they were prepared to trust such blandishments indefinitely, and although Carstares later circulated another letter, this time from Lord Dartmouth, the Secretary of State, expressing reassurances from the Queen herself,[38] there was even less willingness to be set at ease. Deciding that it could not wait passively for an outcome that was becoming ever more likely, the autumn Assembly Commission commissioned Carstares, Professor Thomas Blackwell of Aberdeen and Robert Baillie of Inverness to take up residence in London and be ready, as events unfolded, to use every means at their disposal to lobby on the Kirk's behalf against any Toleration or restoration of patronages[39].

---

35. 8 May 1711, Rbt. Harley to Principal Carstares. *HMC.*, Laing MSS., ii, 161.

36. *Edinburgh Presbytery Minutes*, 25 April 1711, SRO, CH2/121/8.

37. 22 May 1711. Thos. Blackwell to Rbt Harley. *HMC* Portland MSS. xv, part 4, 695

38. Wodrow, *Analecta*, Oct/Nov. 1711, i, 370.

39. Blackwell's correspondence from London can be found in *Miscellany of the Spalding Club*, i, (Aberdeen: 1841), 197–223.

The Parliamentary Session of 1711–12

The Toleration Act

As the 1711–12 session of parliament began, Harley (now Earl of Oxford) was faced with increasing problems. It was essential for him to gain acceptance of his peace terms with France to end the War of the Spanish Succession, but his administration was being severely harassed by the Whig opposition. He had created twelve more peers to bolster the strength of his support, but still he needed the Scots lords as well. Unfortunately for him, the latter had organized a boycott of Parliament in protest at its refusal to allow the Duke of Hamilton to sit in the Lords under the patent of Duke of Brandon. Oxford saw that if he was to survive, then somehow the boycott had to be broken. A judicious dispersal of favors soon brought the desired result, although the Earl of Mar claimed that the real reason behind the peers' return was to prevent the chance for a toleration being lost for ever.[40] Whatever was the truth behind their action, the Scots' return was decisive. Although Oxford listened sympathetically to the objections of the Assembly Commission's London representatives, he knew he could not now renege on the commitment which the queen had earlier made on his behalf not to oppose the Bill. The Lords also heard counsel present the Scots' complaints about the Bill's legality (on 13 February), but although the final result might not have been all that Balmerino and his followers would have wished,[41] the *Episcopal Communion (Scotland) Act* became law on 3 March 1712.

At first sight, the Act appears as an unqualified triumph for episcopalian fortunes in Scotland: now adherents could meet unmolested to use the English liturgy (provided their clergyman was properly ordained and had taken the Oaths), nor was a presbyterian kirk session any longer to have the support of the secular law in the enforcement of its authority or disciplinary procedures. However, as J.S. Shaw points out,[42] it is equally possible to argue that the legislation in fact did

40. *HMC.* Mar and Kellie MSS., Mar to his brother, the Justice Clerk. 14 February 1712. 497; On the bribery of the Scots peers, see Gilbert Burnet, *History of his Own Time.* 881.

41. See Szechi, *Jacobitism and Tory politics,* 110–2; MSS. of the House of Lords. ix, 196, No. 2858, Episcopal Communion (Scotland) Act.

42. John Stuart Shaw, *The political history of eighteenth-century Scotland* (Basingstoke: 1999), 90.

episcopalians a disservice. By settling their right to worship outside the national church, it by the same token confirmed their status as non-conformists, an inferiority that was underscored by the Act's insistence that registration of their banns, births and baptisms were still to be made at the parish church. Moreover, the parish church itself would continue to be financed by a system of teind levy that made no exemptions for those of the other communion.

There was also the matter of the Oaths of Allegiance. This was an issue that was to have profound implications for both churches. Naturally, the Jacobite wing in Parliament had no wish to see their Scottish sympathizers unable to profit from the Toleration through the presence of a specific requirement to abjure the Stewarts. However, when it proved impossible to keep such an oath out of the Bill, they responded by making sure its terms remained equally unpalatable for presbyterians. Apart from the Erastian overtones of government-promoted oaths, the main problem for the latter was that the abjuration was to be linked to the English *Act of Settlement* of 1701, which required the sovereign to be of the communion of the Church of England. More will be said below about the implications of the Oaths. Before moving, however, from the Toleration Act to the restoration of patronage, it must be asked whether the former merited the same accusation that has been leveled against the latter, namely, that it was a clear breach of the terms of the Union.

As with the Patronage Act, much rests on the interpretation of what constitutes law that is unalterable. However, there is also a difference between the Toleration and Patronage Acts: whereas the latter is concerned primarily with one issue, the former also raises questions about the nature of a National Church.

To take first the central matter of the toleration itself, there does seem to be a defensible case made by T.B. Smith in his lecture (see above) that the Toleration did not violate the Union, since it "did not derogate from the recognition of the Church of Scotland as the established church."[43] On the other hand, if Smith's claim is accepted, it is possible that the way is then opened for a case to be made against the legality of that clause by which Parliament removed the civil sanction from the Kirk's courts. If it is possible to say that a body can be the established church without being the only church, then it is reasonable

43. Smith, 112, n. 29.

to suppose there are, nonetheless, some exclusive privileges attaching to its status which other communions have not. The Act certainly recognized this by continuing the Kirk's historic rights concerning finance and registration of births and marriages, yet an exception was made in regard to its parochial authority. By removing the state's traditional confirmation of the National Church's courts, it might be possible to argue that Parliament had departed from its fundamental commitment to maintain a church governed by such courts, in that it had undermined their authority. This reasoning, similar to the objection recorded by Bishop Gilbert Burnet# against the restoration of patronage (see note 19 above), possibly presents the best case for challenging the validity of the Toleration Act, but whether it provides sufficient grounds for sustaining the claim made before the Lords[44] that it "quite alters the government of the Church of Scotland," is another matter.

As a postscript, it is noteworthy that on purely practical grounds, Parliament probably had little choice but to remove the civil sanction in its entirety. If it had retained it intact, then episcopalians would have remained vulnerable to persecution by presbyterian courts; yet if it had confined its reinforcement to the Kirk's own adherents, then it would have been open to miscreants simply to declare themselves members of the other communion to escape further attention.

To sum up, it is difficult to be dogmatic about the Toleration Act of 1712 and its relationship with the terms of the Treaty of Union. Nonetheless, it is probably true to say that whereas it altered the character of the church established in 1707, it did not necessarily destroy its constitutional status. The vital question is whether establishment is the same as monopoly.

The Patronage Act

Having successfully penetrated the Kirk's defenses with the Toleration, the Scots Jacobites pressed on with a bill to restore patronage. According to Burnet, the principle of a Scottish Toleration Act was by most English perceptions entirely reasonable. However, the subsequent proposal that more inroads be made, was met with circumspection, particularly among the

---

44. MSS of the House of Lords, ix, 196.

Whig bishops, who feared that in going too far, there might be a backlash against the Church of England by any future administration.[45]

The Scots were nevertheless determined to press for more, and they did so with a resolution that was fed by a secondary campaign they were conducting. This was to heighten dissatisfaction with the Union among moderate opinion in Scotland[46] and thereby, through making out that he would dissolve it, enhance the Pretender's appeal. Lockhart made it a particular task: "I pressed the Toleration and Patronage Acts more earnestly, that I thought the Presbyterian Clergy would be from thence convinced that the establishment of their Kirk would, in time, be overturned, as it was obvious that the security thereof was not so thoroughly established by the Union as they imagined."[47] The propaganda campaign in London was duly stepped up, not only attacking the idea that patronage was incompatible with the Scottish presbyterian settlement, but also insinuating that the 1690 arrangement was really part of a subversive, presbyterian process whereby presentations were stolen from the heritors and given to "the meanest of the people." The Kirk deserved, the argument went, to pay the price for its "saucy carriage" towards the nobility, and if it continued to set servants against their masters, worse would rightly follow. A variation of this theme was the portrayal of the ministers as greedy for power. They were admonished to rein in their ambitions and welcome the return of patronage as being for their own good: "'tis safe and wholesome, it will cool your blood and make you soft and easy, and thereby put you under obligations to thank your sovereign physicians."[48]

On 13th March, permission to bring in a Bill to *Restore the patrons to their ancient rights of presenting ministers to the churches vacant in*

45. W. Cobbett, *Parliamentary History of England*, (London 1806–12), 371. Wodrow, *Analecta*, i, 321–22.

46. Burnet, *History*, 882. As well as the Patronage Act there was the *Yule Vacance Act* [Ann.10, Anne Reg. 563, ii, Session I]. It received the royal assent on the same day as the Patronage Act. These, Burnet says, were intended 'only to irritate.' Another plan was to have the Bishops' Rents, which since 1689 had been mostly diverted to the Kirk, resumed by the crown.

47. Lockhart Papers. i, 417–8; also ii, 20, where he underlines the need to convince Presbyterians that the best hope of dissolution was through King James.

48. [George McKenzie, Earl of Cromartie], *The Scottish Toleration truly stated in a letter to a peer* (London: 1712), 14; Anon., *Good news from Scotland: or the Abjuration and the Kirk of Scotland reconcil'd* (np. 1712); Anon. *Remarks upon the representation made by the kirk of Scotland concerning patronages* (np. 1712).

that part of Great Britain called Scotland[49] was granted by 152 votes to 82. Its proposers were the MP for Dumfriesshire, James Murray, who eventually became, in exile, the Old Pretender's Secretary of State; the MP for Forfarshire, John Carnegie of Boysack, who came out in the '15, and the MP for Inverness Burghs, George Mackenzie of Inchculter, who was a Jacobite sympathizer. From this point the Bill's passage was swift, probably in order to be complete before the Assembly in May: on 20th March it was read for the first time; four days later its second reading was passed by 198 votes to 80; on 3rd April it went to committee; on 7th April, the third reading was passed by 173 votes to 76, and the Bill went to the Lords. Meanwhile, the Assembly Commission had been wrong-footed by the speed of the Bill's passage, and its three petitions on the subject (one each for Queen, Commons and Lords) only reached the London representatives on 2nd April.[50] The one for the Queen was at once dispatched, but she gave no response beyond a vague reassurance to the May Assembly of her protection, having already told the three ministers on 18th March that, as far as she was concerned, it was purely a Parliamentary matter. Since it was too late to present the Commons petition, the one to the Lords was lodged on 11th April, only to be refused for being incorrectly addressed to the "Peers of Great Britain," instead of to the "Lords Spiritual and Temporal." Swallowing their scruples, the representatives changed the wording and resubmitted it the next day.[51]

49. It is not clear who was responsible for the drafting of the Bill. GWT Omond, in his *Lord Advocates*, i, 298–9, says that although he was not Lord Advocate at the time, Sir David Dalrymple# was consulted about it. This would seem likely, as the government had already commissioned an "Advocate's Opinion Concerning the Patronage Acts" from him in 1710 [*HMC. Portland MSS.* x, 7 July 1710. 220]. Omond is also confident that Dalrymple was responsible for at least the clause limiting the time allowable for presenting to 6 months.

Dalrymple was a pro-Union Court Whig. His stance on the issue of patronage was enigmatic. At the conclusion of his Advocate's Opinion, he advised the government not to take the 600 merks compensation lest this caused complications in any subsequent restoration, yet the following year he published a lengthy pamphlet condemning any return to presentations. [*An account of lay patronages in Scotland and of the fatal differences thay have occasioned betwixt the church and lay patrons; with observations on the arguments for restoring them in 1711* (np. 1711)].

50. Thos Blackwell to Provost Ross, 3 April 1712. *Spalding Club Misc.* 216. They had been sent on the 27 March (*State Papers*, SRO. RH2/4/300).

51. Cobbett, *Parliamentary Debates*, 370–71. On the representatives' discomfort, see Wodrow, *Analecta*, ii, 48.

In the debate, Gilbert Burnet, who sat as Bishop of Salisbury, opposed the Bill as strongly as he could. He had perceived the Jacobite ulterior motive to ferment resentment for the Union, and was apprehensive of what might endanger it. However, his studied moderatism and pedantic manner was out of sympathy with the mood of the House, and notwithstanding the addition of the Church's petition and the opposition of five of the bishops, the Bill passed by 51 votes to 29.[52]

The terms of the Act were fairly straightforward. Patrons were obliged to present a qualified person within six months of a vacancy occurring, and the presbytery was bound to receive and admit him. If no presentation were made, then the right to present fell to the presbytery. Patronages previously belonging to archbishops, bishops or other "dignified persons" were to belong to the Crown. Similarly, the right of any patron who was popish or presented while unqualified would fall (for that time) to the Crown. Finally, the Act awarded a bonus to patrons in that it still continued the teind concessions made to them in 1690 and 1693 in compensation for the removal of their right of presentation. Under the arrangement [see above], they received the whole tithes of their parishes, after which they were to deduct a stipend for the minister. During a vacancy, they were to dispose (at their discretion) of the stipend money on pious uses.

On 14 April, the Bill returned to the Commons, where it was accepted as slightly amended,[53] and sent to the sovereign. The Queen waited until the Assembly was over, then gave the royal assent on the 22 May. The Act had become law.

---

52. 15 April 1712, Sir Hugh Paterson, Whitehall, to the Justice Clerk, *HMC.*, Mar and Kellie, p 498. He says the Bill was '... carried by near two to one, tho' they had gott the whole W[hig]s convinced to opose it. The Bishop of Salisbury was one of the greatest sticklers against it, which I believe made it not goe the worse.' On Burnet's character, see Introduction to his *History*, passim, and J MacVeigh's *Scottish Family History*, (Dumfries: 1891) i, 492. Burnet's opposition to the Bill was also probably related to the fact that he clearly was no admirer of patronage, see his *History*, 911.

53. J. Cunningham in his *Church History of Scotland*, (Edinburgh: 1859) 362, says that through intervention by the Duke of Argyll, the Lords amended the Bill so that the presentee should not just be "qualified," but "presbyterian." See also RH. Story, *William Carstares*, (Edinburgh: 1874), 341. The MSS of the House of Lords, ix, 235, confirms that the amendment was agreed by both houses, but reproductions of the Act retain the original wording, "qualified."

Summary

Leaving aside the Jacobite desire to sow disdain for the Union, it is difficult to see how the restoration of patronage was to be avoided. On the one hand, for the great majority of Scottish property owners, the only honorable and decent way for a vacancy to be filled was through the judgment of men of quality like themselves, and in comparison with presentations, the 1690 system left too much to be desired.[54] On the other hand, the more episcopalians identified with Anglicanism, then the more likely it became that a government which dealt heavily with English non-conformists— as it did in the *Occasional Conformity Act* (1711) and the *Schism Act* (1714)[55]—would be amenable to easing restrictions on those Scots they saw as fellow Anglicans. The resulting Toleration Act was crucial, since its passage had the effect of opening a door in the Scottish ecclesiastical edifice, a door which now did not require too much of an additional push to open wider.

Could the Kirk have prevented the legislation of 1712 if it had dug in its heels at the time of the Union and extracted a more specific security for itself? Whereas such a scenario would certainly have augmented the moral force of its subsequent outrage, the possibility is stopped short by the fact that the Church was not in a position in 1706 to dictate terms: if it had overplayed its resistance to what was on offer, it risked being portrayed in London as unruly opponents of the Union, and in that case, there was the danger that the Crown might turn its favor to their episcopalian rivals and all would be lost.

The character of the post–1712 national Church was doubtless very different from the one the Assembly hoped it had secured in 1707. On the other hand, it could comfort itself with the thought that at least it was still a presbyterian one.

---

54. This is not to deny that some patrons were able to continue as though their right to choose the minister had never been removed. A striking example was at Rothes in 1709/10, where Aberlour presbytery agreed to waive the *jus devolutum* and invited the Earl of Rothes to select whom he wished.

55. 10 Anne c. 6; 13 Anne c. 7.

CHAPTER EIGHT

THE CLOSING DAYS OF April 1712 were an anxious time for Oxford as he contemplated the commencement of the General Assembly on 1 May. The royal seal on the Patronage Act had yet to be given, but no one doubted the inevitability of its becoming law. Fearful of what the Assembly's reaction might be, he wrote nervously to Carstares, asking what could be done to keep it from excessive unrest. Carstares suggested that the Duke of Atholl be appointed Lord High Commissioner on the grounds that since he had been an opponent of the Union, his stock with the more hardline members would be high. This was duly arranged, and Atholl in turn managed to have the moderate William Hamilton#, Professor of Divinity at Edinburgh University, elected Moderator.[1] The Assembly clerks, meanwhile, had received around forty submissions from presbyteries, of which the great majority called upon the meeting to stand up and resist the encroachment of patronage upon the Church's liberties. However, in what was to become a recurring pattern of wariness among the Church's superior courts, the Assembly decided, after much heart-searching, to pass to the Assembly Commission the responsibility of deciding what to do about both patronage and the Toleration.

Convening immediately after the Assembly, the Assembly Commission also found itself unable to make up its mind how to respond: to do nothing could be interpreted as weakness, yet too strong a protest might provoke even greater assaults upon the Kirk's constitutional integrity. Accordingly, it stalled until its July meeting. Meanwhile, the tension and anxiety building up in the parishes continued to make itself known. Several presbyteries wrote wondering how to react if a presentation were given in. The synod of Angus and Mearns wrote urging the Commission to "give as full and plain advice as possibly you can . . . how to behave when the patrons offer their presentations."[2] Aberdeen synod wrote nine

---

1. *HMC.*, Portland MSS., x, 433. Carstares to Oxford, 15 May 1712; Story, *Carstares*, 350; *HMC*, Portland MSS, v, 172, Atholl to Oxford, 2 May 1712; for a full biography of Hamilton, see my entry in the *ODNB*.

2. SRO, General Assembly Papers, CH1/2/32, Pt. 2, ff 167–8, 2 July 1712.

days later expressing their distress and confusion. Some of their number argued for presentations being simply ignored, while others stood for popular consent. Given such an atmosphere, they considered there was an urgent necessity for "very particular and serious advice from the Commission in this matter."[3] The Commission could not ignore the letters, but confusion reigned as to what advice could or should be given. Eventually, the meeting gratefully grasped the opportunity to bow out of the responsibility given it when it was suggested that it was properly the task of the Assembly to make general rules for the Kirk, and not the Commission. Accordingly, it was resolved to take no action other than to give advice in individual cases, if sought. Otherwise judicatories were to keep out of trouble with patrons, and hold fast to all other Assembly Acts since the Revolution: "Further than this it was not thought safe to goe."[4]

Apart from the fear of a backlash at Westminster, the main grounds for such circumspection stemmed from a passage in the Toleration Act itself. This was because the Act's Abjuration clause had now, in effect, put the presbyterian and episcopal communions in the same balance. If presbyterian ministers both refused the Oath and furthermore renounced Parliament's authority in relation to its Act on patronage, it was more than possible that their rivals might qualify *en masse*, and then portray themselves as the only true loyalists to state and crown in Scotland. Under close scrutiny from all sides, the Kirk knew it had to be extremely careful: "The commission of the Kirk has done nothing, therefore, my Lord, they have done no ill, which their enemies wait for. The Episcopalian clergy will take the abjuration if the others refuse it in any number."[5]

Since fastidiousness over the Oath was a source of considerable harm to the Kirk's reputation among English observers, it is worth noting why the Oath presented such problems.

The Abjuration Oath

There were several reasons for the discomfort it caused to many presbyterians. The most pressing were, first, an instinctive dislike of the state imposing any conditions upon the integrity of the Church, but most of all of it intruding a secular qualification upon those who were seen as divinely called to office. This was tantamount to Erastianism. Secondly,

3. Ibid. ff. 174, 11 July 1712, synod of Aberdeen to Carstares.
4. *Analecta*, ii, 71.
5. *HMC*, Portland MSS, v, 230, Alexander Cunningham to Oxford, 3 October 1712.

as mentioned above, the phraseology of the Oath contained a reference to the English *Act of Settlement* of 1701. The implications of this inclusion were that the juror was not only pledging himself to maintain all laws which upheld the episcopally-governed Church of England (a commitment incompatible with the Solemn League and Covenant), but that he was also approving the stricture that any future sovereign be a communicant member of that church. To give agreement to such proposals was for many the equivalent of declaring that the painful struggles of the previous generation had been for nothing. Thirdly, there was annoyance that since such an oath was properly a test for dissenters, it was insulting to apply it to members of a church that was legally established. Fourthly, some felt that submission to the Oath could be taken as a homologation of the Toleration Act as a whole, and therefore to approve of its allowance of the Anglican liturgy in Scotland. Finally, there were those who despised the Oath on the ground that their subscription might thereby suggest they approved of the Union itself.[6]

The whole question of whether it was right to take the Oath or not threw ministers into agonies of indecision. Many were placed in the quandary of whether they should refuse it and face the possibility of deprivation, or subscribe and risk infuriating their congregations, who were frequently more vigorous in their dislike of it than their ministers. Some, like the thirty ministers from Edinburgh presbytery who took the Oath on the 28 October, recorded a qualification beforehand, designed to disassociate them from its more contentious parts. The validity of the ploy was, however, highly questionable and earned derision from all sides.[7] In the event, between a third and a half refused to subscribe. Since all but a handful of episcopalians remained non-jurant, the one relief the Kirk had was that a situation of armed truce, to use Daniel Szechi's phrase,[8] developed whereby the authorities felt it wisest to refrain from zealously prosecuting either side, lest a chain of retaliatory processes be set in motion. Six years later (see below) further legislation provided some relief from the problems the Oath engendered, but much damage had been done by the

6. *Draught of ministers' (non-jurants) declaration*, Wodrow, *Correspondence*, i, App. I, 643.

7. Eg., Anon., *A letter from a gentleman in Edinburgh to his friend in the country concerning the way and manner in which the Abjuration Oath was sworn by the ministers in the shire of Edinburgh* (Edinburgh: 1712).

8. D. Szechi, "The politics of `persecution': Scots episcopalian toleration and the Harley ministry, 1710–1712," in *Persecution and Toleration*, Studies in church history, xxi, ed., W. J. Sheils, (Padstow: 1984), 285.

controversy. The Kirk was wounded internally, by the sometimes bitter split between non-subscribers and those who felt clear to conform, and externally, by the suspicion and disapproval aroused in London by the extent of its non-jurancy.

Meanwhile, there was the immediate problem of the return of presentations, and how to respond to them.

The First Presentations

An enduring myth about the 1712 restoration of patronage is that patrons generally kept their heads down in its early years, having judged it wise not to add to the passions surrounding the Toleration Act by starting to make presentations. The accuracy of this tradition, however, is highly questionable. If there was a self-denying ordinance, it lasted only through the June and July of 1712, for in the six months following, presentations were lodged by: the Earl of Glencairn, for Port Glasgow (Greenock); John Stewart of Blackhall, for Mearns (Paisley); Sir David Dalrymple, for Morham (Haddington); Viscount Stormont, for Kilsyth (Glasgow); the Earl of Selkirk, for Crawfordjohn (Lanark); the Earl of Aberdeen, for Ellon (Ellon); Sir William Forbes of Craigievar, for Fintry (Aberdeen); the Duke of Roxburghe, for Galashiels (Selkirk); the Duke of Atholl, for Dull (Weem); James Ferguson of Pitfour, for Arbuthnott (Fordoun), Peter Forbes of Balfour for Edzell (Brechin), the magistrates of Glasgow for Blackfriars (Glasgow) and the magistrates of St Andrews for the town's second charge. There were also three Crown presentations, for Burntisland (Kirkcaldy), Dunsyre (Biggar) and Kettle (Cupar). The St Andrews city fathers had the additional distinction not only of being the first to lodge a presentation (14 August) but also of being the first to have their choice settled by one (4 September)—the council's aggressive tactics undoubtedly assisting their candidate's progress.[9]

As can be seen, the great majority of the above presentations were for lowland areas. In the north and west regions, there was naturally much frustration among episcopal patrons that they could not supply parishes with those of their own communion, especially as vacancies were so numerous - indeed, in presbyteries like Tain, Sutherland and Dingwall, the gaps were such that the indigenous ministers doubted whether they could

---

9. They threatened to arrest the minister sent by presbytery to moderate a call at large. They then proceeded to draw up a presentation for their candidate, who was the Dean of Guild's son, Laurence Watson. *Fasti*, v, 240; *Analecta*, ii, 99.

even continue as viable courts of the Church.[10] The only option for these patrons was on the one hand to hope that there was truth in the rumor that Parliament would shortly allow episcopal presentees [see above], while in the meantime, as in the case of Avoch (Chanonry) and Alness (Dingwall), they could let the presbytery proceed to settle but demand it be recorded that this did not prejudice their right to present in the future. Alternatively, there was the option of falling back on the ploy of "sham" presentations (prolonging a vacancy by presenting those who were certain not to accept).[11] As a last resort, a non-juring patron could emulate the example of John, the fifth Viscount Arbuthnott, who in 1715, simply built a new church for episcopalians like himself in a corner of the parish.

For the patrons listed above who tried to make successful presentations, the path was nonetheless fraught with difficulties, which the church courts did not scruple to exploit. Sir David Dalrymple's presentation of Robert Kirk to Morham failed because an Assembly Act of 1694 had ordained that highland parishes should have first call on Gaelic speakers, of which Kirk was one. The attempts of Glencairn and Roxburghe faltered through their being judged as having an invalid right to present. Although presbytery and patron agreed on the candidate, Selkirk's presentation was roundly ignored, and presbytery proceeded without it. Stewart thoughtfully allowed the congregation of Mearns time to call, then presented their choice, but presbytery was not won over and refused to countenance the scheme.

Right at the start, these early cases revealed not only an inevitable diversity of procedures, but again starkly exposed the jurisdiction hazards which tend to emerge when a process is shared by two different authorities, namely, church and state. In the case of Morham, since there was no question as to the presentee's ability to speak English, it could not have been argued that he was *unqualified* (the only legal grounds allowed to the Church for refusing him), yet his candidature was still successfully blocked.[12] In the affairs of Port-Glasgow and Galashiels, the local pres-

10. SRO, *Assembly Papers*, CH1/2/32. Pt. 2, ff. 165, "Letter from Presbytery of Tain to the Assembly Commission," 10 September 1712. The presbytery of Sutherland had only one Presbyterian minister active.

11. W. MacGill, *Old Ross-shire and Scotland, as seen in the Tain and Balnagowan documents* (Inverness: 1909), 44. Tain, Dingwall and Chanonry presbyteries complained to the 1716 Assembly about the damage caused by sham presentations in their area: *Assembly Registers*, 7 May 1716.

12. Moreover, the 1694 Act only made a recommendation, not an injunction, to presbyteries regarding Gaelic speakers. It is perhaps worth adding that the Court

byteries were each faced with conflicting claims for the right to present. Despite pressure from the claimants, eventually they (rightly) judged the issue to be solely a matter for the civil courts and did nothing until resolved there.[13] As for those presbyteries who favored defiance and tried to exclude presentations altogether, the unpalatable question at once arose, would this detract from the incumbent's entitlement to the stipend? It remained an issue of heated debate until formally confirmed by a ruling of the Court of Session in 1735: a minister's collation, and therefore entitlement to the stipend, stemmed from the joint action of presentation to the living and institution to the spiritual charge by the presbytery. Thus, according to the 1735 judgment, if a presbytery were to refuse a proper presentation and admit another, the patron was entitled to retain the stipend, as if vacant.[14]

The First Crown Presentation

The Crown had around a third of Scotland's parishes in its gift. Given that this was at a time when the Kirk knew it had to be cautious in its response to the new legislation, it might have been thought that it would look upon government-sponsored presentees with particular circumspection. In the event, William Duguid was not only to earn the distinction of being the first royal presentee after 1712, but he was also the first of all presentees to be rejected by the Church on the grounds of indiscipline. Admittedly, he was of such unseemly character that the Kirk had little choice but to refuse

---

of Session decided, in 1772 and 1825, that the presentation of a monoglot English speaker to a Gaelic charge could be declared invalid. In his *Parochial Law*, Dunlop considered it was nonetheless procedurally wrong to invalidate the presentation. In such circumstances, the correct conduct should be for the presbytery to sustain the presentation, but reject the candidate as unqualified for that pastoral office. [268–69].

13. Port Glasgow was situated within the parish of Kilmacolm, of which Glencairn was the patron, but since the church itself was built and financed by Glasgow's magistrates, they insisted the presentation could only be theirs. In 1717 the Earl agreed to renounce his right in return for 600 merks, but it was not until the middle of the century that the Council's privilege of presenting was settled. At Galashiels, Roxburghe's claim to be patron was challenged by Sir James Scott of Gala. It was Scott who emerged triumphant in the courts. See Registers of Paisley Presbytery SRO., CH2/294/7, 21 November 1711–26 March 1717; *Extracts from the records of the burgh of Glasgow, 1691-1717*, 486ff.; T. Craig-Brown, *History of Selkirkshire or chronicles of Ettrick Forest*, (Edinburgh: 1886), i, 424ff.

14. Moncrieff v. Maxton, 15 February 1735, Morison, *Decisions of the Court of Session*, xxiii, 9909. The issue had in fact been decided the previous century, for which see Duncan, *Parochial Law*, 318.

him, but the well–publicized process could not have come at a more inappropriate time for the Kirk's standing in Court circles.

After converting from Catholicism, Duguid became a protégé of the evangelical James Webster of the Tolbooth Church in Edinburgh, and went on to study for the ministry. Webster soon began to harbor doubts about his disciple's probity, yet before anything came of his suspicions, Duguid became the subject of one of two competing calls for the vacancy at Burntisland in January 1712, he being the nominee of the strong Jacobite element in the burgh.[15] The Church had procedures for vetting candidates for charges [see Appendix VI] and Duguid's moral deficiencies would normally have been quickly uncovered and used to terminate his involvement. However, thanks to chance, incompetence, and the latter's manipulative skills, the Kirk found itself embroiled in a long and damaging procedural wrangle over the following year, in which Duguid constantly portrayed the church courts as persecutors and himself as one whose only crime was to accept a presentation.

It was a dispute that should have been avoided, not least because Duguid's misdemeanors were anything but discreet. When at last investigations were completed, they were to reveal a voluminous catalogue of misdeeds, of which a random selection included: sexually assaulting a servant wench; disporting himself "stark naked" in front of his landlady; frequent drunkenness, including when he "drank til he vomit" ("the smell whereof was very noisome"); an incident when he "spoke and carried very indecently" to his hostess, putting his hand on her naked breast while nursing her child, then kissing her "very immodestly" ("particularly by attempting to put his tongue in her mouth"); his being drunk after preaching at Burntisland, swaying about on his horse, then making his water so that witnesses "saw his nakedness"; swearing at bowls, using expressions like "By God, it was my bowl"; drinking the Pretender's health; calling the synod of Fife "a pack of knaves and rascals" and assaulting his landlady by throwing her on the bed, putting his hands under her clothes and exposing his nakedness.[16]

Some of these allegations had percolated to the surface by May 1712, but when the Assembly Commission investigated, none of the witnesses

15. Wodrow, *Analecta*, ii, 199. The calls came before the Presbytery of Kirkcaldy on the 22 January 1712. The other candidate was the evangelical Ebenezer Erskine of Portmoak.

16. See: SRO, Assembly Papers, CH1/2/32, Pt. 3, ff. 230ff; Edinburgh Presbytery Minutes, CH2/121/9, 4 November 1713; Andrew Lowe, *A Vindication of the Church of Scotland from the Groundless Aspersions of Mr William Dugud* (np. 1714).

appeared, so the case was aborted. It accordingly fell back upon Kirkcaldy presbytery to make the next move - thus allowing Duguid to play his trump card. At their meeting of the 14th. August 1712 (and in the face of more disturbing revelations), Duguid presented the presbytery with the tempting opportunity to be rid of him forever. If the court were willing to issue him with an extract of license and testimonial of good character, he would give up his designs for Burntisland and leave the area for good. Judging the chance too good to miss, the presbytery complied on the 11 September.

Duguid and his supporters, however, had no intention of honoring the arrangement. On the 20 October, Sir Alexander Erskine, the Jacobite MP for Fifeshire wrote to Oxford putting pressure on him to grant Duguid a Crown presentation for Burntisland. Erskine reminded the Lord Treasurer how he had lost several Town Councils recently, and that if the presentation were not sent quickly, "the putting in a minister there falls jure devoluto in the presbytery's hands, and if that be you may be assured from me you will infallibly lose that town likewise."[17] Oxford thereupon gave way, leaving Duguid to reappear before a stunned Kirkcaldy presbytery on 27 November, armed with a presentation. To add to their discomfort, presbytery now realized they had made a disastrous error of giving him a testimonial, for any attempt to have him rejected at his ordination trials on the grounds of moral unfitness, would look absurd.

As the case thereafter ground through the church courts, Duguid and the Jacobite interest made much of the claim that by impugning their candidate's character unjustly (after all, he had a testimonial) as a reason for delaying his settlement, the Kirk was in reality striking not only at presentations, but indirectly at the queen. It was a sensitive point that sent tremors through the Church to the extent that when the matter was referred to the December Commission, the meeting shied away from making any comment or decision, despite, as Wodrow recalled, its previous commitment to give advice on individual cases.[18]

The affair finally came up to the 1713 Assembly amidst uncomfortable publicity for the Church, Duguid's followers having by this time sent petitions to both queen and Parliament.[19] However, Duguid's ill-disciplined personality was to provide a fortuitous opportunity for the Assem-

17. *HMC*, Portland MSS, v, 238. Alexander Erskine, Lord Lyon, to the Earl of Oxford, 20 October, 1712.

18. *Analecta*, ii, 120.

19. Assembly Papers, SRO., CH1/2/32, 230 ff.

bly to escape its predicament. Parading his defiance to a gross degree, he thereby presented the meeting with the justification it needed to revoke his probationer's license by reason of his "insolent carriage to the supreme Judicatory of this church."[20] Although Burntisland had not seen the last of Duguid—he returned there to exercise an episcopalian ministry, having been ordained in 1714 by the bishop of Carlisle—at last the awkward saga was effectually over.

The controversy had been a salutary lesson, not just to the Church but also to the Court. For the latter, Duguid's vaunting of the presentation in the face of his victims' allegations ("I laugh at all these things, for now I have the Queen's letter"[21]) was an embarrassment. To Oxford in particular, it would all have been a further signal that his grasp on Scottish affairs and political patronage was not what it had been. There had been no Scotch Secretary since the death of Queensberry in July 1711, and it does appear that a slackening of control was the result.[22] Accordingly, Oxford now turned to the Earl of Mar#, whom he had been using as his agent on an informal basis, and had him officially appointed the new Secretary on 23 September 1713.

Mar took a close interest in ecclesiastical affairs, and a few months later wrote to every Scottish Sheriff, desiring an accurate account of all parishes in the queen's gift and the value of their stipend. They were also to inform him when and how these become vacant, and—an important matter from the point of view of favors—who were the principal heritors.[23] Crown presentations were now to be dealt with in an ordered fashion: there was to be no repeat of the Duguid fiasco. Before he was able, however, to build up a systematized web of influence in church affairs, Queen Anne died on 1 August 1714 to be succeeded by the Hanoverian George I. Finding no place for himself in the new regime, Mar shortly afterwards went off to join the Rising of 1715.

20. Assembly Registers, 9 May 1713.

21. Edinburgh Presbytery Registers, SRO., CH2\121\9, 16 December 1713.

22. "Is it more than coincidence that the two great Scottish crises in Oxford's ministry occurred at a time of interregnum in the office of Scottish secretary?": Clyve Jones, "'The Scheme Lords, the Neccessitous Lords, and the Scots Lords': The Earl of Oxford's Management and the 'Party of the Crown' in the House of Lords, 1711–1714," in *Party and Management in Parliament, 1660–1784*, ed. Clyve Jones (Leicester: 1984). 133.

23. State Papers, Scotland, (SP.55). i, Sept. 1713—Sept. 1714, SRO., RH.2/4/390. *From the Earl of Mar, Whitehall, Circular to the Sheriffs of Scotland in Relation to the Churches in the Queen's Presentation*—13 March 1714.

The Special Commission

Mar was not, in fact, the first to give thought to how a Crown presentation system might work. As early as 28 June 1712, Carstares had written to Oxford warmly commending an idea that the Treasurer had once expressed to him that a special commission might be set up to supervise presentations to ministers for vacancies in the Crown's gift.[24] When Oxford appeared to be in no hurry to pursue the project, Carstares wrote again two months later, suggesting that in the meantime the government could always exercise some "connivance" and let its patronage fall to presbyteries, *jure devoluto*.[25] Oxford had no inclination to tie his hands in either manner, yet at the same time was too astute to let it be thought he was wholly unsympathetic to the notion. Consequently, he allowed the hope to continue that he might consider the creation of at least some form of special commission, probably comprising four or five well-disposed nobles and officers of state[26]. Those who knew of the idea saw the Lord High Commissioner to the Assembly as the obvious centerpiece to such a body, as indeed did the Lord High Commissioner himself, the Duke of Atholl.[27] Superficially, there was every reason for a man like the Duke (who held the position in 1712, 1713 and 1714) to command the confidence of the Kirk. He had opposed the Union. He had also voted against the Patronage Act, and indeed affected to be so distressed by its passage that he was, he claimed, uneasy at accepting the Commissionership. However, there can be little doubt that, whatever was his public posturing, Atholl's personal motivation rarely deviated from that of self-interest. His vote against patronage was meaningless, the Earl of Ilay, for example, had done the same while privately declaring he was in favor of it.[28] Moreover, Atholl's ostentatious scruples against taking the Assembly appointment did not distract him from a keen interest in the financial and other rewards he expected to receive from it.[29]

---

24. *HMC.*, Portland MSS, x, 276. Sir James Steuart carried the idea further by suggesting that since some patrons had dubious entitlement to their patronage, the queen should be considered "Universal Patron" and that no one else could present unless they were first approved and "instructed." (Portland MSS, 289. Sir James Steuart to the Earl of Oxford, 28 March 1713).

25. Ibid., 277, 19 August 1712.

26. Wodrow, *Correspondence*, i, 608. Wodrow to Linning, 2 November 1714.

27. *HMC.*, Portland MSS, v, 291. Duke of Atholl to Oxford, 12 May 1713.

28. *The London Diaries of Wm. Nicolson, 1702–18*, eds., C. Jones and G.S. Holmes, (Oxford: 1985), 5 March 1711, 555.

29. *HMC.* Portland MSS, v, 179, Atholl to Oxford, 2 June 1712; Wodrow,

It was, however, the Duke's behavior over the settling of the vacancy at Dull on his estates, that showed up in stark clarity how unlikely it could be that the proposed special commission was a credible proposition.

The notorious dispute over Dull hinged upon the bitter offence felt by the Duke that, in his absence, a call for the parish had been arranged on its becoming vacant in the Spring of 1711. He considered this an insult to his authority and set about undermining it. While disputing the call before the synod of Perth and Stirling the following year, he realized that, thanks to the new legislation, he now had a right of presentation. Accordingly, he deserted his appeal and issued a presentation to the Rev. Patrick Stewart of Auchtergaven. When, however, Stewart refused to move, Atholl was forced to turn once more to his appeal. Unfortunately for the Duke, the Dunkeld presbytery of October 1712 decided that the refusal in effect cleared the way for them to continue the original settlement.

On receiving the Presbytery's sentence, the Duke declared it a personal insult, sought legal advice and plotted revenge on those he judged most responsible.[30] His trump card, however, was the Assembly. On the 5 May 1713, two days before the settlement, the Duke's commissioners appeared and lodged a petition for it to be sisted. Fearful of crossing the occupant of the Commissioner's throne, the Assembly duly granted the sist and referred the cause to the Assembly Commission. "Great folk have great power," Wodrow later remarked in disgust.[31] He was even more appalled at the Commission, when, "a great deal of, I doe not say partiality, but a considerable biasse, appeared to[wards] her Majesty's Commissioner."[32] In the event, after a titanic struggle at the August Commission lasting three days, the Duke did not get his way, and the candidate he opposed was allowed. Nothing daunted, however, his response was to appeal to the House of Lords, which, although it ultimately came to nothing, was hardly fitting conduct for a Lord High Commissioner of the Church's supreme court. After this, the Duke was reappointed Commissioner for another year, but,

---

Correspondence, i, 274, 30 April 1712; the following year Atholl's interest was unabated: "'he will not accept of the post of Commissioner again, if your Lordship do not obtain his being gratified either as to former or new demands," *HMC*, Portland MSS, x, 290, Carstares to Oxford, 28 March 1713.

30. E.g., "I doubt not we shall fall on a way to get him [Rev. Archibald Campbell of Weem] out of that parish, and I shall concert with your Lordship at our next meeting not to pay him any stipend." SRO., Breadalbane MSS., GD112/39/267/1/1. Atholl to Breadalbane, 3 October 1712.

31. *Correspondence*, i, 5 May 1713, 452.

32. *Analecta*, ii, 201.

unsurprisingly, enthusiasm for the concept of a special commission, built around Atholl and other landowning nobles, had by now ebbed away.

Issues From Early Presentations

In the absence of detailed guidelines, both church and patrons were left to negotiate a terrain where ecclesiastical procedure and property laws overlapped. The resulting confusion could often produce results which were unexpected, or even outlandish. In the lowland areas, the most notable of these was the case of Kettle in Fife.

The presentation for Kettle was issued on the 22 January 1713.[33] Despite it being from the Crown, Cupar presbytery declined, merely on the presentation, to take the presentee on trials. The synod had ordered presbytery to proceed, but the latter, considering the opposition among the parishioners, simply refused. The synod then referred it to the Assembly, who gave it to the Commission to determine finally. Although the Commission affirmed the synod's sentence, still presbytery did nothing, so the case finally came back to what was the Assembly of 1716. For reasons that had much to do with politics, the Assembly reversed the Commission's decision. It was a vote that at once raised an important question that was to trouble the Kirk's upper courts for decades: was it right for the Assembly to reverse, or even discuss, a decision by the Commission if it had already awarded it power to determine *finally*? Did the Kettle decision mean that the Kirk had undermined its own authoritative structure?

In order for the meeting to give itself a chance to extricate itself from what was now a major difficulty, the Lord High Commissioner, the Earl of Rothes, used his powers to extend the Assembly by an extra day. A prolonged wrangle ensued, but out of which a form of words emerged upon which the court was prepared to agree. This declared that the Assembly had not considered the *validity* of the Commission's sentence, but "in regard of the difficulties that had occurred in the execution thereof, they do now recommend to the synod of Fife to take all prudent methods to remove the same."[34] This was still not ordering the presentee's settlement, nor yet was it a refusal to order it, so, to general relief, the crisis passed. The issue of the Commission's authority, however, was still far from resolved.

There was a number of presentations which, ironically, worked against the patron and instead helped presbyteries in areas where hostile

33. *Register of the Privy Seal*, SRO. PS.3/7.

34. *Assembly Registers*, 16 May 1716. In the event, the presentee was not settled.

lairds had determined to thwart their efforts to plant parishes with presbyterian incumbents.

At Edzell (Brechin presbytery) for example, the laird had for some years kept the church locked while the intruding episcopal minister conducted services in his great hall at Edzell Castle. When in November 1712 he started to have presentations lodged for the charge (being unqualified, he passed his right to another), presbytery was able to pursue a policy of indefinite delay on the grounds that it could hardly proceed to the settlement of a church to which it was denied access. By the end of 1714, they at last had the charge filled and a promise from the laird that the incumbent would be left unmolested.[35]

Brechin presbytery also found the Patronage Act had given them the upper hand in respect of Kinnaird parish. There, one of the delaying tactics employed by the patron, the Earl of Southesk, was a continuing insistence that the church was not in fact vacant. However, as soon as a presentation was lodged, as happened on the 13 January 1715, presbytery seized upon this as homologating its being without a minister.[36] The advantage thus gained was enough to enable presbytery at last to have Kinnaird settled on the 5th. April 1716, after being effectively thwarted since the time of the Revolution.

Again, when a vacancy arose at Kirriemuir (Forfar) in May 1713, instead of a pattern unfolding whereby the patron, the Earl of Panmure, would almost certainly have prolonged the vacancy by making unsustainable presentations whilst, in the meantime, giving the stipend to the episcopal intruder, presbytery took the initiative. At the same time as they continually shifted the dates of their meetings so that, according to Panmure, they could avoid having to receive his presentation, they accepted and sustained a presentation from the pro-Hanoverian Duke of Douglas, who also had interest in the area. The Duke's presentee, the Rev. George Ogilvie of Benvie, was admitted, amidst furious opposition, on the 17th September 1713. The Earl retaliated by denying Ogilvie access to glebe, stipend and church keys, but the latter nonetheless survived to exercise a ministry that lasted until his death in 1771.[37]

35. Brechin Presbytery Registers, SRO., CH2\40\6, 7 October 1713, 21 February 1715; A. Jervise, *History and traditions of the land of the Lindsays*, (Edinburgh: 1882), 55; Lord Lindsay, *Lives of the Lindsays*, (London: 1858), ii, 259.

36. SRO., CH2\40\6. 13 January 1715. It was a sham presentation, since the presentee had already refused it.

37. Sir Hew Dalrymple, *Decisions of the Court of Session, 1698–1718*. (Edinburgh: 1792) Case cxlviii, 203: "Mr George Ogilvie, Minister of Kirriemuir, v. the Heritors of

Finally, in the strangest outcome of all, there was a case where a presbytery found itself having to defend a presentation before the church courts. The incident arose in 1713 out of the situation at Old Machar (Aberdeen), where an episcopal intruder had been ensconced for some time. In an apparent move to remedy the impasse, the Masters of Kings College, who were patrons, presented the Rev Alexander Mitchell of Belhelvie to the first charge in May 1713. Anxious to be rid of the intruder, the presbytery of Aberdeen approved the design and translated Mitchell. However, there was a problem in that Mitchell's parish opposed the loss of their minister and commenced a series of appeals. As these progressed through the church courts, the Assembly of 1714 had the experience of hearing Aberdeen presbytery's approval of the presentation defended by Professor Thomas Blackwell of Marischall College—one of those who two years earlier had been in London arguing the Kirk's case *against* presentations before the queen and parliament. Mitchell was ultimately admitted to the charge on the 31st August 1714.[38]

Summary

Thus it was that the new era of presentations got under way. Split by the Abjuration Oath, and fearful of further encroachments upon its privileges, the Church's higher courts froze, while the inferior ones were left to respond as they saw fit. Most presbyteries, being hostile to presentations, tried to avoid giving them an acknowledged place in the settlement process, or if they felt constrained to include them, did so accompanied by a protest. The remainder, although a small minority, submitted to the practice without complaint. Of these, some were more than willing to co-operate with the patron, and Aberlour presbytery actually wrote to the patron when a vacancy occurred, and "entreated" him to present whomever he liked, but few went as far.[39]

Where collusion took place, it was usually for pragmatic reasons rather than principle. Using a presentation to resolve the situation at Old Machar

said parish, Earl of Panmure, John Lumsden and others:" 25 June 1715; Alan Reid, *The regality of Kirriemuir* (Edinburgh: 1909), 71.

38. General Assembly Registers, 10 May 1714; *Fasti*, vi, 20. On the finely-balanced power struggle between the Presbyterian/Whig and Jacobite/Episcopalian factions among the Masters of King's at this time, see: R.L. Emerson, *Professors, Patronage and Politics - The Aberdeen Universities in the 18th. Century*, (Aberdeen: 1992), 25–26.

39. Registers of the presbytery of Aberlour, 15 April 1714 and 5 May 1714, quoted in *Patronage Report*, App. i, 36.

was a case in point, although a more typical example was the understanding worked out between Duns presbytery and the patron of Longformacus. In 1714, the patron offered a bargain whereby he would co-operate in paying off the episcopal incumbent and rebuild the ruinous manse, in return for which, presbytery would refrain from using the *jus devolutum* without informing him and, indeed, allow him six months to act after their declaration of intent to fill the charge. He further undertook to do everything to plant a minister who would be agreeable to them.[40] Presbytery agreed and eventually a presentation was made. After trying the inclinations of the people and receiving no objections, presbytery went as far as commending the presentation to the presentee, who accordingly accepted it. After trials, he was ordained to the charge on the 29th. April 1715.

Contrary to the myth that, "For nearly twenty years the act restoring patronage remained almost a dead letter in the statute-book. It was very seldom acted upon,"[41] or, that the Act's "immediate results were insignificant,"[42] it is not true to claim that patrons *in general* shrank back from making their presence felt as vacancies arose. Apart from the desirability of having the minister of their choice installed, there was also the concern that their status might be weakened if they did not at least attempt to present. A record of a presentation could be important in any later dispute over entitlement. This was because patronage was, as already mentioned, a heritable right, and, since the passing of legislation by James VI in 1617, if such a right were held continuously for forty years, then a claimant could declare it was his by *prescription*, that is to say by long-standing custom or usage. Naturally, there was a complication with a presentation right since it could only be exercised intermittently. Nevertheless, although it took until 1828 for the courts to rule formally that more than one presentation was required to establish a prescriptive right,[43] it would not have required excessive foresight on the part of patrons to recognize that the more interventions they made, the stronger their claim to a title was likely to become. Accordingly, with regard to the early years after 1712, although church records (and especially the *Fasti*) might not show that a presentation formally accompanied a particular minister's settlement, it did not mean that a presentation was never issued. Often

40. Duns Presbytery Minutes. SRO. CH2/113/4. Letter, received 1 June 1714.

41. Cunningham, *Church History*, 278.

42. Story, *Carstares*, 351.

43. Macdonell of Glengarry v. Duke of Gordon, 26 February 1828, see Dunlop, *Parochial Law*, 212–14.

it was, although it would require a detailed perusal of all documentation surrounding each vacancy to obtain a precise assessment. Nevertheless, a revealing indication that the Act was anything but a "dead letter" can be seen in a complaint about it that the Assembly sent to the monarch within three years of its enactment. The language suggests that patrons had hardly been inactive:

> It is an hardship to be imposed upon.......and that frequently by patrons, who have no property nor residence in the parishes; and this besides the snares of Simoniacal Pactions and the many troubles and contests arising from the power of patronages and the abuses thereof by disaffected patrons putting their power in other hands, who as effectually serve their purposes; by patrons competing for the right of presentation in the same parish: and by frequently presenting ministers settled in eminent posts, to mean and small parishes, to elude the planting thereof: by all which parishes are often kept long vacant, to the great hindrance of the progress of the gospel.[44]

44. *Act concerning the grievances of this church, from Toleration, patronages, etc.* General Assembly Papers, SRO., CH1\1\26. 15–7, 14 May 1715, Sess. 10.

CHAPTER NINE

THE TOLERATION AND PATRONAGE Acts were not the only burdens to make life difficult for the Kirk in the period after 1712. In the first place, the continued advance into the higher church courts of political rivalry, evident during the settlement of Cramond (and, indeed, in the last stages of the Dull and Kettle cases), undermined consistency and tended to turn the final parts of any case into a lottery. Over the next forty years, the *Squadrone* and Argathelians [followers of the Argyll interest] engaged in a fierce competition for supremacy. Their posturing and regular employment of lawyers to promote their cause changed the character of church courts so that debates frequently evolved into adversarial set–pieces, where, to many eyes, the welfare of the Church took second place to a successful outcome for the participants:

> It's lamentably evident that statesmen and persons of rank and quality have of a long time been essaying to involve this church and the judicatories thereof in their parties and designs, and make tools of ministers to carry on their secular purposes. Anybody who has made any observations upon our Assemblys, Assembly Commissions and synods of late years cannot but see what efforts have been made this way in multitudes of cases . . . And you'll scarce now meet with a case, but in the opening of the debate upon it, in ten minutes' time, you'll see a partying of ministers and great men.[1]

Each side would go to considerable lengths to gain a moral advantage, or alternatively, cause a slight to the other. When the *Squadrone* Duke of Montrose succeeded Mar as Scotch Secretary in September 1714, it became vital for the party's credibility in London that it appeared able to hold the Kirk in check, and that the new king would not be embarrassed by any querulous petitions about the Toleration or patronage. However, just when the Earl of Rothes, Montrose's placement as Lord High Commissioner, thought he had succeeded in diverting such a petition from the 1715 Assembly onto the Commission, the "wild men" among the ministers

1. *Correspondence*, ii, 28 Sept 1717, 323.

mysteriously received letters from a source in London, telling them the time was in fact ripe for a petition, and one should at once be sent directly to the king. Not surprisingly, the recipients set about responding as the letters advised, and a war of words re-ignited. Although Rothes's will eventually prevailed, it was not without a disorderly struggle. To no one's surprise, Rothes later uncovered Ilay as the mystery *agent provocateur*.[2]

Not only did such feuding damage the Kirk's ability to speak or act with consistency, but it also took up inordinate amounts of the senior courts' time, often to the detriment of more important business. A typical example occurred at the start of the following Assembly, when, in the draft reply to the king's letter, the mere mention of the Duke of Argyll's prominent part in the crushing of the Jacobite Rising provoked fury among the *Squadrone* supporters and their demands to have it removed triggered two and a half days of angry wrangling.[3]

A second major difficulty for the Church was the inability of the English establishment to understand the niceties of presbyterian non-jurancy. However much unqualified presbyterians tried to distinguish themselves from their Jacobite counterparts, in government circles they remained the object of deep suspicion. This in turn acted as a damaging distraction from the issues the Kirk wished to focus upon. Thus when the Assembly Commission of 1715 did send a memorial of the Kirk's grievances[4] to the king via the Secretary of State, Montrose wrote back to say that the first priority was to find a remedy for the difficulties raised by the Oath. The other matters, such as patronage, would simply have to wait.[5] It was the same pattern two years later, when the Assembly Commission sent its representatives south to lobby both politicians and royal family regarding the grievances. They were told that "the great spring and cause of our complaints and disorders, was the difference about the Abjuration; that whatever grivances were spoken of, the Abjuration was at the bottom, and that there was a necessety of taking an effectual course as to that."[6]

2. Montrose MSS, SRO., GD220/5/458, Rothes to Montrose, 12 May 1715, 13 June 1715; State Papers, SRO., RH2/4/311, Rothes to Montrose, 5 May 1715.

3. Wodrow, *Correspondence*, II, 200–2

4. "Concerning the Grievances of this Church, from Toleration, Patronages, etc." *General Assembly Papers*, SRO., CH1/1/26, 14 May 1715, Sess. 10, 15–17.

5. Home Office Correspondence, SRO, RH2\4\391; Montrose to Carstares. (nd. c.1715).

6. "Diary of the Rev William Mitchell," *Miscellany of the Spalding Club*. (Aberdeen: 1841). i, 228, 18 February 1717. The petition did reach Parliament, but consideration was delayed for a month, during which time Parliament rose.

A third burden was that, by 1715, the Kirk was losing ground in the battle to assert itself in the episcopal areas. Its courts were beset by funding problems and no longer able to pursue legal processes to remove intruders and suppress disorders. Eventually, a circular was sent to presbyteries, appealing for money, and giving a telling summary of the difficulties they had to endure:

> The Church's debts..are . . . very considerable, counting here only those for defraying the expenses of sending preachers to the North, processes before the Parliament against Professor Anderson at Aberdeen, Mr. Currie at Haddington, Mr Logan at St. Ninians, rabblers against the Presbytery of Aberlour, and brethren of the Presbyteries of Kirkcaldy, Brechin, Aberdeen, Fordyce, Ellon, intruders into the churches of Burntisland, Old Aberdeen, Slaines, Raffen and others, processes for relief of oppressed brethren in the Presbyteries of Orkney, Caithness, Skye, Ross and other places . . . and there is now no fund for carrying on processes for removing of intruders, and prosecuting such as insult our church and constitution thereof.[7]

It was becoming a desperate picture, particularly as the Kirk's opponents appeared to be, by contrast, financially organized to meet whatever consequences might ensue from their actions.[8]

Modifying the 1712 Act

The Church's situation, however, suddenly took a turn for the better. In September 1715, Mar raised the Jacobite standard at Braemar, and the '15 Rising was launched, only to peter out six months later. In the aftermath, the estates of prominent Jacobite nobles like Southesk, Mar, Panmure, Seaforth and Nithsdale were forfeited, thus removing from many intruding episcopal ministers the main source of their security and protection. Furthermore, the government placed (for a time) a restriction on counties in their creation of JPs. To curtail their appointment of those hostile to

7. Engrossed in Minutes of Edinburgh Presbytery, 27 July 1715; SRO, CH2\121\9.

8. See the circular to Presbyteries from the General Assembly Commission, dated 2nd. June 1714, which complained that, underpinning all the intrusions and rabblings, there seemed to be "a general combination by enemies to run us down by force, contrary to law, and we have grounds to think that they do contribute money for supporting their party in those illegal practices." (The circular is engrossed in the Minutes of Edinburgh Presbytery, SRO. CH2\121\9, 23 June 1714).

presbyterianism and the Hanoverian regime, each candidate for the office was now to be cleared by the Lord Justice Clerk.[9]

Although there was no sudden reversal of Kirk fortunes, Parliament had been shaken by the Rising, and the loyalty to the Crown shown by the great majority of presbyterians forced many at Westminster to look upon the Kirk's circumstances, albeit grudgingly, with more understanding and sympathy than before. Thus, when the Assembly Commission sent representatives to London in 1717 to lobby for the abolition of grievances like patronage, the atmosphere with which they were received was noticeably more benign. Although it quickly became clear that a straight repeal of the Patronage Act was out of the question, nonetheless two *Squadrone* MPs, Patrick Haldane of Gleneagles and George Baillie of Jerviswood, were sufficiently sympathetic to set about putting before Parliament an amendment of the Patronage Act, whereby "no presentation by a patron, or appointment by a presbytrie on their devolved right, shall have effect in law, without the consent and concurrence of the majority of heritors in the parish; and the kirk session is to name one of their number who is [to] be reckoned as one heritor."[10] Despite its reducing the role of the eldership, this was still seen as a welcome step in the direction of diluting patrons' autonomy. However, the design quickly became entangled in *Squadrone/* Argathelian warfare, with the latter, as a spoiling action, duping the Kirk's representatives into a delay which saw the Parliamentary session finish before anything could be brought in.

Nevertheless, despite the frustrations encountered by the Commission's envoys, the *status quo* was not to last much longer. The Rising had signaled that issues affecting church and state north of the border could hardly be ignored. Accordingly, the legislation which did finally reach the statute book was the 1719 *Act for Making more Effectual the laws Appointing the Oaths for Security of the Government to be taken by Ministers and Preachers in Churches and Meeting Houses in Scotland* [5 Geo R, iv, sess 4 parl 5, c.29]. First, the unpalatable reference to the English *Act of Settlement* was removed from the text of the Abjuration oath and replaced with the requirement that the party taking it engaged to defend the succession of the Crown in the heirs of the late Princess Sophia, they being protestants. The change now made the Oath acceptable to all but around thirty to forty of the "unclear" ministers.

9. Whetstone, *Scottish County Government*, 36.

10. "Diary of the Rev Wm. Mitchell," 232; 240. The representatives were, William Hamilton, professor of Divinity at Edinburgh and Mitchell, who was one of the ministers of Edinburgh.

As for patronage, the legislation regulated the 1712 Act by declaring that patrons who were unqualified or who made absurd presentations could not thereby interrupt the time for presenting, but that the *jus devolutum* would take place as if no such presentation had been offered. Further, any patron who presented, after 1 June 1719, anyone who had not qualified, or who had not declared acceptance of the presentation, or who was then or about to be minister of another parish, could not thereby hold up the time allowed for presenting. The last limitation was the cause of occasional argument later, in that it was possible to claim that it forbade the presentation of *any* minister who was already in a charge. There was, however, never any real doubt that the clause's intention was rather to prevent those extensions of vacancies which arose when a settled minister agreed to come, but his congregation launched proceedings before the church courts to prevent the transportation. Under the legislation, an incumbent could still be presented, but the patron could no longer use any opposition to the move as a means of extending the six months allowed him.[11]

Superficially, the modification to the Patronage Act regarding acceptances might not have appeared to be of great significance. However, many seized upon it as tantamount to the liberation that had long been hoped for. Their reasoning was that since a presentation could only be valid if accompanied by an acceptance, then, provided no one gave their acceptance, the right to plant the parish would always fall to the presbytery. Although it was a plausible enough stratagem, in practice there were difficulties. On the one hand, as will be seen in the next chapter, the hope that nobody, however anxious to find a charge, would break ranks and accept a presentation was absurdly naive. Secondly, there was a sizeable minority within the Kirk who were reluctant to rejoice at the power of election being given to presbyteries while there remained no fixed pattern of how it was then to be exercised. By what means would the presbytery's choice be arrived at? What role would be played by heritors, elders, or the people? This had become an issue of growing importance since the Revolution, for, as was mentioned in chapter five, understanding of what exactly was meant by calling had become a subject for discussion and reflection, particularly among those of a covenanting tradition. It would be important, therefore, to look again at the way popular understanding of it had been moving.

---

11. Dunlop, *Parochial Law*, 252, 268.

Calling and Electing

It will be remembered that a case for popular election had been made during the Restoration period by John Brown of Wamphray (see Chapter 4).
Brown's views became a major influence amongst the radical wing of the
covenanting movement and, as one who was later to be called by some the
father of Cameronianism,[12] his writings continued to be treasured into
the eighteenth century. Central to Brown's understanding of calling was a
high doctrine of the ministry. He regarded it as a sacred invitation from
God, thus demanding from each congregation a respect, if not reverence,
for the office-holder himself. As well as this divine call, there was, he considered, a "mediate call," consisting of election by the people together with
ordination by the presbytery. That conjunct action was to be seen as the
work of God Himself and as such there could be no interference by an
external party.[13] This last point was of no little significance in that it shows
Brown opposed patronage not merely because he idealized popular election, but because he regarded as sinful and abhorrent any intrusion into
the Church's sacred business by those who had not been divinely set apart
by the Church for such a purpose.

Brown's position was why many from the covenanting tradition objected to the 1690 electoral arrangements: it was not simply because the
people had not a vote, but because a crucial proportion of those who did
possess it (ie., the heritors and, in the burghs, the town council) had not
been appointed by the Church to exercise any sacred office, but had been
thrust forward by the state.

It is noteworthy that when John MacMillan of Balmaghie left the
Revolution Church in 1708 (ultimately leading to the formation of the
Reformed Presbyterian Church), although his published reasons[14] for
leaving made no specific complaint about the people's electoral rights, the
scandal of Erastian interference in every aspect of church affairs was the
core of his complaint. It therefore comes as no surprise later to find, in the
Reformed Presbyterian Church's detailed manifesto, the conviction that

---

12. Douglas, *Light in the north*, 180.

13. see, Ian B. Doyle, "The doctrine of the Church in the later covenanting period"
in, *Reformation and revolution*, 223–27.

14. John MacMillan, "Protestation, declinature and appeal, 24 September 1708,"
in *The covenants and the covenanters; covenants, sermons and documents of the covenanted reformation*, ed., James Kerr, (Edinburgh: 1895), 434–42.

such was the thoroughgoing Erastianism of the 1690 Act, its effect was merely that it "changed the form of patronages," nothing more.[15]

Whereas the witness of men like Brown and MacMillan kept discussion turning over, it is not easy to say when demand for congregational elections evolved into a coherent campaign. On the other hand, it was certainly the case that debate on the topic gathered momentum from 1715 to end of the decade. An illuminating insight into the discussions that were going on can be found in an exchange of letters in 1719 between two opponents of patronage, William Wardrobe and James Erskine of Grange#, a lord of Session. These were two men who were part of what might be called the evangelical wing of the Kirk. The subject of their dialogue was the proposed erection of a new parish, Whitburn, at the western end of the large parish of Livingstone (Linlithgow), an area with a covenanting tradition. A group of heritors and other residents,[16] having subscribed the funding required to support the venture, were insisting that the patron was not to be permitted to act in the choice of any minister. This therefore begged the question, how was he to be chosen? The intention of the project's supporters was to give the franchise to the heritors, elders, liferenters and deacons, with the heads of families consenting. This left Grange and Wardrobe (who was one of the project's factors) to explore a range of questions: why let the heads of families concur but not choose? Why restrict any privilege to the *heads* of families? Was a franchise of all residents workable, for what right would temporary residents have? What established residence? The two men wrestled with such questions without agreeing any particular conclusions, but Grange was unconcerned. For him, the priority was to have the arguments aired and discussed: the time was overdue for the anti-patronage lobby to give more detailed consideration to what was to replace presentations, otherwise, "we cry out against patronages in vain."[17]

15. *The act, declaration and testimony of the Reformed Presbyterian church of Scotland*, (np. 1761), sect. 6.

16. They had formed a Board of Managers, under the factorship of: "Thos. Baillie of Polkemmet, John Davie, portioner of east Whitburn, Wm. Wardrop of Torbinhill (late Deacon Convener in Edinburgh) and Wm. Wardrop, Apothecary in Edinburgh." See, NLS., 1.22, "Memorial shewing the reasonableness and necessity of a new erection in the west end of the parish of Livingstone." 25 August 1719.

17. SRO., GD124 15/1186/1 William Wardrobe, apothecary in the Grassmarket, Edinburgh to James Erskine of Grange, 3 April 1719; Grange to Wardrobe, 24 April 1719. Whitburn parish was not erected until 1731. In 1759 the patron obtained a landmark judgment whereby as patron of the original parish he still had the right to present to the new one. (Dunlop, 222).

For the historian, there are questions which arise at this point, particularly, why did those of the stamp of Grange and Wardrobe want to go further than the franchise pattern suggested by the Whitburn sponsors? Was it simply because they were evangelical in outlook? It is a complex issue to investigate, since there was not in the Kirk at this time a distinct party of evangelicals, so much as a body of people who had evangelical opinions—opinions that were, moreover, both diverse and fluid. Thus, it was possible to be evangelical and against popular elections, just as it was possible to be the opposite and in favor of them. Nonetheless, what can be said is that there were probably several factors from the 1715–20 period which served to harden and confirm support for congregational suffrage. The characteristic of these factors was that they involved discomfort at the way the Kirk seemed to be responding to the doctrinal issues of the time, and, as a result, these encouraged a reluctance among anti-patronage campaigners to place the same power as formerly in the hands of heritors—or presbyteries.

The Kirk and Theological Controversies

One ground for anxiety was a suspicion that the Kirk was not paying enough regard to the need for theological orthodoxy. It is noteworthy that when, like Wardrobe, the Rev John Wyllie of Clackmannan corresponded with Grange on the merits of an all-inclusive franchise, he also added the plea: "go on as ye have don in strengthening the hands of the zealous orthodox ministers in opposing noveltie in doctrine and discipline."[18] The tone of his writing is of someone who has lost confidence in the way matters of doctrine and discipline were being handled. In that regard, he would have been thinking particularly about three high–profile cases that had recently come before the Church's senior courts. These were those concerning Professor Simson [1715; 1716–17], the Auchterarder Creed [1717], and the re–publication of the book, the *Marrow of modern divinity* [1718].

Professor John Simson was appointed to the chair of divinity at Glasgow university in 1708, but from 1714 to 1717, was twice investigated for teaching Socinian and Arminian doctrines. To the annoyance of the traditionalists who had led the attack, he was found guilty of some

---

Grange (see biographical note) was Lord Justice Clerk (1710–14) and an MP from 1734 to 1747. Wardrobe made his house available for Edinburgh meetings of evangelical ministers.

18. *HMC.*, Mar and Kellie MSS, 8 May 1721, 521.

minor faults only, and was allowed to continue teaching (although he was pursued again in 1726, this time successfully). Simson's alleged Arminian errors (which emphasized, among other things, free will as opposed to predestination) caused the presbytery of Auchterarder to react by putting an additional test of Calvinist orthodoxy upon candidates for licensing or ordination. Before long, however, a probationer complained to the 1717 Assembly about the imposition, where not only was the complaint upheld, but the presbytery was told that what it had said about sin and grace was an "abhorrence . . . unsound and most detestable."[19]

The mounting dismay felt by some at the way the Church seemed to be deserting its theological heritage, was then intensified by the Assembly's handling of the re-publication in 1718 of a seventeenth century work, the *Marrow of modern divinity*. The book, by the English presbyterian, Edward Fisher, gave a treatment of grace which seemed to the 1720 Assembly to be an incitement to anti-nomianism and the devaluing of holiness as necessary to salvation. It accordingly condemned it. Under the leadership of the Rev Thomas Boston# of Ettrick (Selkirk), Ralph Erskine# of Dunfermline, first charge, and his brother, Ebenezer Erskine# of Portmoak (Kinross), the book's supporters reacted by handing in a *Representation and petition*, signed by twelve ministers,[20] to the following Assembly, complaining that the book's gospel truths had been misunderstood. A year later, the 1722 Assembly confirmed the condemnation and furthermore rebuked the Representers for their aspersions against the Assembly and their erroneous doctrines.

It should at once be noted that it would be mistaken to assume that the Simson, Auchterarder and Marrow controversies *by themselves* damaged the confidence and loyalty of those on the pious or evangelical wing of the Church. To be evangelical was not necessarily to be a proponent of the *Marrow*, for example, and indeed there were those like Allan Logan of Culross, first charge, (Dunfermline) and Thomas Linning of Lesmahagow, first charge, (Lanark) who actively opposed it. Rather, as David Lachman's work on the *Marrow* suggests, its supporters "could be considered simply as a group of men of similar views in regard to the doctrines of grace

---

19. The candidate was asked to affirm that "I believe that it is not sound and orthodox to teach that we must forsake sin in order to our coming to Christ, and instating us in covenant with God." Pitcairn, *Acts of Assembly*, 14 May 1717, 519.

20. James Hog, Ralph and Ebenezer Erskine, James Wardlaw, James Bathgate, Thomas Boston, Gabriel Wilson, Henry Davidson, James Kid, John Bonar, John Williamson and William Hunter.

who were drawn together as much because of geographical proximity as because of their doctrinal views."[21]

On the other hand, if the factor of the *way* in which such cases were dealt with by the Kirk's leading figures is added into the equation, then it becomes clear why this fuelled not only disenchantment, but also a fading of confidence in the way the Church's courts prosecuted their business. The fact was, whenever evangelicals had tried to raise concerns about doctrine, or any of the things they considered blemishes on the face of a pure Kirk, they had found the senior courts of the Church organized to thwart them. It was no accident. As is clear from correspondence to and from successive High Commissioners to the Assembly,[22] it had been the constant wish of the government that the Church's senior courts should eschew any kind of zealotry. In the limited perception of government ministers, the obvious course for achieving this was by the smothering of virtually any kind of activity by non-jurants and those they considered as "wild men." Not only did this desire have an influence through all the controversies of the decade, but it is significant to note that virtually all those who led the charge against the *Marrow* supporters, for example, were leading figures in the Church establishment: men whose appointment to important charges, such as Edinburgh, or university posts or royal chaplaincies, had benefited from political favor.[23]

To many, especially those evangelically-minded, so long as the decisions of the higher courts of the Church were in the hands of such men, expedient would repeatedly take precedence over principle. Their dismay at the Church's heart-searching over doctrine, and the manipulation evident in the courts, knitted together to foster doubt whether there could be a satisfactory return to such practices as the 1690 system for vacancy–filling. This distrust was stimulated by the Kirk's response to the passing of the 1719 *Act for Making more Effectual the laws Appointing the Oaths* etc.

21. David C. Lachman, *The Marrow controversy*, (Edinburgh: 1988), 125.

22. Eg., GD 220/5/472, Principle Stirling to Montrose, 25 April 1715; GD 220/5/458, Rothes to Montrose, 3 and 12 May, 1715; SRO., RH2/4/311, Rothes to Stanhope, 5 May 1716.

23. They included: Principal James Hadow (St Andrews), Principal John Stirling (Glasgow), Principal George Chalmers (King's College, Aberdeen), Principal Thomas Blackwell (Marischal College, Aberdeen), Principal William Wishart (Edinburgh), Professor David Anderson (King's College), Professor William Hamilton (Edinburgh), James Smith (Cramond), William Mitchell, James Bannatine, John Flint, James Hart and William Miller (Edinburgh city), John Gowdie (Earlston), James Ramsay (Kelso), Allan Logan (Culross), Alexander Anderson (Falkland), John Hunter (Ayr), Thomas Linning (Lesmahagow). see Lachman, 158–9.

It was clear the 1719 Act would inevitably increase the frequency of a presbytery's exercise of the *jus devolutum*. Accordingly, the Assembly of that year decided to look again at measures it had drawn up on the subject for consideration by presbyteries in 1711. Because of the passage of the Patronage Act, the debate on these had fallen into suspense. It was now revived. However, it at once became obvious that the Kirk was not interested in reconsidering the privileged role heritors enjoyed in the previous election process. Except for a greater emphasis on the heritors being well–affected, the Overtures sent down in 1719, contained the same deference to their opinions as the earlier version. On the basis of returns received, the 1720 Assembly did add amendments, but when the proposals went down once more to presbyteries, the text still placed the heritors and elders firmly at the centre of the election process. The most heads of families could hope for was the right to suggest a leet to presbytery and to have their views heard when a candidate had been chosen for them, both rights only becoming operative if there was no eldership in existence.[24]

The unimaginative character of the proposals within the *Overtures concerning planting of vacant churches, especially tanquam jure devoluto* came as a major disappointment to those increasingly drawn into the debate on popular rights. Their dismay was not only concerned with the retaining of the role of heritors, but also at the way the original proposals seemed determined to increase *ministerial* powers, through rights of veto: "The laws have given us a Laick Patron which we justly complain of as a great grievance, and here the Overtures give us an Ecclesiastick Patron as if the former were not sufficient grievance."[25] Further disillusion was generated by a clause within another set of overtures which were issued at the same time. The *Overtures concerning kirk-sessions and presbyteries* were concerned with regularizing the status of general kirk-sessions, that is, the single body which came into existence when individual sessions within a city sat together. Among its terms was the provision that a minister, or ministers, could veto a sentence of the general session if they disagreed with it. For evangelicals like the Rev William Wright of Kilmarnock, or the Rev John Warden of Gargunnock (Stirling) who took issue with Wodrow about it,[26] *The Negative*, as the clause was called, was an unwarranted

24. Assembly Registers, 21 May 1719; Pitcairn, *Printed Acts of the General Assembly*, 23 May 1711, 458; 23 May 1720, 539.

25. NLS., 3.2492, *A letter of remarks upon some of the Overtures anent calling of ministers.* (na., np., nd., prob. 1720–21).

26. Wodrow was one of the authors of the *Overtures concerning kirk-sessions etc.* See *Correspondence*, ii, 567 ff; Rev William Wright, minister at Kilmarnock, *The*

expansion of ministerial authority and another depressing example of the way in which the liberties of the Christian people were being ignored.[27] In the event, both *Overtures* were shelved, but not without "A great deal of party humour, heats, and sensless debates about the overtures promotted with unaccountable violence, more than any thing ever I have been witnes unto, since I came to observe things,"[28] as Wodrow reported.

Most churchmen of evangelical opinions steered clear of supporting the *Marrow* or the Representers. However, this had not prevented them from feeling distaste at the self–seeking, party–motivated interference that had been taking place mainly, but by no means exclusively, at senior levels of the Church's decision-making process since 1715. As far as another correspondent of Grange's was concerned, not only was the equality of ministers being extinguished by the antics of these leading figures, but in the way the Kirk was being managed, religion was "neglected wholly, or is at best but taken up in masquerade and changes colours as the times do, or as the humours of Princes or great men dictate to them." In his view it was time for all the good ministers who keep quiet and sit still to resist.[29]

In terms of resisting, few would have considered the option suggested by Boston, who on seeing his comments on the *Overtures* rejected by the Commission, observed that reform was unlikely "till the present constitution be violently thrown down."[30] Nevertheless, as passions moved on in the 1720s from theological to settlement issues, the dubious conduct many ministers had seen made them continue to question whether the 1690 regulations were still appropriate. This in turn led them, whatever their theological leanings, to look with increased attention upon the role of the people. Thus it is significant that by 1730, even in Fife where division between those for and against the *Marrow* was fiercest, those who were doctrinal adversaries could nevertheless be found making common cause in objecting to forced settlements.[31]

---

negative discussed in two parts (Glasgow: 1721).

27. For a full discussion into the controversy, see, A. Ian Dunlop, "The general session, a controversy of 1720," *RSCHS*, xiii, (1957–9), 223–29.

28. Wodrow, *Analecta*, ii, January 1720, 339.

29. SRO., GD124/15/1236, Erskine of Grange MSS. Letter to Grange (na., [?] Rev Andrew Darling of Kinnoul, nd., c. 1721).

30. Thomas Boston, *Memoirs*, 338.

31. Eg., *Analecta*, iv, 136. See also Lachman, 473.

The Importance of Influential Churchmen

Before looking further at how vacancy-filling had been progressing during this time, more should first be said about the way in which those who
were prominent men in the Kirk were able to exercise leverage upon its
courts. The primary position of influence was the moderatorship of the
Assembly, and it is instructive that of those listed above in connection
with the *Marrow* proceedings [see n. 23], no less than nine had been or
were later elevated to the chair, some repeatedly. Although the election
was technically a free vote by the Assembly, it was a major responsibility of the Lord High Commissioner to use every influence to ensure that
the right person prevailed. To that end, the Commissioner would have in
mind someone like Principal Wishart#, whose great merit, according to
his report of 1724, was that he "would be entirely managed by me."[32]

On the other hand, missing the moderator's chair did not prevent a
dominant figure from swaying affairs within the Assembly. Because of his
seniority, not only was he more likely to be chosen as a member of each
Assembly, it was also highly probable that he would be placed on important committees, such as those appointed to prepare bills and overtures.
Even so, it might be wondered why, in open debate, so large a body as the
Assembly could be affected by individuals, especially as the great majority
of commissioners [delegates] changed each year. Indeed, writing in 1725,
Wodrow says that there were not above five or six that year who were
present the Assembly before. However, he also provides an understanding
as to how influential those few could be: "this [change in commission-
ers] gives . . . the greater superiority to the few that ordinarily are chosen,
because they, and they only, almost, are acquaint with the thread of affairs
and methods of procedure; and the bulk of members this way are much
strangers to the churches affairs till they come up, and [this] lays a good
many members open to be wrought upon by a particular set of persons."[33]

It is significant that this was a situation that held true for another
quarter of a century: ". . . no young men almost ever ventured to speak
but when at the bar until after 1752. The custom invariably was for the
Moderator to call for the opinion of two or three of the old men at the
green table who were nearest him, and after them one or two of the judges,

---

32. SRO., RH2/4/316, *State Papers*, Earl of Findlater to Secretary of State Stanhope,
12 May 1724.

33. *Analecta*, iii, 200.

or the King's Advocate and Solicitor, who were generally all of a side and, and were very seldom opposed or answered.'[34]

As for the Assembly Commission, senior churchmen there found themselves in an even better position to dominate proceedings. Although the meeting which convened immediately after each Assembly was usually well-attended, for the remaining three (August, November and March), numbers could be extremely low, especially in winter. In 1703, for example, it was repeatedly difficult to find a quorum,[35] even though this was set as low as 21.[36] This naturally meant that those ministers situated in and around Edinburgh would always have a potential advantage over others in pushing their views forward. Although the quorum was raised in 1711 to 31 (21 had to be ministers), it still remained a simple matter whereby, if a moderator had enough friends, " . . . he might signify to some members to come up, and so get the Commission to vote what he pleased."[37] It was for this reason that succeeding Commissioners always regarded the "shuffling off" of awkward items of business onto the Commission as the next best thing to defeating them at the Assembly.[38]

Ironically, when it came to selecting the membership of the Commission,[39] a real effort had been made in 1705 to make the sederunt as representative as possible. The Assembly's *Act concerning the regulation of the Commissions of the general Assemblies, and the attendance of members thereon* established a system whereby each presbytery's representatives at an Assembly would meet with their colleagues from the other presbyteries in their synod and name two or three of their number to serve on a committee. This committee would nominate members of the Commission, using leets provided by synods (in 1731 the committee numbered 34 ministers and 7 elders, of whom two were to be the Lord Provost of Edinburgh and the Solicitor General). As well as trying to appear equitable, the circuitousness of the selection system was designed to avoid any appearance of presbyteries simply creating another Assembly. However, how far it was successful in promoting fairness, can be judged from the remarkable incident which came to light at the 1718 Assembly, when the

34. *Autobiography of Dr Alexander Carlyle of Inveresk. 1722–1805*, (Edinburgh: 1910), 264.

35. Assembly Commission Registers, SRO. CH1\3\6.

36. Of which 15 must be ministers. Pardovan, 238.

37. Wodrow, *Correspondence*, II, 233.

38. eg., SRO., GD220/5/458, *State Papers*, Earl of Rothes to Scotch secretary Montrose, 12 May 1715.

39. For a note on the membership of the Assembly itself, see Appendix VII.

synod of Merse representatives discovered that one influential churchman they had deliberately left off their leet, the *Squadrone* James Ramsay of Kelso (who had been on the Assembly Commission for fifteen years), had suddenly been included, while a person they had selected had been left out. The Lord High Commissioner quickly intervened in the gathering fuss, drawing attention to the fact that Ramsay was a king's chaplain and therefore should have due recognition. Accordingly, a way was found to keep him in, and the scandal was smoothed over.[40]

Settlements After 1715

Before proceeding to the next decade, when political maneuvering within church affairs came into its own, there are two post–1715 settlement disputes which stand out. Of these, the first is notable for the legacy it left behind, while the other demonstrates that, at this stage, suspect influences were not always to be assumed when a minister was inducted amidst popular resistance.

When Principal William Carstares died on the 23 December 1715, Montrose, the *Squadrone* Scotch Secretary, realized he could now usefully re-distribute the preferments Carstares left behind. Accordingly, the loyalty of William Mitchell# of Edinburgh's Old Kirk, second charge, was cemented with the gift of Carstares' deanery of the Chapel Royal. Mitchell, like Edinburgh's Professor of Divinity, William Hamilton (who in November had been given the position of King's Almoner),[41] was an important churchman to have as an ally, and he was to prove himself steady during the embarrassing affair of Kettle church at the 1716 Assembly.[42] It was therefore with some relief that Rothes, the Lord High Commissioner for the 1717 Assembly, managed to have Mitchell elected that year's moderator. The impending business that caused particular apprehension for Rothes was the resistance to the settlement of John Hay, the Earl of March's presentee for the town of Peebles. Hay was very much of the *Squadrone* camp, being formerly chaplain to the Marquis of Tweeddale, as well as a protégé of Rothes's aunt, Lady Mure. Any defeat would therefore have been highly embarrassing. Despite Mitchell having to vacate the chair, being a

40. Wodrow, *Correspondence,* ii, 382, 27 May 1718.

41. SRO., GD220/5/652, GD220/5/600, Montrose MSS; RH2/4/310, State Papers, 21 February 1716. See also my entry in the *ODNB.*

42. It was he who moved the (defeated) overture to order the presbytery to obey the synod.

party to the case, the vote went the Commissioner's way, and the reluctant presbytery of Peebles was told to obey the synod's order to proceed with Hay's settlement.

The anxiety at once arose, however, that since opposition to Hay was so deeply entrenched, both in the town and the presbytery, there was no guarantee that the Assembly's order would be complied with. Failure being by now unthinkable for Rothes and his party, an expedient had to be found. This came in the form of a special Act of Assembly which appointed seven ministers of the presbytery of Edinburgh to join with any concurring members of Peebles presbytery in order to effect the ordination.[43] When it took place on the 26 June 1717, it was the first example of what later became notorious as a "riding committee," the name deriving from the committee having to ride to the parish from outside the boundaries of the presbytery which was refusing to effect the settlement.[44] There were to be many more.

Meanwhile, at Bathgate (Linlithgow) a vacancy-filling dispute was unfolding which was in many ways a classic example of the collision of views which obtained in the Kirk during the period. With its covenanting background, the Bathgate area was always one in which passions would be easily aroused. Accordingly, when, in February 1717, the patron persuaded some elders to sign what was styled an invitation to his preferred candidate, then abandoned any pretence at consultation and issued a presentation (which the presbytery accepted), an atmosphere of rage and opposition quickly materialized. The intensity of the parishioners' antagonism successfully disconcerted the presbytery, but when the case was passed into the hands of the synod of Lothian and Tweeddale, the situation was at once entirely different. Since the synod's roll included the cream of the capital's ecclesiastical and legal establishment, the protesters found themselves out of their depth. Labeled "McMillanites" for their demands for what they called a fair vote, and unable to recruit a suitable advocate to appear for them in any appeal to the Assembly, their cause had little chance of success. According to a supportive pamphleteer, the synod was "bullied by some lawyers, etc, sitting as Judges tho' acting rather like parties . . . pleading for patrons and their rights (sound presbyterian elders

---

43. Assembly Registers, 11 May 1717; Hetherington, 204; A. Williamson, *Glimpses of Peebles, or Forgotten Chapters in its History*, (Selkirk: 1895), 25.

44. Warrick, *Moderators*, 232; *DSCHT*, 719. On the Peebles case alone, it is hard to see how authors like Dunlop could claim that, "For nearly 20 years after the passing of the Act of Queen Anne, no instance occurred of a presentee being settled against the will of the congregation." *Parochial Law*, 294.

indeed)." As for lodging even a simple petition with the Assembly, the protesters suspected it would only be handed to the Commission "where they could never expect justice impartially, considering that it is managed by a few in and about Edinburgh of whom they have got their fill already."[45] The presentee was at last installed on 26 December, but not before presbytery had been obliged to enforce the calling of his edict for ordination with the presence of a troop of dragoons.

However, despite the impression conveyed by the pamphleteer just quoted, it should be emphasized that the Bathgate affair was one of several which were in fact handled fairly and were not the victim of the base treachery that nineteenth-century polemicists often portray. There could be an honorable governing spirit behind the conduct of the Kirk's superior courts in such affairs for which credit is often not given. In truth, men like William Mitchell, who became the pre-eminent churchman after the death of Carstares, were firm opponents of patronage on principle. On the other hand, they were unable to accept that the Church could disregard the law, any more than that the Church's adherents could disregard ecclesiastical discipline, and so they acted accordingly. It was of course a happy coincidence for them that their views were not unwelcome to the political establishment, especially when their candidature for advancement was being considered. Nevertheless, not everyone was venal all of the time. What is true, however, is that, as the third decade of the eighteenth century dawned and the management of Scottish society moved into a new climate, it was to become increasingly difficult for ambitious ministers to place noble motivations above every other.

Summary

Despite the firm stand taken by many presbyteries, the absence of any spirited backlash against the re–introduction of patronage among the Kirk's higher authorities astonished observers like Wodrow. In 1717 he looked back and shook his head over "the strange indolence and negligence fallen in among us in judicatories these several years" regarding the issue. "In a word, we all complain of our hazard, and yet will not effectually set ourselves to the proper measures for relieving ourselves and this church and posterity. Patronages are complained of once a year in our Assemblys; and patrons, and those who favour them, begin to be easy,

---

45. NLS., L.C.3335.19, Anon., *A letter to a minister of the gospel, concerning the parish of Bathgate* (Edinburgh: 1720).

and let us complain on."[46] However, Wodrow was being unrealistic in his expectations. In the Abjuration Oath, the London administration had unintentionally achieved a masterful spoiling action. Before its passage, the Kirk was already under pressure, in the face of episcopalian propaganda, to present an image of stability and loyalty to the established order. Now it was obliged to continue doing so while large numbers of its ministry, for reasons obscure to those in the south, were disdaining the requirements of the law of the land. In such circumstances, spirited resistance to the Patronage Act would have brought little advantage to any but those hostile to the Kirk's interests.

Presbyterian loyalty to the government during the Jacobite rising of 1715 did arrest the Kirk's declining fortunes, but its continuing weakness had the effect of making it more susceptible to political manipulation as well as frustrating those who wished to see the Church assert itself in doctrine and discipline. This meant that even when the 1719 Act enabled most non–jurors to qualify, there lingered among the evangelical fraternity a residue of dissatisfaction. This arose from a feeling that, in its relationship with the secular world, the Church had somewhere lost its integrity: traditional Calvinist tenets were being adulterated, major decisions were being made on the grounds of expediency rather than principle, and those who had no approved status or authority within the Church were nonetheless considered worthy to take part in ministerial selection. The result was that a divide opened up between those who opposed patronage yet believed in preserving the rights of heritors, and those who also opposed it but who championed the rights of the Christian people—seeing this as an important part of the process of rescuing the Church from its Erastian entanglements.

The split was to prove highly damaging to the anti-patronage cause. First, as Richard Sher has noted,[47] it removed the possibility of a half-way house emerging between patronage and popular elections, forcing many to side with the government and the *status quo* rather than be branded as zealots. Secondly, as was to be seen in the period leading to the Secession of 1733, it distracted attention away from presentations as such, and onto the issue of the privileges of landownership, the raw nerve upon which compromise was always least likely. Above all, it played into the hands of the regime of the Campbells, which from 1724 was to drive all before it—with one hiccough—for the next twenty years.

46. 28 September 1717. *Correspondence* ii, 324

47. Richard B. Sher, *Church and university in the Scottish Enlightenment*, (Edinburgh: 1985), 49.

CHAPTER TEN

In this chapter it will be seen how political rivalry encouraged those in government to interfere increasingly in the workings of the Kirk, not least in the matter of settlements. To understand how this came about, it is necessary to return to the political situation in Scotland after 1707.

The Political Background

As already mentioned, when the Duke of Queensberry died in July 1711, his Secretaryship was abolished, and the administration of Scotland given to Henry St John, first Viscount Bolingbroke. It is possible that Lord Treasurer Oxford was assisted in making his decision by Daniel Defoe's warning to him that, "The Scotch Secretary again would be the channel through which all Scotch business must pass before it could reach the sovereign; this would make the Secretary as it were the ruler of Scotland."[1] However, if Oxford's dispensing with a Scottish Secretary was to make Scotland more directly dependent on himself, the plan simply did not work. On the one hand the volume of work required was too great on him, while on the other, it became clear that an acknowledged intermediary on the spot in Scotland was preferred by supplicants, and that the absence of one caused a lack of direction in Scottish affairs.

Pressure began to build for the return of a Scottish Secretaryship, although what settled the issue was Oxford's concern over the burgeoning power of Bolingbroke. Reviving the Scottish post and making it the single channel of patronage north of the border would have seemed a suitable means of checking him. This was duly done in September 1713, with Oxford's fellow Tory, the Earl of Mar, the appointee. Mar's weakness was that, as a Court servant only, and not someone with a large power-base[2], he was expendable. Thus when Queen Anne was succeeded in 1714 by George I,

---

1. MA. Thomson, *Secretaries of State, 1681–1782*, (Oxford: 1932), 32.
2. P. W. J. Riley, *The English ministers and Scotland, 1707–1727* (London: 1964), 254.

there was little incentive to retain him, and while he went off to the '15, the government turned to the *Squadrone* and the Duke of Montrose.

The Duke of Argyll's successful role in defeating the rebels aroused sufficient kudos to bring down Montrose in less than a year, but the *Squadrone* countered with a slandering campaign which ended in 1716 with the Campbell brothers, the Duke of Argyll and the Earl of Ilay, dismissed from their posts and the Scotch Secretaryship going to Roxburghe. Ilay was not dismayed. "Politics," he wrote during the war of attrition which then ensued between the *Squadrone* and Argyll interests, "is a continual petty war and game, and as at other games, we will sometimes win and sometimes lose, and he that plays best and has the best stock has the best chance."[3] Since the Campbells were the family with by far the best stock in terms of land and influence, he knew it would simply be a matter of time before power would pass back into their hands.

Their chance came when in April 1721, Robert Walpole was made first Lord of the Treasury and Chancellor of the Exchequer. Since Roxburghe and the *Squadrone* opted to align with the Treasurer's rival, Lord Carteret (later Earl Granville), Walpole turned increasingly to the Campbells. Ilay became Scottish Privy Seal, and Argyll Master of the Household. The brothers were to work loosely in tandem until Duke John's death in October 1743. Although the partnership was hugely effective, it was not always an easy alliance, and relations became increasingly strained as the latter descended into mental illness towards the end of his life. Nevertheless, they undoubtedly needed each other to uphold the strength of Campbell influence, and much of the slippage which opened the way for the rise of the marquis of Tweeddale in 1742 can probably be traced to when the two split in 1739.

In raising the position of Ilay to his manager of Scottish affairs, Walpole nevertheless was cautious enough not to endue him with too sweeping an authority. With Roxburghe's dismissal in 1725, the Scottish secretaryship was abolished once more, and although Ilay provided the main channel for patronage, he had still to work through the two English Secretaries of State, especially the Duke of Newcastle#. He was to be enormously powerful, but at the end of the day, Ilay was still a supplicant of patronage, not a dispenser. Despite such limitations, that the set-up came to work well was undoubtedly due in part to the shared aptitude both Newcastle and Ilay had for the business of management. It has been said of Newcastle that, "Above all he realized that success for the party depended

3. *HMC* Bute MSS, 618.

not merely on the results of elections, but on the constant refreshment of elected members by a judicious distribution of favors."[4] Ilay was of the same cast, as a newssheet was to comment: "All the electors attend his levee, his generosity is unbounded, as is his power. The private commissions he has to execute will make you wallow in riches . . . and preferment, besides a pension, will be your reward."[5]

More pertinently, Newcastle had a particular concern for ecclesiastical appointments. Although it is true Ilay had not Newcastle's privilege of grooming clergymen who one day could provide votes for him in the Lords, nonetheless, the settlement of ministers as chaplains, teachers and parochial clergy was of similar importance in his game plan. Clerical appointments were valuable not just in insinuating right–minded candidates, but also provided a currency for obliging friends and discountenancing enemies. As the Argathelians sought to advance their presence in university, local government, and elections to both upper and lower houses, it will be seen that, in repeated instances, a judicious use of clerical patronage provided real advantages.

The Settlement Disputes At Lochmaben, Aberdeen and Old Machar

As already suggested, when Walpole sought to consolidate his position after 1721, he did not preside over a simple transfer of favor from the *Squadrone* to the Argyll interest in Scotland. Not having a particularly high regard for either, he attempted to create a balance between the two factions, which meant that Roxburghe was retained as Scotch Secretary. Far from creating peace and stability, however, the policy caused relations between the two sides to deteriorate to such an extent that the General Election of March/April 1722 was to be the most bitterly contested of the whole eighteenth century.[6] The elections went badly for the *Squadrone*, but with Roxburghe still in office, they continued to fight their corner with all the vigor they could muster. It was this background which turned two settlement cases, namely Lochmaben and Aberdeen, into struggles of dramatic intensity. No quarter was asked or given, to the extent that

4. Basil Williams, *Carteret and Newcastle, a contrast in contemporaries*, (Cass: 1966), 30.

5. *The Patriot*, 7, 25 July 1740, 132.

6. R. H. Scott, "The politics and administration of Scotland 1725-48," PhD diss. Edinburgh 1982, 313.

not only were some of the Lochmaben case papers deemed unsuitable for reading out to the 1723 Assembly on account of the "indecent expressions" they contained, but, at the dispute's conclusion, both Lochmaben presbytery and the synod of Dumfries were ordered to record as little as possible of the documentation "that all memory of the differences that had arisen might be utterly extinguished."[7] This suppression, along with its convoluted character, explains why the Lochmaben affair in particular has invariably been misunderstood.

The important parish of Lochmaben became vacant four months after the 1722 General Election. James Johnstone, second Marquis of Annandale, who regarded the burgh as his personal fiefdom, had made a presentation for the charge only to find it challenged by one issued by Roxburghe on behalf of the Crown. Although Annandale's claim to the patronage was poor, he took deep offence, and intimidated the presbytery into holding back from proceeding. However, the synod, to which the Crown agents appealed, was much influenced by *Squadrone* supporters, and so ordered presbytery to continue with the royal presentee, the Rev William Carlyle of Cummertrees. Presbytery appealed to the 1723 Assembly, whose Moderator that year was the *Squadrone* James Smith of Cramond. The Assembly passed it to the Commission, who decided that the way to deal with all the presentations (a third had now been offered by David Murray, the fifth viscount Stormont), was for presbytery to go back and try the inclinations of the people and report back to them at their August meeting. This apparent regard for popular sensibilities was not entirely ingenuous, since it was obvious that the ordinary parishioners were overwhelmingly for Carlyle. However, Annandale and Stormont devised the ploy of dropping both their candidates and combining to support another one, Edward Buncle, a probationer. In presbytery's eyes, this development justified their now moderating a call at large, and in doing so, decided that the votes which mattered belonged to the men of "quality" (i.e., heritors and councilors) of which the majority were for Buncle. Then, despite an order from the Commission to refrain from doing anything, they went ahead and ordained him to the parish on the 27th September 1723, having put him through his trials with unprecedented haste. Synod responded by referring the matter back to the Commission, who, on the 13th. November, declared the settlement null and void and ordered the presbytery to admit Carlyle, which failing, it was to be effected by a

7. Assembly Registers, 20 May 1723; *Fasti*, ii, 214.

committee of synod. Carlyle was duly admitted on the 10th. March 1724. Roxburghe's authority had prevailed.

The Marquis, however, had not finished. The Town Council (which he dominated) and presbytery appealed against the conduct of the Commission to the 1724 Assembly, where the ensuing debate, heavily colored by political maneuvering, lasted three days. When it became clear that he was unable to prevent the Assembly deciding the Commission had exceeded its powers, Robert Dundas, the *Squadrone* Lord Advocate, proposed a face-saving resolution whereby if both calls were set aside and a new one moderated, he would see to it that there would be no attempt by the Crown to interfere by issuing a presentation. This was accepted, with the addition of a rebuke for the presbytery of Lochmaben for its irregular and precipitant conduct.

Thus the affair was concluded, and Patrick Cuming# of whom much more was later to be heard, was translated from Kirkmahoe, Dumfriesshire, to fill the charge the following March.[8]

Nineteenth century historians were later to make much of the Lochmaben case on the grounds that it demonstrated that the Church of the time was still forthright enough to stand up for the importance of the call when a presentee was disliked by the people.[9] Notwithstanding the fact that the ordinary parishioners were actually in favor of the Crown's candidate, such a conclusion is naive. To gain a truer reflection on the case, one need but note the remark of Wodrow, that the whole affair seemed only "insisted on by one side, to give a thrust to the present set of people in office, under the King,"[10] or again, there are the comments on the case made in a private memorandum for the Scott of Harden family, written around

8. Assembly Registers, 20 May 1723, 21 May 1724; SRO., RH2/4/400, Townshend to Earl of Findlater, 21 May 1724; Anon., "*A true and fair representation of the case concerning the settlement of Lochmaben with a gospel minister*" in a letter from a gentleman in Annandale to his friend at Edinburgh (np. 1724); Analecta, ii, 385; John Wilson, *The churches of Lochmaben*, (Dumfries: 1981), 40; "Lochmaben Council minutes," ed., J. B. Wilson in *The transactions of the Dumfries and Galloway Natural History and Antiquarian Society*, 3rd. series, lii, (1977), 154ff.

Carlyle was translated to Prestonpans (Haddington) and was the father of the celebrated Alexander Carlyle of Inveresk; Buncle replaced Cuming at Kirkmahoe.

9. Thus Cunningham, *Church History of Scotland*, ii, 281: "the people were not satisfied with the [Crown] presentee; and when two competing calls came up before the Assembly, it was thought most judicious to set both aside"; see also, Henry Moncrieff-Wellwood, *Account of the life and writings of John Erskine*, (Edinburgh: 1818), App., 438.

10. *Correspondence*, iii, 22 May 1724, 130.

1730. Although the anonymous author writes as a *Squadrone* partisan, the insights he provides can for the most part be confirmed. Writing about the Assembly, he seeks to explain what motivated one group over Lochmaben:

> [it was] merely in odium of the D. of R . . . h and the then ministry, by these very persons with whom the management of our kirk affairs is now entrusted [ie., the Argyll interest] who at that time humored the zealous brethren in all their whims and violently bore down all the men of moderate principles for serving the above named purpose. For some time after this, those who were generally called My Lord I . . . 's party in Scotland joined in all matters with the Hot clergy and took every opportunity to embarrass such measures as those of a different character were engaged in."[11]

This curious partnership was made possible in the Lochmaben controversy, because the so–called pious brethren's opposition to Carlyle's candidature was primarily motivated not by indignation at his presentation, but by their belief that a presbytery's authority had been trampled on by great men manipulating the Commission in order to promote his cause.[12] It was a perception that suited the Argyll camp in that it enabled them to make trouble without appearing to oppose patronage. For their part, the brethren were doubtless glad of the support, even though it obliged them to turn a blind eye to the blatant manipulation their allies employed at the 1724 Assembly, whereby, according to the Scott of Harden memo, "everything was managed, nay the very minutes were dictated to the Clerk by George Drummond#, Lord Provost of Edinburgh, who was for some time after usually styled the Moderator of the Lochmaben Assembly."

Hard on the heels of the Lochmaben case came the Aberdeen (East) settlement controversy of 1724–6. Equally convoluted and bitterly contested (and similarly misinterpreted by nineteenth-century commentators), it became notorious as the "Norland Lochmaben." Particular intensity was added to its outcome by the fact that Roxburghe's fall occurred midway through its duration, and since the presentee had been nominated by Aberdeen Town Council, a *Squadrone* stronghold, the Campbells knew that this was a crucial opportunity to demonstrate their strength. By this time Ilay had found the Scottish agent he had been looking for in a young

11. SRO., GD157/1392, Scott of Harden Papers, "A short memorandum relating to the situation and management of Church affairs in Scotland at least so far as the King's ministry or those employed by them seem to have been concerned." (na., nd. c.1730).

12. *A true and fair representation of the case concerning the settlement of Lochmaben.* (np. 1724)

advocate called Andrew Fletcher of Saltoun. Fletcher was not from a promising background, in that his uncle was the famous anti-union republican of the same name, but he readily gave assurances as to the correctness of his own thinking.[13] He came to Ilay's notice after marriage to Elizabeth Kinloch, the Earl's cousin, and a year after the two men met, Fletcher was made a judge [1724] taking the title Lord Milton; two years later in 1726 he was appointed a Lord of Justiciary, became Lord Justice Clerk in 1734, then Keeper of the Signet in 1746 until his death in 1766.

From the start, Milton shared his patron's interest in the correct handling of church affairs, and after watching the conduct of the Lochmaben case at the Assembly of 1724, came to the conclusion that, despite what Drummond had achieved, the priority requirement was a better marshalling of ministerial support within the Church's supreme court: "had it been organise[d]," he wrote in frustration to Ilay, "many weak brethren would [have] been stumbled."[14] Before long, he had the chance to put his strategy into operation, and it was to do with two important vacancies which arose in quick succession at Aberdeen. Clearly, Milton saw them as his opportunity to show what he could do. The fact that, at this early stage, he failed to achieve success in one case and made a mess of the other, possibly yields an understanding why, for the rest of his political life, he pursued similar cases and causes with an unrelenting tenacity. Certainly, there is no doubt that both incidents caused deep embarrassment to his patron. However, as will be seen later, there would be times to come when his reluctance to let go would act to his disadvantage.

The Aberdeen East affair had begun in June 1724, when Aberdeen presbytery found it had two competing calls before it, of which the one for James Chalmers of Dyke (Forres), the Council's candidate, was ostensibly the stronger, since it was not only supported by a presentation from the magistrates but also had the majority of elders. However, the Argyll interest countered by once again playing the evangelical card, and promoted James Ogilvie of Footdee (later St Clements), a chapel preacher popular with "meeting house people . . . and . . the meaner sort."[15] Milton's first task was to see that pressure was put on both Aberdeen and Forres presbyteries to make sure that they obstructed any moves by the Council to push

---

13. NLS Saltoun MSS. 16529, passim. How far he was from the chauvinism of his uncle can be seen in MS 16571, no.155, where his son's teacher at Winchester school writes: "he has not lost all his scotch yet, but is much improved in his language." (13 Nov 1737).

14. NLS., Saltoun MSS, 16529. 23 May 1724.

15. *Analecta*, iii, 283.

Chalmers' settlement along quickly. Then, when the frustrated magistrates brought the matter up to the 1725 Assembly, Lord Grange was put forward to lead the attack on Chalmers's candidature, portraying Ogilvie as the people's choice and demanding to know why the magistrates and elders had been given the sole right of call, as if the 1690 regulations still existed? The *Squadrone* Lord Advocate, Robert Dundas, argued equally forcefully in favor of Chalmers and why the 1690 franchise pattern still applied, but to no avail. Although the issue of who should be callers was left unresolved (as will be seen, it returned to haunt the Church a few years later), enough was done to rally the pious brethren to the Argyll cause, and the Assembly ruled that there was to be a new moderation of a call, during which the inclinations of the people were to be sounded. Scenting victory, Milton wrote to his man on the Council, Bailie William Forbes, coaching him how, in the meantime, he could damage the magistrates further by circulating defamatory propaganda about them. He also reassured him how he could arrange to have any electoral success they might have in the future declared void.[16]

Milton's plans, however, received a setback at the moderation, when many of Ogilvie's supporters were found not to be communicants, and so, with their votes disregarded, it was Chalmers who prevailed. When Aberdeen and Forres presbyteries continued their delaying tactics, the case went back up to the Church's superior courts, except that this time, it was to the Commission. This was bad news for the Argyll camp, since the often poorly-attended Commission tended to be dominated by those in and around Edinburgh, and their leading figures, the "bishops of Edinburgh," were largely *Squadrone*. Provost Drummond had managed to manipulate the membership of the 1724 Commission so that *Squadrone* luminaries like James Smith were excluded, but the 1725–6 one had proved more difficult. As a result, the Commission sustained Chalmers's call and ordered the settlement to proceed. Responding, according to Wodrow, to instructions from Milton in Edinburgh, Forres presbytery thereupon resorted to the ploy of petitioning its superior courts for advice, in his view "a plain designe to put the affair by [past] the Commission and land it in the next Assembly."[17] The ruse was not, however, to be a success.

The problem for Milton was that the Commission suddenly decided to discuss the issue at a special, *pro re nata* [for a matter that has appeared] meeting on the 30 March. Not only was he unable to muster his troops in

16. NLS., Saltoun MS. 16531. 10 September 1725.

17. *Analecta*, ii, 285.

time, but by then Ogilvie had gone to another charge. Although he tried to prevent the meeting raising a quorum, he was out-maneuvered and it went ahead. Unsurprisingly, all objections to Chalmers were swept aside, and the members of the Commission in the synod of Aberdeen and the presbytery of Fordoun were commanded to join with Aberdeen presbytery in seeing that the settlement was carried out on the 21st. April 1726, which it was.

There was, however, still the Assembly to come, and Milton had no intention of giving up. Once Mitchell had been fixed as moderator (he had recently defected from the *Squadrone* and was anxious to please), the rest was not too difficult. The anti-Chalmers side played the populist card of demanding the Commission's decision be recalled, because it had not considered the views of all the heads of families in the parish, but had (in addition to the Council and session) restricted itself to the opinions of actual communicants. Once again the support of the brethren was mobilized against the apparent discrimination, and this was enough to sway the Assembly to disapprove the Commission's conduct on the grounds that it had been too precipitate and had not paid due regard to the inclinations of the people.[18] Unfortunately for Milton, the Assembly did not thereafter proceed to reverse the settlement, for the reason that, originally, it had appointed the Commission to determine *finally* in the Aberdeen case. The implication of this was that its conduct could therefore be disapproved, but to reverse its decision would (as was previously thought with the Kettle case) be to undermine its status and function as a church court. Thus Chalmers remained, much to Ilay's chagrin: "I perceive the levites have been very rediculous about the Aberdeen affair," he afterwards fumed to Milton, and decided it was time to take action against those who had opposed him: "Professor Hamilton will soon pay the price of his impertinence . . . '[19]

How Ilay proceeded to show his power to reward or blight ministerial careers will be shown shortly, first however, it should be made clear that although the evangelical wing of the Kirk played a crucial part at decisive moments in the Aberdeen East case of 1726, it is mistaken to make the deduction that this was part of a spontaneous assertion of popular rights. The fact was, it suited the Argathelian managers to use, for a period, the sentiments of the pious brethren to achieve goals which happened to coincide. Past commentators have often read into the Aberdeen decision

18. General Assembly Registers, 15 May 1726.
19. NLS., Saltoun MSS. 16533. Ilay to Milton. 14 May 1726; 22 May 1726.

that it was a high-water mark in the Kirk's concern for the rights of ordinary parishioners.[20] Cunningham, for example, equates the case with
that of Twynholm (Kirkcudbright presbytery), saying that such was the
bullish mood of the Assembly, it disregarded the patron's presentation for
there, and that the man who had the voice of the people was inducted in
preference. Once again, this is a misapprehension. In fact, the Assembly
requested the patron, Lady Mary Hamilton (acting with her son Basil),
to drop her presentation in favor of the preference of the parish, Andrew
Boyd. Since she readily agreed to do so "out of regard for the Assembly," it
is hardly accurate to suggest that she was disregarded.[21]

Whereas it is certainly true that much support was expressed by both
sides in favor of the call of the people, it is wise to be cautious about making assumptions about the true mind of the 1726 Assembly. As was seen
above, the Argyll faction espoused the cause of the heterogeneous heads
of families simply because they provided a source of support for Ogilvie,
rather than because they represented the authentic voice of the congregation. That was undoubtedly for Chalmers. Despite appearances, in the
end, the least substantial triumph belonged to the evangelicals. The real
agenda was the battle for political dominance in Aberdeen.[22]

A similar lack of understanding has led historians to be equally
mistaken about the character of the settlement at Aberdeen's Old Machar
[1728–9], although, ironically, the Argyll camp themselves became lost in
confusion at a critical moment.

Old Machar was important to Milton since Aberdeen had proved
to be consistently hard terrain in which to advance Ilay's cause. He had
worked successfully on the Town Council[23] in order to have his man,
Colonel John Middleton of Seton, re-elected MP at the 1727 general
election, but "They are such rogues," he later complained to Ilay, "there's
no believing their promises."[24] The Council elections of September 1727

20. eg., Introduction to *The Life and Writings of John Willison*, (Aberdeen: 1817),
vi; John Currie, "Jus Populi Divinum: or, the People's Right to Elect their Pastors,"
(Edinburgh: 1740), 40; Hetherington, *History*, 208–9; Cunningham, *History*, 422–23.

21. General Assembly Registers, 15 May 1726.

22. See also, SRO., State Papers, RH2/4/321; 323; 400; Edinburgh Evening Courant, 18–20 May 1725.

23. See NLS. Saltoun MSS. 16536. 31 July 1727, for insight into Milton's meeting
with Principal Thomas Blackwell of Marischal College, whose niece was the wife of the
Squadrone George Fordyce of Broadford, Provost 1718–9, 1722–3 and 1726–7 (A. M.
Munro, *Memorials of the provosts of Aberdeen, 1272–1897* (Aberdeen: 1897), 195 ff.).

24. Saltoun MSS.16540. 24 February 1729.

enabled Milton to make progress against his main opponents,[25] but he knew he could not afford to rest easy.[26] Accordingly, when Old Machar (or St. Machar's) the premier charge in Aberdeen became vacant in early 1728, he made it an issue of major importance this time to have his choice, Principal George Chalmers of King's College, installed there.

At first the College tried to proceed on the strength of the call being for Chalmers, however, when the validity of some of his votes was challenged by his opposers, they fell back upon a presentation. Milton's enemies hounded Chalmers at the next presbytery meeting, forcing him to concede that patronage was "justly reckoned a grievance and not agreable to the constitution of our church." Chalmers's defense was that a presentation was necessary in law to make the settlement effectual, and since also the support for him was "attended with so affectionate a call of the most considerable part of the parish, I think it my duty to signify . . . my gratitude to the said patrons for the honour they have done me." [27] His description of the support for his candidature was a brazen re-casting of the facts[28] and failed to impress Aberdeen presbytery. It promptly gave the call to Chalmers' rival. King's College accordingly appealed to synod. At their meeting on the 2nd. October, the synod (which Wodrow's correspondent, James Brown, regarded as corrupt and unscrupulous) reversed the Presbytery's sentence and ordered it to install Chalmers. The Principal was duly installed in March 1729, inevitably provoking the other camp into appealing to the Assembly.

Since both the Moderator of the Assembly, James Alston of Dirleton (Haddington) and the Lord High Commissioner, the Earl of Buchan, were allied to Ilay, gaining the result should not have involved particular difficulty. However, through a disastrous misreading of signals, Ilay's troops proceeded to march in the wrong direction. Because of a private quarrel with Chalmers, Buchan's daughter, Lady Katherine Fraser, had formed an aversion to the Principal and had persuaded her father to use his influence to oppose him.[29] On seeing the obvious way in which the Commissioner

25. J.S. Shaw, *The Management of Scottish Society, 1707–1764,* (Edinburgh: 1983), 110–11.

26. see, R.L. Emerson, *Professors, patronage and politics, the Aberdeen universities in the eighteenth century,* (Aberdeen: 1992), 51.

27. CH2\1\7. 10 July 1728.

28. ". . . he had the Magistrates, Town Council, most of . . . the Trades, 12 elders and most of the heads of families against him," NLS., Letters to Wodrow (1728–9), Quarto xviii, James Brown, Aberdeen, to Wodrow, 4 March 1729.

29. *Analecta,* iv, 55.

resisted the settlement, many simply assumed this was the official policy, and so, anxious to please, fell in with it.[30] The result was that the settlement was rescinded and a new moderation ordered.[31]

To be thus routed by "the caprices of our viceroy"[32] came as a great shock and embarrassment to Milton and Ilay, and hurried plans had to be set in motion to have Chalmers re-elected at the moderation.[33] A struggle of remarkable ferocity ensued,[34] in which Chalmers was ultimately re-elected on the 23rd. September and re–admitted by a special committee of synod on the 13 November. The opposers brought the case back to the Assembly on the 18 May 1730, amidst a welter of objections and accusations. This time there was no mistake, and Chalmers's settlement was confirmed, but it had all been a ragged and clumsy process.

What was also annoying for Ilay was that the Assembly's unexpected annulment of Chalmers's induction to Old Machar passed into folklore as, to use the phraseology of the later historian Hetherington, "a clear affirmation of the principle that the opposition of the people was, in the estimation of the Church, more powerful to prevent, than a presentation could be to secure, a settlement."[35] As has been seen, the reality of the situation was quite different, yet evangelicals could see that, regardless of the reasons behind it, the incident was too good an opportunity for them not to use it as an example to encourage their supporters. Years later, Ilay was still deeply frustrated about the debacle. Writing from Edinburgh at the time of the 1733 Secession, he fumed to Secretary of State Newcastle: "four ministers who behaved themselves very insolently in regard to the laws concerning the settlement of ministers are suspended; it seems plainly to me to be the fruit of that seed which was sowed in the Earl of Buchan's

30. "Memorandum on Church Affairs." The author describes how all the "zealous chaplains" followed Buchan in "this false step."

31. General Assembly Registers. 15 May 1729.

32. Saltoun MSS.16541. James Innes to Milton, 7 May 1729.

33. Saltoun MSS. 16540. Sub-Principal Fraser of King's College to Milton, 30 May 1729.

34. Amidst the ebb and flow of battle, a breakaway presbytery formed itself and ordered Chalmers to appear. When he refused, they suspended him for contumacy. See, Archibald Murray, *The state of the case of the parish of Old Machar* (np. 1730), which is a reply to, [Anon.], *A letter from the north in answer to another from a friend in the south, concerning Principal Chalmers, his call to Old Machar, and the conduct of the presbytery of Aberdeen and the people of Old Machar thereanent* (np. 1730). See also, J. Farquhar, W. Osborn, R. Melville, J. Bisset (signatories), *A fuller and truer state of the case of the parish of Old Machar* (np., 1730).

35. W.M. Hetherington, *History*, 209.

Assembly, I believe your Grace has often heard me complain of the proceedings at that time."[36]

Appointments to Chaplaincies

In the aftermath of the Aberdeen East case, Ilay was determined to do what he could to protect himself against the embarrassment of further plans going awry in the senior courts of the Church, and so set about using his stock of ecclesiastical preferments to recruit support and move loyalists into key positions. Although it had not been customary in recent times for royal chaplains to be removed from their posts, he was true to his threat regarding Professor William Hamilton. Both he and the *Squadrone* James Ramsay of Kelso, were removed from their royal appointments and replaced with James Alston of Dirleton and James Hart of Edinburgh.[37] The ploy was but the beginning of a careful dispensing of what Milton called "confections."[38] In September 1727, both William Mitchell and another *Squadrone* chaplain, Principal John Stirling of Glasgow University, died, thus providing Milton and Ilay with more recruitment opportunities. Especially fruitful was Mitchell's deanship of the Chapel Royal, whose large stipend Ilay arranged to have divided so as to create three chaplaincies instead of one. The beneficiaries were the Rev. Thomas Linning of Lesmahagow, Professor David Anderson, King's College, Aberdeen and the Rev. William Millar of Edinburgh. At the same time, the demise of Glasgow University's Principal opened the way for the placement of a Campbell (Rev. Neil Campbell of Renfrew) at the heart of that *Squadrone* establishment.[39] The Rev. William Gusthart of Edinburgh received Stirling's chaplaincy, having previously written to assure the Earl and his brother "how much I am and ever have been theirs."[40] The fact that Gusthart, Hart and Linning were prominent evangelicals made the purchase of their allegiance a useful piece of diplomacy, although for non-jurants like Linning, some moral adjustment on their part became necessary: "one thing about him very remarkable is that having been appointed one in a Royal Commission for visiting the College of Glasgow . . . Linnen positively refused to

36. BL., Newcastle MSS.32688. Ilay to the Duke of Newcastle, 8 September 1733.

37. Hart received Hamilton's position of King's Almoner, a paid post involving the disbursement of charity money.

38. MSS.16529. Milton to Ilay, 11 April 1724.

39. Saltoun MSS. 16535. Ilay to Milton, 26 October 1727.

40. Saltoun MS. 16536, William Gusthart to Milton, 9 October 1727.

qualify to the government . . . but . . . very soon after got a chaplainry with a salary of £70 which effectually gave him new light and then for the first time he swallowed the unclean morsel which he used to say had so much defiled his brethren."[41]

By contrast, the Rev. Allan Logan[42] stood by his principles and refused to take the Oath merely for advancement. Nonetheless, Wodrow's summation of the 1727–8 appointments remained cynical: "We see, nou, that the two brothers cary all before them . . . And what a poor pass we are at, when six Chaplains and an Almoner shall byas persons to act for partys in Church Judicatorys!"[43]

Self-interest encouraged other conversions besides that of Linning and, before that, Mitchell. The fright given to Hamilton ensured a hasty change of heart, and as soon as April 1727, Ilay was writing to Milton, relating how he persuaded Walpole to create another chaplaincy especially to gratify Hamilton, "our new friend."[44] Hamilton was further rewarded with the chair of the 1727 Assembly. At the next Assembly, the moderatorship went to another Edinburgh Argyll man, Principal William Wishart. In 1729, it was James Alston once more. In 1730, it was back to the capital, and Professor William Hamilton again.

Meanwhile, Hamilton had set up a meeting between Milton and another *Squadrone* "bishop of Edinburgh," the Rev. James Smith of Cramond. Milton was gratified to hear from Smith that he was ready to change sides, but wondered in a report to Ilay if "pardon . . for bygones"[45] should not be withheld until Smith had proved himself by his actions. In the event, Smith's chance came when Ilay decided to bring to Edinburgh another desired agent, the Rev. John Gowdie# of Earlston.[46] Since Gowdie was tainted, in some eyes, by his defense of the supposedly heretical Professor Simson at the 1728 Assembly, Smith's influence would be crucial. The design succeeded, and at the same time as Gowdie was brought, in 1730, to Lady Yester's, Smith was duly rewarded with the charge of the city's New North Church, a move which in turn allowed Hamilton to be

---

41. Memo, SRO., GD157/1392.

42. Allan Logan was ordained to Torryburn (Dunfermline) in 1695 and transported to Culross in 1717. He became Logan of that ilk in 1727 and was a frequent author of pamphlets. He died 1733.

43. *Analecta*, iii, 8 November 1727, 454–5.

44. Saltoun MS. 16535, 1 Apr. 1727; MS. 16749, March/April 1727 (Milton to Ilay).

45. Saltoun MS 16547, "1731" clearly is 1730; Milton to Ilay.

46. See my biography of him in the *ODNB*.

obliged by having his son Robert fixed at Cramond. Smith went on to be given the moderator's chair in 1731 and was made professor of Divinity at Edinburgh the following year.

By such ways, Ilay and Milton built up their power base within the Kirk. While they were doing so, many of those within the Church who opposed presentations continued to look for ways to neutralize its effects without engaging in actual resistance. One possibility to be explored was the matter of acceptances.

Acceptances

It was seen earlier that, following the 1719 Act, there were those like Lord Grange who hoped that presentations could be defeated by the simple expedient of all probationers and ministers uniting in a refusal to accept them. It was, however, soon to prove unrealistic. By 1723, candidates (as at Morebattle in Kelso presbytery) were lodging *qualified* acceptances, that is, acceptances dependent upon the presentation's confirmation by a call from the congregation. Alarmed at the possible consequences of the trend, the 1724 Assembly requested the Commission to propose an overture recommending what might be done as to ministers and probationers who showed a willingness to accept presentations,[47] yet nothing was to come of the move. Instead, as was feared, once cracks in the principle of non-acceptance had begun to appear, further erosion was not long in coming.

The parish of Old (or West) Kilpatrick (Presbytery of Dumbarton) became vacant on the 11th. December 1726. The original presentee gave a qualified acceptance only to withdraw when he found a lack of support for his candidature within the congregation. As a replacement, The patron, the Earl of Dundonald, had the choice of John Millar, probationer, or John Pinkerton, the chaplain of his friend Sir James Maxwell of Pollok. In order to exercise his right yet avoid the same nuisance occurring again, the patron insisted that this time any presentee was to give an acceptance that was full and unreserved. When Pinkerton scrupled to do so, Millar drew up a form of words which managed to contain qualifications, yet was firm enough in its central assertions to satisfy Dundonald's lawyers. Despite this success, however, Millar was obliged both to apologize to an outraged presbytery for his boldness and give an assurance that his acceptance was not, in fact, to be understood as absolute. Only then was the settlement allowed to proceed, although in Wodrow's eyes, the damage

47. Assembly Registers, 26 May 1724.

had been done and the whole incident was a "wide step" towards unreserved acceptances.[48]

Wodrow was correct in his foreboding to the extent that when Principal Chalmers intimated his consent to the presentation for Old Machar in 1728, it will be noted that although his letter of acceptance made "much noise and give great umbrage to thinking men,"[49] he was not forced to withdraw it. It would, of course, have been difficult to make an example of Chalmers since he had the weight of Milton's party machine behind him. This was confirmed shortly afterwards, when Aberdeen presbytery tried to come down hard upon Thomas Ray (Chalmers's cousin) and removed his preacher's license for making an acceptance to a presentation for New Machar. Milton simply arranged for the next Commission to order its restoration and, even though the meeting had only been asked for its advice, it furthermore ordered his admission by riding committee.[50]

There was one, determined church court that almost got the better of the Commission on the issue of acceptances. When John Burgh gave in an unreserved acceptance for the charge of Foulis Wester (Auchterarder) in 1730, the situation was passed to the synod who promptly suspended him. The May 1731 Commission seized upon the fact that the synod had originally been asked for its advice only and declared that the suspension was therefore invalid.[51] The synod, however, had the perfect counter in its contention that the suspension had not been for accepting the presentation, but for contumacy. When originally examined by a synod committee, Burgh had apologized, declared patronage a grievance and said he was "heartily sorry he had done anything that might contribute in the least to the wreathing or continuing a yoke about the church's neck."[52] The apology was repeated before the plenary court, but when he was asked actually to withdraw his acceptance, he displayed "prevarication and juggling":

48. *Analecta*, iii, 478–9; 494.

49. NLS., Letters to Wodrow (1728–9), Quarto xviii, James Brown, Aberdeen, to Wodrow, 4 March 1729.

50. After Ray's settlement in October 1729, presbytery retaliated both by refusing to enroll him and by accusing him of "powdering his periwig on the Sabbath day." He was acquitted by the 1730 Assembly (but was later deposed for immorality and deserting his charge, in 1736). *Fasti*, vi, 66; Archibald Murray, *The case of Mr. Thomas Ray, minister of the gospel at New Machar* (np. 1730); J. Farquhar, W. Osborn, R. Melville, J. Bisset, *The state of the case of the parish of New Machar and Mr. Thomas Ray and the conduct of the presbytery of Aberdeen in relation to there* (np. 1730).

51. Wodrow, *Correspondence*, To Charles Masterton, iii, 2 June 1731, 489.

52. NLS., General Assembly Papers, *The case of the parish of Fowlis Wester* (12 May 1731).

synod accordingly decided he was guilty of deceitfulness, since he had professed repentance, "yet the penitent rolls the sweet morsel under his tongue."[53] Thus it was on the grounds of disrespect to the synod, a disciplinary matter, that Burgh had been deprived of his license. This meant that the Commission's decision could surely be appealed. However, the synod were shocked to find their case undermined through the record of the sentence on Burgh in the synod's minute book being worded in an ambiguous and "lame" manner. It transpired the Clerk had cast it in that form, according to one synod member, after being visited and subjected to pressure by someone "who was concerned for the patron."[54] The establishment had won again.

Burgh's presbytery (Auchterarder) was prepared to bide its time, and, as will be seen later, was resolved not to let qualified acceptances evolve into unconditional ones without a struggle. However, to the dismay of those who had hoped a firm stance was the key to relief from presentations, political control of the higher courts combined with a remarkable diversity across the Church in responding to acceptances, ensured the idea came to nothing as a national movement. An area where particularly there was variety of opinion, not only regarding acceptances, but patronage in general, was the Borders. There, the presence of sensitive consciences was often to set colleague against colleague in the starkest way.

The South and West

Probably the sharpest demarcation between fellow ministers manifested itself in the synod of Merse and Teviotdale [Duns, Chirnside, Kelso, Jedburgh, Earlston and Selkirk presbyteries]. The popular pietist movement of the praying societies had traditionally been strong in the area, and although figures like Boston were strongly against division and confrontation, the hardline nature of popular sentiment within many parishes made it difficult for their ministers to remain detached. This was particularly the case after the 1719 Act, when much popular indignation was directed against ministers who had decided to accept the re-framed Oath.[55] This

53. SRO., Miscellaneous General Assembly Papers, CH1\2\78, Rev Thomas Finlayson (Dunbarney, Perth) to Rev James Bannatine, 21 March 1740; Rev. Lachlan MacIntosh (Errol, Perth) to Bannatine, 6 March 1740.

54. Ibid. Rev James Mackie (Forteviot, Perth) to Bannatine, 12 March 1740. Burgh eventually abandoned the presentation—*Fasti*, iv, 272.

55. "Great was the stumbling and offence of the people in the Forest and Teviotdale,

pattern of hostility against particular sections of the ministry (as opposed simply to patrons or presentees) was a significant feature of settlement disputes in the Borders. In the violent resistance that occurred, in 1725, over the planting of Morebattle (Kelso), for example, the pro-establishment ministers[56] were blamed as the aggressors. On the other side, when there was resistance to the presentation for the vacancy at Fogo (Duns) in 1721, the presbytery's evangelical ministers[57] were held responsible for stirring up all the trouble.[58]

Eventually, popular disgruntlement within the synod area percolated to the surface in the form of a petition to the 1725 Assembly. It was signed by almost four hundred elders from the presbyteries of Jedburgh, Selkirk and Earlston, and craved, in the light of the synod's arbitrary conduct, that proper measures be taken for the tightening and defining of planting procedures, and that such regulations be honorably adhered to. Moreover, it was their belief that the fault for the mutual alienation in the synod

---

on account of the oath." Boston, *Memoirs*, 341.

56. I have here used this awkward phrase as a means of avoiding the description "moderate" since it is a word that can be misused. R.B. Sher, argues forcibly that the term "Moderates" should only be applied to "the party of Scottish Presbyterian churchmen that emerged shortly after 1750 under the leadership of William Robertson and his friends," [*Church and University in the Scottish Enlightenment*, (Edinburgh: 1985), 16; see also, I.D.L. Clark, "Moderatism and the Moderate Party in the Church of Scotland, 1752–1805," CU Phd. Thesis, 1964. It must be said, however, that such phrases as "person of moderation" [NLS. MS.16548, William Baillie to Milton, 15 June 1732], "men of moderate principles" [SRO., GD 157/1392, Memorandum of early 1730s], and "upon the moderate side"'[NLS. MS.16550, William Hamilton to Milton, 13 May 1732], were in general currency by the early 1730s, and clearly were intended to denote an adherence to pro-establishment, conservative sentiments. It is in this context that I shall occasionally use the term, but with a lowercase "m."

See also, H.R. Sefton on the use of the term "Old Moderates," as distinct from the later "New Moderates," in "The Early Development of Moderatism in the Church of Scotland," Glasgow University Phd. Thesis, 1962, esp. 2. Also, N. Morren, *Annals of the General Assembly of the Church of Scotland*, (Edinburgh: 1838), i, 318–21.

57. Although there were those like Boston, whose views had much in common with those of the other camp, by the mid-1720s, the groupings could probably be classed as follows:

Evangelicals: James Noble, Eckford [Jedburgh]; Thomas Boston, Ettrick [Selkirk]; William Hunter, Lilliesleaf [Selkirk]; Gabriel Wilson, Maxton [Selkirk]; Henry Davidson, Galashiels [Selkirk]; Walter Hart, Bonkill [Duns]; William Gusthart, Crailing [Jedburgh] (trans. to Edinburgh in 1721).

Moderate men: James Ramsay, Kelso; John Glen, Stitchell [Kelso]; Robert Colville, Yetholm [Kelso]; Walter Douglas, Linton [Kelso]; William Baxter, Ednam then Sprouston [Kelso]; John Pollock, Roxburgh [Kelso].

58. Duns Presbytery Minutes, SRO, CH2/113/5. 2 January 1722.

was not simply patronage itself, but could be directed to those clergy who indulged in the "detestable practice of solliciting in order to obtain presentations from patrons and [their] undue manner of patching up and sustaining pretended calls from the people, by virtue whereof . . . parishes are woefully set at variance among themselves, [and] very bad impressions made upon the minds of many others of their neighbourhood about, concerning their pastors."[59]

As well as pointing out the ministers' defects of character it will be noted that there was also reference to the erratic and unpredictable way in which vacancies could be handled.[60] This was a frustration that was shared across the country. Indeed, at the same time as the petition, Wodrow was also recording his dissatisfaction that, "cases are so various about settlements, that scarce one rule can be laid down."[61] The Scott of Harden memo complained similarly: "those [churchmen] chiefly entrusted in this country . . . are at no pains to preserve in the Kirk one, regular and uniform way of acting, but are zealous and remiss in causes perfectly parallel, only as idle party views and the serving of particular persons influence them."[62] This absence of consistency throughout the church courts was yet another cause of damage to popular perceptions of the Kirk, to which was added the further annoyance of knowing that, even if it had used wrong procedure, the decisions of the Commission would not lightly be reversed if it was believed its status would then be threatened.

There was yet another important ingredient which added to the disturbances within the Borders area and it became a further source of hostility towards a section of the synod's ministers. It stemmed from what had been happening in neighboring Galloway. It was there that landowners' enclosing of land in order to maximize profit on the cattle trade had led to violent protest and vandalism by dispossessed tenants and cottars. The Levellers' Revolt, as it came to be known, caused consternation both in Edinburgh and London, and troops were eventually employed to quell the

59. General Assembly Registers, 17 May 1725.

60. Formally in 1715, and thereafter by implication, the Assembly had emphasized the need for presbyteries to obtain the consent of the people when planting charges, yet it had not itself felt constrained by the absence of any call when deciding the cases of Fogo and Morebattle. cf., Cunningham's assertion: "Between 1712 and 1730 . . . no case is known of a settlement without a call," *History*, 422.

61. *Correspondence*, iii, 19 May 1725, 206. See also, *Analecta*, iii, May 1725, 195: "if Patronages continou, the church will of necessity be oblidged to lay doun rules which they have not yet done to ridd marches [define boundaries] as to such are callers."

62. Scott of Harden memo.

tide of disturbances. Early in 1724, the presbytery of Kirkcudbright had appointed a fast with a view to promoting a good harvest—not unusual in rural areas at seed-time—but had also allowed each parish minister to add on "parochial reasons" for the observance. Most ministers thereupon added as a reason "the great devastations made of Christian people by enclosures."[63] By the time news of this had reached Edinburgh, it was represented as the Galloway ministers stirring up the people against the landlords. A shocked Assembly promptly passed an Act condemning the tumults and, in ordering it to be read from pulpits, strictly forbade any minister from giving any expression of encouragement to the miscreants, but rather that he should show the people their sinfulness.[64] Since it was already thought locally that the ministers should have spoken out more against the greed of the proprietors (who were naturally supported by the authorities),[65] the Assembly's action fuelled disillusion in the south and west, and almost certainly added to the fury of the many zealous brethren in Morebattle against the synod, when it tried to install the presentee of the Secretary of State, the Duke of Roxburghe. "Never," reported one observer, "was there such a spirit of rebellion against all order and government as rages universally in this country." Eventually the trouble was to die down, but only, the same writer feared, until "they are again blown up to madness by something from the Assembly."[66]

The resentment engendered by the Kirk's weakness in resisting powerful patrons who, like Roxburghe, insisted on the implementation of their presentations, naturally facilitated the exodus of parishioners to the meeting houses. Indeed, in the case of Morebattle, as early as August 1725, the elders were being investigated for refusing to do their duties, and by April 1727 their application to demit office and go elsewhere had been accepted.[67] The crowning despair for evangelically–minded churchmen,

63. NLS., Saltoun MSS., 16529, Milton to Ilay, 30 May 1724.

64. Assembly Registers, 27 May 1724; Wodrow, *Correspondence*, iii, 27 May 1724.

65. Anon., *News from Galloway; or the poor man's plea against his landlord, in a letter to a friend*, [np., c. 1724]; Anon., *An account of the reasons of some people in Galloway, their meetings anent public grievances through enclosures* (np., 1724). Ian Whyte in his article, "Rural transformation and lowland society" feels that it was generally recognized that landowners had overstepped the mark. See, *Modern Scottish History 1707 to the present*, eds., A. Cooke, I. Donnachie, A. Macsween, C.A. Whatley, i, 95.

66. *HMC.*, Roxburghe MSS., xiv, 54–5, Sir William Bennet of Grubet to Countess of Roxburghe, 18 April 1725; 13 May 1725.

67. J. Tait, *Border Church Life*, (Edinburgh: 1911) i, 57. They were initially deposed by the presbytery, on 3 May 1726, but the synod on appeal recommended the deposition be removed and the elders be allowed to demit. Presbytery complied on the 19 April 1727.

locally and nationally, however, was now to come with the conduct of the vacancy at Hutton (Chirnside) in 1727.

Hutton

Hutton became vacant on the 3rd. September, and was of immediate personal interest to Milton in that he was seeking a charge in the area for Robert Waugh, the chaplain to his father-in-law, Sir Francis Kinloch of Gilmerton. The patronage of the church was held jointly by the Crown and the Earldom of Home. Since the curators of the under–age 8th. Earl included another relative of Milton's, Ninian Home of Billie, there was little difficulty in having the presentations drafted and lodged with the Presbytery on the 30th. January 1728.

Milton's action provoked the *Squadrone* Earl of Marchmont into organizing a rival call to his own minister, the Rev, John Hume of Polwarth, and, following the earlier ploy of the Argathelians, recruited support for it among the evangelical brethren, claiming Hume was the people's choice. The dispute came to the 1728 Commission who ordered Waugh's installation. Contrived delays and allegations of scandal led, however, to nothing being done until it came before the 1730 Assembly, on appeal by Hume's supporters. In reality, the appellants had a good case for having the Assembly overturn the Commission's sentence. On the one hand, the 1729 Assembly had, in attesting the Commission's minute book, already refused to approve its conduct regarding Hutton. Furthermore, as they pointed out, such a ruling could do little harm to the Commission's integrity since, unlike Aberdeen and Kettle, no actual settlement had taken place.

The outcome, however, was a manipulative triumph on the part of the moderator, Professor William Hamilton. When it came to the vote, the Commission, who should have been excluded as parties, were allowed to stay by Hamilton on the grounds that their division of opinion was so balanced as to make no difference to the outcome. In fact, the result, in Waugh's favor, was decided by four votes. When the losers later studied the sederunt, they discovered a "cheat [had been] put on them, and they would have gained more than the four votes, by which Not Reverse carried."[68]

The result left the evangelical wing of the Assembly outraged. They had centered the issue upon the Kirk's ignoring its own principles in allowing the wishes of the people to be overruled by the tyranny of patronage.

68. *Analecta*, iv, 128; Assembly Registers, 22 May 1730; Printed Assembly Commission Paper: William Grant, *The case of the parish of Hutton* (np. 1730).

Now they found that political chicanery had made their arguments pointless. Deciding to fight back, around a dozen returned the next day and attempted to register dissent at the decision, but the Assembly, considering that to allow such an action might disturb the peace of the Church, refused to record the dissents.[69] Understandably, this heightened the group's indignation, and determined them to publish and circulate nationally their reasons of dissent[70] along with an invitation for sympathizers to join with them.

Seeing that the incident was not to be forgotten, the Assembly panicked, becoming fearful that the use of dissents might be turned into a damaging weapon if the practice were allowed to be used unchecked. Accordingly, two days later, it passed an Act, appointing that, "reasons of dissent against the determination of Church judicatories . . . shall not be entered in the register, but be kept *in retentis*, to be laid before the superior judicatories."[71] Clearly, few things could be more alienating for a group that made much of scruples of conscience than to be denied means of expressing them. As Hetherington was later to comment: "This Act contains evidently the essence of ecclesiastical despotism, and is contrary to the very spirit of a church court, which being essentially a court of conscience . . . it never can with propriety refuse to its members the right of exonerating their own conscience."[72]

The aspirant dissenters agreed, as evidenced by the events which followed thereafter and which culminated in the 1733 Secession. Thus the Hutton case was a landmark, in that it brought much festering anger about patronage, as well as mounting disillusion with the integrity of the Kirk, to a head. Milton had won the Hutton affair, but his success was not without its repercussions.

---

69. SRO., State Papers, (RH2\4\330) Earl of Loudoun to ? Ilay, 23 May 1730; Assembly Registers, 23 May 1730.

70. These were (1), that the Commission should have been excluded from voting, and (2), that the settlement was contrary to the principles of the Church, which were that no one should be admitted to a charge solely on a presentation without the consent of the people. According to Wodrow, the seminal group of dissenters were: "Mr James Hog, Mr Ebenezer Erskin, Mr A. Darling, Mr Moncreife of Kilfergie, Mr Henry Erskin, Mr J. Forbes, and some others from the North; Mr H. Hunter, Mr Allan Logan, Coll Erskin, Mr Ch. Erskin of Edenhead, and others." *Analecta*, iv, 128.

71. Pitcairn, *Assembly Acts*, Sess. 15, May 25, 1730, 612.

72. Hetherington, 209

Summary

The controversies of Lochmaben and Aberdeen highlighted several realities about the Scottish Church. First, they underlined how, notwithstanding the absence of bishops, prominent individuals wielded enormous influence, and that whoever controlled those men could rely upon a high rate of success in the Kirk's senior courts. Secondly, they showed that, sooner or later, the Church would have to settle the matter of who precisely was eligible to be classed as a legitimate caller, when calls were moderated.

Amongst many—and not just those of an evangelical disposition—all the settlements outlined above served to continue what was discussed in the last chapter, namely a sense of disillusion with the integrity of the Kirk. Laxity over theological issues, refusal to stand fast against the principle of patronage, the venality of leading churchmen, the blatant manipulating of church courts and traditions by political rivals, the refusal to clamp down on acceptances, the disallowing of dissents—all combined to trouble the conscience of a large proportion of the ministry. What was beyond the Kirk to agree upon, however, was a fitting and unifying response.

CHAPTER ELEVEN

For authors like John Brown in his classic *An historical account of the rise and progress of the Secession* (Edinburgh: 1775), the schism that was to begin in 1733 stemmed from a culmination of those discontents which had been building up since the Union among the evangelical fraternity, and where the final straw was an Assembly Overture which sought to place the franchise for ministerial elections (when the right of presentation had fallen to the presbytery) solely in the hands of heritors and elders. Since this denouement could not have been unconnected with the Ilay/ Milton administration's policy on settlements, it requires to be considered what contributions they made to what ultimately triggered the drama of 1733, and whether it was deliberate or accidental.

The Approach to 1733

Ilay was now to be heavily involved in two settlement disputes, Renfrew and Edinburgh's West Kirk, and whereas it was the latter that caused particular scandal, both displayed not only manipulation but also a remarkable incompetence. This last was to add particular force to the evangelicals' complaints, since it nullified their opponents' repeated argument that the state's managing the Church in an orderly way was for its own good. They now could ask, how could it be for the Kirk's good, if government management showed itself to be bungling and confused?

Ilay's first mistake concerned a successor to Neil Campbell of Renfrew, who, thanks to the Earl's patronage, had been made principal of Glasgow University in January 1728. Renfrew was a sensitive area, being one of the four burghs which made up, for him, the "ticklish"[1] parliamentary seat of Glasgow District. After several months, Ilay thought he had found the right man for the situation in the Rev. John McDermid of Ayr, second charge, and proceeded to issue and, in the face of dogged opposition from most of the parish, promote his presentation though the

---

1. NLS., Saltoun MS 17532, Notes on Parliamentary Elections, 1727–54.

church courts. Unfortunately, however, it was only after Ilay had publicly committed his forces to pushing the settlement through the 1730 Assembly, that McDermid revealed that, having thought more about it, he was happy at Ayr and would really prefer not to go to Renfrew. He accordingly withdrew his acceptance. It was a bombshell that effectively rendered the cause hopeless. The Assembly thereupon vetoed the translation, leaving the Argyll camp embarrassed and humiliated.[2]

Worse was to follow shortly afterwards over what was to become one of the most famous settlement disputes of the eighteenth century, that of Edinburgh's West Kirk (also called St. Cuthberts).

The West Kirk Settlement Case

When a vacancy arose in the first charge of the West Kirk, Ilay and Milton decided they could do worse than indulge the preferences of the holder of the second charge, Neil MacVicar. For some time, MacVicar had given every indication that he was a loyal and useful lieutenant, and had, in 1729, well-earned his reward of the post of King's Almoner in succession to the deceased Hart. He was also the only Gaelic-speaking minister in the city and was therefore a useful influence to have within the highland community. Accordingly, Ilay and Milton agreed to humor him when he asked that the candidate for the first charge be Robert Jardine# of Glencairn (Penpont)—someone who, like him, was of an evangelical bent. Because of his leanings, MacVicar was also keen that the settlement should proceed on the basis of a call rather than presentation, although he would not object if it followed the moderation. MacVicar was asking a lot from his patrons, but, assured by him that Jardine's popularity was overwhelming, they again agreed, provided time was allowed for Milton to win round those of the large heritors who were doubtful about having someone of Jardine's persuasion. Rallying support for the plan, however, was not to prove as straightforward a task as Milton hoped, and as he was drawn increasingly into the situation, he compounded his difficulties by making two serious errors of judgment.

---

2. William Grant, *The case of the heritors, elders and other parishioners of Renfrew: their complaint to the General Assembly, 8 May 1730* (np. 1730); SRO., State Papers, (RH2/4/330), Lord High Commissioner to Ilay, 19 May 1730; *Analecta*, iv, 73–4, 127; Saltoun MS 16543 Professor Hamilton to Milton, 16 May 1730, MS 16542, Archibald Campbell to Milton 25 April 1730.

First, despite being himself unconvinced about the value of support-ing Jardine's candidature, he ignored and overruled the strong aversion that loyalists like Hamilton and Smith had to bringing a zealous man to Edinburgh.[3] It was a decision which meant that, as the case opened out, damaging rifts to appear. Secondly, in order to protect the king's patronage right, he should have insisted on the six months expiring before any mod-eration of a call took place. As it was, since he wanted to spare MacVicar (who claimed ill-health) the stress of ministering single-handedly for any longer, he agreed with Ilay that a statement be made that the king had resolved not to present for that occasion and that a call could proceed at once.[4] This meant that when they did eventually resort to using a presenta-tion, it was portrayed (despite their attempts to disclaim responsibility) as an example of gross perfidy.

Problems began at the moderation of the call, which was on the 24th. November 1730. Initially, everything was as expected: all but three elders and the vast majority of the petty heritors favored Jardine, while the great heritors, and those of the Town Council who had a franchise, were for the Rev. Patrick Wotherspoon (or Wedderspoon), a minister without charge but known as a man of moderate principles.[5] However, the meeting was then thrown into confusion when both sides started challenging the valid-ity of the other side's votes. Uncertain what to do, presbytery had no choice but to delay further. What happened next altered the entire situation.

At the end of November, Ilay was still writing from London telling Milton he was happy to keep his distance over the West Kirk affair and let matters take their course.[6] However, in early December he was outraged to receive a copy of a "very malicious" anti-patronage leaflet which was being circulated in Edinburgh. In it he found that he and his brother, as well as Newcastle and Hamilton were "thrashed." The Earl had no doubt that MacVicar's patronage of the populist faction in the West Kirk affair had helped encourage such boldness,[7] and that the original decision to be accommodating over the settlement had only served to foster unruly con-

---

3. MS. 16544. Milton to Ilay, October 1730. Interestingly, Milton in the same letter reveals that he did harbor doubts about Jardine: "If he prove troublesome as I fear he may, poor MacVicar will be the first who will feel it."

4. Ibid.

5. Saltoun MS 17601, memo on ecclesiastical matters, nd.

6. MS.16542. Ilay to Milton. 26 November 1730.

7. cf., Scott of Harden Memo, GD157/1392: "ever since his preferment [MacVicar] has been at the head of a mob in his parish against the authority both of church and state."

duct. He duly resolved to avenge himself on MacVicar and his evangelical friends by having a crown presentation issued to Wotherspoon, knowing that someone of his moderate principles would be especially irritating to them. The awkward problem of Ilay's having agreed not to interfere with a presentation was to be solved by Milton's telling the Wotherspoon faction to apply directly to the Duke of Newcastle for one, thus allowing the Earl to distance himself from it. Meanwhile, public opinion could be encouraged to blame the pamphlet's author for provoking the government's reaction.[8]

The presentation was duly issued on the 1st. January 1731, and the subterfuge of Ilay's guiltlessness was even given added credence by the Earl ordering Hamilton to spread the word that his patron was furious at being bypassed in such a way.[9] Ilay's plan was working, but he had underestimated the scale of the anger he was about to unleash. The volatile MacVicar and his zealous friends seized upon the presentation as a betrayal of the assurances that one would not be issued and pointed to it as proof that the word of the king's ministers of state could not be trusted. Suddenly, things appeared to be spiraling out of control. An alarmed Milton wrote to Ilay warning that "if some method be not fastened on to quiet this matter there will be a great[?] complaint from the elders of the Kirk of Scotland to the Assembly about patronages." He therefore begged him to take a firm grip on matters rather than leave them to chance and in the hands of others.[10]

Milton was especially worried at what the approaching Assembly might do about the situation at the West Kirk, the case having been referred there. However, Loudoun#, the Lord High Commissioner, was able to achieve the usual winning formula of getting it remitted to the Commission where, he assured Ilay, "it will be perfectly safe."[11] The Commission duly ordered Wotherspoon to be settled, but when Edinburgh presbytery decided to hold back from putting into effect what was so passionately opposed, it came back to the Commission of March 1732 for a decision on how to respond.

For Ilay and Milton the situation was now a mess. On the one hand, they were itching to clamp down upon the Jardine faction ("Any tenderness

8. Saltoun MS. 16542, Ilay to Milton, _ December 1730.

9. "The conduct of Ld. Milton and his friends in this affair was generally ascribed to their patron's being disobliged that the D. of Newcastle had been applied to [for] the presentation and had given it without his advice - Nay, I was told by Principal Hamilton that this was the sole cause of it," Scott of Harden Memo, GD157/1392. The writer says he knew the truth was in fact the opposite.

10. Saltoun MS. 16545, Milton to Ilay, 8 April 1731.

11. SRO., State Papers, RH2/4/330, Loudoun to Ilay, 13 May 1731

they have met with has only served to make them more obstinate."[12]) yet on the other, it was hardly credible for the Earl to maintain his pose of dismay at the hated presentation while at the same time have his lieutenants obviously on orders to push it through. On the other hand again, it was his duty to ensure that a royal presentation was not trifled with. Given the difficulties, his only option was to place his managers in the absurd position of having to prevaricate while in the meantime watching the controversy continue towards boiling point.[13] The desired result was eventually obtained, however, and Wotherspoon was at last ordered to be settled by a riding committee. It duly took place on the 30 March.

Ilay and Milton's victory was nonetheless a hollow one. Not only had they let a presentation involving the Crown become an object of embarrassment and public controversy, but they had in the process sowed dissatisfaction among their leading loyalists, who from the start had been far from happy at the way the affair was being handled. Their distaste was ill-hidden, as Milton's spy at the March Commission, reported: "three of our chaplains . . . laboured the point [against the presentation] with more keenness than I thought became them.[14] Alston, who was admittedly an erratic ally,[15] went so far as to abstain at the vote. He afterwards wrote to explain, saying that although he was a King's Chaplain, if he appeared in the Church courts merely as a puppet, what regard would his words ever command in the king's service?[16] His patrons were, however, unimpressed, and no further preferment was ever given to him. The displeasure was underlined at the following Assembly, when, having put himself forward as a candidate for moderator, Alston found that Ilay had sent orders that Principal Neil Campbell was to be elected instead, which he was.[17]

Good relations with the royal chaplains were further strained when it was noted that three out of the four who belonged to Edinburgh presbytery refused to join with the special committee to settle Wotherspoon. Following Alston's example, Millar and Gusthart also wrote afterwards to explain that their conduct had been on grounds of conscience, and that the Earl

12. MS.16548. Milton to Alston.__ February 1732.

13. See, Laing MSS., (Edin. Univ. Library), ii, 18/3, Report of meeting of the Assembly Commission on 8 March 1732.

14. MS. 16548, Colin Campbell to Milton, 9 March 1732.

15. "tho' unquestionably a very clever man, [he] is one of these politicians who by endeavouring to appear sometimes on one side and sometimes on another, seldom fail to render themselves odious to all parties," Memo, GD157/1392

16. MS. 16548., 9 March 1732.

17. See, JS. Shaw, *Management of Scottish Society*, 104.

could still be assured of their loyalty.[18] Their attempts at rapprochement did not deter Ilay from toying with the possibility of retribution.[19] In the end, however, he restrained himself.

Meanwhile, the vexations surrounding the West Kirk affair were still far from over. When the Rev. James Dawson of Langton (Duns presbytery) went to the church on the 12th. March 1732, to read the edict for Wotherspoon's settlement, a riot of such violence ensued that the Town Guard opened fire, killing one and wounding four.[20] The news of the affray caused widespread shock, and the immediate effect was to deepen the divisions within public opinion over the case as well as harden each side's resolve. The Town Clerk of Edinburgh, George Irving of Newton, typified the establishment side's desire for a sterner stance on patronage by declaring the necessity now was "for going thorough stitch" in asserting the authority of the law.[21] In London, the reaction was equally belligerent. Vaughan [see n.19] wrote some weeks later speaking of the great scandal caused there by the reports of the Kirk's impertinence in dealing with the king's presentations, and warning that "some of the sub-ministers had infused such notions and such stories as made most people here think a short bill necessary for ascertaining and [?]securing both the King and the subjects' undoubted right of patronage."[22]

On the evangelical side, passions were also rising and support began to be rallied for what Hamilton predicted[23] would be a violent push at the 1732 Assembly to undo the settlement. Immediately, the Master of Ross, one of Milton's leading managers at the 1732 Assembly, began working furiously to gain the co-operation of both the recalcitrant chaplains and the evangelicals, warning them that good behavior now would "tend much to free them from any great inconveniences by the patronages for the future, and to preserve to them the esteem and favour of their friends above." He reported that his words did seem to have some restraining effect, but he was "much plagued with the North Country ministers who are all zeal and

18. MS.16549. 2 May 1732.

19. "it was generally given out by his friends at Edinburgh, and was told to myself in particular by Mr. Vaughan [a Customs Commissioner and close friend of Ilay] that Ilay was much disobliged with the Chaplains and that some of them would be turned out," Memo, GD157/1392.

20. MS. 16547. Gwynne Vaughan to Milton, 14 March 1732 [the letter has been wrongly included in a bundle of letters for 1731].

21. MS.16550.Irving to Milton, 14 March 1732.

22. MS.16547. 8 May 1732 [incorrectly filed under 1731 correspondence].

23. MS.16550. William Hamilton to Milton, 27 April 1732.

fire about the West Kirk."[24] Some of them were "as wild as bucks."[25] His spirits were not raised at the opening of the Assembly when he saw that there were "four Erskines at the Assembly, two lay and two clergy, more than enough to raise fire in any society whatever. Buchan's brother [an Erskine] seems as mad as any man I have seen out of Bedlam."

Just when a battle of unprecedented ferocity seemed about to break, Providence intervened with dramatic timing. Affected, according to the *Fasti*, by the opprobrium he had attracted through the affair, Wotherspoon took ill and suddenly died on the 12th. May, causing the case to be abandoned. Although doubtless highly relieved at the news, Milton moved swiftly to head off any repeat of former difficulties. The Commissioner, the Marquis of Lothian, was duly sent to speak with MacVicar and bluntly tell him to forget having any say in who his future colleague would be.[26] Consequently, the great heritors were allowed a free hand to make a choice, and they settled upon the James Dawson who had served the Edict at the riot. He was admitted the 15 February 1734, on a call.

The Aftermath of the West Kirk Case

Wotherspoon's demise, and its timing, brought elation to the evangelical camp. Ross gloomily reported that they regarded what had happened as "a signal providence of God in their favour to spirit up the people to, what they call, their Christian liberty."[27] All that was now required was a rallying-point around which they could unite with a view to building up further credibility and support. This appeared almost immediately in the guise of an overture passed on from the previous year's Assembly *Anent the method of planting vacant churches.*

Since at least 1727, the senior courts of the Church had been pondering the difficult question of how exactly presbyteries should proceed when the right of planting came to them *jure devoluto*. For some, the tried path of the 1690 rubric was the obvious choice, especially if landowners were to be won round. To others, however, such regulations were nothing more than a version of patronage.[28] The debate might well have rumbled

24. MS.16551. Master of Ross to Milton, 2 May 1732.

25. MS.16551. 11 May 1732

26. MS.16551. Ross to Milton, 13 May 1732.

27. Ibid.

28. Adam Gibb, *The present truth: a display of the Secession Testimony; in the three periods of the rise, state and maintenance of that Testimony* (Edinburgh: 1774), i, 25.

on for some time more had the Argyll camp not been alerted, at the start of the 1731 Assembly, that more embarrassment for their administration was possibly on the way.

Soon after the court had convened, it came to light that a move was afoot to petition the king about the grievance of patronage. There had been such moves before, but this time there was an alarming number of new members present, all determined to push the petition through, and there was no guarantee that it could be quashed in the way the previous ones had. That the petition might succeed was unthinkable. Accordingly, a plan was hatched by Charles Areskine#, Ilay's solicitor general, whereby the hotheads who had come armed with anti-patronage speeches were to be diverted onto committees appointed by the Assembly to prepare an overture on the subject of planting churches *jure devoluto*. Areskine calculated that this would allow them to discharge all their passions on the issue of presentations, yet deny them the public platform of the Assembly on which to do it. Having given vent to their feelings, he was convinced they would then be more tractable. The strategy seemed to work:

> In these meetings, the brethren were at last told it ill became them to throw out hard things against patrons, when in the event of no presentation within six months, the right which by law devolved upon presbyteries was used by them in an arbitrary manner, the Church having never settled a rule where they lawfully might do it, and that no man could believe they meant anything other than to grasp at more power. This persuaded them, and was thrown in to divert them from pursuing the schemes they had down to themselves.[29]

The upshot was the overture *Anent the method of planting vacant churches*. Exhausted by two days' debate, the warm men on the committees agreed to the overture's reverting to the 1690 regulations as the template for congregational elections, but doubtless did so on the assumption that when it was sent down to presbyteries for discussion and approval,[30] the majority would be against it. When, a year later, they directed their attention to the presbyteries' returns, hopes were high of adding to the encouragement derived from the West Kirk affair. Initially, it might have seemed

---

29. SRO., State Papers, RH2/4/330, Charles Areskine to Ilay, 13 May 1731.

30. Under the 1697 Assembly *Act anent the method of passing Acts of Assembly of general concern to the Church and for preventing of innovations* (commonly called the *Barrier Act*), any new binding rules in worship, doctrine, government and discipline had first to be sent down to presbyteries for consideration.

that all had gone their way: six approved the overture *simpliciter*, twelve approved but with amendments, thirty-one disapproved and eighteen made no return. In the event, however, it was Ilay's administration who were to win the day, boosted by a highly questionable victory two days before, in the settlement of Kinross, whose presbytery (Dunfermline) was regarded by Milton's aides as a hotbed of evangelical fervor and a thorn in their side.[31] Since this triumph amply demonstrated the impotence of the warm brethren on the floor of the senior courts, Milton's people realized they had now within their grasp what they believed would "take the power out of the people's hands and settle many disorders,"[32] namely, a turning of the overture *Anent the method of planting, etc.* into a standing Act. The path towards that conclusion had been facilitated by the vagueness of the overture's original wording, which said that if presbyteries did not make a return to the 1732 Assembly, the overture was to be "laid before the next General Assembly to be passed into a standing act or not, as they see cause."[33] Claiming that this allowed the eighteen unrecorded returns to be treated as approvals, the Assembly voted to turn the overture into an Act. It did so amidst a storm of protests, including a speech by Ebenezer Erskine which contained some of his most quoted lines:

> What difference does a piece of land make between man and man in the affairs of Christ's kingdom, which is not of this world? Are we not commanded in the Word to do nothing by partiality? Whereas here is the most manifest partiality in the world. We must have "the faith of our Lord Jesus Christ," or the privilege of his Church, "without respect of persons;" whereas by this act we show respect to the man with the gold ring and the gay clothing, beyond the man with vile raiment and poor attire . . . It is not said that He hath chosen the heritors of this world, as we have done; but He "hath chosen the poor of this world, rich in faith, and heirs of the kingdom." And if they be

31. The Commission received a petition from the patron and his supporters which they simply treated as a call and had the candidate installed by riding committee. Assembly Commission Reports, *A short state of the case of Kinross* (np. 10 August: 1731), 3. Assembly Papers, *The case of the parish of Kinross*, 11 May 1732; *A short answer to the case of Kinross, published this day at 11 o'clock, 11 May 1732*; *Fasti*, v, 66. NLS. Saltoun MS. 16545, Roger Aytoun, Dalgety, to Milton, 27 November 1731.

32. MS.16551, Ross to Milton, 13 May 1732; MS.16550, William Hamilton to Milton, 13 May 1732; State Papers, RH2\4\330, Lothian to ?Ilay, 16 May 1732.

33. *Acts of Assembly*, 14 May 1731.

heirs of the kingdom, I wish to know by what warrant they are stripped of the privileges of the kingdom.[34]

It will be seen from Erskine's words how much the cause of popular elections, and the intensity of the rhetoric, had developed over the fairly brief period since Ilay's coming to power. It was the 1731 overture which most fuelled passion and debate. As well as a *Humble representation and petition* against it, signed by fifty ministers, there was also given in to the 1732 Assembly a *Public testimony of above 1600 Christian people against the Overture of the General Assembly 1731.* The latter in particular exemplified the language that was now being used. It portrayed the overture as only serving to "shut the gospel door of entering the Lord's house, [and to] open a window of human contrivance to thieves and robbers", to which, however, a printed reply warned that the complainers displayed "a tongue filled with venom . . . zeal without knowledge . . heat without light . . invectives without force of reason."[35]

The difference of opinion over the issue of popular franchise had not only become sharp but also highly personal. For the evangelical/populist camp, the greatest opprobrium was reserved for the hand–picked Edinburgh ministers and royal chaplains. As far as the former was concerned, all the Kirk's corruptions and defections followed from the latter's venality.[36] To be fair, it should again be remembered that many of those who followed the policy of the political establishment, whether highly placed or not, did so in the belief that keeping the Church free from fractiousness and dissent helped to protect it from the punitive repercussions that were often threatened from London.[37] Moreover, there were those like John Currie#, minister of Kinglassie (Kirkcaldy), who was an evangelical, a good friend of Ebenezer and Ralph Erskine and wrote fulsome tracts against patronage, as in *A full vindication of the people's right to elect their own pastors* (Edinburgh 1733) and *Jus populi divinum* (Edinburgh 1727), yet who abhorred the idea of schism and inveighed equally passionately against those who believed that any grievance could justify it.

34. Quoted in Cunningham, *History*, 284.

35. George Logan, *The public testimony of above 1600 Christian people against the overture of the General Assembly 1731 made more publick and set in its due light being a full confutation of their arguments adduced for the divine right of popular elections* (Edinburgh: 1733).

36. Saltoun MS. 16551 Master of Ross to Milton, 11 May 1732.

37. eg., SRO., State Papers, RH2/4/400, Newcastle to Professor William Hamilton, 9 June 1730.

The Secession

If the Argathelians hoped that the passage of the *Act anent the method of planting* would quieten the Church, the short-term effects were the opposite. The particular causes of rage were threefold. On the one hand, there was the fact that the Act had not simply revived the terms of the 1690 parliamentary Act, but had actually reduced the people's contribution: whereas before, the heritors and elders were, in an unspecified manner, to name and propose the minister (the congregation approving), now they were to hold a conjunct meeting (where the heritors would frequently be a majority) and then elect and call—the people's approval being sought only afterwards. Secondly, there was no attention given to the glaring problem of heritors who were of a different religious persuasion, or non-resident, being nevertheless able to vote on equal footing with an ordained elder. Lastly, none of those protesting against the Act were allowed to register their dissent in the Assembly record.[38]

A furious Ebenezer Erskine returned to his parish and soon after published a sermon saying the supporters of the Act were attempting to "jostle Christ out of His government." Then at the Autumn meeting of the synod of Perth and Stirling, he preached, as moderator, a sermon in which he declared that the Act was a wound to Christ and the privileges of His subjects, that since it wanted His authority it had no authority at all, and were Christ present, He would say that by it, "He is rejected in His poor members, and the rich of the world put in their room."[39] Although the synod was resolutely opposed to patronage, such comments could not be ignored and Erskine was censured, against which sentence he appealed to the next Assembly.

In what was something of a parallel with the preceding Assembly, before Erskine's case was heard by the 1733 one, the continuing controversy at Kinross was brought before the meeting. Not only had the presbytery of Dunfermline still refused to accept the incumbent, but some members were also allowing his parishioners to receive religious ordinances in their parishes. The question was whether the Assembly would treat the presbytery's scruples with a sensitivity similar to that previously shown towards

---

38. Adam Gibb, *The present truth*, i, 26; Anon., *A mutual negative in parish and presbytery in the election of a minister in opposition to episcopacy on the one hand, and independency on the other, instructed from both Books of Discipline by some member of the last General Assembly who protested against the Act anent the method of planting vacant churches* (Edinburgh: 1733).

39. Cunningham, 287–88.

non-jurants. In the event, not only was the presbytery ordered to enroll their colleague at once, but they were to be sternly rebuked, forbidden to dispense ordinances to other parishioners and prohibited from recording any dissent.

The Assembly's uncompromising mood continued into the hearing of the Erskine appeal and his censure was upheld. Erskine thereupon handed in a protest, to which three of his supporters adhered, namely, William Wilson of Perth (1690–1741), Alexander Moncrieff (1695–1761) of Abernethy (Perth) and James Fisher (1697–1775) of Kinclaven (Dunkeld). The Assembly responded by instructing the August Commission to suspend the four if they did not repent, and if they remained defiant, the November Commission was to declare them no longer ministers of the Church. The Commission found itself obliged to do both, and so on the 6 December, at Gairney Bridge, near Kinross, the Associate Presbytery was formed.

Thus the first secession from the national Church began to take place. It was provoked by a succession of failings and defections, most of which have been outlined above, and summarized in the seceders' *Testimony* of 1734, where the emphasis is on their disassociating themselves not from the constitution of the Church of Scotland, but from the prevailing party in her judicatories which had ignored the sanctity of Christian conscience, allowed heritors and elders to impose the people's spiritual guides upon them, promoted the violent intrusion of presentees, censured ministers protesting against what was sinful, used the Commission to settle ministers when presbyteries refused, corrupted the doctrines of the Confession of Faith and permitted preachers to entertain their hearers with "dry harangues of almost mere heathen morality."[40]

For his part, Ilay was glad to see the trouble-makers go. When Erskine appeared before the Assembly Commission of August 1733, Ilay, according to one observer, "attended all the diets and run down Erskine prodigiously." After deriding Erskine for his hypocritical zeal and labeling his followers a vile rabble, he concluded with the warning, intended for general consumption, that "the practice of presbyterian ministers ever since the Revolution had gone so much in that way of courting the mob that if the Union had not saved them he did not doubt in a very little

---

40. John Brown, *An historical account of the rise and progress of the Secession*, (Edinburgh: 1775 and 1788) 24; *A testimony to the doctrine, worship, government and discipline of the Church of Scotland..or reasons...for their protestation.* (Edinburgh: 1734).

time he would have seen the Presbyterian Government of the Church abolished."[41]

However, If the Earl finished 1733 thinking that its events would lead into a new era in effective management of ecclesiastical affairs, he was to receive a rude awakening. Far from tightening his grip on the Kirk, he was soon to find that, for an extraordinary two-year period, he was in danger of losing it.

Summary

The Ilay/Milton style of administration might appear reprehensible to modern eyes, but was hardly remarkable by most eighteenth–century standards. However, it did require a simple necessity: competence. The lesson of Renfrew and the West Kirk was that both showed a slippage in concentration and judgment that added a seasoning of derision to the anger of the evangelicals. Moreover, it showed that the regime was vulnerable. Such things certainly did nothing to hinder the path to secession. Defiance was in the air, and, as Ilay was to find, it was not going to disappear as he had hoped.

41. Central Region Archives, GD189 2/132, Unsigned letter [?Alexander Bayne] to William Murray of Polmaise, 10 August 1733.

Chapter Twelve

Back in October 1725, Ilay had written to the Duke of Newcastle in London describing to him the administration he was setting up in Scotland. It would be one, he assured the Duke, that would be better informed and more efficient than any that had existed before.[1] As described above, he was to be as good as his word and, assisted by the large resources of the Campbell clan, he and his brother were able to achieve a dominance in Scottish affairs that few were able to challenge. Suddenly, however, the period 1734–6 saw a slippage in control. The regime's authority was shaken at several levels, but most noticeably in church affairs. This chapter will consider the likely causes, look at what happened, and consider why the period did not endure.

The Origins of The Loosening of Control

In a sense, one contribution to the regime's temporary undoing was its own success. Even where mistakes had been made and situations mishandled, it was the final judgment of the Assembly or Commission which mattered and manipulating these was the Argyll interest's strong point. On the other hand, it should have been more obvious to Milton, who, after all, was Ilay's man on the spot, that winning cases or achieving desired settlements by *force majeure* were not always advantageous if the decisions behind them were widely perceived to be ill-advised. The discomfort displayed by his own men in the West Kirk dispute was a glaring example. There is no doubt that he was a sub-minister of supreme ability and guile, but if he had a flaw, it was an almost irrational reluctance to give up a cause he had begun, even though the cost of victory might have become more than it was worth. An instance of this was the settlement at Port-Glasgow in 1731, where he continued to push a presentee, even though his

---

1. SRO., State Papers, RH2/4/321, Ilay to Newcastle, 28 October 1725. Ilay also told Newcastle that he had recruited Milton and regarded him as someone "on whom in all respects I could depend more than any person in this country."

trusted local adviser had warned him the situation was hopeless.[2] An absurd state of affairs ensued whereby, after pressure from Milton, Glasgow Town Council insisted on their right of patronage and tried to curtail the presbytery's actions with a Court of Session sist, despite the fact that the same document (when finally revealed) also contained a declaration that they were not the sole patrons in the first place. It was a foolish and clumsy attempt to bluster and deceive, and inevitably left Milton looking inept.[3]

A similar situation took place regarding the vacancy at Troqueer (Dumfries). Despite good advice not to by-pass the long-designated successor to the previous incumbent, he persisted in advancing his chosen presentee through the senior courts until the Commission ordered a riding committee to perform the admission on 19 April 1734. This merely created a universal fury that triggered an arson attack on the manse offices and stackyard, a violent assault on the minister while he tried to perform his parochial duties, and an eldership that, until his death in 1742, refused even to meet him. Meanwhile both presbytery and synod declined to enroll his name, believing (as did most observers) that a gross injustice had been done to the previous minister's loyal assistant by his being overlooked.[4] Such events damaged confidence in the regime's good judgment among its supporters, but more importantly, it made nonsense of their claim that its management of church affairs was designed only to promote peace and order.

A second contribution was that the problems Ilay began to have after 1733 in the political arena, would have had an emboldening effect on those considering a challenge to his hegemony in ecclesiastical matters. As the 1734 General Election approached, anti-Ilay agitation had been growing, and particularly so among the peers, within whose circle insurrection broke out for a time.[5] From its launch in February 1734, the *Thistle* newssheet published unrelenting attacks on the administration, drawing attention to every attempt in the Lords to embarrass Walpole and his adherents. Meanwhile a committee of discontented peers published a declaration attacking Ilay's disreputable conduct, and claiming that in return

2. Saltoun MS 16547, Rev Robert Paton to Milton, 26 July 1731.

3. Saltoun MS 16547, Rev Robert Paton to Milton, 17 November 1731; *Analecta*, iv, 275 and 291.

4. Saltoun MS 16551, Vaughan to Milton, 15 April 1732; J. L. Mangles, *Troqueer Parish Church, Dumfries*, (Dumfries: 1971), 26–8; Assembly Registers, 16 May 1735, 24 May 1736; *Fasti*, ii, 303.

5. Sir James Fergusson of Kilkerran, *The 16 Peers of Scotland, 1707–1959*, (Oxford University Press: 1960) 77.

for supporting what the Earl called the King's List, there was evidence of: "money given to many, promised to more; offers of pensions, places, civil and military preferments, acts of grace, reversals of attainders."[6] In the event, the *Squadrone* alliance of Hamilton, Tweeddale, Aberdeen, Marchmont, Strathmore, Queensberry, Montrose and Roxburghe failed to inflict much damage on Ilay, but it was a difficult time for the regime, not least when, after the election, the dissident peers proceeded to lodge a petition with Parliament that it be declared void. They protested that Ilay had sent an agent with money to corrupt the electors, and that the sixteen representative peers had been chosen entirely by that influence, and consequently had no right to sit.[7] The House of Lords dismissed the petition in 1735, but Lord Hervy in his Memoirs noted that the embarrassment and "apprehensions" caused at Court by the whole episode were extensive.[8]

The Argathelians were also to experience intense pressure in the Commons elections, and it is instructive that in the Dunfermline Burghs in particular, Tweeddale was able to make spectacular inroads for the *Squadrone* (or Patriots, as they were now often called) largely through playing a role as defender of the evangelical wing's rights against bullying and interference by Ilay in the Church's courts. Lord Grange, who had meanwhile given the warm brethren a fillip (and dealt Ilay a severe blow) by defecting from the Argathelians to the opposition, told Tweeddale that to win the seat, it was not necessary for him to support the evangelicals' views, but only to attack the measures threatened against them.[9] On the other hand, Grange could well see the advantage to be gained by organizing allies at the forthcoming Assembly: "If we get something done to remove the offence of the strict people . . . about the Act 1732, and in consequence get the four outed ministers brought in again, it will be a vast slur on Ilay and greatly recommend the Patriots to the country."[10] Encouraged by the rumors that Tweeddale would lead the Assembly into reinstating Ebenezer Erskine, a local hero, the voters enabled his candidate to take three of the five burghs. Only by resorting to a false return did Ilay manage to reverse the outcome, and have his own man elected.[11]

6. Marchmont, *A selection from the papers of the Earls of Marchmont*, ed. G. Rose, (London: 1831), ii. 4–9; see also *The Thistle*, 27 March 1734.

7. John, Lord Hervy, *Memoirs of the reign of King George II*, (London: 1931), i, 295

8. Ibid. ii, 434–35

9. NLS Yester MSS 7044. Jas Erskine of Grange to Tweeddale. 26 Aug 1733

10. Yester MS. 7044, Grange to Lord Tweeddale, 29 March 1734.

11. A full description of the election and the religious dimension to it, can be

While the above was unfolding, the 1734 Assembly convened in an atmosphere much altered from that of previous years.

The Assembly of 1734

The change in character is usually ascribed to shock throughout the Church at the Secession and a desire to make amends[12] for it, yet, although this was almost certainly a factor, it was not the complete picture. Writing in 1736 about the altered atmosphere, William Grant# (the Kirk's procurator and later, a senator of the College of Justice as Lord Prestongrange) summarized how he saw it. There were, he said, three groupings within the Church, the Warm and Moderate parties, and the Political Clergy: "[the latter] are not actuated by any regards to religion or their country, but influenced by little mean hopes of being made king's chaplains . . . or, being in possession of such places, must, in order to maintain them, act whatever part they are commanded by men in power."[13] He considered that these were to blame for the increasing forcing on of presentations without any semblance of parochial concurrence, and for the undermining of presbyteries' authority. Thus it had happened that, "these considerations roused many of the moderate party, and all the warmer brethren: the kirk-sessions were in a flame: the political party-men opposite to the court joined them: warm elders were returned for Synods and Assemblies; and thus, in the two last Assemblies, every thing has been determined against the presentations which they could venture to determine."[14]

Grant was correct in claiming that a conscious effort had been made to have more men of an evangelical stamp chosen as representatives to the senior church courts. Indeed, an example of how intense the choosing process became was highlighted by the *Caledonian Mercury*. In an article entitled *A Case without Precedent*, it reported on the bitter infighting which occurred in Perth presbytery after James Mercer of Aberdalgie, who had taken a leading part in the proceedings against Ebenezer Erskine,

---

found in Ronald Sunter, *Patronage and Politics in Scotland, 1707–1832*, (John Donald: 1986), 211–30; see also A. T. N. Muirhead, "Religion, politics and society in Stirling during the ministry of Ebenezer Erskine 1731–54." MLitt diss. (Stirling: 1983), 454ff.

12. Burleigh, *Church History*, 281; Hetherington, 211; Cunningham, 440.

13. William Grant, *Remarks on the State of the Church of Scotland with respect to Patronages, and with reference to a Bill now depending before Parliament* (London: 1736), 7.

14. Ibid. 8.

had "artfully" contrived to have himself and three colleagues elected by seven brethren at an unexpected hour. The warm members had thereupon marshaled their forces, elected another four in tune with their views and sent them as well. It was left to the Assembly to sort out which group it was prepared to recognize.[15]

As the 1734 Assembly began, the success of the evangelicals' membership offensive was at once obvious to Lothian, the Lord High Commissioner. He nervously reported to Ilay that he was very uncertain how things were going to turn out: "it plainly appears that there is a majority of those who are warmly disposed, and Thursday last, they carried for a moderator of that temper."[16] The moderator in question was James Gordon of Alford, whose 1732 pamphlet had castigated the corruption evident in the church courts and proposed a wide spectrum of reforms.[17] Although reviled by the Argyll camp for his views (later that year they succeeded in having his election to the chair of divinity at King's College annulled[18]), Gordon ensured the Assembly's new enthusiasm did not overstep the bounds of legality. Thus, in the first case, he wisely guided the court into rejecting petitions for a call at large to Cambusnethan (Hamilton). Although the patron was not insisting on his choice (his interest was more in maintaining his right), the issue remained that the six months had not elapsed and a presentation had been lodged and could not be safely ignored.[19]

On the other hand, when the case of Auchtermuchty (Cupar) then came to be heard, suddenly there was an opportunity to break the pattern of past years. On the orders of the Commission, a riding committee had just settled an unwelcome presentee there. Despite irregularities about the case, the Commission's apologists led their customary catch–all defense that whatever the plaintiffs claimed, "the Commission did not act in the capacity of a committee but as a sovereign judicatory, having all power

15. *Caledonian Mercury*, 7 May 1734. see also, John Brown, *Rise and Progress of the Secession*, 27; The Assembly, when asked to adjudicate between the representatives, preferred the election of the latter.

16. SRO., State Papers, RH2/4/333, Lothian to Ilay, 4 May 1734.

17. James Gordon, *The state and duty of the Church of Scotland, especially with respect to the settlement of ministers set in a just light* (Edinburgh: 1732). Among his suggestions were that, probationers on trials should be asked questions distancing them from presentations, in event of popular election, only intelligent representatives of the parish should have a say, also they should live in the parish and be members of the Kirk; dissents should be allowed, and finally, presbyteries should not only choose commissioners to the Assembly, but should also select the members of the Commission.

18. Saltoun MS 16556, James Chalmers to Milton, 25 October 1734.

19. Assembly Registers, 5 May 1734.

delegated on them, so that it was unprecedented, even incompetent to reverse their judgements."[20] This time, however, the Assembly was not to be deflected, and the Commission's decision was not only disapproved, but the presentee's settlement overturned.[21]

More was to follow. Both the 1730 *Act Discharging the Recording of Reason of Dissents*, and the 1732 *Act anent the Method of Planting Vacant Churches*, were annulled, and the synod of Perth and Stirling were given authority to bring Erskine and the other three Seceders back in to the Church. It was further declared that in future when a presbytery felt it could not comply with a Commission's sentence, the case should lie over until the Assembly following, and not go to the next Commission—a severe blow to a case's management by the regime.[22] An Overture was even introduced which proposed to regulate the conduct of Commissions, but this was not proceeded upon.[23]

Finally, acting on a suggestion from the synod of Perth and Stirling[24], an instruction was given to the Commission to petition Parliament with a view to the abolition of patronage.

Conscious of the poor impression of his administration such a petition would project in London, Ilay was more alarmed about the Assembly's last resolution than any of the others, especially as it also contained a request for the Crown to waive its right of presentation even if patronage were not repealed. Accordingly, when the Commission considered the project on the 14th. August 1734, a fierce resistance was led by Milton's deputy as Keeper of the Signet, Alexander MacMillan of Dunmore.[25] The familiar arguments that such presumption would only antagonize parliamentary opinion against the Kirk were used, but the Commission nonetheless voted to proceed with the instruction, and James Gordon of Alford, Lauchlan MacIntosh of Errol and John Willison of Perth were appointed to take the address to London.

---

20. *Caledonian Mercury*, 13 May 1734.

21. Assembly Registers, 10 May 1734.

22. *Caledonian Mercury*, 20 May 1734. This was expanded two years later into Act XII, Sess. 10, 24 May 1736, which further stated that the Commission should desist from appointing special or "riding" committees, but leave the matter to the following Assembly. [SRO., CH1/9/11].

23. Assembly Registers, 14 May 1734.

24. Cunningham, 439, n.

25. *Caledonian Mercury*, 15 August and 19 August 1734.

The Petitions

They arrived in London in January 1735, but, meeting with little co-operation, were unable to present the petition to the Commons until the 10th. April.[26] At that point, however, the representatives' fortunes appeared to improve, in that the house heard the petition and agreed to consider a Bill on the subject. To that end, "Mr Plumer, Mr Ereskine, Mr Forbes, Mr Areskine, Sir James Ferguson and Mr Hume Campbell were ordered to prepare and bring in the same."[27] When the Bill appeared, its terms indicated that a return to something very near the 1690 legislation was envisaged. To minimize anxiety among the landed interest, what changes there were made no concession to the agitation that had been taking place in favor of popular election. Not only was there to be no broadening of the heritor/elder franchise enshrined in the 1690 abolition, but the role of the session was restricted so that the number of elders voting should never be allowed to exceed the number of (qualified) heritors. As for the heritors, the Bill's framers were clearly mindful of the disruption caused by numerous petty heritors in the West Kirk controversy, and so declared that eligibility to vote was to depend upon their possessing a freehold worth not less than £10 sterling *per annum*. There was no reference to heritors' denominational affiliation nor was mention made of teinds or vacant stipends.[28]

The Bill was presented by Plumer on the 18th April, but due to lack of parliamentary time, progressed no further. Whether deliberately contrived or not, the delays which had been forced upon the representatives on their arrival in January had proved decisive.

Meanwhile, in Scotland the Bill and its franchise provisions had invigorated the debate on what should be the best electoral system for planting churches, should presentations be abolished. The Kirk's legal adviser,

26. Assembly Registers, 15 May 1735; *Caledonian Mercury*, 12 April 1735.

27. *History and proceedings of the House of Commons from the Restoration to the present time*, ix, na., (London: 1741), viii-ix. Walter Plumer (?1682–1746) was MP for Appleby and "a strong supporter of the non-conformists"; James Erskine (c. 1678–1754), later Lord Grange, was MP for Clackmannanshire, 1734–41; Duncan Forbes of Culloden, was Lord Advocate and MP for Inverness Burghs, 1722–37; Charles Areskine (1680–1763) was Solicitor General and MP for Dumfriesshire, 1722–41; Sir James Fergusson (c.1687–1759) was a Lord of Session and MP for Sutherland, 1734–5; Alexander Hume Campbell (1708–60) [twin brother to Hugh, Lord Polwarth] was a lawyer and MP for Berwickshire, 1734–41. (Romney Sedgwick, *The House of Commons, 1715–1754*, (HMSO 1970) ii, 357; ii, 14–16; ii, 43; i, 420; ii, 30; ii, 159).

28. *Caledonian Mercury*, 29 April 1735. see also William Grant, *The present state of the Church of Scotland etc*, 27–8.

William Grant supported the Bill's blueprint. The distinguished professor of Moral Philosophy at Glasgow University, Francis Hutcheson#, not only supported it but published a clarion call to all heritors to appreciate how important it was for them to take interest in the issue, if they wished to arrest a slide into unrestrained patronage. By rousing themselves to support the Bill, they would keep power of election out of the hands of the populace, while at the same time enlarge their own influence in a parish and make the ministry attractive to their own sons. Even patrons would still retain much influence, except it would be "of a more neighbourly and gainly sort."[29]

Another publication, in the form of an imaginary debate between Ebenezer Erskine and a university principal, tried to devise a voting system which involved everyone, with the impact of their respective vote being in proportion to their status.[30] For those who also favored a wide franchise yet doubted the law would ever be changed, another writer argued that the Church should make the best of things and simply allow all objectors to a presentee's settlement to go elsewhere.[31] Yet another viewpoint was that the Church's best interest lay in emphasizing to Parliament how steadfast its loyalty to king and government had been, and then leaving it to Westminster to decide how best to remedy the problem of patronages.[32] There were dangers surrounding the latter tactic, however, in that episcopal pamphleteers were already disseminating counter-propaganda in London circles, with one pamphlet in particular claiming that presbyterians were anti-monarchial, that the Assembly's London representatives were of bad character and that any abolition of patronage would only feed ministers' insolence and lead them to make even more unreasonable demands.[33]

While this was going on, the time had come round for the 1735 Assembly. Ebenezer Erskine later wrote that care had again been taken to

29. Francis Hutcheson, *Considerations on Patronages Addressed to the Gentlemen of Scotland, etc.* [np. 1735].

30. "Philumen Scotsman," *Grange: or, the schemists on calling of ministers and presentations in Scotland*, i, *On calls*, (Edinburgh: 1735).

31. Anon., *A Letter to a Scots Clergyman, lately ordained, Concerning his behaviour in the Judicatories of the Church*, (Edinburgh: 1735).

32. Anon., *A plea for the Church of Scotland against patronages, with reasons for relieving her from them and repealing the Act made in the reign of Queen Anne 1712 whereby patronages were restored, and full answers are made to all objections*, (London: 1735).

33. Anon., *Ancient and modern presbytery considered, being a true and candid representation of the principles and practices of the presbyterian clergy in Scotland with relation to their settlement of churches by popular elections. To which is added a brief answer to the most material objections in their late plea against patronages* (London: 1735), 35.

ensure that as many as possible of his like–minded brethren were sent as commissioners, and that it was expected that they would make great strides in giving the people back their Christian liberties.³⁴ He was however, to be bitterly disappointed. Some of Erskine's requirements that, for example, the Assembly show penitence for its past misdeeds, were over–optimistic. Nonetheless it is clear that this meeting did go about its business with an air of caution rather than the zeal of the previous year. This was especially noticeable in the way contentious cases were frequently remitted back to the synods or presbyteries from which they originated, rather than be decided at once. The reason for this was that, although the initial approach to Parliament for repeal of the Patronage Act had stalled, it was still hoped that success might be achieved through another petition, this time presented directly to the king. It was therefore vital, in the meantime, to keep controversy to a minimum.

The new address was drawn up and dispatched to London with another team of representatives, namely, Principal Alexander Anderson of St. Andrews, James Gordon of Alford and Colonel John Erskine of Carnock. The project did not go well. In their report to the following year's Assembly, the commissioners related that they had called on all the most important people relative to Scottish affairs, but that they received "no encouragement, countenance or concurrence . . . but on the contrary." Their attempts to meet with the king were constantly obstructed by Ilay, and particularly by Newcastle, who claimed he had shown the king the petition, but that he had answered that he did not meddle in such affairs but left them to his Parliament. After their continuing to insist on seeing the monarch, an audience was granted, but it was amidst a "throng," and they were forbidden either to read the address or speak anything about it. Later, Newcastle sent word that the king's answer was the same as before³⁵. At this, the representatives decided there was no point continuing their efforts and went home. The threat to the 1712 Act was over.

Despite the disappointment of the London commissioners' report to it, the Assembly of 1736 did show some of the same determination to stand against abuses as its two predecessors. Orders were given for a stricter regulation of the process by which Presbyteries elected commissioners to the Assembly, and also how members of the Commission were

---

34. Ebenezer Erskine, *The testimony and contendings of the Rev Mr Alexander Hamilton, one of the ministers of the gospel at Stirling, against the violent settlement of Mr James Mackie in the parish of St Ninians*, (Edinburgh: 1736).

35. Assembly Registers, 20 May 1736. The text of the petition can be found at SRO., CH1/1/26.

to be appointed. Moreover, riding committees were to be abolished.[36] As for patronage, a resolution was adopted testifying to the ills wrought by it on the Church, with the aim that this should be held in readiness for such a time when it was considered advantageous to renew the campaign against the 1712 Act.[37] At the same time, an instruction was given to the Commission to seize every opportunity for obtaining redress from the grievance of patronage. The instruction was subsequently repeated by every Assembly until 1784.

The 1736 Assembly did also pass an *Act against Intrusion of Ministers into vacant Congregations, and recommendation to presbyteries concerning settlements.* This quoted the Acts of Assembly of 1575, 1638, 1715 and the second *Book of discipline*, all of which, it was averred, showed that it was a principle of the Church that no minister should be intruded contrary to the will of a congregation. However, it was simply recommended to all judicatories to have due regard for the principle, while at the same time trying to promote harmony and avoid whatever might excite unreasonable exceptions against an otherwise worthy candidate.[38] In practical terms, the Act was of little far-reaching effect and it is more likely that it was a piece of window-dressing designed to attract the Seceders back to the Church (which it did not do).

What is clear is that the Assembly had now reached its high-water mark in leaning towards evangelical sensibilities. It did issue a rallying call for more gospel preaching rather than that which tended "more to amusement than edification," yet drew back from finding fault with Professor Archibald Campbell# (St Andrews), about whose pronouncements evangelicals repeatedly complained and considered heretical.[39] Again, despite the *Act against intrusion, etc.*, it did its best to avoid confrontation by taking the course of least resistance in the difficult settlement cases which came before it.

The ecclesiastical climate-change, begun in 1734, was coming to an end.

36. 21 May, *Act for Regulating of Elections to Members of Assembly*, (this was appointed to be sent down to Presbyteries, but in the interim to be obeyed. It was ratified 23 May 1738); 24 May, Sess. 10, *Act anent the manner of Electing members of the Commission and Concerning their Powers.*

37. *Caledonian Mercury*, 27 May 1736.

38. SRO., CH1/1/26. *Act against Intrusion of Ministers into Vacant Congregations and Recommendation to Presbyteries concerning Settlements*—25 May 1736.

39. Assembly Registers, *Act Concerning preaching; Act and recommendation for preserving purity of doctrine and concerning Professor Campbell*, 21 May 1736.

The End of the 1734–1736 Resistance

There were several reasons why the altered atmosphere of 1734–6 did not last. Chief among these was the crushing blow of the failed attempt to abolish patronage.[40] Morale sank as the interest and debate over replacement systems which had been taking place appeared now to have been pointless. For the great majority who continued to look upon secession with distaste, the only option which now remained was to return to the loophole afforded by the 1719 Act. However, such a solution depended upon a clamping down on acceptances, and this was made more difficult by the fact that the repeal of the Assembly's 1732 Act, together with the uncertainty created by the attempt on the Patronage Act, had led many parishes and presbyteries to hold back from filling vacancies. As a result, an unusually large number of probationers were anxiously waiting to be placed.[41] Clearly, it was not the best of circumstances in which to make life even more difficult for expectants by outlawing acceptances. Then the situation was made more problematical by what was seen as a lamentable climb-down over the issue in the Assembly's dealings with George Blaikie, presentee for the charge of Madderty (Auchterarder).

According to the publicity which had been growing around Blaikie, he had first seen his unqualified acceptance of a crown presentation to Kinnaird (Dundee) set aside because of opposition in the parish, and then, when presented to Madderty in two years later in 1736, his impudence in accepting this second presentation was punished by the synod of Perth and Stirling by their removal of his license in April 1737. The popular satisfaction engendered by this firmness over acceptances was however transformed into rage and despair when the Assembly of that year, after hearing his appeal, reinstated him.

In actual fact, the reality of Blaikie's story was quite different from what was generally believed, even though the false picture is the one that has endured.[42] His rejection over Kinnaird was through a technicality rather than a challenge to the law, while his later suspension had not been for accepting a presentation but for using "several indecent expressions

---

40. It was a disappointment shared, it should be said, by the Church as a whole, since the majority of its personnel, whatever their party affiliation, had been hoping for some alteration in the law.

41. *Grange: or, the schemists on calling etc.,* ii, (Edinburgh: 1737), 8ff.

42. British Library, [1354.e1], "A Candid Enquiry into the Constitution of the Church of Scotland in Relation to the Settlement of Ministers," in *Tracts Concerning Patronage,* (Edinburgh: 1770); *Patronage Report,* #634; *Fasti,* iv, 277.

and reflections against the judicatories and ministers of this Church . . . which together with his behaviour before the Synod gave offence."[43] It was therefore perfectly reasonable for the Assembly, having issued a rebuke, to reinstate him. However, such was the public perception of the dispute, the decision horrified anti–patronage factions.[44] For them, it seemed that the Kirk was incapable of taking a stand against a man whose apparent motivation was simply "to fleece than feed the flock."[45]

As well as the failed attempts to remove presentations or neutralize them by banning acceptances, there were other reasons why the 1734–6 resistance lost its momentum. In the first place, although they might have lost command of the Assembly or Commission, there was nothing to stop Milton and Ilay continuing to wield influence in those presbyteries and synods where they had a strong interest, as was the case, for example, with Irvine presbytery and the synod of Ayr where their influence gained an important victory in the settlement of Kilmaurs (1735–9).[46]

Secondly, the intransigence of church courts did not discourage them from having recourse to the civil ones, and in the aftermath of the Auchtermuchty case [see above], that is what happened. The loss of face occasioned by the defeat clearly rankled with Ilay, and a swift counter-attack through litigation seemed an attractive response: "I am of opinion that a judicial determination well founded, will at present be the best way to restrain the mad people, at least it will be a good experiment. It seems to me that if a presbytery can settle a minister so far as to give him right to the stipend and glebe contrary to the right of a patron, then, the patron has a civil right . . . but has no remedy when his right is invaded."[47] Accordingly, George Moncrieff of Reidie, the joint patron at Auchtermuchty, was encouraged to take his case to the Court of Session. In the end, the advantage to Reidie personally was slight, in that his sole accomplishment was the gaining of the vacant stipend for a period. On the other hand, for

43. Assembly Registers, 23 May 1737. cf., the case of John Burgh, above.

44. "I view the ruin of this poor church as begun, and hastening on" Edinburgh University Muniments, [DC.1.82/3], "The Private Diary of George Drummond." (1736–38), "RB" to Drummond, 24 May 1737: Drummond thought the return of the license would make "a thorough rent in this poor church" (23 May). 23 elders dissented from the decision at the Assembly.

45. *Caledonian Mercury*, 28 May 1739.

46. see Laurence A.B. Whitley, "The operation of lay patronage in the church of Scotland from the Act of 1712 until 1746, with particular reference to the presbyteries of Duns, Edinburgh and Brechin," PhD. diss. (St Andrews: 1993), 214–18.

47. Saltoun MS. 16555. Ilay to Milton, 5 Dec 1734.

Ilay's purposes, the case was highly significant, since it resulted in a formal declaration that, in order for a minister to have the legal right to stipend and glebe, he had to be duly collated, that is to say, it was not enough that he be presented to the living by the patron, or that he has been instituted to the spiritual charge by the presbytery.[48] It had to be both. The judgment therefore confirmed that if a presbytery chose to refuse a valid presentation, then whoever was subsequently inducted had no right to the stipend, and it could be retained by the patron as if the charge were vacant.[49] The implications of this naturally caused presbyteries some anxiety.[50]

A third contribution to the break-up of the anti-patronage coalition was the fall-out from the Porteous Affair of 1736. In April of that year, Captain Porteous, of the Edinburgh Town Guard, had fired on the crowd during the execution of a smuggler who also commanded much local popularity. The Court of Justiciary condemned Porteous to death, but Queen Caroline, acting as regent, ordered a stay of execution. The incensed mob thereupon dragged the Captain from prison and executed him themselves, an act which provoked great outrage in London. The incident might reasonably be expected to have been entirely secular in significance, but, having repaired to Edinburgh to take charge of the crisis, Ilay saw in it a means of turning it to ecclesiastical advantage.

On the 10 October 1736, the Earl wrote to Walpole: "The most shocking circumstance is, that it plainly appears the High Flyers of our Scottish church have made this infamous murder a point of conscience . . . All the lower rank of the people . . . speak of this murder as the hand of God doing justice; and my endeavours to punish murderers are called grievous prosecutions . . . and I have observed that none of those who are of the High Party will call any crime the mob can commit by its proper name."[51] In his autobiography, Alexander Carlyle of Inveresk says that Ilay saw here a chance to capitalize on the indignation in Parliament aroused by the affair, and harness the penalty of the law to remove the more offensive of the

---

48. Duncan, *Parochial Law*, 318.

49. Morrison, *Decisions of the Court of Session*, xxiii, Moncrieff v. Maxton, 15 February 1735.

50. Referring to the case, the synod of Dumfries instructed its commissioners to the 1735 Assembly to do what they could "for obtaining relief from the grievances that may follow on the late decision [in] the Courts of Session." MS.16562. James McEwen, Moffat, to Milton, 14 April 1735. Further comments on the case's implications can be found in Story, *Church of Scotland—Past and Present*, iv, 74–75.

51. quoted in William Roughead, *The Trial of Captain Porteous*. Series, Notable Scottish Trials [Wm Hodge. 1909].

warm clergy from their charges.[52] There would then be the added bonus of a chance to replace them with those of a more agreeable stamp to him.

Accordingly, on the 25th May 1737, Ilay presented a Bill to the Lords *For the more Effectually bringing to Justice any persons concerned in the barbarous murder of Capt. John Porteous etc.* Included in it was a clause ordaining that, for a year (from 7 August 1737), all ministers had to read the Act from their pulpits on the first Sunday of each month, immediately after the sermon. If this was refused, the penalty for the first offence was disqualification from voting in church courts; for the second, it was deposition. According to George Drummond, the Act was transparently a contrivance whereby those who scrupled to read the Act would be "catched in the trap My Lord Ilay has set for them."[53] Certainly, Ilay well knew that the evangelical clergy would dislike references to Lords Spiritual in the wording of the Act, as well as the sanguinary tone of some of its provisions. He also knew they would take offence at being instructed when to insert so profane a text into divine worship. Above all, there would be deep unhappiness at the Erastian implications contained in the penalties, since discipline of ministers was considered to be the exclusive domain of the church's courts.[54]

What Ilay did not anticipate, however, was that large numbers of *both* moderate men and evangelicals would find the order abhorrent. Carlyle claimed that as many as half the clergy refused to read the Act; the Solicitor–General wrote to the Duke of Newcastle on the 5th November 1737 and said it was one third.[55] George Drummond's information for the first Sunday after the 7th. August, was that of those whose actions were known, 118 had read the Act, 366 had not.[56] Whatever the true figures, Ilay had undoubtedly made a miscalculation, and it was obvious even to him that the full rigors of the Act could not be applied to so many.

Nevertheless, the whole exercise did not in fact turn out to be a failure, but rather had a beneficial spin–off for the Earl, and in two ways. First, it distracted the Church's attention away from virtually all other issues, including patronage. Secondly, it sowed among many ministers a considerable anxiety over what retribution might be exacted on them by

52. *The Autobiography of Dr Alexander Carlyle of Inveresk, 1722–1805*, (TN Foulis, Edinburgh: 1910), 45.

53. Drummond. "Diary," 19 July 1737 and 13 July 1737.

54. For a summary of the scruples felt by clergy, see, Anon., *The Lawfulness and necessity of ministers, their reading the Act. of Parliament for bringing to justice the murderers of Capt. John Porteous*, (np. 1737).

55. Roughead, 139.

56. "Diary," 11 August 1737.

the government for their disobedience. Sensing this, Ilay sought to keep up the atmosphere of apprehension by writing to Milton at the end of September 1737, and telling him to select two or three ministers, and make an example of them.[57] In the end, nothing happened and the whole matter of clerical retribution was handed to the Duke of Newcastle. Although the threat thereafter died away, Ilay and Milton were able to benefit from the lingering uncertainty.[58]

The fourth factor which contributed to change after 1736, was the death in that year of Principal James Smith of Edinburgh University, for, from then onwards, it was the Rev. Patrick Cuming of the Old Kirk who was entrusted with the direction of the Assembly by Ilay.[59] Since his desertion from the *Squadrone*, Smith had arguably become the most influential figure in the Church's senior courts. Due probably to his failing health however, it is clear that in recent months he had not been performing with the same competence as previously.[60] More gifted as a tactician, Cuming was to reverse the situation, knowing that Ilay's authority had to be reasserted yet without causing more splits within the Church. On the enforcement of presentations, he took a tougher, more confrontational stance yet used his persuasive talent to contain hostility among disaffected parishioners. Although himself no enthusiast for presentations, in his view, the law, however distasteful, had to be obeyed by the Church if it was to benefit from the law's protection and security. If the use of riding committees and token calls helped circumvent opposition to a settlement, then he was happy to countenance them. Working closely with Milton, Cuming went on to dominate the ecclesiastical scene in Scotland for the next twenty years (except for the period of the *Squadrone* administration, 1742–6). In the latter half of the 1750s, he was gradually overshadowed by William Robertson, and when Ilay (now Duke of Argyll) died in 1761, the leadership passed to him[61].

57. Saltoun MS.16569. 29 September 1737.

58. "As to the clergy being in danger I know nothing of it, sometime ago I heard that notice would be taken of those who did not read the Act, but nothing as yet has been mentioned in our House in relation to them." Saltoun MS.16572, Capt. Charles Campbell, London, to Milton, 14 March 1738.

59. J. Ramsay, *Scotland and Scotsmen in the Eighteenth Century*, (Edinburgh: 1888), i, 233.

60. see my article on Smith in the *ODNB*.

61. H. R. Sefton, "Lord Ilay and Patrick Cuming: A Study in Eighteenth-Century Ecclesiastical Management." *RSCHS*, xix, 1977, 203–16; Shaw, *Management of Scottish Society*, 105; see also my entry on Cuming in the *ODNB*.

The Period After 1736

So, then, by a combination of skill and good fortune, Ilay and Milton negotiated the difficult period from 1734 to 1736/37 without sustaining lasting harm to their machinery for influencing the settlement of church vacancies. In the field of politics, on the other hand, the consequences of incidents like the Porteous Affair were much more serious, and, as will be seen below, Ilay was to be out of office in less than four years.

In the meantime, however, Milton set about managing the Church as before, only, things were not to be exactly as they had been. The difference was that the post–1736 Church was one in which schism was rapidly becoming a fact (finally occurring in 1740), and the example and constant declamations of the Seceders heightened passions within the Church's courts, which in turn made their proceedings more volatile and difficult to manage. In short, whereas most of the cases in which Milton became involved now ended well for him, the management of them occasionally bears a distinctly ragged appearance. The Blaikie affair was a case in point, in that Milton assumed any obloquy it provoked could be shrugged off like previous controversies, yet such was its intensity, it proved too much for the presentee himself, and, despite winning an order for his settlement at Madderty, Blaikie suddenly decided he had had enough and went overseas.[62] Again, although Milton made sure his father-in-law's presentation to Kingsbarns (St. Andrews) prevailed against the parish's opposition before the 1739 Commission and Assembly,[63] he overestimated what his prestige could now achieve. Not content with achieving his object, he then went on to insist that all attempts to register dissent over the settlement at the March Commission should be refused, but this triggered a furor of such passion that the exhausted Commission eventually resolved it was preferable to neglect his wishes and let the matter drop.[64]

62. *Caledonian Mercury*, 9 August 1739; Assembly Registers, 15 May 1740.

63. Saltoun MS.16574. 16 November 1738, George Logan to Milton. It is worth noting how at the Assembly, the parish argued that the presentee's admission on the 3rd. January 1739 had been in defiance of the Act of Assembly concerning the intrusion of ministers against the will of the people. To this it was successfully countered that the will of the people did not mean their "mere will, or obstinate will, without assigning a reason for their will." In other words, the Assembly insisted that the Act meant there had to be reasons, which the Church would then judge. Milton's father-in-law was Sir Francis Kinloch and was acting on behalf of the creditors of the patron, the Earl of Crawford (*Caledonian Mercury*, 13 November 1738).

64. *Caledonian Mercury*, 15 March 1739. Milton claimed it was because such dissents "had often been found tinctured with the alloy of conceit, vanity and pride."

The most striking example of the erratic grip Milton and Ilay had on church affairs in the turbulent post-1736 period, was the disputed settlement of Currie (Edinburgh). Ilay had always made it clear that he would allow no minister to come to Edinburgh who was of the warm persuasion,[65] but when the obeisant Council and heritors of Currie decided between them[66] to fix on a *bete noire* of the evangelicals, the Rev. James Mercer of Aberdalgie (see above), it quickly became clear their desire to please had superseded wise judgment. Described as a "hot, violent man, a plague to the Presbytery of Perth, and most active always in a bad cause,"[67] Mercer had incurred a widespread notoriety bordering on hatred through his prominent role in the proceedings against Ebenezer Erskine in 1732.[68] Edinburgh presbytery was nonetheless caught off guard by the storm of criticism which followed its sustaining of his presentation[69] and referred the matter to the synod of Lothian, which considered it on the 30th. April 1740. After reflecting upon the submissions, which contained "a peculiar virulence,"[70] the synod set aside the call based on Mercer's presentation. When the Council then appealed to the Assembly, the unexpected decision was made to confirm Mercer's rejection, on the wholly irregular ground that there were difficulties surrounding it.[71]

As Moncrieff suggests in his *Life of Erskine*, the volatility which gave rise to surprising decisions like that of the Currie case was to a large extent "influenced by the state of the country, and by the Secession from the Church."[72] His reference to the state of the country was alluding to

65. George Drummond, "Diary", 20 October 1736.

66. The Council offered a list of four suggestions to the heritors, who, in a private meeting, proceeded to elect Mercer by a majority. SRO., Assembly Papers, CH1/2/78. "Petition to Edinburgh Presbytery by several Heritors, 27 February 1740."

67. from the Memoirs of William Wilson of Perth (one of the Seceders), quoted in John Wilson, *Dunning*, [Crieff 1906], 140.

68. "He was in the highest degree obnoxious, from that circumstance, to every order of the people." Moncrieff, *Erskine*, 450, n.

69. Edinburgh Presbytery Minutes, SRO., CH2/121/13, 30 January 1740; *Caledonian Mercury*, 27 December 1739. Presbytery later produced a defense of their actions, declaring that the discouraging reception given to the "recent remonstrances" put before the King and Parliament in London, had made clear that intransigence on the Kirk's part would cause Parliament to make the yoke of patronage harder by returning to the old practice of prosecuting those who refused to effect settlements. Assembly Papers, CH1/2/78, "Answers to Reasons of Dissent," 1740.

70. *Caledonian Mercury*, 1 May 1740.

71. Assembly Registers, 17 May 1740.

72. Appendix, 450, n.

the groundswell of opposition to Walpole, and, by association, Ilay. It had not been a good period for the Earl: the Porteous Affair had damaged his personal authority, not only in Scotland, but also in London, where it was perceived as a failure in his duty to keep Scotland quiescent: "[the affair] has laid such a foundation of disunity between my Lord Ilay and some of the ministry as will not easily be made up."[73]

Yet another serious problem had been the departure from Walpole's ministry of the Duke of Argyll in 1739. Not only did his brother's absence reduce the resources which Ilay could then draw upon, but his presence among the disaffected greatly encouraged the morale of the opposition.[74] Milton did what he could to serve his patron's interest, but the tide against him was now too strong, and when the general election came in May/June 1741, twenty-seven of the forty-five Scottish members ultimately returned were opposed to Walpole's administration. Walpole clung to power for another six months, but the Patriots/*Squadrone* sensed their opportunity had come, and increased their pressure on the ministry.

Finally, Ilay wrote to Milton on the 4th. February 1742 with the news: "You will hear from all hands this post that the political game is over . . . how soon I may be out I don't know and I believe Lord Tweeddale will succeed me."[75] It turned out that he was correct, and on the 15th. February 1742, John Hay, the fourth Marquis of Tweeddale, was appointed His Majesty's Scotch Secretary. Ilay's immediate inclination was not to throw himself into enthusiastic opposition. By the end of 1743 he was writing to Milton: "I am now too old . . . to wish to set myself up again as a cock to be thrown at."[76] Ilay and Milton did not, however, proceed to disappear from the political scene. The fortuitous occurrence of the Rising of 1745 ensured a second term of office still awaited.

Summary

The period after 1733 was a difficult time for Milton and Ilay. While political pressure from their opponents mounted, they made several errors of judgment. Then when a concerted effort was made by evangelicals to

73. NLS., Yester MSS., MS.14420, Carteret to Tweeddale, 7 May 1737. John Carteret, 2nd. Earl Granville led the opposition to Walpole.

74. Murdoch, *The People Above*, 32.

75. Saltoun MS.16587.

76. Saltoun MS.16591, Ilay [now 3rd Duke of Argyll] to Milton, 26 November 1743.

send a strong representation to the Assembly, they found they were unable to deploy their allies to their customary good effect in controlling the business. Of the enactments which followed, the petitions caused them most concern. Although these came to nothing, they nonetheless were a crowning embarrassment in a period when Ilay and Milton's hold on the Church's upper courts slipped.

When they regained the initiative, they found themselves in a more volatile situation, both politically and in the church arena. Eventually, weakened by the Porteous affair, his brother's defection and the ascendancy of the Patriots after 1741, a tired-sounding Ilay made way for the new regime under the Marquis of Tweeddale.

Postscript: A note on the English experience of patronage Abuses

Although the complaints listed in the 1735 petition[77] about patronage were not to receive redress, the Scots' criticism of the presentation system would not have been received in England with shock and surprise. As mentioned above, Bishop Burnet, when writing of the English Church's defections during the time of Queen Anne, was scathing about the abuse of patronage, calling it a "filthy merchandise of the souls of men, which is too common."[78] The faults he listed were, the unwillingness of bishops to reject unworthy presentees through fear of incurring expense by having to defend their decision in the courts; patrons selling advowsons, not just simoniacally, when the charge was vacant, but bending the spirit of the law by arranging it when the incumbent was close to death; patrons buying advowsons in order to present their children regardless of their suitability, and ecclesiastics buying an advowson and then, to keep within the law, arranging for trustees to present them.

Twenty years later, at the time of the Assembly petition to Parliament, such criticisms were still being voiced. However, a further ground of offence was now added. This was particularly expressed in the widely circulated tract, *The nature of patronage and the duty of patrons, considered in three letters published in the Weekly Miscellany*. Unlike Scotland, possession of a living could also carry with it the right to vote in elections. To the author's disgust, this meant that political considerations had now come to govern patrons' choices as well. Clergymen were receiving the

---

77. See *History and proceedings etc.*, ix, viii, for the text of the petition.
78. Burnet, *History*, 911.

best benefices "for no other consideration besides a firm attachment to a party; a practice so openly avowed one would be apt to think it not only justifiable but meritorious."[79]

Along with the 1735 bill, the tract provided an opening for William Grant (later Lord Prestongrange) to publish a pamphlet, with an English audience particularly in mind, on the issue of Scotland's problems with presentations, and in doing so take a different tack from previous Scottish pamphleteers. Carefully avoiding the implication that the Kirk regarded patronage as an unworthy practice for any church, the emphasis of his argument was that in Scotland, patronage had a different history from its southern neighbor, and as a result possessed a different and less admirable character. Far from being, as *The nature of patronage etc.* had claimed for the English office, a sacred trust answerable to God, the Scots lords mostly had received the privilege from the Crown, after its depredations upon the abbeys, in the form of whimsical grants and upon trifling considerations. Something so lightly gained could, he argued, be lightly taken away again. As to the frequently-quoted argument that landowners who subsidized a living should at least have the right to choose its occupant, Grant again differentiated between the two countries. England had some very wealthy benefices funded by patrons, whereas in Scotland the great majority of incumbents received only what was barely necessary for their support. Finally, Grant sought to downgrade the significance of Scottish patronage by showing how, unlike their southern counterparts, Scots ministers had been kept apart from involvement with the state since the Reformation: no civil right or power went with their office, nor did it make them freeholders and thus eligible to vote. Indeed, ministers were excluded from all civil offices. In England, not only were the clergy more blended with the state, but they could frequently occupy positions of power and influence, especially through the presence of their bishops in the Lords. Patronage therefore held a position of importance in England that was far from the case in Scotland.[80]

79. Anon., *The nature of patronage and the duty of patrons, considered in three letters published in the Weekly Miscellany*, by "Generosus." London: 1735, ii, 11.

80. Grant, *Remarks on the state of the Church of Scotland with respect to patronages, etc.*; I am grateful to the bishop of Stafford, the Rt. Reverend Christopher Hill, for drawing my attention to the excellent article on the evolution of English patronage by Dr. Peter M. Smith of the university of Exeter, "The advowson: the history and development of a most peculiar property," in *Ecclesiastical Law Journal*, xxvi, (2000), 320–39.

Grant's line of argument had some persuasive merit, in that it was not simply a Scottish rant against a practice that the Church of England was prepared to live with and unlikely to jettison. By underlining how it differed in character between the two countries, the Kirk's complaints at once assumed a more reasonable and less strident complexion. Although the 1735 attempt at abolition would probably have failed in any case because of the delaying tactics of Ilay and the Scots nobility, English sympathy for a repeal of the Patronage Act might well have been enhanced had more been made earlier of the arguments put forward later by Grant.

CHAPTER THIRTEEN

BEFORE PROCEEDING TO LOOK at the relationship between the Kirk and the Tweeddale administration on the matter of church settlements, it should not be forgotten that meanwhile, in Jacobite/episcopalian areas north of the Tay, church courts had been obliged to wrestle continually with issues which were different from those which affected their lowland colleagues. Indeed, in many respects, it was a world away from the political ebb and flow of the last chapter, with those laboring at the front line often believing themselves forgotten by those at the center of the Church's decision-making process. By way of a snapshot of the difficulties involved, it is worth taking a brief look at one of the areas, in this case, the county of Angus.

Jacobitism in Angus 1715–45

It might be assumed that the failure of the 1715 rising would have done much to ease the lot of presbyteries north of the Tay in their attempts to fill vacancies with pro–Hanoverian candidates. Certainly, the church courts now had ample authority to depose recalcitrant ministers and teachers, and the forfeiture of estates like those of Panmure and Southesk meant they no longer found themselves in confrontation with the Earls over candidatures. However, presbyteries such as Brechin and Forfar were to find, in parish after parish, that the belligerence and hostility of the parishioners intensified rather than diminished. This made the presbyteries' candidates extremely reluctant to go to charges, and those that did were soon anxious to leave. Meanwhile, disaffection among the indigenous legal officers meant that the new ministers had little chance of enforcing the possession of their stipends, manses, glebes or even churches. By 1721 Brechin presbytery was complaining to the Assembly that Jacobitism and disaffection prevailed there more than ever.[1] There were to be many such complaints from presbyteries in the same situation over the ensuing twenty-five years, their chief dissatisfaction being the Kirk's apparent disinterest in what they

1. SRO, GD CH2/40/7, Brechin presbytery registers, 3 May 1721.

saw as the sources of most trouble, namely, the licensing of unsuitable probationers and the gentry's use of unqualified family chaplains.

Probationers and chaplains

On the matter of probationers, it seems that the Assembly and its Commission were too often ready, merely on a profession of repentance, to license or repone [return to ministerial status] someone of questionable character or loyalty. It was not uncommon for the licentiate then to surface in a different part of the country, having returned to his previous, unreformed state, and embarrass the local presbytery by insisting that it recognize his credentials. A typical example occurred in the vacancy at Maryton in 1724 [see below], where the presbytery was presented with a demand to put on the leet someone who, despite being deposed only five years before, for drunkenness "and saying the King had no more right to the throne than the Moorcock,"[2] was yet able to produce an Assembly Commission Act saying that he had since been reponed to the ministry. The presbytery ultimately managed to thwart the settlement, but there was no escaping the fact that such incidents made the Church's procedures look foolish.

It quickly became a frequent tactic for local gentry gleefully to pitchfork into settlement processes such candidates as they knew presbyteries would find unacceptable. The latter responded by dispatching a series of protests to Edinburgh, complaining that the number of probationers in circulation nationally was far beyond what the Church had need for,[3] and that, "we find from lamentable experience, that, let Presbyteries use all the caution they can in licensing probationers, there will not be wanting preachers who will judge it their interest to comply too much with the humour and inclination of these [disaffected] heretors, and we have instances of their [the heretors] seeking thro' the nation for such preachers as they know would be most unacceptable to the professing people."[4] Later again, another plea was sent, reminding the Assembly that the greatest danger for the Church arose from young students and probationers, so that none should be entered on trials without the greatest caution. They also begged for a tightening of procedures enabling the Church to know who and where its probationers were, as well as a renewal of the Assem-

2. *Fasti*, i, 363. He had been minister of Garvald and Bara (Haddington).
3. Brechin presbytery registers, SRO., CH2/40/8, 15 April 1729.
4. CH2/40/9, 1 March 1732.

bly's regulatory *Act Concerning Probationers etc.*, of 1711, which insisted that none be licensed by a presbytery unless he had resided there for six years, which failing, great care should be taken as to his vetting.[5]

The other source of frustration to presbyteries was that the Assembly did not seem to appreciate the trouble caused by the unregulated employment of tutors and/or chaplains by disaffected families. The lack of interest almost certainly stemmed from the fact that Assembly members from lowland areas tended to regard the practice of employing domestic chaplains as a perfectly acceptable means of supplying worthy candidates for the ministry, since many had themselves had benefited from such sponsorship. Among the gentry of counties like Angus, however, the situation was different. Brechin presbytery had no doubt that these "pedagogues" were "most violently set on propagating Jacobitism not only in their families but the neighbourhood." They also pointed out that there was nothing to stop them holding what could be construed as rival church services, under the guise of family worship.[6] It frustrated the presbytery that the Assembly showed little concern for their insistence that such teachers should be obliged to qualify to the government, and indeed, the disinterest seemed to confirm the feeling among members that neither the Assembly nor the Commission truly appreciated the nature of the political/ecclesiastical situation in localities like their own. For that reason, in another submission to the Assembly in 1735, they asked that the Commission might meet not just in Edinburgh, but in other cities around the country, so that a fuller awareness of what was going on might come from their hearing of cases close to such centers.[7]

Attempts at resistance: the example of Brechin presbytery

Thus it was that Angus, with its frequent pockets of well-organized Jacobite/episcopalian dissent, was an area where vacancy-filling was a difficult and enervating process for the local presbytery. The presbyteries for their part nonetheless did show remarkable resilience, despite their continuing feeling of isolation. Brechin presbytery, for example, clearly decided from an early stage that it would not at any time relax its staunch resistance to

5. CH2/40/9, 5 May 1736; CH1/9/10, 14; *Act concerning probationers, and settling ministers; with questions to be proposed to and engagements to be taken of them.* 22 May 1711.

6. CH1/9/10, 3 May 1724.

7. CH2/40/9, 1 May 1735.

the very idea of settling charges by presentations, and that always (even if this entailed disobedience to the secular law courts) it would set itself the aim of using only the process of admission by election and call. Precisely who were to be entrusted with the right of franchise was not something in which the members were consistent, but this was not always a simple matter, when account had to be taken as to who among the parishioners were well-affected and who were not. Such a difficulty arose at Maryton, where, having found that the heritors had "no other design but to teaze us," the presbytery learned that the ordinary parishioners were ready to approve the leet drawn up for them. Presbytery awarded them the vote, only to snatch it back again when it became obvious that the people were now "under undue influence." Presbytery thereupon abandoned its attempts at a vote and call and simply imposed an incumbent.[8]

The major test of its resolve to resist patronage at all costs concerned the important burgh of Montrose. As what became a battle of wills with the magistrates opened out, presbytery knew that the whole county was watching, and that the outcome was therefore crucial. It came as a shock to find the case was to be lost by the decisions of their own church courts.

When the first charge at Montrose became vacant in August 1730, a crown presentation was issued (to the minister of the second charge) which presbytery refused to accept. The town council, who were patrons of the second charge, however insisted on proceeding to the nomination of a successor for that position on the grounds that it was now vacant. The magistrates were told that presentations were a great grievance to the Church, and that presbytery would "think upon some proper method for remedying that grievance and for discouraging it within their bounds."[9] As the council hit back with appeals and protests, matters threatened to spiral out of control. Accordingly, the synod sent a committee to negotiate an agreement. The resulting compromise was that presbytery would agree to the translation provided the council allowed the free choice of a minister for the second charge.

The election was duly called for the 17 June 1731, and at once the presbytery found itself in the difficulty which arose wherever in the county it tried to moderate a call, namely, how much weight should be given to the vote of a heritor or councilor who was episcopalian? Adhering to its

---

8. CH2/40/8, 5 January and 13 April 1726. The charge was vacant from the 8 March 1724 until 14 September 1726. There was no presentation offered, the patron being unqualified.

9. CH2/40/9, 25 November 1730; 10 March and 7 April 1731.

policy of resisting all encroachments on what it saw was the Kirk's proper rights and privileges, it decided, after an all-night sitting, to reject the votes of three "non-hearers." The result of the decision was that the council's choice lost the election, by one vote. Immediately, the magistrates retaliated by producing a presentation for him. Presbytery rejected the presentation, ignored the magistrates' subsequent appeal to the synod, and proceeded to draw up a call. The magistrates fought back with a sist from the court of Session, to which presbytery answered that since they were a court of Christ, they were not liable to any civil court, and so they would continue, while in the meantime, sending representatives to Edinburgh to enlist the support of the procurator of the Church. As the weeks went by, it became clear that the procurator was less than comfortable about the presbytery's belligerence. Letters were sent from the capital, advising them to take no action until the next synod. The advice was ignored. Only when the presbytery's candidate became anxious at the furor and begged for a delay did the next stage of the settlement come to a halt.[10]

The sentence of the synod, when it came, was uncompromising. The votes of the non-hearers were declared competent,[11] and a special committee was appointed to join with any willing presbyters in order to settle the council's choice on the basis that both a presentation had been issued and a majority call recorded. When the admission took place on the 7th. December 1731, not one of the presbytery took part.

Shortly after, presbytery was required to send its views on the Assembly's *Overture Concerning the Method of Planting Vacant Churches*, and the ensuing submission does not conceal a deep sense of betrayal. It declares at length its indignation that the Kirk did not appear interested in the particular problems which presbytery had to confront through so many of their heritors being of another communion. That such persons should have a place in the election of a minister, they considered both absurd and unique among Europe's reformed churches.[12]

---

10. Ibid., 20 July, 18 August and 1 September 1731.

11. Under the terms of the 1690 Act, this was entirely correct, since the Act only stipulated that heritors (which presumably included councilors) had to be protestant. On the other hand, it was often claimed that the provisions of the 1690 Act had been rescinded by those of the 1712 one. This, it was claimed, left the 1649 legislation as a guide. However, that Act did not ascribe any special role to heritors, and moreover, it must be argued that King Charles' 1661 *Act approving the Engagement etc.* did annul the 1649 legislation.

12. SRO., CH2/40/9, 1 March 1732.

Throughout the 1720s and 1730s, the presbytery continued its fight and avoided any action which might suggest that it would countenance patronage as an acceptable way of filling charges. If, for example, a presentation was issued, as at Kinnaird in 1724, the court simply declined to record it. By such means it fought doggedly to keep its integrity intact. Such tactics, however, could not last indefinitely without the backing of the Kirk's senior judicatories, and when the vacancies at Brechin and Menmuir in 1744 came to be resolved, that deficiency proved decisive.

At its meeting on the 19th. September 1744, presbytery heard that the Brechin magistrates had obtained a crown presentation to the second charge and were demanding a call be moderated to the presentee. Irked that mostly episcopalian magistrates had interfered in such a way, presbytery decided that it would only agree to moderating a call at large. As for Menmuir, the presentation for there was lodged by the patron on 2nd. January 1745. Since it was made out for a minister already settled in a charge, presbytery cited the case of Rayne [see below] claiming that the 1719 Act allowed them to reject it and again moderate a call at large. In both instances, appeals brought the case up to the Assembly. On the 14th. and 17th. May 1745, the Assembly considered both the Brechin and Menmuir disputes, and, without even the necessity of a vote, dismissed all the presbytery's arguments, and ordered them to settle the presentees without delay. The presbytery recorded that it was a sentence which nearly all found "grievous."[13]

Summary

For the presbyteries whose locality contained substantial numbers of those disaffected from the Kirk, the Assembly and Commission decisions such as the ones concerning Brechin and Menmuir, were a crushing disappointment. Throughout the years from 1715, they had constantly lobbied the Assembly about the damage the Kirk was sustaining in their areas through unregulated domestic chaplains, insufficient support for their resistance to presentations, and inadequate concern about episcopal participation in

---

13. Not everyone was of this opinion. The newly-admitted minister of Fern, George Tytler, was a staunch upholder of patronage, and when a despondent presbytery met on the 5th. June, he demanded that the Assembly's decisions be read out in full. The Rev. David Blair of Brechin criticized him for wanting only to hear Presbytery declare its opponents victors: "a thing which all who are well acquaint with human nature will own not to be extremely pleasant, nay a severity which a generous enemy would scarce put upon his vanquished foe."

settlements. For their part, as well as the difficulties of distance and the distraction of other issues, the Church's superior courts had to be wary of the power and connections of titled landowners bearing down upon them. There was also the need for caution lest they be seen adopting a different policy for different areas.

When the admissions to Menmuir and Brechin took place on the 22nd. and 28th. August 1745, most presbyters felt acutely disappointed that their years of resistance had brought so little return. However, a few days previously, on the 19th. August, the Stewart standard had been raised at Glenfinnan, and before long, the situation would be much improved. The failure of the '45 rising was not to affect the reality of patronage, but in its aftermath the Assembly sent down to presbyteries an overture which became, in 1748, the *Act concerning the qualifications of persons claiming to vote in the calling of ministers to vacant parishes*. From then on, no one was to be allowed to vote in any call who, in the year before the vacancy, had: "either twice heard sermon in any meeting or congregation not allowed by the laws, or attended divine worship performed by any Non-jurant minister, or preacher professing himself to be of the Episcopal communion, or where His Majesty King George and the royal family were not prayed for in express words."[14] At last the Church had taken notice.

The Kirk and the ministry of the Marquis of Tweeddale

Another consequence of the 1745 rising was that it confirmed the demise of the administration led by the Marquis of Tweeddale. It is possible to argue, however, that it never properly established itself. Certainly, in the realm of church affairs, it is revealing to compare the marked difference in style between the new regime and its predecessor.

The Marquis took office in February 1742, and although, unlike Ilay, he had the advantage of enjoying the official status of Scotch Secretary, he was not able to use his position to any great effect. R.H. Scott has succinctly summarized the reasons:

> Tweeddale had been appointed Secretary of State not because of any political strength in Scotland but simply because he was the political ally of Carteret[15]. He had no influence in the Cabinet, little support in Scotland and no group of Scots members with

14. Assembly Registers, 18 May 1748.

15. John Carteret, 2nd. Earl Granville (1690–1763), was appointed Secretary of State in February 1742.

which to bargain with the Ministry. Carteret wanted Scotland kept quiet in order to concentrate on the struggle against Pelham...he had no intention of allowing Tweeddale to create an unnecessary diversion by dismantling the Argathelian hegemony in Scotland. Most people in Scotland quickly realized this and saw little point in switching their allegiance from Ilay.[16]

It is also clear from Tweeddale's correspondence that he was indecisive, dilatory and, given the fact that he only visited Scotland once during the tenure of his office, made the fatal mistake of not having a sub-minister of anything like the caliber of Milton to handle affairs in Scotland. Thus although it was the ineptitude of his handling of the Jacobite rising of 1745, which ostensibly triggered his downfall, the defects of his administration were already there, waiting to be uncovered by such a crisis.[17]

There was also a contrast with his predecessors in his approach to the filling of church vacancies. Where the Argathelian regime saw church appointments as an integral part of the business of building support, Tweeddale's view was one of open-minded detachment. Indeed, it is illuminating to detect in Tweeddale's later reflections upon his administration, a somewhat bemused regard for a Church with which neither he nor his premier Scottish adviser, Thomas Hay# of Huntingdon, had previously been particularly acquainted. He consulted Hay about "presentations and other matters related to that Church," even though he understood Hay inclined to the episcopal persuasion: "as I myself was educated in the same principles in England."[18]

Although his religious affiliations did not prevent him from believing it was the presbyterian establishment which ought to be supported north of the border, Tweeddale nonetheless came to the matter of Scottish church affairs with no clearly formed policy. This meant he was constantly obliged to rely upon advice, and, at the start, that which he received from Robert Dundas, Lord Arniston, in April 1742, made a strong impression:

> ... one great occasion of heats and disturbances that have arisen in Church judicatories and parishes about planting kirks hath proceeded from the very bad use that hath been made of the

16. Scott, "The Politics and Administration of Scotland, 1725–48," 493–4

17. See J. M. Simpson, "Who Steered the Gravy Train?" in *Scotland in the Age of Improvement*, 58.

18. British Library, MS.35448, Tweeddale to Hardwicke, 1 November 1754. Tweeddale was writing to Lord Hardwicke recommending Hay's appointment as a Lord of Session.

Crown's patronages: presentations given sometimes as rewards of corruption to a Baillie or Councilor's brother, and sometimes given to anybody named by a voter or a great man without the least regard either to heretors of a parish or people. I wish that may not go on, that no presentation may be given without your knowing the inclinations of the parish as far as may be, but at least of the heretors. And I believe, tho' not anything of that kind can well be said in a letter or speech, yet if the Commissioner were by his instructions allowed to give any assurances among the clergy that if they would come to more temper and quietness in the matter of settlements, that they might expect care would be taken to dispose of Royal presentations so as might best suit the inclinations of the parishes . . . it might be setting out with a good grace and have a good effect.[19]

Tweeddale liked Arniston's suggestions, but on the advice of Hay, stopped short of allowing Leven, the Commissioner, to give out any assurances at the 1742 Assembly about the easing of royal presentations. Hay assured him that any consultative scheme would quickly sink crown patronages, and that, in any case, novelties were not to be tried at that time.[20] Tweeddale accordingly took no action.

This left Leven, however, with nothing in the way of a manifesto to offer that year's presbytery commissioners, despite the fact that they would have come up to the Assembly expecting to see what the new regime had in its shop window. Worse still, Leven appears to have been given very little policy instruction of any kind concerning his handling of the Assembly. Robert Craigie# of Glendoick, Tweeddale's Lord Advocate, had recommended Principal Tullideph of St Leonard's College, St Andrews, as a man of integrity and merit,[21] so Leven arranged his election as Moderator[22], but quickly after that there is an appearance of uncertainty and drift. A particular example of this was the debate on the disputed settlement of Bowden (Selkirk). Although the patron, the Duke of Roxburghe, was not directly involved in politics, nonetheless the Roxburghes had always been renowned as *Squadrone* men. It would have been of inestimable value to Tweeddale at such a juncture to have demonstrated the power of his patronage by championing the cause of the Duke's presentee, James Hume. In the absence of orders, Leven took no action. The result was a

19. NLS., Yester MSS. 7046 15 April 1742.
20. Yester MS.7046, Hay to Tweeddale, 30 April 1742.
21. Yester MSS 7045 17 March 1742.
22. MS.7047, Leven to Tweeddale, 12 May 1742.

confused and emotionally-charged debate, lasting nine hours, and which was only decided in his favor, amidst much acrimony, on the difference of one vote.[23] It was not an impressive start.

The experiences of that Assembly made it abundantly clear that a church luminary had to be found, both to act as a leader around which an interest could cluster, but also as one who could garner information helpful to the regime. In other words, a *Squadrone* equivalent to Patrick Cuming. Arniston was enthusiastic that this should be the Rev. Robert Wallace# of West St Giles', Edinburgh. Craigie argued against him on the grounds that, nationally, all the ministers of Edinburgh were currently ill-regarded, and that there was much jealousy against Wallace, not to mention suspicion over the orthodoxy of some pamphlets he had written. There was also the matter of his friendship with Principal Wishart, who was attached to "another patron."[24] Although Thomas Hay agreed with Craigie's assessment, Tweeddale did not like to cross Arniston and so decided to compromise and employ both clergymen, who were to pass on their information and ideas directly to the Lord Advocate. Although Tullideph was to be the chief adviser, the Marquis later admitted that it was Wallace in whom he had the principal confidence.[25]

As can be seen from studies of him,[26] Wallace was something of a multi-hued character. He was of moderate principles, yet, as seen above, was a leading figure in the resistance to the reading of the Porteous Act. Since he also believed the settlement of a minister was a purely spiritual matter, he had no scruple about ignoring a Court of Session sist on his translation to the New North Kirk.[27] On patronage, although he considered it a grievance, it was still one that was remediless, in his view, and that it was in vain to endeavor to have the law repealed.[28] As for a method of choosing a minister, he felt that the greater the number of people involved

---

23. *Caledonian Mercury*, 19 and 21 May 1742; Morren, 352–4; MS.7047, Leven to Tweeddale, 18 May 1742; Assembly Registers, 14–20 May 1742.

24. Yester MSS 7049 Thos Hay to Tweeddale 7 Aug 1742.

25. British Library, MS. 35448.Tweeddale to Hardwicke, 1 November 1754.

26. H.R. Sefton, "Robert Wallace: An early Moderate," *RSCHS*, xvi, (1966–8); Norah Smith, "The literary career and achievement of Robert Wallace (1697–1771)," PhD diss. Edinburgh: 1973.

27. (See below); Morren, *Annals*, Appendix, 303.

28. from "Some good Hints with respect to Patronages of Churches," a pamphlet written by Wallace c.1734, and quoted in "Clerical Corridors of Power: Extracts from Letters concerning Robert Wallace's Involvement in Ecclesiastical Politics, 1742–43", Norah Smith, in *Notes and Queries*, ccxviii, June 1973, 216.

in the election, the less chance would there be for corruption, yet this was not to suggest he believed in a divine right of popular election. It would seem that he initially harbored reservations when approached by Tweeddale's administration, but that on hearing that it had well–meaning intentions regarding settlements, decided it was an opportunity for him to do good, especially concerning crown presentations.[29]

Managing Settlements

The first necessity was to establish an information network, so that notice of a vacancy could be received in sufficient time to arrange a suitable presentee. Hay was soon to complain to Tweeddale that many opportunities had been lost. Either the six months had expired, or there was no time to consult the heritors, or examine the qualifications of the person who applied for the presentation. This was made worse by the fact that presentation requests were often not sent to him at all, even though "Everybody knows I correspond with your Lop."[30] The unpalatable truth was that Hay had not the stature of Milton, nor had Tweeddale entrusted him with sufficient authority to be his equivalent. Thus, in order to get to the source of patronage quickly, supplicants had been bypassing him and instead writing to their friends in London, requesting them to approach Tweeddale directly. The only solution was an early warning network of correspondents, encompassing all presbyteries. Accordingly, Hay arranged for Wallace to take up the task.

An alphabetical list among Wallace's papers[31] reveals how over the following year he wrote nearly two hundred letters around the country. The information he asked for included the name of each minister, the value of his parish, and whether it was in the king's gift. In another circular, he not only sought timeous notice of any vacancy where the Crown had interest, but also "the inclinations of those whose interest is likely to have the greatest weight in bringing about comfortable and peaceable settlements." This was to include the opinion of the congregation as well as that of the principal heritors.[32] In the meantime, Hay was trying to ascertain the identity of each parish's patron, but found it a taxing responsibility. When he started his investigations, the best he could uncover was a book

29. Sefton, "Wallace," 7.
30. MS.7047, Hay to Tweeddale, 18 and 20 May 1742.
31. Laing MSS. II, 620.29(5).
32. Laing MSS. 620.29(6) and 620.29(7).

index in the SPCK Hall, but its value was limited.[33] Later, Tweeddale's London agent sent him a list, as did the agent for the Church, but both turned out to be inaccurate and defective. There was nothing else for it but to rely on Wallace's letter-writing.[34]

It was, of course, vital to have prompt and accurate information, but there still remained the matter of the use to which it was put. Here again, Tweeddale's management was ineffective. To begin with, three of his major advisers, Craigie, Arniston and Robert Dundas Junior (the Solicitor General) did not get on with each other.[35] Thus Craigie was deeply unhappy about Arniston's whole attitude to church affairs, and complained to Tweeddale that Arniston wanted to "govern" the Church, whereas he thought it "easier to superintend their governing themselves in a peaceable way."[36] Typically, the Marquis's reply was an unrealistic compromise. It was indeed better to let the Church govern itself, but always provided the right men were at the head.[37] It did not seem to occur to Tweeddale that the right men could only be put there by his appointment, yet he had done nothing to dismantle anything of Ilay's hierarchy of royal chaplains, despite Hay's repeated appeals to do so.[38]

Tweeddale's thinking was even more flaccid in the matter of presentations: although they were to wait for the disclosure of the parish's inclinations before intervening in a vacancy, he wanted the king's right to be as little neglected as possible.[39] Thomas Hay had already warned him that this could only be a very general plan, after all, what if the heritors and people disagreed? Secondly, the employment of the royal patronage could be most useful in building up an interest in the country, especially in the burghs. Most of all, always to arrange the agreement of the parish beforehand could actually undermine the king's right, since ministers generally preferred to eschew presentations, and would increasingly feel encouraged to shun them if they started to think the necessity for one was

33. MS.7047, 1 June 1742. (SPCK stands for Society for the Propagation of Christian Knowledge).

34. MS.7053, 1 February 1743; MS.7053, 17 February 1743. Hay mentions here that the Clerk of the Teinds has offered to make up a list from his information, but it was still to be finished.

35. R.H. Scott, 457. they formed "an unhappy group, torn by mutual distrust and jealousy."

36. Yester MSS 7050. 17 Aug 1742.

37. MS.7075, Tweeddale to Craigie, 26 August 1742.

38. e.g., MS.7047, 1 May 1742 and 18 May 1742.

39. Yester MSS 7075 26 Aug 1742.

being relaxed.[40] In this connection he alluded unhappily to the situation in the vacancy at Stranraer (Wigton), where a crown presentation had been procured, but was being kept in reserve, to be used if their preferred candidate were rebuffed. It was clear to Hay that if the existence of a presentation became public knowledge but then was not used, then it would only serve to show that they had the king's presentation, but had not thought it proper to use it.[41]

Although their conduct of the Stranraer vacancy was marked by inefficiency and the absurd antics of Hew Dalrymple, Lord Drummore, who had concerned himself in the affair,[42] the administration managed to avoid humiliation. A similar escape from the consequences of ineptitude followed their attempts to place a candidate at Stichill and Hume (Kelso), yet the outcome was still extraordinary. Suddenly their nominee revealed that he was withdrawing because he didn't like to disoblige the Earl of Home who, he had learned, had once promised Argyll he would give his first vacant living to one of the Duke's protégés. As it was, Stichill was not even in Home's gift, nonetheless Tweeddale, not wanting a confrontation nor yet wishing to lose the king's right, gave the presentation to the Argyll man.[43]

It is perhaps typical that the one occasion when Tweeddale did score a triumph over the Campbells, it was by accident rather than design. Indeed, his intention had been entirely otherwise. When the parish of Kilmodan, or Glendaruel, (Dunoon presbytery) became vacant in December 1742, it was first decided to gratify one of Tweeddale's supporters in the area by issuing a crown presentation to the Rev. Peter Campbell of North Knapdale. However, when Wallace canvassed opinion in the parish, he found that their firm preference was for the protégé of Sir James Campbell of Ardkinglas, who had formerly been the Argathelian MP for Argyllshire (1708–34). Seeking to avoid confrontation, Tweeddale dutifully ignored party differences and presented Ardkinglas' man on the 14th. March 1743. It transpired, however, that in promoting his candidate, Ardkinglas had secretly been pursuing a private scheme regarding the settlement of Kilmodan, and that Ilay knew nothing about it until too late. The Earl was outraged. To see a minister settled in Campbell territory without his knowledge was an acute embarrassment, and on learning of it, wrote

40. Yester MSS 7049 Thos Hay to Tweeddale 7 Aug 1742.

41. MS. 7051. 30 November 1742.

42. On his cavalier attitude and change of mind on the candidature, see, Whitley, diss. 238.

43. See Whitley, PhD. diss., 239.

menacingly to Milton, telling him to find out "to whom I owe the favour of furnishing Argyllshire with a minister."[44] In the event, he took no action, other than a protest to the presbytery.

Notwithstanding what happened unintentionally at Kilmodan, under Wallace's guidance, it remained the administration's objective to be fair and irenical in its dealings with royal presentations, and to that end it was almost entirely successful, as his son was later to record: "all the time he [Wallace] was employed . . . government was not embarrassed, in a single instance, either in obtaining judgement from the spiritual courts in favour of His Majesty's presentees, or in effecting the execution of settlements ordered to be made by the Church."[45] However, as Hay had noted at the beginning, the regime's aim of using its presentation privileges to promote only harmonious settlements was certainly worthy, but it was also naive to suppose that such results could be achieved without the frequent sacrifice of political advantage. For the most part, the administration was content to abide by the policy, but in the case of the vacancy at Rayne (Garioch), the temptation to apostatize from the code proved too overpowering. The reasons for the aberration were both political and personal to Hay.

After Rayne became vacant on the 3rd. January 1743, the Earl of Aberdeen recommended that Tweeddale grant a crown presentation for a relative of the highly influential brothers, Alexander and John Robertson, former Provosts of Aberdeen.[46] The Marquis might well have ignored the request had not Hay, still smarting from the Stranraer debacle, discovered that Drummore had had the effrontery to start campaigning on behalf of Rayne's popular assistant minister, James McWilliam. Hay's fury at Drummore[47] was enough to swing Tweeddale round to the idea of gratify-

---

44. Yester MS.7053, Hay to Tweeddale, 6 January 1743; Saltoun MSS., MS.16591, 11 January 1743, 25 January 1743; 5 November 1743; ____November 1743, 14 November 1743; Fasti, iv, 31. The Duke of Argyll was arguably the patron instead of the Crown, but it would appear that Ardkinglass and the Duke's legal agent, Robert Dunbar, attempted to profit by the Duke's mental decline (he finally died on the 4th. October 1743) by discretely promoting a settlement of their own choosing, through the Crown's claim to the patronage.

45. Biographical sketch of Wallace by his son, quoted in full in Morren, *Annals*, Appendix, 300–6. Henry Sefton suggests that Wallace's one failure was a riot at Kettins (Meigle Presbytery) on the 22 January 1746.

46. Yester MS.7053, 12 February 1743. The Earl added that John Robertson had "the best estate of any merchant I know in Aberdeen"; see also R.L. Emerson, *Professors, Patronage and Politics, The Aberdeen Universities in the Eighteenth Century*, (Aberdeen University Press: 1992), 65, 83.

47. Yester MS.7053, Hay to Tweeddale, 15 January 1743

ing his Aberdeen supporters, and so together they resolved not to settle Rayne by consensus. Although the majority of the parish was against their candidate,[48] Hay and Tweeddale pressed ahead and issued a presentation for him on the 14th. March 1743. Presbytery, seeing the reluctance in the parish to have the presentee, decided to resist his settlement on the grounds that, as he was a settled minister, his transportation was an infraction of the 1719 *Act for making more Effectual the Laws appointing the Oaths for security of the Government, etc.* [see above]. The superior courts of the church however had little difficulty in dismissing the plea and the settlement went ahead.

It is illuminating that despite the regime's intention to avoid the less worthy practices of the previous administration, when the pressure against their candidate was at its height, one of their number (Tullideph) undertook to find out who had concurred with the presentation, so that, as he darkly promised: "means may be taken to quash the opposition."[49] Suddenly, the words and sentiments had a familiar ring.

In connection with the foregoing, it might be wondered if Milton and Ilay remained inactive throughout Tweeddale's ministry, or was the temptation to meddle surreptitiously in settlements too strong?

A first answer to the question must be that Tweeddale frequently did not require Ilay's intervention in order to make things difficult for himself. Men like Drummore had been trusted, when, as Hay was later to remark to the Marquis, it was obvious that he was "your constant enemy."[50] Again, there was a naive expectation of goodwill from those who had lost their office as a result of the change of administration. Thus when, early on, it was decided to gratify Lord Maule over a crown presentation to Kinnell (Arbroath), Tweeddale and Craigie simply assumed that William Grant, who had lost his position as Solicitor General and was a heritor in the parish, would remain quiescent. He in fact created as much trouble as he could.[51] Later, a chastened Craigie reported on the case's perilous progress before the 1743 Assembly: "Mr. Grant refused all accommodation tho' [it was] proposed by his old friends. He was so idle as to say he hoped to see his successors foiled in their first attempt. However, we carried it today by

48. Ibid., 17 February 1743

49. Ibid., 1 October 1743

50. Yester MS.7055, 12 May 1743. Not only did he oppose Tweeddale's choice for moderator of the 1743 Assembly, but Hay discovered that the leader of the opposition to their candidate at Rayne "at bottom cared not a pin what way any Church was settled," but had been stirred up by Drummore—MS.7058, 8 October 1743.

51. Yester MS.7055, Craigie to Tweeddale, 19 May 1743.

a small majority . . . I hope we shall be careful not to run such risks in time coming."[52]

Above all, there was Tweeddale's reluctance to replace Ilay's royal chaplains with his own appointees. Craigie, for once in full agreement with Arniston, wrote advising the removal of the most nefarious,[53] first on the 30th. July 1743, then again on the 11th. August, warning that it was now absolutely necessary to act, since they brought disrepute upon the administration. On the 3rd. September, Robert Dundas junior also wrote with the same recommendation.[54] All were ignored. By the Assembly of 1744, the Commissioner, the Earl of Leven, was complaining that the previous year one of the king's chaplains had had the assurance to vote against his choice for moderator [Wallace], and that since he had still retained his office, now another chaplain had felt encouraged to do the same.[55] Only then did the Marquis act, and in June 1744, Wallace, Principal Neil Campbell of Glasgow University and William Gusthart of Edinburgh Tolbooth were given the offices.[56]

As for direct Argathelian interference in settlements, little appears in Milton's papers that is suggestive of much active intrigue before the end of 1743. It is at this point that a quickening of pace can be detected. The reason was that, despite Ilay's protestations that he was getting old [see above], when he inherited his brother's title and interest in October of that year, he clearly judged the time was opportune to rally Argathelian support—as one of Tweeddale's advisers despondently observed: "I find the old ministry people and those in opposition very closely corresponding together at this place [Edinburgh] at this time as I find all the dependants of the present D. of Argyll in high spirits."[57]

More importantly, it was clear that Tweeddale was increasingly perceived as having lost his authority: "My Lord Carteret's interest and your Lordships," he was told, "must every day diminish in Scotland except something is done to show you have power and exert it for I'm told they

52. Ibid. 20 May 1743.

53. Professor John Goudie of Edinburgh University, John Mathieson of St. Giles, and Robert Bell of Crailing (Jedburgh). Hay calculated that the total number of clerical offices at their disposal was, 2 Chaplains, 1 almoner, the revenues of the Chapel Royal divided among three and their collector. - MS.7047, Hay to Tweeddale, 18 May 1742.

54. Yester MS.7057, 30 July and 11 August; MS.14423, 3 September.

55. MS.7062 10 May 1744.

56. Morren, 304.

57. MS.7059, Arbuthnot to Tweeddale, 3 November 1743.

make no secret to assert it will soon be at an end."[58] Whether Ilay [now Duke Archibald, having succeeded his brother] sought it or not, supplicants for presentation favors began to direct their requests primarily to him or Milton and only in a nominal way to Tweeddale. The most striking example occurred with the settlement of Fern (Brechin) which had become vacant on the 4th. October 1744. Sir James Carnegie, on behalf of himself and the other major heritor, the Laird of Skene, wrote to Tweeddale and requested a presentation for their cousin, the Rev. George Tytler of Premnay (Garioch). The Marquis consulted Wallace, and promptly agreed, expressing the hope that there would be no opposition. In doing so, however, Tweeddale was wholly unaware that the real work of cutting out rival requests and promoting Tytler's cause at Court was being effected through the Argathelian network: "I shall entirely depend upon your Lop's friendship and activity in this matter," Skene had written to Milton.[59]

The nadir of Tweeddale's fortunes came in the Autumn of 1744. When the Argathelian Charles Areskine was appointed a Judge, on the 15th. November, without the Marquis even knowing, it was obvious his control was gone. Carteret fell from power shortly after and although the Marquis remained in office for a further year, it was clear he had little authority left. To judge from the dearth of correspondence, a similar watershed appears to have taken place in ecclesiastical affairs. In what was probably the unkindest cut of all against the regime's policy of settlement by consensus, Tweeddale received a public humiliation in connection with a vacancy at Dalrymple (Ayr). While the parish was in the act of centering upon a candidate, and while the crown presentation was being held back pending the outcome, Sir James Dalrymple (who had no connection with the parish) suddenly produced a presentation for his chaplain, signed by the Prince of Wales.[60] This was doubly damaging to Tweeddale in that, not only did it appear to be derisive of the king's rights, of which he was custodian, but it also implied that he had no knowledge of what actually was taking place at Court.

---

58. MS.7060, Sir John Inglis to Tweeddale, 18 January 1744.

59. Saltoun MSS., MS. 16602, George Skene to Milton, 21 September 1744.

60. Yester MS.7063, Cassillis' [?]secretary to Tweeddale, 3 July 1744.

Summary

Although the administration of Tweeddale is frequently noted for its ineptitude,[61] it would be churlish to be derisive of its benevolent intentions for the Kirk, which were sincerely, if naively, motivated. It should certainly not be forgotten that it was under this administration that an important scheme for the benefit of ministers' widows was established.[62] The fact was, however, the noble experiment of his "peaceable" settlement policy was borne down by the political realities of governing Scotland in the post-Union period. It was not enough to aspire to rule by use of laws and agreed conventions, it was even more important to be able to rule by management and influence. Tweeddale had not the personal or material resources to do either. This meant that much of Scottish society was left the latitude to follow its own wishes and loyalties. This in turn meant that the co-operation required to operate the regime's settlement strategy, was frequently withheld by those men of interest who saw no advantage in being altruistic for its own sake.

The stark truth that the idealism of the settlement plan had been doomed by the realities of the times, was tacitly acknowledged by Craigie when, in the aftermath of the Dalrymple fiasco, he wrote what in effect was the policy's epitaph: "I am very sensible of the bad use that hath upon some occasions been made of His Majesty's gentleness in his exercise of his right of Patronage and that this abuse ought to be rectified, but the proper remedy I cannot at present suggest."[63]

61. Eg., J. M. Simpson, 'Who Steered etc.,' 58.

62. See Morren, I, 303–4.

63. Yester MS.7063, Craigie to Tweeddale, 7 July 1744.

CHAPTER FOURTEEN

SINCE EDINBURGH MINISTERS WERE among the groups which exercised the most influence in ecclesiastical affairs, it would be remiss not to take time to give some consideration to the method of their appointment. As might be expected with positions of such strategic importance, the path towards a settled system for filling them was neither short nor smooth.

Ecclesiastical Patronage and the City of Edinburgh

Despite the disappearance of the Scottish Parliament in 1707, Edinburgh remained a centre of prestige and importance throughout the eighteenth century as the great weight of legal, political and ecclesiastical business still was conducted by way of the capital. In the midst of it was the town council whose members, in addition to the distinction carried by their office, were themselves the holders of considerable privileges. As well as a wide civil and criminal jurisdiction, they enjoyed the right to present to all offices of trust or emolument, the right to elect the MP, and were patrons of the university.[1] They also enjoyed a special understanding with the ascendant political figures of the day, usually the Dukes of Argyll, yet were astute enough not to allow their compliance to be taken for granted.[2] Jealous of the influence and power that had accrued to them since the constitution, or *sett* of the burgh in 1583,[3] the appointment of ministers to

1. See Hugo Arnot, *History of Edinburgh*, (Edinburgh: 1788), Book II, Ch. 3, for detailed specification

2. See Anon., [?George Drummond] "Memorandum of the Present State of the Political Differences in the City of Edinburgh—July 1763," contained in *Selections from the Caldwell Papers*, Part II, i, Maitland Club Publications. (Glasgow 1854), 182–187; Alexander Murdoch, "The Importance of Being Edinburgh: Management and Opposition in Edinburgh Politics, 1746–1784," in *SHR*, lxii, 1: No.173: April 1983, 4.

3. In theory, James VI's Act—the Decreet Arbitral—was supposed to make the

any of Edinburgh's coveted[4] charges was of more than passing interest to them. Indeed, from the early seventeenth century until their triggering of one of the most notorious patronage disputes of the times (the Drysdale "bustle" of 1762–64), the presbytery and the council engaged in a roller-coaster ride which alternated between truce and warfare.

At all times, the central focus of contention was the matter of authority, or more specifically, how it was to be divided between the council and the presbytery. This of itself was not an insurmountable problem; what, however, made it so difficult to resolve was the extent to which the city charges were one entity. In other words, was a minister called to the city or to a specific congregation? If, as was generally accepted, it was to the former, by whose will and authority could he then be moved between congregations? It was this question which cast a constant shadow over the relationship between the council, the presbytery and the city charges themselves.

Before looking at how this was dealt with in the eighteenth century, it is necessary first to look back to what was developing at the start of the previous one.

The Seventeenth Century Background

It was during the reign of James VI that the relationship between the Church in Edinburgh and the council began to be formalized. James always considered the ministers of Edinburgh to have been the instigators of a near-mobbing of him on the 17th December 1596, and so had long been eager to prevent a repetition of the incident by having the town's parish boundaries properly regulated, with each incumbent obliged to live and operate within his own parish, instead of residing at the centre with his colleagues. Despite pressure on the magistrates, however, nothing had been done. Then in early 1625, galvanized by an additional desire to gather support for his attempts to gain more acceptance for the Articles of Perth, he decided to come to an arrangement with the council whereby their co-operation with his wishes on both matters would be well rewarded.

---

reins of power more widely accessible, particularly by emancipating the crafts from their disadvantaged position; in reality, it merely confirmed the government of the city by privileged oligarchies. See further, Michael Lynch, *Edinburgh and the Reformation*, (John Donald: 1981), especially 63–64.

4. "I think I may take it for granted that every minister in Scotland has ambition enough to wish to be in Edinburgh." NLS, Saltoun MSS. 16666, Patrick Grant, Lord Elchies, to Milton, 1st. May 1749.

While the parishes were divided into four with two ministers each,[5] the council were the recipients of some remarkable advantages. Each of the four sessions would be made up of two ministers, six elders, six deacons, and the magistrates. The elders would be elected yearly by the council and the respective parish ministers. Moreover, the session clerk, reader and other offices would also be chosen by the burgh. In vacancies, the new minister would be elected exclusively by the Provost, Bailies and council, and presented to the Archbishop of St. Andrews for collation and admission. Any candidate favored by the council would be obliged to come and be heard, and if called, be unable to refuse. If the High Kirk should fall vacant, the magistrates would be free to choose which minister from the burgh should be locum. Similarly, if a High Kirk minister became infirm, they would be able to meet the problem by having the Archbishop move around the town ministers according to their pleasure; indeed, from then on, the magistrates were to have the right to decide on the parish distribution of all the clergy coming to the city churches. As a final bonus, the council asked that no session should be allowed to pass an act without it first being approved by them.

These generous terms were drafted on the 2nd March, 1625, but unfortunately for the council, James died later in the month, before giving his formal approval. However, not only was King Charles willing to ratify them, but the magistrates were even able to expand them even further, giving themselves, for example, the right to move a town minister to St. Giles whenever it became vacant. They also added the warning that kirk sessions were not to meddle in any civil affair, nor inflict any censure but an ecclesiastical one.[6]

For those who championed the inviolability of the Church against interference by secular authorities, the settlement was a major reversal[7]. On the other hand, neither was it a resounding triumph for the town, in that despite the strictures of the 1625 Act, the majority of the ministers subsequently called by the council continued to refuse to accept, and so the town churches remained severely under strength until after the conflict of

---

5. "Extracts from the Records of the Burgh of Edinburgh, 1589–1603," *Scottish Burgh Records Society* (Edinburgh: 1875 onwards), iv, 269

6. Extracts of Edinburgh Records. 16th. Nov. 1625. vol. v. 286; Also, John Connell, *Treatise on the Law of Scotland Respecting Erection, etc. of Parishes,* (Edinburgh: 1818); and William Maitland, *History of Edinburgh,* (Edinburgh: 1753).

7. see Walter Makey, *The Church of the Covenant (1637–1651),* (Edinburgh: 1979), 159. Chapter 12 of this book provides a fulsome background to the relationship between burgh and Church during this period.

1637–38.[8] Another difficulty was the king's continued insistence that the level of stipends be raised. It is clear from his national policy on teinds' reform, that Charles' general intention was to set the ministry everywhere on a secure financial footing. On the other hand, in the case of the capital, it is likely that he had the additional motive of seeking to dispense with the magistrates' annual subsidy to ministers from the Common Good Fund, something which added extra weight to their hold over their clergy[9]. The eventual outcome was an Annuity Tax on all burgh inhabitants (authorized by the Privy Council on the 18th. March, 1634), but since it did not prove sufficient either, the object was not achieved. Nonetheless, the first crack in the magistrates' solid grip on Edinburgh's ministers did stem indirectly from the measure, for resentment against this and other like taxes added fuel to the hostility that culminated in the Bishops' Wars, which in turn led to a questioning of the role played by the town in church affairs, especially in the matter of vacancy-filling.

The Souring of Church/council Relations

Before long, the Assembly was annoying the magistrates by interfering in settlements, as in the calls of William Bennet in 1640 and George Gillespie in 1641. Presbytery then added to their sense of grievance by translating John Oswald from the Tolbooth Church (which the council had only just built) to Prestonpans, not only without the council's consent but against their will.[10] Relations reached a nadir in 1648, when the council opted to support the Engagement in the face of trenchant opposition from the presbytery. Principal Robert Baillie wrote despairingly to his cousin: "The discord betwixt their magistrates and ministers was much more than I desired to see. Their spleen against one or two of their ministers was great. . . . one of their [ie., the magistrates] great cares has

---

8. Even then the situation was not helped by the raising, on the 24th. December, 1641 of the number of parishes from four to six, with two ministers for each. At the time, only seven ministers' names appear in the council minutes. ("Extracts." vi, 254.) During the Protectorate it was decided to increase the number of parishes to 10. Then it was reduced to 4, on the 12th. September, 1662. By the end of January 1663, however, the number had been raised again, to 6. Of the two ministers for each charge, one was known as the Principal and the other the Second minister.

9. R. K. Hannay and G. P. H. Watson : "The Building of the Parliament House." in *The Book of the Old Edinburgh Club*, vol. XIII (1924), 28–29.

10. "Extracts," 10th. July, 1648. (1642–55), 157.

been to keep their kirks vacant rather than to plant them with any whom they liked not."[11]

Up to this point, the procedure which appears to have evolved for attempting to fill the vacancies in the town, was that the council and deacons of crafts would summon the ministers and six sessions together, inform them whom they were proposing to present to the presbytery, then hear their opinion on it.[12] For their part, the magistrates saw the act of consultation as nothing more than a courtesy, and so responded in some alarm when the ministers and sessions began to seek it as a matter of right: not only did they refuse to see why, any more than other laic patrons, the council should feel obliged to canvass the sessions's opinions, but also "they na wayis acknowledge any power or jurisdictioun in the meittings of the sex sessiouns as ane ecclesiasticall judicatorie."[13]

The latter statement was a move of considerable significance. The council's clear intention was to splinter opposition by refusing to recognize that when the several sessions met as a single body—known as the Great or General Session—it exercised any valid authority. It would thus be easier for the magistrates to manipulate calls to candidates of their liking, since, if it had to go through a particular session, there would be less effort required to influence the outcome.[14] The move was challenged successfully before the Assembly, which ruled that the council's choice had to be agreed by the six sessions before being given to the presbytery.[15]

Before the council could counter the decision, on the 17th. August, the Engagers' expedition into England ended in humiliating failure at Preston, leaving the Church in a commanding position north of the border. Four months later, the magistrates meekly ratified the lists of instructions handed to them by the Great Session of the city churches. By the time of the parliamentary debate on the abolition of lay patronage in the following March, their submission was complete, and, seeing the way the tide was running, they resignedly instructed their commissioners to concur if nothing could otherwise be done.[16] From then on, the council

11. Principal Robert Baillie to Rev. William Spang, letter, dated 23 August 1648, concerning meeting of General Assembly, 14 July 1648, in, Peterkin, *Records of the Kirk of Scotland*, Vol. I, 526–27.

12. Extracts. 13 July, 1647. vol. 1642–55, 128.

13. Ibid., 10th July, 1648.

14. A. I. Dunlop, "The General Session: A Controversy of 1720", in *RSCHS.*, Vol.13, (1957–59), 234.

15. Peterkin, *Records*, Baillie to Spang, 526.

16. Ibid. 8th. March, 1649.

had to be careful to consult the sessions in the choosing of a minister, and take one of their number with them, when they went to prevail upon a candidate to come. At the same time, the Assembly Commission's close vetting of every proposed translation extinguished any lingering hope that the capital's status might entitle it to call whomsoever it chose.[17] The tide, however, was soon to turn yet again.

The debacles at Dunbar and Worcester savaged the Church's credibility and ushered in the Cromwellian protectorate. In 1653, the Assembly was dissolved and forbidden to meet again. Meanwhile, the relationship between the council and the Church, already soured, continued to the Restoration under a cloud of intermittent bickering. Nevertheless, the former continued to abide by the same general principles for the filling of vacancies, and in March 1660, still arranged to have full consultation with the burgh ministers not only over the selection of two new ministers, but also over which parishes they were to occupy. Again, despite King Charles's ecclesiastical changes over the following two years, there is little sign that the council eagerly seized the advantages handed to it by the restoration of patronage and the rescinding of all legislation since the Bishops' Wars.

However, by October 1662, the dearth of ministers available to serve the capital had become acute, owing to the deposition of all but one of the city clergy, and the ongoing refusal of ministers from other areas to accept calls there. The council therefore decided that their only option was to insist upon their previous privilege of having the right to compel whomsoever they chose to come, and at the same time, "becaus the present necessities of the Counsell cannot admit of the tediousnes of former formalities," they ordered presentations to be drawn up and delivered to their most recent selections without further ceremony.[18] The spirit of the times ensured that the magistrates' decision went unchallenged and they continued to fill vacancies in the same way up to the Revolution.

After 1690

At the start of the reign of William and Mary, the signs were set fair for a new era of co-operation between the council and the churches for which

17. For examples, see "Extracts," vol. 1642–55; the minutes for 7th. November,1648, and 9th. January, 1650, and the respective footnotes.

18. "Extracts," (1655–65). 6th. October, 1662. 306–7. The privilege of compelling candidates to come to the capital appears to have disappeared at the Revolution - see the case of William Mitchell, 10th. April, 1691.

it had responsibility. If the 1690 abolition of patronage might have been greeted with municipal dismay, it does not appear in the council records. This was because the council's role in the new arrangements was still considerable. Not only did the 1690 Act guarantee them a role as joint electors in a vacancy,[19] but they were to continue unchallenged in their right to move ministers from one city parish to another, and to erect parishes as they saw fit.[20] Such advantages took the heat out of the situation and allowed an atmosphere of flexibility and variety in the way the council and the General Session set about filling vacancies which then arose. The procedural variations included:

a) the council made a choice and presented the names to the Great Session for approval (1st October, 1690);

b) the council proposed a leet of names, the individual sessions considered it and added more, then the General Session voted on the successful candidates (11th and 13th January, 1692);

c) the council considered the leet drawn up by the General Session and indicated a short-leet from which it would be most suitable to make a final selection (21st November, 1692);

d) the Provost "acquainted the Session . . . that the Rev. Mr. George Hamilton, minister, and principal of the College and Parish of St. Leonards in St. Andrews, may probably be obtained if called . . . The Session calls him." (21st September,1696);

e) the council and General Session convened, and at the same meeting a leet was drawn up and a selection made (28th March,1699).[21]

The spirit of co-operation which gave rise to such flexibility went on to include the placing of ministers, who, called to the the city as a whole, had still to be assigned to individual parishes. Thus, after the Rev James

19. "This act shall be but prejudice of the calling of ministers to Royal Burghs by the Magistrates, Town Council and Kirk Session of the burgh . . . and where there is a considerable part of the parish in landward, that the call shall be by Magistrates, Town Council, Kirk Session and the Heritors." APS.1690., c.23, *Act concerning Patronages*.

20. See Extracts. vol.1689–1701, 23rd January, 1691,57, and especially, 5th. and 12th. August, 1691, 71–72. Also, 17th August,1692. 98; & concerning the New North Kirk, 25th March, 1698. 227 and 20th December, 1699. 257.

21. a).: "Extracts." 1st October,1690, vol. 1689–1701, p.48, b). to e).: from 'The Registers of the General Kirk-Session of Edinburgh', reprinted in *The Scottish Antiquary, or, Northern Notes and Queries*. vol.13. (1898).

Hart was called to the city from Ratho, and his admission fixed for the third Sunday of September 1702, the council's representatives came to presbytery on the 9th. September and declared their inclination that he be planted in the South West (Old Greyfriars) Parish. Presbytery did not hesitate to agree with the desire.[22]

It was in 1706 that friction started to arise. The trigger was grumbling by the presbytery over items such as the council's taking it upon themselves to select the holders of offices like that of kirk treasurer as well as the parish precentors and beadles. According to presbytery's researches, that right had belonged to the General and individual sessions up until the Restoration.[23] A year later it was further complained that since the council would only agree to one clerk (also appointed by them) for what was now eight sessions, the registers were woefully ill-kept. Presbytery felt it was time the magistrates began the consideration of reforms in these and other matters.[24]

Possibly to underline their dissatisfaction, the presbytery took the opportunity, later that month, to drag their feet over the magistrates' declaration that they intended to move Principal William Carstares from the South West Parish to the New Kirk. Presbytery insisted that he could not be moved without the formalities of a call, reasons for it given and answered, and an act, by them, of transportation. The magistrates replied that the whole city was only one parish, ministers were called to it, and then settled by the presbytery in one congregation or another at the council's desire.[25] It was a confrontational moment, but appreciating that a church with so distinguished a congregation[26] as the New Kirk would be as well to have someone of the caliber of Carstares, the presbytery ultimately relented and the principal was transported.

Matters settled for a further two years until the presbytery revived its former complaints about the appointment of church officials. They accepted the present council was ready to choose only candidates acceptable to them, but were concerned that those hostile to the Kirk might in future form the council and abuse the privilege.[27] The court also aired other

22. Edinburgh Presbytery Minutes, SRO., CH2\121\4. 9 September 1702.

23. Presbytery Minutes, CH2\121\5. 14 August 1706.

24. CH2\121\6. 10 December 1707.

25. Ibid., 17 December 1707.

26. 'the nobilitie, Lords of Session and others of the best qualitie doe frequent the said Kirk.' "Extracts," [1701–1718], 10 December 1707, 144.

27. CH2\121\7. 13 July 1709.

grievances, and requested consultation to remedy them. Before this could take place, tensions were raised by the council, as patrons of the College of Edinburgh, presenting the Rev. William Hamilton of Cramond to the Chair of Divinity. At the meeting of the 21st. September 1709, four ministers complained that though the council professed to have taken their advice, as required of them by the royal charter of 1566, they had disregarded the list of names the four had submitted. They therefore petitioned presbytery to uphold their rights. The complaint was added to the growing list of matters needing to be adjusted between the two bodies.

Little seems have come of any discussions between council and clergy. There was a sporadic interchange of letters, particularly concerning the matter of the council's right of moving ministers within the city,[28] but both sides appear to have preferred to perpetuate a state of truce for the next five years.

The peace might well have continued longer had it not been for the aversion of the Rev. James Hart (1663–1729), one of the ministers of Greyfriars, to losing his colleague, Matthew Wood. When in 1714, the council declared to the presbytery their desire to have Wood moved to the Tron Kirk, Hart resisted, complaining that he, the elders and congregation should be allowed to have their reasons against the move heard, as was proper procedure.[29] In response, the council insisted on their desire, saying it had been their privilege, since the Reformation, to transfer clergy as they saw fit. Presbytery eventually agreed. Hart accordingly appealed to synod, chiefly on the grounds that there had been no process, call or citation of his parish, and that the Act of Council was a gross encroachment upon the Church's jurisdiction since it amounted to an act of transportation, whereby the magistrates claimed they could move ministers at their pleasure without reference to the presbytery other than to inform it of their decision.[30] At the synod of Lothian, which met on the 4th. November, the council's representatives made the point that the same practice had been followed since the Reformation, yet this was the first appeal against it. The synod agreed, and rejected the appeal.[31]

Hart's actions were, however, a watershed in the council's dealings with the presbytery over ministerial appointments, and before long, the

28. For example, the synod launched an investigation into the issue in 1711; see Minutes of Synod of Lothian, SRO., CH2\252\8. 1 May 1711.

29. CH2\121\9. 18 August 1714.

30. Ibid. 22 September 1714.

31. SRO., CH2\252\8.

whole issue of how the Edinburgh city charges were to be supplied with clergy had boiled over into what was to be a long and acrimonious feud.

The approach to an agreement

By December 1716, the presbytery was complaining to the council about the delay in filling the town's two vacancies. As referred to above, the traditional way of filling vacancies was that each Particular Session (usually consisting of six elders and six deacons[32]) submitted their recommendations (up to three per charge) to a specially-convened meeting of the General Session. Then the Session and council together made the final choice, after which, without having to go back to the presbytery to approve the election,[33] the call(s) were dispatched. An important element in the system, however, was that although, from 1708, quarterly meetings of the Great Session continued to be held, these were for general business only. Vacancy matters were dealt with at special meetings, and the calling of these was the prerogative of the council.[34]

Around the beginning of 1717, leets had been submitted by the Particular Sessions for the city's two vacancies, but after that, nothing had happened. When, in the summer of 1718, the presbytery sent some of their members to ask the council why, the reception they encountered was less than effusive. The representatives reported that the magistrates had said that they were glad to see any of the members of presbytery "but did not know what concern the Presbytery had in the vacancies of the town, and that they had Reverend and worthy ministers of their own with whom they could converse with on that subject."[35]

The magistrates did, however, reveal to the representatives that the cause of their inaction was that some of the Particular Sessions had leeted

---

32. Deacon: "His Business is to collect the Offerings for the Poor at the Church Doors . . . to enquire into the Necessities of the Parishioners, to visit and take an Account of the Condition of poor sick People . . . to distribute to them as the Kirk Session shall appoint . . . to assist at the Communion . . . In Kirk Sessions he has no Vote, only may give his Advice if asked, except in Matters relating to the Poor: Nor has he any Stipend from the Parish." John Chamberlayne, *Present State of Great Britain*, (London: 1755), 67.

33. This was affirmed after being challenged in 1711 by Lanark presbytery, when they received a call from Edinburgh to Rev. John MacLaren of Carstairs. See, Lanark Presbytery Minutes, SRO., CH2\234\5, 18 April 1711.

34. *The Scottish Antiquary or Northern Notes and Queries*, vol. 13, 82.

35. CH2\121\9. 6 August 1718.

two sets of recommendations for one charge. This had caused offence, first, because it was unprecedented and done without consultation (the town ministers hotly denied the latter); secondly, it was bound to cause stipend difficulties eventually; and thirdly, because the recommendations involved the professors of Divinity and Church History, the design was clearly to settle them in the New Church, with its distinguished congregation. This last would be an encroachment upon their own right to decide where the ministers should go. They therefore had no intention of proceeding until new leets were submitted.[36]

While the presbytery was reflecting on the situation, the council followed up their declaration with a move that was clearly designed to spoil the plan for planting the two professors in the New Kirk. On the 20th. August 1718, they intimated to the presbytery that they had transported the Rev. William Mitchell from the Old Kirk to the New Kirk, and that "the reasons for their so doing were so weighty that they expected the Presbytery's concurrence and Mr. Mitchell's complyance, and that the expedience of this translation was so obvious, that they judged it needless to trouble the Presbytery with the reasons thereof."[37] Presbytery took deep offence at the wording, as did Mitchell over his being used as a device to undermine the leets. It was further pointed out that none of the parties involved had previously been apprised of the move. When invited to respond, the council's representatives delivered the dark warning that: "the not complyance with this translation might occasion undesirable effects." Presbytery nonetheless declined to back down and voted not to grant the transportation on the grounds that the council was claiming a power inconsistent with the Church's presbyterian constitution.

The council appealed to the next synod, where the issues were contended with a fulsomeness that required almost fifty pages of the presbytery minute book to report. The essence of the pleadings was that the council appealed to custom, while the presbytery stood on the principle of presbyterian authority. In the latter case, presbytery argued that the council's actions were worse than naked patronage, in that at least patrons accepted that presbytery alone could settle the presentee in a parish, but the council's conduct meant that they imagined that they could do so.[38] Synod's response was to delay any action pending discussions with both parties.

36. Extracts, [1701–1718], 23 July 1718, 356.
37. CH2\121\9.
38. CH2\121\10. 29 October 1718.

Eventually, it was reported at the meeting of the 6th. May 1719, that in the interests of peace the magistrates had dropped their appeal. However, the presbytery insisted on synod pursuing the matter until some satisfactory arrangement was established. A committee was appointed, but when unceremoniously warned by the council not to interfere, kept its distance[39]. This left matters unresolved until the following year, when an attempt was again made to do something about the vacancies in the city. Against presbytery's advice, a meeting of the General Sessions was called on the 30 August 1720, and although two ministers were elected, presbytery withheld its approval.

Since at this point it looked as if the dispute was about to wind back to its original beginning, both sides recognized that some jointly agreed regulations were long overdue. A meeting was held on the 2nd. November, out of which a code for filling vacancies was thrashed out. This was that, in future, when the Particular Sessions submitted their leets, the council would then lay them before the presbytery with the request to appoint a date, place and moderator for a meeting of the General Sessions, who would then make a final selection. For their part, the council would undertake to ensure that no city vacancies would be long unfilled, and that if leets are not lodged with the presbytery within two months of their preparation, the presbytery can still proceed to call a meeting of the General Sessions. Also, in future, all ministers called to Edinburgh would be settled by a service of admission, to be held in the New Kirk. Moreover, when the magistrates desired someone to be translated from one parish to another, they would first discuss it with the city ministers, obtain the consent of the parish to which he is to go, and acquaint the session of the minister's current parish. Thereafter they would approach the presbytery and ask them to make the translation effectual.[40]

The regulations of 1720 were an instant success. Both sides were clearly anxious to begin afresh, and for the next decade and a half, calls and translations were for the most part conducted in a spirit of harmony and co-operation.

The truce, however, was eventually to come to an end, and it was a letter sent to Lord Milton in 1736 which set in motion the regulations' demise.

39. CH2\252\8. 6th. and 7th. May 1719.

40. Edinburgh City Archives, Edinburgh Town Council Minutes, vol.48, 2 November 1720; also, CH2\121\10, 2 November 1720.

The End of The 1720 Agreement

The Rev. George Wishart of the Tron Kirk, a staunch Ilay loyalist, wrote on the 4th. September to Milton saying that his brother William, currently serving a dissenting congregation in London, wanted to return to Edinburgh. His brother would cheerfully accept the Principal's chair along with a city charge, although would not be willing to take one without the other. Wishart heartily commended the idea to Milton, suggesting he use his influence with the council, although he accepted it might prove a difficult maneuver in face of the growing strength of the evangelical faction in the town.[41] As Milton well knew, although his correspondent refrained from mentioning it, the evangelicals had no love for Wishart.[42] and therefore would harbor little inclination to favor his brother. Milton was however, anxious to continue his clawback of the initiative temporarily lost during the 1734–1736 period [see above], and so decided to press ahead with the project.

On the 10th November 1736, the council elected William Wishart to the principalship of the university, and then set about the other task of his call to one or other of the two vacancies then in the city, which were the New North Kirk (or West St. Giles or Haddo's Hold/Hole) and the Tolbooth (or Northwest Kirk). At the meeting of the General Sessions, called for the 6th. January 1737, the plan of the council was to have the candidates for the two charges elected separately, thus making it easier to scrutinize waverers and influence their voting. To their anger, the presbytery however insisted that there would be less suspicion of bias if each voter were to be called upon only once, at which moment he would register his choice for both vacancies.[43] This complicated any manipulation of the voting, and a frustrated Milton later wrote to Ilay: "The uproar the mad people made against Principal Wishart being a minister of Edinburgh has given us employment enough for some time, and if those who have their bread from your Lop. had not opposed us we might have got both Wishart and another Moderate man which would have casten the balance in the Presbytery on the Moderate side."

41. Saltoun MSS.16568.

42. See Shaw, *Management*,103, and the threatening letter which called Wishart and his colleagues "soule sellers."

43. Edinburgh Council Minutes, vol. 57; CH2\121\13. 5 January 1737.

As it was, Milton was forced to treat with the evangelicals so that in return for his having Wishart elected, they could have their own Alexander Webster as the other candidate.[44]

At this point yet more contention broke out. Of the two vacant churches, the Tolbooth was firmly of an evangelical disposition and had already made clear its disinclination to receive any "declaimer or mere morality teacher,"[45] of which variety they had reason to believe Wishart was.[46] This left the New North Kirk as an alternative, except that, at their meeting of the 23rd. February 1737, presbytery heard that it was also averse to accepting Wishart. The council's response was that his call should nonetheless proceed, and if the resistance still continued there were other ways of settling him in the city. The presbytery were understandably wary about such a plan, since all transportations had properly to be justified with reasons for their being allowed, and plainly this could not be done if no parish was actually desirous of having the candidate concerned. Accordingly, it was decided to consider the calls separately, and since the Rev. Alexander Webster, currently at Culross, was unanimously wanted at the Tolbooth where his father had previously ministered, presbytery sustained his call and held Wishart's in suspense.

The Wishart affair remained undetermined for another year until the 1738 Assembly, which vindicated him of some allegations that had since been made regarding his orthodoxy and ordered presbytery to proceed to his admission to Edinburgh forthwith. Presbytery complied by admitting him as a minister of the city on the 13th. July 1738. The question remained, however, where was Wishart to go?

In a move designed to pre-empt Wishart's arrival, the New North Kirk had petitioned presbytery on the 28th. June 1738, saying they had applied to the magistrates for their concurrence in their desire to have the Rev. Robert Wallace translated from New Greyfriars. They moreover asked presbytery to do what they could to further the desire and in the meantime repel attempts to settle their church in any other way. Presbytery accordingly approached the council, who replied that they might have been willing to co-operate with Wishart's succeeding Wallace at New Greyfriars, except that they understood it was not willing to receive

44. Saltoun MSS. 16569. Letter copies, Milton to Ilay, January and February 1737.

45. Ibid.

46. Morren, *Annals,* i, 311, says that he tended to confine himself to moral illustration.

Wishart either.[47] This being the case, the council was resolved to cut short any further argument and were determined that Wishart be settled at the New North Kirk forthwith. Disliking the council's tone, presbytery, at their meeting on the 30th. August, retaliated by going ahead and translating Wallace there instead.[48]

On the 1st. September 1738, the council met in a state of rage at what they saw as a manifest violation[49] of the 1720 regulations, and instructed their lawyers to seek from the Court of Session, a suspension of the presbytery's sentence, a reduction of the 1720 regulations and a declarator of all the town's rights and privileges of presenting, calling and translating. Presbytery's reply was to label the magistrates' act of applying to the civil courts "the most daring blow given to the constitution of the church since the Reformation,"[50] and appointed the procurator of the Church to represent them. In response, the council decided that it was time the seats in the New North Kirk were repaired, and had it announced that the church would be closed until further notice.[51] Wallace nonetheless went there and lodged his extract of transportation with the Session, who received him as one of their ministers.

Matters were spiraling out of control by the time the presbytery met on the 27th. September. The meeting was a stormy one, aggravated, as one of Milton's agents told him, by the fact that the evangelicals were averse to peace and only wanted to inflame the dispute further. Eventually, however, a "pacifick committee" was appointed to meet with the council in the hope of finding a remedy to the points under contention.[52]

At the initial meeting of both sides' representatives, the council offered to drop their suspension and let the issue be decided by an ecclesiastical court provided the presbytery in the meanwhile withheld Wallace's translation. Presbytery's committee replied that it was now too late to do so, and besides, there was no mention of the council's dropping their Reduction and Declarator. There the discussions ended. The full presbytery met

47. CH2\121\13. 26 July 1738.

48. According to Morren, *Annals*, i, 303–4, the underlying cause of the Magistrates' antipathy to Wallace's translation was his prominent part in the campaign to resist the reading of the Act for apprehending those involved in the Porteous murder. This had been further aggravated by his criticisms of Walpole's administration.

49. Edinburgh Council Minutes, vol. 59.

50. *Caledonian Mercury*, 12 September 1738.

51. Ibid. 18 September 1738.

52. Saltoun MSS. 16574. George Irving, Town Clerk, Edinburgh to Milton, 29 September 1738.

on the 4th. October and in another heated debate considered whether the magistrates had given them grounds to suppose it was worth continuing negotiations. It was successfully moved that there were no such grounds, unless, as one member argued, the presbytery was prepared to read the magistrates' supposed concessions backwards, "in which case they might have an affinity with the boatmen of North Leith who while they looked one way tugged another."[53]

On hearing the presbytery's decision, the council made up its mind to press ahead with its Bill of Suspension before the Court of Session, only to realize that with Wallace's translation already so far advanced, it was hardly worth the trouble of continuing, especially as the Court of Session would not extend its initial sist of the presbytery's sentence. It accordingly dropped the Bill and decided once again to make Wallace's charge of New Greyfriars its target for Wishart. At first, presbytery rebuffed the magistrates' desire on account of its impudent expressions and offensive claims as to their patronage of all the city churches. However, since the latter then produced a petition and concurrence with their project from New Greyfriars itself, the presbytery had little choice but to agree to the settlement, despite complaints from one member that the magistrates had "led the presbytery a dance" before the courts.[54] Wishart was finally admitted on the 13th. July 1739.

Meanwhile, the Lords of Session were still to give their judgment regarding the Declarator and the Reduction. The council's argument was that the right of patronage had always been their inalienable possession since 1636, and that whereas, as in 1720, they could *voluntarily* restrain themselves in their exercise of it, it still remained open to them to make settlements by presentations, by the regulations, or by both.[55] On the 12th. February, the Lords delivered their verdict and unanimously found for the complainers. The 1720 regulations were reduced and the magistrates were restored to their "ancient right" of patronage.[56]

53. *Caledonian Mercury*, 5 October 1738.

54. *Caledonian Mercury*, 8 February 1739.

55. See: "Memorial for the Magistrates, Council and Community of the City of Edinburgh, 1738". Edinburgh City Archives, "Miscellaneous Mss."

56. *The Scots Magazine*, i, February 1739.

After The Verdict

The council had won their point, but since it was obvious that opposition from the evangelical faction was not about to disappear, they also knew that a bald desertion of the 1720 regulations was not a realistic proposition if endless trouble and expense were to be avoided. The result was that the progress of settlements and translations over the next twenty years followed an irregular course, as if each side were constantly testing the other's resolve. The first confrontation occurred in 1744, when the council, supported by petitions from the congregation's kirk session, requested Principal Wishart's translation from New Greyfriars to the Tron be made effectual by the presbytery. Presbytery agreed but took exception to the council's phraseology, which stated that the magistrates had resolved, on their own authority, to appoint, translate, place and settle Wishart at the Tron. After lengthy negotiations between the two bodies, presbytery eventually proceeded with the translation, but only on condition they would first be permitted to supervise the precise wording of the call lest it imply the council possessed privileges to which it was not entitled.[57] The 1720 arrangements did of course allow for the council to initiate a transportation, but the keys to its smooth operation were consultation and careful wording. Presbytery's sensitive conscience would be satisfied only if it could be demonstrated, on the one hand that a projected move conformed to the wishes of the congregation and was acceptable to the parish losing its pastor, and, on the other, that the Church alone had the authority to join a minister to a congregation.

As the years went by, this tension between the Church and the town over each other's rights regularly held up settlements while negotiations took place.[58] It was not, however, until 1758 that relations became especially strained, when the synod of Lothian and Tweeddale took a dislike to the cavalier fashion in which the council had arranged for the Rev. Hugh Blair to be translated from Lady Yester's to the College Kirk, and then to

---

57. SRO. CH2/121/15, Edinburgh Presbytery Registers, 25 July 1744, 27 February 1745; Town Council minutes, 20 February 1745.

58. Eg., in 1747, the council decided to transport the minister installed at New Greyfriars to Old Greyfriars. Intimation of this was sent to the presbytery along with a request to moderate a call from the leets originally drawn up by the Particular Sessions for the Old Greyfriars vacancy, but which they now asked to be applied to the New. Presbytery responded by declaring that the power of translating was vested in them only. When the council then produced evidence that its desire was supported by all the parties affected, presbytery had little choice but to co-operate. Edinburgh Town Council registers, lxvi, 15 April 1747.

the New Church (St Giles' or High Kirk) instead, when it suddenly became vacant, all in a matter of months.[59] The synod accordingly annulled Blair's tie with the New Church and ordered his settlement at the College Kirk. An outraged council went to the Assembly, won its appeal against the sentence and Blair was returned to the New Church.[60] The situation nonetheless remained volatile and, as other issues concerning their authority began to bear down upon the council, it was perhaps to be expected that matters came to a head four years later in the passionate dispute that was to be known as the Drysdale Bustle.

For some time the council had been going through a difficult period. Already unpopular for its fiscal measures, condemned as elitist, corrupt and ripe for reform of its electoral procedures, the death of the council's patron, the Duke of Argyll, in 1761 inevitably left it looking vulnerable to its opponents. It therefore became vital for the magistrates to avoid appearing to fail in the delivery of any promise to their new patron, the Earl of Bute. Accordingly, when they were asked to have a candidate favored by William Robertson's# "Moderate" interest [see below], the Rev. John Drysdale of Kirkcaldy, called to the city, they were anxious to please. However, since they were not hopeful about persuading the increasingly radical General Sessions to agree, they decided that the only solution was to issue a presentation in December 1762. The move united a wide spectrum of opposition forces in a resistance which, for all its intensity, was insufficient to affect the outcome and the magistrates had their way. However, as R.B. Sher has pointed out in his article on the affair,[61] times were changing in the city.

After Argyll's death in 1761, Milton had continued to be a person of power and influence, yet his hold on, and therefore protection of, Edinburgh town council had thereafter carried an uncharacteristically uncertain appearance until his retirement from public life in the mid–1760s (he died in 1766). This meant that the council could not afford to

59. Although Blair had been translated on 28 January 1756, he (as was now standard practice) was not to start work until his former church was filled. It was during this intervening period that the New Church became vacant and the council changed its mind.

60. NLS., MS 17601, Milton's Letter Books, memorial dated May 1758; Edinburgh University library, Laing MSS, ii, 18/12, Minute of Edinburgh presbytery, 21 April 1758; Morren, ii, 161–62.

61. RB. Sher, 'Moderates, managers and popular politics in mid-eighteenth century Edinburgh: the Drysdale 'Bustle' of the 1760s', in *New perspectives on the politics and culture of early modern Scotland*, ed., John Dwyer et al, (Edinburgh: 1982), 180ff.

ignore the unexpectedly widespread opposition they had encountered in the Drysdale affair from the ranks of tradesmen, merchants and ordinary burgesses as well as the General Sessions. They were accordingly more cautious when using their power to present in the following decades, and indeed, as in 1766, were happy to court popularity with the Sessions and Merchant Company by eschewing it[62] altogether.

It is of interest that while the above was taking place, a parallel controversy was unfolding in Glasgow. Up until this point, elections to that city had also been on the basis of a joint decision by the council and General Sessions. Then, in 1762, the council triggered a furious debate by announcing that it would issue a presentation for the latest vacancy. Ned C. Landsman has described how, as in Edinburgh, the council emerged victorious, yet had also created more difficulty for itself in the long term by providing a rallying point for protest among the growing number of radicals whose opposition to patronage had broadened out into the general cause of liberty. Unlike the earlier Seceders, who saw patronage as an obstruction to the Kirk's return to her pure and proper condition, these campaigners regarded it in a quasi-political light. For them, it was part of an establishment edifice which denied people a liberty of conscience or Christian liberty that applied not only to presbyterians but to all protestants.'[63]

What happened in the 1762 Edinburgh and Glasgow settlement controversies would not bring about the demise of municipal management by a self-serving oligarchy, but the magistrates' confidence in being able to staff their city's churches as they saw fit was certainly shaken. As the century progressed, pressure for political reform would not go away. Thus, as Sher suggests, it may well be that in the unfolding story of popular agitation for political change in Scotland, the Drysdale incident should be regarded as an underrated but highly important landmark.[64]

62. See, Morren, ii, 286, n.

63. Ned C. Landsman, 'Liberty, piety and patronage: the social context of contested clerical calls in eighteenth-century Glasgow', in *The Glasgow Enlightenment*, ed.s, Andrew Hook and R. B. Sher, (East Linton: 1995), 218.

64. Sher, 'Drysdale "Bustle,"' 203.

Chapter Fifteen

After Tweeddale

When, in January 1746, the discredited Tweeddale at last resigned as Scotch Secretary, Archibald Campbell, now third Duke of Argyll, was already in London and available for office. First, however, he had to await the unfolding of the celebrated power struggle[1] between George II and his ministers, an episode which established the ascendancy of Henry Pelham# and his brother, the Duke of Newcastle. Ostensibly, this outcome should have been favorable to Argyll's fortunes. However, any hopes he may have entertained of a swift return to his previous prominence were not to be realized and for the next two years his influence floundered. An explanation for this can probably be detected by looking at Argyll's standing at Court, in Scotland and in Parliament.

First, there was his relationship with the Court. Later that year, the *Squadrone* Earl of Marchmont recorded how Lord Chesterfield had told him that: "the King had a most mortal hatred to him [Argyll], worse than to any man in his Dominions, and that I had an affection for the Duke in comparison of the King."[2] Clearly, although Pelham had emerged as victor from his confrontation with the king, he still required to maintain a working relationship with the Crown. It would be of no advantage to him to feed the king's near-paranoia about Argyll (George II later described him acidly as 'Vice Roy in Scotland'[3]) by restoring to his patronage the largesse he had previously enjoyed. Some measure of caution was required.

1. See, for example, Dorothy Marshall, *Eighteenth Century England*, (London: 1962) 208–10, for a description and assessment.

2. SRO. GD 158/2519. Diary of Hugh, 3rd. Earl of Marchmont, vol. VII, 27 October 1746. (Chesterfield at this time succeeded Lord Harrington as Secretary of State for the Northern Department).

3. *History of Parliament: The House of Commons, 1715–1754*, ed. R. Sedgwick, (London:1970), I, Pelham to Newcastle, 24 July 1747, 159–60.

Secondly, although the Duke had gone to London on the outbreak of the Rebellion to safeguard his position there, his absence from Scotland left behind a damaging vacuum. Milton performed excellent service in assisting the Duke of Cumberland's successful suppression of the revolt,[4] but this brought little benefit to his patron in London. It was Milton and Cumberland who received the ensuing acclamation, and, for the initial period after Culloden, it was with them that authority rested for sorting out Scottish affairs.[5] When the elections of 1747 took place, it was Cumberland who chose five new Scottish representative peers and influenced the result of several parliamentary contests.[6] Cumberland's rivalry only receded after he had fallen out with Newcastle in 1748.

Thirdly, Argyll's standing within Parliament was damaged by the fact that, although he enjoyed good enough relations with Pelham, estrangement had arisen between him and the powerful Newcastle. This handicap was aggravated by Newcastle's decision to identify with Cumberland's insistence that severe legislative measures were the best way to deal with post-rebellion Scotland. Argyll was thus in an awkward position. He had no wish to be perceived in Scotland as having concurred lightly with the more punitive measures, yet he nonetheless could little afford to stand too boldly against the tide of Scotophobia in London. As it was, his patent dislike of the 1747 Bill for the Abolition of Heritable Jurisdictions was gleefully cast in an ill light by his enemies.[7]

To make matters worse, Argyll's rivals from the *Squadrone*, fearful of a restoration of his former hegemony in Scotland, had also been working to weaken his position. On the 22nd. October 1746, Marchmont had talks with Pelham. It became clear to the Earl that Pelham, on the one hand, would not think of going past Argyll in Scottish affairs,[8] yet was also determined to avoid the acrimonies of the past by promoting a much broader dispensation of government favors and places. Marchmont was unsure if the Lord Treasurer was being realistic in imagining that Argyll would voluntarily co-operate in a more relaxed regime, answerable directly to the ministry in London. He told Pelham that his *Squadrone* colleagues were

---

4. See Shaw, *Management*, 167–68.

5. After Cumberland returned south in July 1746, he continued to exercise authority through his secretary, Sir Everard Fawkener.

6. Murdoch, *The People Above*, 35. The peers were, Leven, Gordon, Lauderdale, Rothes and Aberdeen.

7. Murdoch, 35.

8. Marchmont, *Diary*, vii, 22 and 27 October 1746.

prepared to be agreeable, and that their only desire was that they should receive a share of royal largesse without having to pay court to Argyll. However, this would only be feasible if Pelham were genuinely firm in curtailing the Duke, otherwise, Marchmont knew Argyll's hostility would be implacable if any Scottish appointment was made without his approval. He also warned that it was all very well for Pelham to say he wanted the Earl and his brother (Alexander Hume Campbell, MP for Berwickshire) brought into the administration, but unless Argyll's wings were clipped first, it could not be done.

In the event, Pelham decided to achieve his intentions for Scotland by means of diplomatic barter, in May/June 1748. The *Squadrone* Robert Dundas of Arniston was made Lord President. In return, Argyll's secretary, John Maule, was made a Baron of the Exchequer. Since Milton's health had been suffering, he was allowed to resign the Lord Justice Clerkship and received instead the post of Keeper of the Signet,[9] with the added bonus that it be for life. The Argathelian Charles Areskine was made Lord Justice Clerk in his stead.[10] In addition, Pelham persevered in his policy of confining the Duke by extending the ministry's influence, ensuring, for example, that elected peers, judges and other law officers were appointed from a wider range of interests and loyalties. His view, as he told Lord Chancellor Hardwicke in 1753, was that, "Though I have great regard for his Grace and think him the most able, and willing to serve there as any in Scotland, yet I do not think it is necessary always to have his fiat in the disposition of offices."[11] When all was said and done, however, the 1748 compromise was still much to Argyll's advantage: not only did it end the damaging period of uncertainty about his credibility[12] and status, but, despite the inroads on his hegemony, it clearly acknowledged that he could not be ignored in any effective administration of Scotland.

9. This gave him the power to appoint all the sheriff clerks and JP clerks. The Earl of Findlater wrote to Newcastle and complained that many thought Milton's resignation "was too dear bought." (BL., Newcastle MSS, MS 32715, Findlater to Newcastle, 8 July 1748).

10. BL., Newcastle MSS, 32712, Earl of Findlater to Newcastle, 14 July 1747; NLS. Saltoun MSS, 16655, Lord Arbuthnot to Milton, 26 May 1748. On Milton's workload, see Shaw, *Management*, 168–71.

11. RH. Scott, 550. The quotation is from BL. Hardwicke MSS.,35423, f 160, 10 June 1753.

12. As late as April 1748, Patrick Cuming was writing to Milton complaining bitterly that their former influence in Church affairs was slipping away; see Saltoun MSS, 16657, 22 April 1748.

On the other hand, the Golden Age of Argyll and Milton's dominance in church affairs was not about to return. They would still have much success in imposing their wishes, yet times were changing: in the first place, the restrictions on their power meant they were unable to recapture the momentum of their old party machinery. Indeed, a glance at the initial years after 1748 reveals several instances where their former efficiency and sureness of touch seemed to be lacking. Thus when the principal of Marischal college, Aberdeen, died in August 1748, it seemed an ideal opportunity to regain the city for the Argyll interest, by arranging for the post to be given to the incoming provost's son–in–law. To Argyll's embarrassment, however, Newcastle gave the appointment to someone else, which left him scrambling to arrange another preferment (King's Almoner) for his candidate, by way of compensation. In the event, the Argyll interest did win the town, but the Duke's failure over the principalship was reported to Patrick Cuming as being a major loss of face.[13]

The settlement of Duns (Duns presbytery) was another example. The Duns controversy was to be the most famous settlement case of the 1740s. Milton owed a favor to Andrew Dickson, the minister of Aberlady, and so decided, when the desirable charge of Duns became vacant in April 1748, that it would be a suitable reward for his son, Adam. He accordingly prevailed upon John Hay of Belton, who had the right of patronage, to give him the presentation. The only problem was that Belton's possession of the right was based on questionable circumstances. Alexander Hay of Drumelzier was the recognized patron, but scrupled to take the oaths enabling him to exercise his right of presenting. In the previous vacancy (1737) he solved the problem by disponing the right to another, Lord Blantyre (and his heirs), now he repeated the device by disponing it to Belton. Belton however approached Duns presbytery with documentation claiming he had the patronage through a disposition, not from Drumelzier, but from the present Lord Blantyre. In the ensuing confusion, presbytery unsurprisingly decided that the circumstances suggested collusion had been present in both vacancies, and that Drumelzier was simply commissioning his friends to perform his wishes. That the disposition to Blantyre had been a

13. BL., Hardwicke Papers, MS 35446, Findlater to Hardwicke, 25 September 1748 and 28 October 1748; NLS., Saltoun MSS, MS 16657, Provost William Chalmers to Milton, 20 August 1748; MS 16668, Provost Archibald Robertson to Patrick Cuming, 31 January 1749, Scott of Scotstarvit to Milton, 19 February 1749. The principalship was given to the professor of Greek, Thomas Blackwell, who was the first layman to hold the office. Argyll's man, Robert Pollock, professor of Divinity, eventually succeeded in 1757.

sham then appeared to be confirmed when presbytery heard that Drumelzier had thereafter continued to exercise a patron's right of uplifting the
vacant stipend. Accordingly, Belton's presentation was ignored, prompting
him to apply to the Court of Session for a declarator of his right.

Although it was obvious that collusion had occurred,[14] Milton had by
now little choice but to encourage Belton's action. The reason was that, as
had frequently happened in the past, *Squadrone* sympathizers had by this
time aligned themselves with the opposition to the presentation and had
even been suggesting that a successful resistance might help to unhinge
patronage altogether.[15] Perhaps predictably, in February 1749, the law
lords found for Belton, which in turn left the Assembly little choice but
to order Dickson's admission. The presbytery would not, however, give up
and appealed the Court of Session's judgment to the House of Lords who,
in March 1750, overturned it on a technicality. Milton hurriedly ensured
the defect was made good and the Session's judgment was allowed to stand
after all, but yet again he and Argyll had come perilously close to major
embarrassment.[16] Moreover, they had not enhanced their reputations by
becoming involved in a case where the success of the patron's antics had
caused distaste and some alarm in London.[17]

14. That Belton had only accepted the patronage to serve a purpose was clearly
demonstrated by his signing an "Obligation" on 3 September 1748, binding his heirs
to return it to Blantyre on his death (Hay of Duns Castle Muniments, TD86\44\402).
Belton's legal advisers successfully argued, however, that even though collusion was
provable, the law did not specifically condemn it.

15. One such was the Rev. James Laurie of Langton, whose opposition was intensified by his having attempted to solicit the presentation for Duns and being spurned.
(Hay of Duns Castle Muniments, TD86\44\7, "Memorial for John Hay of Belton, 22
March 1749") [I am most grateful to the Hay family of Duns Castle for access to their
family papers].

16. Hay of Duns Castle Muniments, TD86\44, bundles 7, 10, 85, 402; NLS., Saltoun
MSS, MS 17601, 5 November 1748; MS 16657, 4 May and 10 June 1748; MS 16663, 2
May, 25 May, 26 and 27 July 1748; MS 16665, 17 January, 26 May and 22 December
1749; SRO., CH2\113\7, Duns Presbytery Registers, September 1748 ff.; *Scots Magazine*, 1749, 235–40; Morren, *Annals*, i, 141–53. Dickson was admitted on 21 September
1750. As with his predecessor, the induction took place under military protection, and,
again similar to the previous admission, it prompted the formation of a dissenting
congregation. (*FES*, ii, 10).

17. see the memorial for Lord Chancellor Hardwicke: BL., Hardwicke MSS, MS
35891, bundle 78, "Note relative to collusive presentations in Scotland," Anon., nd.,
?1753–60. A similar concern prompted the Assembly to instruct its Commission to
draw up an overture "for applying to Parliament to have the law of Patronages so explained as to prevent unqualified patrons from substituting others *pro haec vice*." A
draught overture was produced on 14 March 1751, yet nothing seems to have come of

In a similar way over the soon to be notorious settlement of Lanark, they allowed themselves, for political reasons, to be drawn into a dispute which, once begun, had to be continued to what became an absurd conclusion. When the charge became vacant in 1748, the town council decided to thwart the apparent patron, John Lockhart of Lee, by trying to claim that they possessed the patronage. When it looked as if they would fail, they invited the Crown to claim the right to present, whereupon Milton and Argyll, glad to please their allies on the council, did so. The presbytery were, however, confident from the evidence of their records that Lockhart's right was valid and so proceeded to install his presentee, despite much local opposition, on 7 October 1750.[18] Nine months later, the Court of Session declared that the patronage belonged to the Crown. The civil courts could not then remove Lockhart's presentee (Robert Dick, probationer), but it could decide the fate of the now vacant stipend. On 29 July 1752, the Lords of Session generously decided that Dick should have it until the end of his incumbency. Determined not to let go, however, Argyll instructed the Lord Advocate to appeal to the House of Lords, where the judgment was reversed. The stipend thus reverted to the Crown, leaving Dick to survive on his own income.[19] Although a transportation to Edinburgh was arranged for him in 1754, the proceedings made the administration appear vindictive and moreover ensured that the outcome was frequently cited in future debates on patronage as an example of its baleful effects.

In another change from former times, Argyll was to find that resistance to presentations was becoming bolder, of which there was no more striking example than the response made to the presentation made by himself when the Lowland congregation at Campbeltown became vacant in February 1749. The embarrassment of being opposed from within his own heartland provoked the direst of threats from the outraged Duke, yet both the elders and the ordinary members put up a determined resistance. The reason was that the congregation was mainly comprised of

---

it. (SRO., CH1\3\25, Assembly Commission Registers, 1747–1757).

18. The admission was supported by the senior courts of the Church, but owing to the passion of the presentee's opponents, it took place in the Tron church in Glasgow.

19. Henry Moncrieff Wellwood, *John Erskine* 427 ff.; Morren, i, 169–80; Tytler, *Decisions of the Court of Session*, iii, (1738–1770), 273; John Connell, *Treatise on the law of Scotland respecting the erection, union and disjunction of parishes: the manses and glebes of the parochial clergy, and the patronage of churches* (Edinburgh: 1818), 533 ff., note his comparison with the case of the second charge at Culross, where the patron successfully sued for the vacant stipend on 26 June 1751.

descendants of covenanting sympathizers who had fled from persecution in Ayrshire and Lanarkshire in the seventeenth century. This was their first experience of a presentation, and they resolved to resist it. Eventually, amidst "a great uproar" the session succumbed to the pressure and abandoned their stance, thus paving the way for the presentee's admission. The affair had nonetheless put Argyll in an awkward and potentially humiliating position, since both sides in the struggle well knew that the Duke "would not incline to have an appeal from his country tossed in the Assembly house if possible it could be prevented."[20]

It was not only congregations that were more spirited in their intransigence. Argyll found the Kirk's senior courts were also harder to manage, a fact that was especially demonstrated by his failure to smother what was to be known as the Augmentation Scheme. The background to the project was that ministers' stipends had been diminishing in value during the 1740s, and although it was technically possible for individuals to apply to the Court of Session for increase, the trouble and expense involved made such a course uninviting. Parliamentary legislation accordingly seemed the solution, and many felt emboldened to support a petition to Parliament on the grounds that the Kirk's loyalty to the government during the '45 was surely deserving of such acknowledgement.[21] Unsurprisingly, the landed interest were strongly opposed to it, and Argyll's Lord High Commissioner to the Assembly, the Earl of Leven, did his best to stifle the project when it came to the 1748 and 1749 Assemblies. However, the 1750 meeting was determined, and despite Leven's threats and cajoling, the petition went ahead. Although there was never any danger of the representation being successful, that it was made at all was an embarrassment for the administration in Scotland.

Ironically, the affair of the Augmentation Scheme in fact turned out to be something of a turning point for the regime in that it enabled it to regain some of the initiative it had let slip in managing the Kirk over the years after the end of the '45. In the first place, Leven suddenly found his job had become easier as a result of the way the Assembly had been split by the Scheme along unexpected lines: some establishment men (like Cuming) supported it because they wanted to raise the social standing of their

20. *FES.*, iv, 52; Saltoun MSS, MS 16664, Archibald Campbell to Milton, 25 August 1749, 4 September 1749, 28 October 1749, 28 November 1749; Duke of Argyll to Archibald Campbell, 28 August 1749; MS 16668, Peter Stewart to Archibald Campbell, 24 August 1749. The presentee was Rev. John MacAlpine of Arrochar (Dumbarton).

21. Carlyle, *Autobiography* , 237–38; Thomas Burns, *The Benefice Lectures* (Edinburgh 1905), 105.

colleagues, whereas some evangelicals opposed it because they distrusted the notion that ministers should be members of polite society with all its liberalism and secular influences. Secondly, by raising the specter of a greater enforcement of the law on patronage as a *quid pro quo* should the augmentation project succeed, the regime found it had sown near panic amongst the Church's ranks.[22] The tactic could be used again (which it was). Thirdly, and most importantly, the Scheme coincided with the rise of a group within the Church itself who were determined to arrest the trend of indiscipline amongst its subordinate courts, especially over the issue of patronage.

The Moderate party

It was during the Assembly of 1751, that a circle of concerned ministers and elders met in an Edinburgh tavern to plan how they could reassert the Assembly's authority, which they believed had too often been compromised by ministers' being permitted the luxury of disobeying its instructions on the ground of conscience. For them, a typical example of this misguided leniency was once more likely to occur when the Assembly heard the case against John Adams of Falkirk (Linlithgow), who had disobeyed an order to preside at the ordination of the presentee to Torphichen. The group, who came to be known as the Moderate party,[23] resolved to demand that Adams and the presbytery be suspended for six months. Although they were to lose that vote, the impression they made was sufficient to convert many to their point of view and when a similar case of disobedience came before the following year's Assembly, the result was very different.

The presbytery of Dunfermline had refused to obey the Commission's instruction to settle the presentee for Inverkeithing, yet when the Commission were informed of the offence in March 1752, they had refrained from issuing a censure. The new group, headed by William Robertson of Gladsmuir, gave in their dissent (later published) and complained to the 1752 Assembly. On Monday, 18 May, the Assembly ordered the presbytery to proceed to the ordination, and at the same time enlarged the presbytery's

22. See Morren, i,188 ff.

23. They were, Provost George Drummond, the Master of Ross, Gilbert Elliot, jnr. of Minto, Andrew Pringle, Rev Mssrs John Jardine, Hugh Blair, William Robertson, John Home, Adam Dickson of Duns, and George Logan of Ormiston, Alexander Carlyle of Inveresk and four others not named (Carlyle, *Autobiography*, 257). For more on their role as a party, see I.D.L. Clark's "Moderatism and the Moderate party in the Church of Scotland 1752–1805," PhD diss., (Cambridge 1963).

quorum in order to ensure that at least two of its recalcitrants would be obliged to conform. When nothing had been done by the day appointed, the court decided it was time to act. Among the Dunfermline ministers who made submissions, there were six who defended themselves by referring to the Assembly Act of 1736, which cautioned against the intrusion of ministers against the wishes of the congregation [see above]. Rather than mollifying the meeting, however, this had the opposite effect and the members voted to make an example of one of them by deposing him.[24] It is not obvious why Thomas Gillespie# of Carnock was ultimately selected for the punishment, other than his having the effrontery to lodge another representation which repeated almost the same points, however, K. B. E. Roxburgh's biography of Gillespie suggests that Robertson's revulsion for Independency may have had a bearing, since Gillespie had received both theological training and ordination within that tradition south of the border.[25]

In the event, Gillespie's departure (he went on to form the Relief Presbytery in 1761) and the subsequent suspension of three of Dunfermline presbytery seems to have had the salutary effect intended. Leven wrote exultantly to Hardwicke after the next Assembly to report that it had been "moderate beyond expectation."[26] Although the furor raised by the case had provoked many overtures from presbyteries and synods, the Commissioner found that, by using the same threat of a rigorous application of the 1712 Act as had worked with the Augmentation Scheme, he was able to persuade the meeting to ignore them. The next year's Lord High Commissioner was also to report on the calm and peaceableness of that Assembly's conduct,[27] and certainly, as the Moderates continued to grow in influence, a period of consistency in the enforcement of presentations ensued.

For the Moderates themselves, their ascendancy was not to come to its height until Robertson was made principal of Edinburgh University

---

24. The Moderates' reply to those who appealed to the 1736 Assembly Act was to argue that: "it is by no means specified how great the concurrence should be; or that opposition, even from the majority of the congregation, shall be regarded, unless their objections be solid and verified." See Anon. (? John Hyndman, West Church, Edinburgh) "A just view of the constitution of the Church of Scotland, and of the proceedings of the last General Assembly in relation to the deposition of Mr Gillespie," in *Scots Magazine*, xv, February 1753.

25. K. B. E. Roxburgh, *Thomas Gillespie and the origins of the Relief Church in 18th. Century Scotland*, (Berne: 1999), 82.

26. BL., Hardwicke MSS, MS 35447, 5 June 1753

27. BL., Newcastle MSS, MS 32735, Earl of Hopeton to Newcastle, 3 June 1754

in 1761, the same year as Argyll's death. Until that year the Duke had remained the main fount of political patronage, and the group were on good terms with him and Milton. Now, for the first time, there was a party within the Church which, as I.D.L. Clark and R.B. Sher have argued, was not simply the ecclesiastical arm of some great man, but an interest with a mind of its own.[28] Moreover, after the *Douglas* affair of 1756–1757,[29] Argyll's close confidant and agent in church matters, Patrick Cuming, progressively lost influence, leaving Robertson to fill the vacuum.

The Moderates' independence was further aided by their maintenance of direct links with the well-connected Earl of Bute in London, which meant that when there was a change in administration with the accession of George III in October 1760, and Bute rose to become secretary to Northern Department (March 1761) and first lord of the treasury (May 1762), their position remained secure. As for Milton, he also was able to survive the loss of his patron and remain as useful to Bute (who was Argyll's nephew), however, age was catching up with him, and his effectiveness slowly dwindled until his death in 1766.

After 1750

Under Pelham, Milton and Duke Archibald were still a force to be taken notice of in church affairs, yet their dominance was not to recover the consistency they enjoyed in their heyday. Eventually, it was to be Robertson and his allies who brought a measure of stability to the Kirk's situation regarding unpopular settlements. The anger they provoked did not diminish, but now at least there was consistency in what the senior courts were prepared to allow. Cuming's policy of countenancing riding committees had proved discredited (Torphichen was to be its last occurrence), since it

---

28. Clark, "Moderatism," 52; Sher, *Church and university*, 56ff. The other main interest was the Popular party. This was less a party and more a loose and theologically diverse grouping who opposed patronage. Many, though not all, favored a popular franchise for the election of ministers. See John R. McIntosh, *Church and theology in Enlightenment Scotland: The Popular Party, 1740–1800*, (East Linton: 1998), 19–21.

29. John Home of Athelstaneford (Haddington) wrote a play, *The Tragedy of Douglas*, which was performed in Edinburgh on 14 December 1756. Home and other ministers who went to see it were criticized by evangelicals who considered the theatre too disreputable to be countenanced by men of the Church. Cuming joined in the criticism, probably out of jealousy for their intimacy with Milton and Argyll, but the action backfired upon him.

seemed to suggest that, in patronage matters, the Kirk would issue orders, yet be prepared to make other arrangements if they were disobeyed.

Despite the new firmness, the underlying dissatisfaction with presentations did not go away, and the price for asserting the authority of the senior courts was the growth of desertions from the established Church. By the mid-1760s, there were one hundred and twenty meeting houses.[30] The alarm felt by many within the Kirk over the exodus was expressed in the abortive Schism Overture of 1765 which made patronage the cause of the defections and called for an investigation. Robertson led the charge against it, rehearsing the familiar arguments that patronage promoted good order, raised men of quality to their respective parishes, and that the Church was already well protected by its right to license only fit probationers.

The overture failed, but it is noteworthy that in their reply to Robertson, the proponents of the overture stated that "the time was long passed in which they [the people] excepted against any man merely for his getting a presentation" and that opposition by this stage was no longer directed against the law of the land but the ways in which presentations were abused.[31] The proposers were also opposed to handing the franchise over to parishioners in an indiscriminate way. This was an indication that in some ways the evangelical wing of the Kirk and the Moderates were less polarized than has sometimes been thought.[32] However, if Robertson hoped that general opposition to patronage would eventually lose its momentum, it was not to be. In the following decades, the American and French Revolutions and the growth of agitation for political reform were to stir passions which spilled over into the issue of ministerial elections. As the new century progressed, the Industrial Revolution also meant that traditional parish structures lost their significance in the populous parts of the cities, and where the Kirk set up new congregations the sway of the patron could be challenged or ignored. Change was in the air, and the arguments of the "non-intrusionists" became increasingly vocal. In response, Parliament ordered a Select Committee in 1834 to investigate patronage in Scotland and report.[33] The result, published within six months, failed to

30. Morren, ii, v.

31. Ibid., 339.

32. E.g., David Allan, *Scotland in the Eighteenth Century: Union and Enlightenment*, (Pearson Education: 2002),70: "In reality . . . neither the political nor the cultural affiliations of the two clerical parties were necessarily antithetical. Often they amounted to only a difference of emphasis."

33. Its remit was "to consider the past and present State of the Law of Church

extrapolate any meaningful conclusions from the mass of evidence it had collected and so achieved nothing. Meanwhile, as a further addition to the mix, the specter of Catholic emancipation had intensified debate over the idea of disestablishment. Those who argued for it, known as voluntaries, claimed that patronage epitomized the danger of a Church being too entangled with the state, and that separation was the only way to ensure the Church could enjoy her rightful independence.

Faced with what they saw as a rising tide of dangerous radicalism, the successors to Robertson's Moderates dug in their heels. When in accordance with the Assembly's Veto Act of 1834, presbyteries were refusing to settle presentees rejected by the parochial heads of families, the Court of Session was summoned to intervene. It was hard to argue that this was anything but Erastian interference, and from this point onwards, the dilemma of how to respond to it troubled ministerial consciences throughout the country. Nemesis came in the great Disruption of 1843 when over 470 ministers walked out, but it is important to remember that many of those who left to form the Free Church, were not opposed in principle to the notion of a Church established and protected by the state, only to where the line was drawn between the two. Patronage may have led to the upheaval of the Disruption, but its role was more as catalyst than cause. Thus it was not the eventual abolition of patronage in 1874 that was to ease and settle the relationship between Kirk and state, but The Church of Scotland Act of 1921, which effectively recognized the Church's independence in spiritual matters,[34] and thereby cleared the way for what was now United Free and Auld Kirk to work towards re-union.

Patronage in Scotland, and to enquire how far that system is in accordance with the Constitution and Principles of the Church of Scotland, and conducive to its usefulness and prosperity, and to report their observations thereupon to the House." *Report*, ii.

34. On this subject it is worth reading Jeffrey Stephen's article, "Defending the Revolution: The Church of Scotland and the Scottish Parliament, 1689–1695", *SHR*, vol. 89, April 2010, 19–53, where he shows that the Kirk's relations with the Scottish parliament after the Revolution were such that the two bodies were able to work together without encroaching upon each other's domain.

Conclusion

The 1690 Legacy

MAINLY BECAUSE IT WAS established, not by popular acclaim but through expedient, the problem with the 1690 church settlement was that it left behind a legacy of unresolved tensions and resentments.[1] These were added to by the abolition of patronage, where, despite the frequent belief that "The feeling in Scotland was so unanimous against patronage, that it could not be resisted,"[2] the truth of the Act's passage was that it derived from the "ambition, ignorance and miscalculation"[3] of those who would have preferred to retain it. To summarize it differently: anti–patronage presbyterians had won no debate on the most fitting mode of ministerial election, nor had they triumphed by virtue of moral or political superiority. They had instead been largely the beneficiaries of a political misadventure. In later years, the Kirk simply ignored this point, and sought to represent the reimposition of patronage as an attempt to sabotage a right which, in response to popular desire, it had been justly awarded. That this was a historical perception which the landed interest simply did not share, is most apparent in their almost unanimous rejection of the opportunity to sell their right of presenting for the 600 merks. If they were persuaded that their right had been lost through no stronger force than careless mischance, then, it is not hard to understand how they might believe that, as soon as the time was right, the error would quickly be made good, and that therefore to sell out would be folly. Certainly, hopes of restoration were high as early as 1703.[4]

1. Riley, *King William*, 4
2. Begg, *History of the Act of Queen Anne 1711*, 5
3. Riley, *King William*, 42.
4. Wodrow, *Correspondence*, ii, to Col Erskine, 28 Sept 1717, 325

Again, once patronage had been restored, it is illuminating to see the resolutely disinterested response from virtually all those canvassed by the Rev. William Mitchell and his colleagues on their mission to London in 1717. Although the Kirk might argue that the 1712 Act was an aberration imposed by crypto-Jacobites taking revenge on pro-Hanoverian Presbyterians,[5] that fact that this made little impression, could well indicate that however presbyterian propaganda might portray the abolition of 1690, for the property-owning section of Scottish society, it was *that* Act and not the one of 1712, which was the real, politically–conditioned aberration.

Another way in which the Revolution settlement contributed to the complexity of issues behind church settlements was in its establishment of the role of the heritor in the vacancy–filling process. The heritors' inclusion in the legislation was the culmination of a process which had begun earlier in the century, as Rosalind Mitchison has described: "The two strands of landowner, 'barons' . . . and lairds . . . combined in the new definition of heritors, proprietors of land on whom was placed the burden and privilege of maintaining the ministry and the church. This change was not only the promotion of a class, but the bringing forward of the concept of property as against feudal superiority . . . In their new status it was clear that property had become the basis of power."[6]

It might have seemed to many that the inclusion of this new social presence was, if not advantageous to the Kirk, then at least fair to the heritors, given the fact that it was they who financed the local church's work and ministry. However, if another development of the period is brought into the equation, namely the burgeoning importance of the law,[7] it is possible to see why the formal establishment of the heritors' place in church affairs from the start contained the potential for friction. What the 1690 abolition did was to engraft into the selection process, not those who had been set apart to a divine office, but a grouping whose ecclesiastical rights and status were based entirely on property and the civil law. As soon, therefore, as the Church emphasized its spiritual independence (its

5. See the General Assembly's *Testimony against Patronages*, 14 May 1715: "the zeal of the Established Church of Scotland for, and their steady adherence to, the protestant succession, did expose them to the resentments of the disaffected party."

6. *Lordship to Patronage*, 67.

7. "There are five ways in which the centrality of the Law to 18th. Century Scottish life can be seen – agricultural improvement, political management, the importance of property, commercial development and the relationship in law with England." A. Chitnis, *The Scottish Enlightenment*, (London: 1976), 81

"intrinsic power"), and the separate authority of its own courts, a clash of values and jurisdictions became immediately exposed.

Another problem was that the equal division of franchise between Session and heritors meant that the price of such balance was that any confrontation could rarely be resolved without long and tiresome proceedings.[8] The fact was, there was a necessity for some adjustment within the system which would have clarified how a decision was to be reached when heritors and elders found themselves grouped against each other. Weighting the balance towards one of the parties would probably have been the simplest remedy, in which case, the advantage would almost certainly have gone to the heritors. From the tone of the Assembly's Overture of 1711, *Concerning the Planting of Vacant churches*, it would appear that it did recognize both the problem and the possible remedy, but lacked the initiative to act, other than by stressing the importance of the heritors' views.[9] When in later decades, pamphleteers like Lord Prestongrange argued for the repeal of the 1712 Act, they also recognized this inadequacy about the 1690 system, and, rather than advocate a simple return to it, proposed giving the advantage to the heritors.[10]

Even without the restoration of patronage in 1712, at some stage, it would have been necessary for the Kirk to confront the difficulties engendered by the inclusion of heritors in the vacancy-filling process. Indeed, it is hard to see how a workable, alternative to patronage could have established itself which denied landowners the opportunity to make a decisive contribution to an election's outcome. It was the Kirk's misfortune that it did not recognize the situation earlier after 1690, and then have the boldness to effect a remedy.

Resistance to Patronage

The question which repeatedly presents itself is: why did the Kirk did not take stronger action to resist the injustice it believed had been done to it by the passage of the 1712 Act? The answer is that there were several reasons. In the short term, there was the misfortune of the Abjuration Oath.

---

8. As was seen with the disputes at Channelkirk, Cramond and Inchinnan, the logical solution for some was to break the deadlock by artificially creating more of their own number.

9. Assembly Papers, SRO., CH1/9/10, 23 May 1711.

10. "it is just to make some restriction upon the numbers of elders who should be admitted to vote." William Grant, Lord Prestongrange, *Remarks, etc.*, 14

It was tagged onto the Toleration Act almost as an afterthought, yet as a means of constricting the Church's actions, it was highly effective. So long as a large proportion of ministers scrupled to take it, the Kirk's moral position was severely weakened. Violation of the Patronage Act as well as the Toleration Act would have given an opportunity to the episcopalians to reinstate themselves by first subscribing, then affecting the role of loyal citizens. Moreover, since the government's chief desire was to see the Church quiescent, by playing upon this defection, as well as hinting at the possibility of worse afflictions, it knew it could stifle much presbyterian intransigence.

Secondly, for the Church to take on the ruling establishment and be successful, as it was over the reading of the Act for apprehending Porteous' murderers, and during the 1734 and 1735 Assemblies, it needed to find at least some degree of unity within its superior courts. However, from the end of the '15 onwards, the task proved increasingly difficult. Primarily, there was the discord created by *Squadrone*/Argathelian rivalry, but there was also the distraction and division caused by the doctrinal controversies of 1715 to 1718,[11] which in turn accentuated the divergence in preaching and churchmanship between what were to be called moderate men and Evangelical/Popular Party adherents. On the matter of patronage itself, there were those who favored a conciliatory approach in order to convince government that the Church could be trusted to be responsible in its behavior and respectful of landowners' privileges; there were those who favored compliance because it was the law,[12] and by contrast, there were those, like Wodrow and Brechin presbytery, who believed that anything other than firm resistance would be interpreted as weakness. Finally, unanimity was not helped by procedural uncertainty within church judicatories as they struggled to cope with settlement disputes, the resolution of which was made harder by both the growing presence of legal representatives and the reluctance of the senior courts to lay down legislative guidelines.

The factor of uncertainty also made the decisions of the Church's courts more vulnerable to manipulation, since it vested added authority in senior churchmen, and in particular those having the prestige of a professorship, chaplaincy or superior charge (especially one within the city of Edinburgh). Since the current administration would have the patronage

11. ie., The John Simson cases, The Auchterarder Creed and the Marrow Controversy.

12. Their argument was that since the Kirk was established and protected by law, it was in its own best interest to uphold its enactments. Understandably, the strongest proponents of the argument tended to be the proteges of political luminaries.

of many of these preferments, it is easy to see how the situation could be worked to advantage.

Above all, it was uncertainty as to the constitutional status of the Assembly Commission which handed church managers their most successful aid. Since the smaller and more erratically-attended Commission was easier to control than the Assembly, its decisions could usually be relied upon to go the desired way. If the Commission's judgment was revealed as manifestly unjust, the danger was that Assembly might reverse it. On the other hand, however, since it was considered undesirable to do anything which might suggest that the Commission was not a valid judicatory, in practice the Assembly consistently recoiled from rescinding the Commission's sentences.[13]

Political Management

The next question to ask must be, why was the partnership of Ilay and Milton so successful in managing the Church? First, since the regime had so much general patronage at its disposal, it could afford to work on the principle that, as was seen with figures like Hamilton, Smith, Gowdie, Linning and Mitchell, most men had their price. If preferment was desired, there was simply nowhere else for such men to go. Secondly, there was a determination on the part of many to believe that the House of Argyll was by history and tradition[14] the friend of the Kirk, and should continue to be trusted. Thirdly, unlike Tweeddale, the regime was able to profit greatly from the network of contacts and information provided by so large and powerful a family as the Campbells. Fourthly, Milton and Ilay, unlike Tweeddale, were not handicapped by any visionary desire to assist the Church in some way, but rather saw settlements as simply a tool to be used to strengthen the regime.

The regime could, however, make mistakes. One was to believe that the loyalty of its agents could be stretched indefinitely, which, as the rebellion over the West Kirk case showed, was not always true. Again, if Milton himself had a flaw, it was a reluctance to disengage from a cause in which he had concerned himself. The forcing through of the Hutton case followed by the suppressing of dissent against the decision, had a crudity and heedlessness for the consequences which contrasted with his customary acumen. Again, the revulsion caused by the conduct of such cases

13. Except for the 1734-36 period

14. It was also recalled that Ilay had voted against the Patronage Act.

as Port-Glasgow and Troqueer, as well as the John Burgh affair, together showed that, however venal the Church might become, something more subtle was required for its management than blatant corruption.

The Tweeddale regime, by contrast, seemed to believe that there was a possibility that the Kirk could be administered by appealing to the finer instincts of those associated with it. He was to be disappointed. His reluctance to replace Argathelian appointees, along with a naive trust in the goodwill of figures like Drummore and the former Solicitor General, were simply taken by observers as confirmation of a lack of authority and competence. In an earlier age, it might have been feasible to implement Craigie's strategy "to superintend their [the Church's] governing themselves in a peaceable way," but the time was certainly past. Whereas it must be admitted that Tweeddale and Wallace did manage to avoid the occurrence of notorious settlement disputes, yet it is hard to avoid the impression that such a situation was unlikely to have continued indefinitely. Whatever Wallace's personal merits, confidence in him was indissolubly linked to confidence in the Marquis, and the fact was that by the end of the second year of Tweeddale's administration, confidence in him had evaporated, and increasingly attention turned back to the Argathelian interest for the direction and general patronage, which, by this stage, many seemed uncomfortable without.

External Issues

Naturally, national issues of party did not have a bearing upon every settlement by patronage. In Edinburgh, the desire to protect the rights of the Council against any encroachment involved them in patronage disputes, mainly with the presbytery, which regularly transcended matters connected with the influences of party politics. In the south of the country, the pietist traditions of the praying societies along with the profound changes brought by the process of improvement, ensured that the settlement process could be colored by a range of characteristics which frequently superseded all else. The same was true of the areas typified by the presbytery of Brechin, where the overshadowing source of contention remained the existence of widespread disaffection both towards presbyterianism and the Hanoverian succession. Given the advantage theoretically handed to their episcopalian opponents (provided they qualified) by the restoration of patronage, it is of interest to observe how much it was possible for a presbytery to achieve by a resolute determination to resist the depredations of presentations, even if it meant disobeying the weight of the law. Admittedly, the presbytery was facilitated by having much less to distract it in the form of *Squadrone*/Argathelian warfare than many other areas. However, that it was able to lose so little ground to the work of patronage until immediately before the '45, despite a continuing lack of interest from the senior courts of the Church,[15] demonstrates what could be accomplished when any court was able to present a unified front.

It was perhaps to the Kirk's misfortune that this was a feat the Assembly and Commission only felt capable of achieving, from 1734, for one, brief period. If, twenty years earlier, the accident of chance had been more benevolent, and the Kirk had not been burdened with the Abjuration Oath, a similar unity might conceivably have seen it emerge from the '15 with the Patronage Act removed from the statute book.

Successful Presentations

It must be asked whether there were many settlements in the first half of the eighteenth century where a presentation was deployed, yet which proceeded without difficulty? If that scenario is defined as being where a settlement proceeded without confrontation arising between any of the parties, then it must be said that this occurred in the majority of cases. However, it should also be noted that in most of these instances, the presbytery either did not record the presentation in their minutes or did so with a disapproving comment. Even if it did not attempt active resistance, it would very often only proceed with a gesture or statement of protest. Again, it was even possible that a presentation might actually be suited to a presbytery's wishes. Thus the presbytery of Selkirk, having in 1725 roundly condemned patronage as "a remaining branch of the Roman anti-Christ's usurped authority over the Church of Christ and the consciences of men,"[16] swallowed its principles seven years later and accepted without comment a presentation to the parish of Ettrick and Buccleuch. The crucial difference was that the presentee was a popular son# of the previous incumbent, the revered Thomas Boston, who had successfully laboured to keep his Cameronian parishioners from schism. This made it virtually impossible for the presbytery to do other than co-operate with the wishes of the congregation and patron if it wished to avoid causing more damage

15. Even the Kirk's petition to Parliament of 1736 took no interest in addressing the need to remedy the problem of episcopal interference in presbyterian vacancies.

16. Selkirk Presbytery Registers, SRO., CH2/327/5, 5 October 1725

than could ever be justified by adherence to its scruples. Again, although the circumstances were very different, a similar pressure was felt by the presbytery of Meigle in 1743. In a region where whig, presbyterian ministries were frequently shunned, when the Earl of Strathmore as patron of Airlie, presented, to popular acclaim, a member of a family of well–known, local ministers,[17] the presbytery were quick to realize the opportunity and progressed the settlement.

The Kirk without Patronage?

It remains, in conclusion, to be asked, how substantially different would the history of the Kirk have been during the first half of the eighteenth century, had the 1712 Act been swiftly annulled? As might be expected, it is clear that the number of settlement disputes would have been lower. However, this is not to suggest that they would have been rare or that schism would have been avoided. As was indicated above, a vacancy-filling process might be colored by any one of a number of discontents current from the period, ranging from resentment against agrarian improvements to whether the candidate had subscribed the Abjuration Oath. In such situations, often the presentation acted as the stimulant for trouble, rather than the sole cause. To put it another way, the Church of the period was neither a happy nor settled one, and would have been so even without the presence of patronage.

If, however, the 1712 Act had been annulled, it is interesting to speculate as to the system which might have replaced it. Since the Patronage Act had already condemned the previous system as "inconvenient," a direct return to it was hardly feasible without loss of face. Moreover, as already suggested, its even-handedness was a disadvantage when heritors and elders were not in agreement.[18] An amended formula would thus have been almost certain, in which case, it is difficult to see how this would have led to anything other than a greater measure of influence going to the indigenous men of property where parishes fell vacant.

Given the scenario of that enhanced leverage, it is reasonable to make two suppositions. First, with regard to the claim by later proponents of patronage that it helped to bring more men of learning and superior social

---

17. The Revd David Thomson's father was minister of Meigle, his grandfather had been minister of Alyth and his brother became minister of Kingoldrum.

18. A heritor could, of course, be also an elder.

standing into charges, it is very possible that the same outcome would have happened under the replacement regime.

Secondly, the more the landed interest became established in the process of ministerial elections, the more likely it is that a political machine like Ilay's would have concerned itself in their outcome. In other words, it is not especially likely that a Scottish Church without patronage in the period to 1750 would have been the model of freedom and independence that the more romantic of nineteenth-century historians have sometimes supposed. Indeed, even if the Kirk had been given permission to devise any formula it chose for supplying ministers to vacant parishes, the difficulties involved in keeping it away from the long shadow of that influence, would have been considerable, if not insurmountable.

Appendices

Appendix I

Henderson, Alexander, *The Government and Order of the Church of Scotland*, (Edinburgh: 1641).

What follows is a summary of section ii, "Of the calling of officers of the church." It should be noted that the section purports to give a description of the situation that already obtained at the time. However, since practice frequently varied between presbyteries, what is described is probably the author's ideal picture of what he would like to see as the standard practice.

Summary

In almost all presbyteries there are students of divinity. If they reside permanently within the presbytery's bounds, they are expected to attend all its meetings, otherwise they attend when they return for the vacations.

When, after examination, they are considered fit to attend, they are invited to the presbytery's "exercise" [regular meetings of the ministers for bible study], and occasionally asked to preach publicly. By such means they become known to the people. Out of these expectants, one may be nominated by the eldership of a vacant church "with the consent and good liking of the people."

The nominee's name is given to the presbytery, who examine him as to his skill in latin, greek and hebrew, interpretation of scripture, doctrine, preaching, history and, above all, his life and manner of conversation. If found qualified for the charge, he is sent there "that the people, hearing him, may have the greater assurance of his gifts for edification."

After the congregation have heard him, one of the presbytery's ministers is sent there to preach and serve an edict that if any have objection as to the nominee's literature, doctrine or life, or have reason why he should not prove to be a profitable minister to the parish, they are to appear before the presbytery at a specified date, to be heard. Upon the day appointed, the presbytery officer calls three times for any submissions. If any objection is found to have weight, the ordination is suspended until investigated.

The foregoing is so that none be intruded upon a parish without the voice of the elders or the consent and approval of the congregation. If the nominee is already a minister elsewhere, and his worth well known, the above process may be left out.

On the day of the nominee's election and ordination, a fast is appointed to be kept, and a minister from the presbytery preaches an appropriate sermon. The nominee is then summoned forward, and required to affirm his willingness to serve the gospel in the parish. The congregation are then asked if they will receive the candidate and submit to his ministry. The answers being given satisfactorily, the presbytery then approach and ordain him by the imposition of hands, followed by the right hand of fellowship. The service is then closed.

It will thus be seen that ministers are not admitted without assignation to a particular flock, nor does ordination go before election. The act of ordination follows the simplicity exercised by the apostles.

Patronage is a hindrance which has to be borne with for the meantime, even though it is not part of the Church's discipline. The presbytery still retains the power of examination and trial, and the people have the right to object against a candidate's doctrine or life "or that their consent may be heard." Furthermore, "if he be found *reus ambitus* [a party canvassing for office], or to have gone about to procure a presentation, he is repelled and declared incapable of that place."

No pastor may intrude upon a flock, or remove elsewhere at his own pleasure. Deserters are disciplined. If a minister is called or desires to move elsewhere, this can only be done by the wisdom and authority of the Church's courts, and not without the consent of the minister's current congregation.

A transported minister is not re-ordained, but at the service of admission, the presiding minister commends, with prayer, people to minister, and minister to the people (who have already declared their desire to receive him). The right hand of fellowship is then given to him.

Pastors reaching infirmity continue in office for their lifetime, but are given, with the people's consent, someone to assist them by the presbytery.

The same procedures are followed in the election and admission of other officers, such as elders and deacons. If there are none, then the minister, along with those of the soundest judgement, and with the consent of the rest of the people, chooses them. Otherwise, the minister and the existing eldership choose additional members, again with the consent of the people. On the day of admission, they are 'solemnly received with lifted up hands, giving their promises to be faithful.'

Appendix II

Act of Parliament abolishing the Patronage of Kirks, at Edinburgh, March 9, 1649.

The estates of Parliament being sensible of the great obligation that lies upon them by the National Covenant, and by the Solemn League and Covenant, and by many deliverances and mercies from God, and by the late Solemn Engagement unto Duties, to preserve the doctrine, and maintain and vindicate the liberties of the Kirk of Scotland, and to advance the work of reformation therein to the utmost of their power ; and, considering that patronages and presentations of kirks is an evil and bondage, under which the Lord's people and ministers of this land have long groaned ; and that it hath no warrant in God's word, but is founded only on the canon law, and is a custom popish, and brought into the kirk in time of ignorance and superstition ; and that the same is contrary to the Second Book of Discipline, in which, upon solid and good ground, it is reckoned amongst abuses that are desired to be reformed, and unto several acts of General Assemblies ; and that it is prejudicial to the liberty of the people, and planting of kirks, and unto the free calling and entry of ministers unto their charge : and the said estates, being willing and desirous to promote and advance the reformation foresaid, that every thing in the house of God may be ordered according to his word and commandment, do therefore, from the sense of the former obligations, and upon the former grounds and reasons, discharge for every hereafter all patronages and presentations of kirks, whether belonging to the king, or to any laick patron, presbyteries, or others within this kingdom, as being unlawful and unwarrantable by God's word, and contrary to the doctrine and liberties of this kirk ; and do repeal, rescind, make void, and annul all gifts and rights granted thereanent, and all former acts made in Parliament, or in any inferior judicatory, in favours of any patron or patrons whatsoever, so far as the same doth or may relate unto the presentations of kirks : and do statute and ordain, that no person or persons whatsomever shall, at any time hereafter, take upon them, under pretext of any title, infeftment, act of Parliament, possession or warrant whatsoever, which are hereby repealed, to give, subscribe, or seal any presentation to any kirk within this kingdom ; and discharges the passing of any infeftments hereafter, bearing a right to patronages, to be granted in favours of those for whom the infeftmnets are presented ; and that no person or persons shall, either in the behalf of themselves or others, procure, receive, or make use of any presentation to any kirk within this kingdom. And it is further declared and ordained, that if any presentation shall hereafter be given, procured, or received, that the same is null, and of none effect ; and that it is lawful for presbyteries to reject the same, and to refuse to admit any to trials thereupon ; and, notwithstanding thereof, to proceed to planting of the kirk, *upon the suit and calling, or with the consent of the congregation, on whom none is to be obtruded against their will.* And it is decerned, statued, and ordained, that whosoever hereafter shall, upon the suit and calling of the congregation, after due examination of their literature and conversation, be admitted by the presbytery upto the exercise and function of the ministry, in any parish within this kingdom, that the said person or persons, without a presentation, by virtue of their admission, hath sufficient right and title to possess and enjoy the manse and glebe, and the whole rents, profits, and stipends, which the ministers of that parish had formerly possesst and enjoyed, or that hereafter shall be modified by the commission for plantation of kirks . . . and because it is needful, that the just and proper interest of congregations and presbyteries, in providing of kirks with ministers, be clearly determined by the General Assembly, and what is to be accounted the congregation having that interest; therefore, it is hereby seriously recommended unto the next General Assembly, clearly to determine the same, and to condescend upon a certain standing way for being a settled rule therein for all times coming.

Appendix III

Directory for the election of Ministers, by the General Assembly, at Edinburgh, August 4, 1649.

When any place of the ministry in a congregation is vacant, it is incumbent to the presbytery, with all diligence, to send one of their number to preach to that congregation, who, in his doctrine, is to represent to them the necessity of providing the place with a qualified pastor ; and to exhort them to fervent prayer and supplication to the Lord, that he would send them a pastor according to his own heart : as also, he is to signify, that the presbytery, out of their care of that flock, will send unto them preachers, whom they may hear ; and, if they have a desire to hear any other, they will endeavour to procure them an hearing of that person, or persons, upon the suit of the elders to the presbytery.

2. Within some competent time thereafter, the Presbytery is again to send one or more of their number to the said vacant congregation, on a certain day appointed before for that effect, who are to convene and hear sermon the foresaid day ; which being ended, and intimation being made by the minister, that they are to go about the election of a pastor for that congregation, the session of the congregation shall meet and proceed to the election, the action being moderated by him that preached ; and if the people shall, upon the intimation of the person agreed upon by the session, acquiesce and consent to the said person, then the matter being reported to the Presbytery by commissioners sent from the session, they are to proceed to the trial of the person thus elected ; and, finding him qualified, to admit him to the ministry in the said congregation.

3. But if it happen that the major part of the congregation dissent from the person agreed upon by the session, in that case the matter shall be brought unto the presbytery, who shall judge of the same ; and if they do not find their dissent to be grounded on causeless prejudices, they are to appoint a new election, in manner above specified.

4. But if a lesser part of the session or congregation show their dissent from the election, without exceptions relevant and verified to the presbytery ; notwithstanding thereof, the presbytery shall go on to the trials and ordination of the person elected ; yet all possible diligence and tenderness must be used to bring all parties to an harmonious agreement.

5. It is to be understood, that no person under the censure of the kirk, because of any scandalous offence, is to be admitted to have a hand in the election of a minister.

6. Where the congregation is disaffected and malignant, in that case the presbytery is to provide them with a minister.

Appendix IV

Act of the Scottish Parliament 1690, C. 23.

Our Sovereign Lord and Lady, the King and Queen's Majesties, considering, that the power of presenting ministers to vacant churches, of late exercised by patrons, hath been greatly abused, and is inconvenient to be continued in this realm, do therefore, with the advice and consent of the Estates of Parliament, hereby discharge, cass, annull, and make void the foresaid power, heretofore exercised by any patron of presenting ministers to any kirk now vacant, or that shall hereafter happen to vaick within this kingdom, with all exercise of the said power : And also all rights, gifts and infeftments, acts, statutes and customs, in so far as they may be extended or understood to establish the said right of presentation ; but prejudice always, of such ministers as are duly entered by the foresaid presentations (while in use) their right to the manse, gleib, benefice, stipend, and other profits of their respective churches, as accords : And but prejudice to the patrons of their right to employ the vacant stipends on pious uses, within the respective parishes, except where the patron is Popish, in which case he is to employ the same on pious uses, by the advice and appointment of the presbytery ; and in case the patron shall fail in applying the vacant stipend for the uses foresaid, that he shall lose his right of administration of the vacant stipend, for that and the next vacancy, and the same shall be disposed on by the presbytery, to the uses foresaid ; excepting always the vacant stipends within the bounds of the Synod of Argyle : And to the effect the calling and entering ministers, in all time coming, may be orderly and regularly performed, their Majesties, with consent of the Estates of Parliament, do statute and declare, that in case of the vacancy of the particular church, and for supplying the same with a minister, the heritors of the said parish (being Protestants), and the elders, are to name and propose the person to the whole congregation, to be either approven or disapproven by them ; and, if they disapprove, that the disapprovers give in their reasons, to the effect the affair may be cognosced upon by the

presbytery of the bounds, at whose judgment, and by whose determination, the calling and entry of a particular minister is to be ordered and
concluded. And it is herby enacted, that if application be not made by the
eldership, and heritors of the parish, to the presbytery, for the call and
choice of a minister within the space of six months after the vacancy, that
then the presbytery may proceed to provide the said parish, and plant a
minister in the church, *tanquam jure devoluto*. It is always hereby declared,
that this act shall be but prejudice of the calling of ministers to royal
burghs, by the magistrates, town-council, and kirk-session of the burgh,
where there is no landward parish, as they have been in use before the year
1660. And where there is a considerable part of the parish in landward,
that the call shall be by magistrates, town-council, kirk-session, and the
heritors of the landward parish. And in lieu and recompense of the said
right of presentation, hereby taken away, their Majesties, with advice and
consent foresaid, statute and ordain the heritors ; and liferenters of each
parish, and the town-councils for the burgh, to pay to the said patrons,
betwixt and Marinmas next, the sum of 600 merks, proportionally effeiring to their valued rents in the said parish, *viz.*:- two parts by the heritors,
and a third part by the liferenters, deducing always the patron's own part,
effeiring to his proportion as an heritor, and that upon the said patron his
granting a sufficient and formal renunciation of the said right of presentation, in favours of the said heritors, town-council for the burgh, and kirk-
session: And it is hereby declared, that as to the parishes to which their
Majesties have right to present, upon payment of the said 600 merks to the
clerk of the thesaury, their Majesties shall be fully denuded of their right
of presentation, as to that parish ; and as to other patrons, if they refuse to
accept the said 600 merks, the same is to be consigned in the hands of a re-
sponsal person in the parish, upon the hazard of the consigners, not to be
given up to the patron, until he grant the said renunciation ; allowing, in
the meantime, the heritors and kirk-session to call the minister, conform
to this act : And ordains letters of horning to be direct at the instance of
the patron, against the heritors and others, who shall not make payment
of the said 600 merks, after the said term of Martinmas next, and likewise
at the instance of the heritors, and others willing to pay, against those who
are unwilling. And in case the patron be unwilling to accept the said sum,
or the heritors, and others aforesaid, unwilling to pay, ordains letters of
horning to be direct, at the instance of their Majesties' solicitor, against
either of them. And further, their Majesties, with advice and consent
foresaid, statute, enact and declare, that the right of the teinds of the said

parishes, which are not heritably disponed, shall, by virtue of this present act, belong to the said patrons, with the burden always of the minister's stipends, tacks, and prorogations already granted of the said teinds, and of such augmentations of stipends, future prorogations, and erections of new kirks, as shall be found just and expedient, providing the said patrons, getting right to the teinds, by virtue of this present act, and who had no right thereto of before, shall be : Likeas, they are hereby obliged to sell to each heritor the teinds of his own lands, at the rate of six years' purchase, as the same shall be valued by a commission for valuation of teinds ; and whereas there are certain lands and annual-rents holden of the said benefices, and beneficed persons, from which the patrons might have some benefit arising to them ; It is hereby ordained, that the right of superiority of the said lands and annual-rents shall belong to their Majesties in all time coming, with all the whole casualities and emoluments thereof, notwithstanding of any former act of Parliament in the contrar; reserving, notwithstanding, to the patrons the feu-farms, and feu-mails of the said superiorities, aye, and while they receive payment and satisfaction from their Majesties, of the price thereof, at the rate of 100 merks for each chalder of victual over head, and for each 100 merks of feu-mail, except where the said feu-farms are a part of the minister's modified stipend, or where the minister is, and has been in possession thereof, by the space of ten years, or where he has the full benefice, in which cases they are to be irredeemable. Excepting, likewise, from this act the superiorities belonging to the deanry of Hamilton, and the provostry of Bothwel, whereunto the Duke of Hamilton has right, which are no ways hereby prejudged.

Appendix V

An Act to restore the Patrons to their ancient rights of presenting Ministers to the churches vacant in that part of Great Britain called Scotland. [1712]

Whereas by the ancient laws and constitution of that part of Great Britain called Scotland, and presenting ministers to vacant churches did of right belong to the patrons, until by the 23d act of the 2d session of the first Parliament of the late King William and Queen Mary, held in the year 1690, entitled, "An Act concerning Patronages," the presentation was taken from the patrons, and given to the heritors and elders of the respective parishes ; and in place of the right of presentation, the heritors and liferenters of every parish were to pay to the respective patrons a small and inconsiderable sum of money, for which the patrons were to renounce their right of presentation in all times thereafter : And whereas, by the 15th act of the 5th session, and by the 13th act of the sixth session of the first Parliament of the said King William, the one entitled, "An Act for the encouraging of preachers at vacant churches be-north Forth ;" and the other entitled, "Act in favours of preachers be-north Forth," there are several burdens imposed upon vacant stipends, to the prejudice of the patron's right of disposing thereof : and whereas that way of calling ministers has proved inconvenient, and has not only occasioned great heats and divisions among those who, by the foresaid act, were entitled and authorised to call ministers, but likewise has been a great hardship upon the patrons, whose predecessors had founded and endowed those churches, and who have not received payment or satisfaction for their right of patronage from the foresaid heritors or liferenters of the respective parishes, nor have granted renunciations of their said rights on that account : Be it therefore enacted, by the Queen's Most Excellent Majesty, by and with the advice and consent of the Lords Spiritual and Temporal, and Commons, in this present Parliament assembled, and by the authority of the same, that the aforesaid act, made in the year 1690, entitled, "Act concerning Patronages," in so far as the same relates to the presentation of ministers by heritors and others therein mentioned, be, and is hereby repealed and made void ; and that the aforesaid 15th act of the fifth Session, and the 13th act of the sixth Session of the first Parliament of King William, be, and are hereby likewise repealed and made void ; and that in all time coming, the right of all and every patron or patrons to the presentation of ministers to churches and benefices, and the disposing of the vacant stipends for pious uses within the parish, be restored, settled, and confirmed to them – the aforesaid acts, or any other acts, statute, or custom to the contrary, in any wise notwithstanding ; and that from and after the 1st day of May 1712, it shall and may be lawful for her Majesty, her heirs and successors, and for every other person or persons, who have right to any patronage, or patronages of any church or churches whatsoever, in that part of Great Britain called Scotland (and who have not made and subscribed a formal renunciation thereof under their hands), to present a qualified minister or ministers to any church or churches whereof they are patrons, which shall, at any time after the said 1st day of May, happen to be vacant ; and the presbytery of the respective bounds shall, and is hereby obliged to receive and admit in the same manner such qualified person or persons, minister or ministers, as shall be presented by the respective patrons, as the persons or ministers presented before the making of this act ought to have been admitted.

Provided always, that in case any patron or patrons have accepted of, and received any sum or sums of money from the heritors or liferenters of any parish, or from the magistrates or town-council of any borough, in satisfaction of their right of presentation, and have discharged or renounced the same under their hand, that nothing herein shall be construed to restore such patron or patrons to their right of presentation, - any thing in this present act to the contrary notwithstanding.

Provided also, and it is hereby enacted, by the authority foresaid, that in case the patron of any church aforesaid shall neglect or refuse to present any qualified minister to such church that shall be vacant the said 1st day of May, or shall happen to be vacant at any time thereafter, for the space of six months, after the said 1st day of May, or after such vacancy shall happen, that the right of presentation shall accrue and belong, for that time, to the presbytery of the bounds where such Church is, who are to present a qualified person for that vacancy, *tanquam jure devoluto.*

And be it farther enacted and declared, by the authority aforesaid, that the patronage and right of presentations of ministers to all churches which belonged to archbishops, bishops, or other dignified persons, in the year 1689, before Episcopacy was abolished, as well as those which formerly belonged to the Crown, shall and do of right belong to her Majesty, her heirs and successors, who may present qualified ministers to such church or churches, and dispose of the vacant stipends thereof for pious uses, in the same way and manner as her Majesty, her heirs and successors, may do in the case of other patronages belonging to the Crown.

Declaring always, that nothing in this present act contained shall extend, or be construed to extend, to repeal and make void the aforesaid 23d act of the second session of first Parliament of the late King William and Queen Mary, expecting so far as relates to the calling and presenting of ministers, and to the disposing of vacant stipends, in prejudice of the patrons only.

And be it farther enacted, by the authority aforesaid, that all and every patron and patrons, who have not taken, or shall not take, at any time before his or their presenting a minister or ministers to any church or churches aforesaid, the oath appointed to be taken by persons in public trust, by an act made in the sixth year of her Majesty's reign, entitled, "An Act for the better security of her Majesty's person and government," shall, and are hereby obliged, at their signing such presentation, to take and subscribe the aforesaid oath before the sheriff of the shire, stewart of the stewartry, or before any two or more justices of the peace of the county or place where such patron resides ; and in case such patron or patrons, who have not formerly taken the aforesaid oath, refuse or neglect to take the same at signing of such presentation, that the same shall be, and is hereby declared to be void, and the right of presentation, and of the disposing the vacant stipends for that time, shall belong to her Majesty, her heirs and successors, who may present a qualified person to such church or benefice, at any time within the space of six months after such neglect or refusal – any thing in this present act, or in any other act, to the contrary notwithstanding.

And whereas the right of patronage of churches may belong to Papists, be it therefore enacted, by the authority aforesaid, that any person or persons, known or suspected to the Papists, and who have a right of presenting ministers, shall be obliged, at or before his or their signing any presentation, to purge himself of Popery, by taking and signing the Formula, contained in the third act of the Parliament of Scotland, held in the year 1700, entitled, "Act for preventing the growth of Popery :" and in case such Popish patron or patrons shall refuse to take and subscribe the Formula aforesaid, the same being tendered to him or them by the sheriff of the shire, stewart of the stewartry, or any two or more justices of the peace within their respective jurisdiction, who are hereby empowered to administer the same, the presentation, and the right of disposing the vacant stipends, shall, for that time, belong to her Majesty, her heirs and successors, who may present any qualified person or persons within six months after such neglect or refusal, - any thing in their present act, or any other act, to the contrary notwithstanding.

Appendix VI

Entering the Ministry

For any candidate for the ministry, the path to ordination was a long one and involved several steps:

1. Education

The Assembly's *Act concerning Probationers and settling Ministers; with Questions to be proposed to and Engagements to be taken of them* of 22nd May 1711 (SRO. CH1/9/10), stipulated "That none be admitted to Trials in order to be licensed, but such as have attended the Profession of Divinity for six years . . . after they have passed their course of Philosophy at the College." A century later, in 1818, clearly little had changed: "A young man, intended for the Church, after completing his education at grammar school, is required, before he enters on the study of theology, to attend a university for at least four years. During that time he is supposed to complete his studies in the Greek and humanity classes, and afterwards to apply to the study of logic, moral philosophy and natural philosophy . . . He is then placed in the divinity college . . . This course of study in theology requires an attendance of four years; and till it is completed he cannot be received on probationary trials or receive a licence to preach." [Wellwood, Henry Moncrieff, *Account of the Life and Writings of John Erskine*, (Edin.1818), Note CC, 410, 526]

2. Preliminaries to Trials for Licence

Before a candidate could be considered for licence by a presbytery, he should have resided within the bounds for at least six years, or be able to produce equivalent testimonials and a request from another presbytery that he be licensed. The presbytery then appointed a committee to conduct a private examination of the candidate to make sure of "his Orthodoxy, Knowledge in Divinity, particularly the modern Controversies . . . and what Sense and Impressions he has of Religion upon his own Soul" [1711 Act]. If satisfied thus far, the presbytery then circularized the other presbyteries in the synod, intimating their intention to take him on trials.

3. The Trials

Walter Steuart of Pardovan ("Collections and Observations Methodized, etc.", Book I, 201) describes the proceedings as they were conducted around 1709:

> "1. The Homily, which is a discourse upon some text of Holy Scripture assigned unto him by the presbytery, and delivered before them in private.
>
> 2. The Exegesis, which is a discourse in Latin upon some common head appointed him by the presbytery and delivered before them, at which time also he gives in the substance of his discourse, comprised in a short thesis or doctrinal proposition in paper, which he is to defend, at the presbytery's next meeting, against two or three ministers who are appointed to impugn his thesis.
>
> 3. The Presbyterial Exercise and Addition, the exercise gives the coherence of the text and context, the logical division, and explanation of the words, clearing hard and unusual phrases, if any be, with their true and proper meaning according to the original language, and other parallel places of Scripture, proposing and answering any textual questions that occur, and then a plain and short paraphrase upon the text: This is ordinarily the work of one half hour. The addition gives the doctrinal propositions or truths, which, without straining, may be deduced from the text so explained, with reasons, applications and pertinent improvement and application, as the other half hour will allow.
>
> 4. A Lecture, or exposition of a large portion of Scripture, ordinarily a whole chapter.
>
> 5. A Popular Sermon. These three pieces of exercise, viz. Presbyterial exercise, lecture and popular sermon, are to be in the pulpit before the people.
> 6. He is to be tried in his knowledge of the original languages, by interpreting a portion of the Greek New Testament *ad ap-*

erturam libri [at the opening of a book], and reading and expounding a portion of some Psalm in Hebrew. Of his knowledge of sacred chronology, ecclesiastic history, especially of our own church, answering extemporary questions, of the meaning of the hard places of Scripture, on heads of divinity, polemic or practical, on cases of conscience, on church government and discipline [he is to be tried], and is likewise to be tried as to his piety, prudence, and former Godly conversation . . ."

4. The Call

Once a probationer received a call to a charge, and the call was approved, the vacant church's presbytery put him on trials for ordination. These were largely identical to the trials for licence.

Since the Church regarded presentations as a grievance, there was no legislative standard set for the time or manner of their receipt. Presbyteries accordingly followed their own inclinations. A common practice was for the presbytery to treat a presentation as equivalent to a petition from a section of the parish, craving a hearing of a candidate and/or requesting a moderation of a call to him. The crucial point was then whether the presbytery staged an election with the named person as the sole candidate, or whether it proceeded on the basis of a leet. It was the latter course which naturally aroused patrons' anger.

For the wording of a specimen call, see Pardovan, Book I, 183. For an example of the wording of a presentation, see Floors Castle Muniments, (WRH, TD 87/9/1275), Tutors to Robert, Earl of Roxburghe presenting to Lilliesleaf, Sprouston and Bowden, 1690.

5. Ordination

The call and ordination trials having been sustained, a representative from the presbytery served an edict upon the vacant parish, intimating the ordination, and inviting any with objections as to the candidate's life or doctrine to submit them to the next meeting of Presbytery. If no valid objections were lodged, the Presbytery proceeded to the ordination, usually within ten days.

Carlyle's Example

A useful example of a Divinity student's progress to the ministry during the 1740s, can be found in the *Autobiography of Dr Alexander Carlyle of Inveresk, 1722-1805*, TN Foulis. Edinburgh. 1910.

The taking of a position as a tutor/chaplain was a practice commonly adopted by students as a means of supporting themselves:

> "My father had sometimes expressed a wish that I should allow myself to be recommended to take charge of a pupil, as that was the most likely way to obtain a church in Scotland; but he did not press me upon this subject, for as he had been four years in that station himself, tho' he was very fortunate in his pupils, he felt how degrading it was. By that time I had been acquainted with a few preceptors, had observed how they were treated, and had contracted an abhorrence of the employment - insomuch that, when I consented to follow out the clerical profession, it was on condition I should never be urged to go into a family, as it was called, engaging at the same time to make my expenses as moderate as possible." 62.

Carlyle mentions how his father had hopes of getting a bursary to put him through divinity at the College of Glasgow. The one hoped for (through the Duke of Hamilton) was for two years at college, then one year abroad. If the bursary could not be procured, then college along with live-in tutoring was to be the main alternative. Carlyle's dislike of the idea was strong: "We thought we had observed that all tutors had contracted a certain obsequiousness or basseuse, which alarmed us [he and his friends, William Robertson, John Home and George Logan] for ourselves. A little experience corrected this prejudice, for I knew many afterwards who had passed through that station, and yet had retained a manly independency both in mind and manner" 69–70.

However, the bursary was apparently obtained. After returning from university abroad, Carlyle says he was obliged "to spend a part of this summer, 1744, in visiting the clergy of the Presbytery of Haddington, as the forms required that I should perform that duty before I was admitted to trials." The idea was that the ministers would be able to examine him personally. 100.

When he passed trials in summer 1746, he was, in the October presented by John Hay of Spot to Cockburnspath. Hay had known Carlyle's father when he had been tutor to the family in 1714–15. Carlyle did not want to go to so obscure a charge, but his father and grandfather were against "resisting Providence" [which showed they had the same providential view of presentations as calls]. Then in early 1747, a friend of his father, Andrew Gray (later at Abernethy), heard that the minister of Inveresk, Frederick Carmichael, was being promoted by Lord President Forbes for a church in Edinburgh. Carlyle senior was encouraged to try and arrange Inveresk for his son. He therefore used his friendship with Lord Drummore to induce him to write to the patron, Francis, 2nd. Duke of Buccleuch, as well as his brother-in-law, the Duke of Queensberry. Both returned favourable replies to Drummore. Extra leverage was obtained with Queensberry through Carlyle's kinsman, Provost Bell of Dumfries, who was very close to the Duke. Carlyle withdrew his acceptance to Cockburnspath in January/February 1747, and was ordained in August 1748. 211–18.

Appendix VII

Commissioners to the Assembly

In its Act anent the Representation of Presbyteries in the General Assemblies, the 1694 Assembly decided, on the 2nd. April, Act V, that the allocation for each Presbytery should be:

Presbyteries with 12 parishes or less could send 2 ministers and 1 elder;

Presbyteries with 18 parishes or less could send 3 ministers and 1 elder;

Presbyteries with 24 parishes or less could send 4 ministers and 2 elders;

Presbyteries with over 24 parishes could send 5 ministers and 2 elders.

In 1712, the Assembly, by Act VI of the 8th. May, added the allowance that Presbyteries with more than 30 parishes could send 6 ministers and 3 elders.

Collegiate charges could be counted as 2 parishes.

(There were 84 Presbyteries).

Appendix VIII

Biographical Notes

Annandale, William Johnston, 2nd Earl of, (1st Marquis from 1701) (1664–1721) President of the Council 1693–9, and 1702–6. Lord Treasurer 1696–1705. Lord Privy Seal, 1702, 1715–21. A principal secretary of state in 1705. Scots rep. peer 1708–13, and 1715–21. Was Lord High Commissioner to the GA in 1701, 1705, 1711. Keeper of the Great Seal 1714–16; opposed Act of Union. Wodrow says he refused Q Anne 's appointment as LHC to the GA in 1712 because he was ashamed to look them all in the face, considering the encroachment made on them by the Act.

Areskine, Charles (1680–1763): distinguished lawyer and MP for Dumfriesshire (1722–41) and Tain Burghs (1741–2); cousin of the Earl of Mar; Argathelian; solicitor-general 1725–37; Lord Advocate 1737–42; became a Lord of Session as Lord Tinwald in 1742; app. Lord Justice Clerk 1748.

Athole, Dukes of. John Murray, 2nd Earl, was made a Marquis by Chas. II in 1676. Passed over at the Revolution, he became a Jacobite until his death in May, 1703. His 2nd son, Charles was made 1st Earl of Dunmore; his 4th son William married the heiress of Nairne and thus became Lord Nairne. His 1st son, John succeeded him as 2nd Marquis. While still Lord Murray, he found favour with King William, and was made Secretary of State, High Commissioner to Parliament, and Chancellor of the University of St Andrews. He was also made Earl of Tullibardine and viscount Glenalmond. In April 1703, Q Anne made him Marquis of Tullibardine, then in July, after father's death, she made him Duke of Athole. Having been accused by Queensberry of being involved in a Jacobite conspiracy, he became a firm enemy to the govt., then a fierce opposer of the Union. His opposition to the latter was however bought off with £1000. He was chosen one of the

16 peers in the 3rd and 4th GB Parliaments, made a Privy Councillor in 1712, made Privy Seal in 1713, and LHC in 1713 and 1714. He was twice married and had 6 sons and 1 daughter, Susanna, who married the E of Aberdeen. His 1st son John fell at Malplaquet in 1709. His 2nd son Lord William was in both risings and died in the Tower in 1747. His son Lord Charles was in the 15 and died in 1720. Another son, Lord George, was general of the Pretender's army. He died in the Tower in 1747. His 3rd son, James, succeeded him as 2nd Duke in 1724.

Baillie, Robert (1599–1662): Principal of Glasgow University; initially in favour of episcopacy, then changed his mind; appointed to Glasgow's divinity chair in 1642; representative to the Westminster Assembly; joined Resolutioners but refused bishopric after Restoration; tried to prevent forced imposition of episcopacy without success.

Baillie, George, of Jerviswood. (1664–1738). son of the famous Robert, executed in the 1680s. MP for Berwickshire, 1708–34. Squadrone. By virtue of his marriage to Grizel Hume, he was son-in-law to Patrick Hume of Polwarth, 1st Earl of Marchmont. He was Lord of the Treasury 1717–25.

Blair, Hugh (1718–1800): minister and Robertson Moderate: ord. to Collessie 1742; trans. to Edinburgh Canongate 1743–54; Lady Yester's 1754–8; St Giles, High Kirk 1754–1800; app. professor of Rhetoric at EU 1760; was esp. celebrated as a preacher.

Boston, Thomas (1676–1732): evangelical minister and writer, was at Simprin before trans. to Ettrick in 1707; Ettrick had Cameronian background, but he consistently argued against schism; non-jurant, champion of the *Marrow*, anti-Simson; his most famous work was *Human nature in its fourfold state* [1720]

Boston, Thomas, jnr. (1713–67), minister and son of the above; was ord. to Ettrick on father's death in 1732; trans to Oxnam 1749; after his call to Jedburgh was blocked n 1755, the people erected a meeting-house, and he served there; eventually teamed up with Thomas Gillespie to form the Relief Presbytery.

Brown, John (c.1610–79): minister of Wamphray; banished in 1663 for opposing episcopacy and went to Holland where he remained until his death; exercised his writing ability to defend the Covenanters

Burnet, Gilbert (1643–1715) Bishop and historian; episcopal minister of Saltoun (1665–9) then Professor of Divinity at GU; went to London in 1674; moderate in outlook, he criticised any whose conduct was excessive or immoral; became close to William of Orange, who made him bishop of Salisbury in 1689.

Calamy, Edmund, DD., (1671–1732) English non-conformist writer and historian; while studying in Holland, met Carstares, who unsuccessfully tried to induce him to take a chair at a Scots university; visited Scotland in 1709 on Carstares' invitation, according To *ODNB*, this gave him an opportunity "for preaching moderation;" was honoured with degrees from Edinburgh, Glasgow and King's College.

Campbell, Archibald (d. 1756): professor of church history at St Andrews; ord. to Larbert 1718; app. to St Andrews 1730; annoyed evangelicals by criticising their style of preaching; most famous work was *The apostles no enthusiasts*, which was alleged to contain irreverent and heretical sentiments.

Campbell, John (1678–1743): 2nd Duke of Argyll; statesman and major Scottish landowner; app. LHC to Scottish Parliament 1705; for his assistance in the Union was made Earl of Chatham; served with Malborough on continent; made commander-in-chief of forces in Scotland after accession of George I and led victorious army at Sheriffmuir; rose to political ascendance in Scotland after 1725 with his bro. the Earl of Ilay; made master-general of ordinance 1725–30; governor of Portsmouth 1730–7; field-marshal 1735–6; impetuous and volatile, he fell out with Walpole 1739–40 and despite later being made commander-in-chief of all the forces, he resigned his offices and retired.

Campbell, Archibald, Earl of Ilay (1682–1761): Became 1st Earl in 1706. Bro of 2nd Duke of Argyll, became 3rd Duke in 1743. Scots representative peer 1707–13, and 1715–61. Lord of the Treasury 1705–6; app. a lord of Session 1708; Lord Justice General 1710–61. Lord Clerk Register 1714–16; took part in battle of Sheriffmuir; app. Lord Keeper of the Privy Seal 1721; commissioned by Walpole to carry through the imposition of the malt tax in Scotland, after which his power and influence earned him the reputation of being the uncrowned king of Scotland; helped found the Royal Bank of Scotland; used Lord Milton as his chief agent north of the border.

Carstares, William (1649–1715): minister and principal of Edinburgh University; suffered during Restoration period; became chaplain in

Holland to William of Orange and a close confidant until William's death; instrumental in establishing and maintaining Scottish presbyterianism; very influential in Kirk affairs; pro-Union; moderator of the Assembly four times.

Carteret, John, 2nd. Earl Granville (1690–1763): became Baron Carteret in 1695; entered Lords 1711; appointed secretary of state in 1721; lord lieutenant of Ireland 1724; led opposition in the Lords to Walpole from 1730 to 1742, when again became secretary of state until1744; president of Privy Council 1751–63.

Craigie, Robert, of Glendoick (c. 1685–1760): *Squadrone* legal adviser to Tweeddale when secy. of state 1742–6; advocate 1710; became deputy to solicitor general Robert Dundas 1719; MP for Tain Burghs 1742–7; app. Lord Advocate 1742–6; Lord President of the Court of Session 1754–60.

Cuming, Patrick (d 1776): minister and church history professor, he became Argyll's chief agent in church affairs after the death of James Smith in 1736; ord to Kirkmahoe 1720; trans to Lochmaben 1725; brought to Edinburgh's Old Kirk 2nd charge 1732; opposed patronage but believed the Church must obey the law, thus favoured the use of riding committees when conciliation failed, and the maintaining of a call, even when signed by few; supported Augmentation Scheme, which Carlyle said increased his popularity, but his jealousy of the rising William Robertson coloured his judgement so that he lost face, split from his deputy John Hyndman and came to be known as Dr Turnstile for his erratic behaviour; became professor at EU in 1737; was moderator 3 times.

Currie, John (1679–65): minister and evangelical; ord. to Kinglassie in Fife 1705; friend of the Erskine bros., but disapproved of schism; anti-patronage and wrote in favour of the people's right to elect their own minister

Dalrymple, Hew, Lord Drummore. Bought Westpans in E Lothian (parish of Inveresk), and called it Drummore. Took it as his title when he was raised to the Bench in 1726. Close friend of Carlyle's father, William. Gained much prestige among the clergy by supporting the Augmentation Scheme in 1749. Carlyle said he was the lay leader of the Moderate Party and that he used to socialise much with clergy during the GA, and always had elders in tow, eg, Sir James Colquhoun and Colin Campbell, Commissioner of Customs.

Dalrymple, Sir James (1650–1719) 2nd son of the 1st Viscount Stair; historian and lawyer. Bt of Nova Scotia in 1698.

Dalrymple, James (1619–1695) 1st Viscount Stair. began as a covenanter, soldiered between 1639 and 1641, then a regent at GU for 6 years, after a year of study this infantry captain became and advocate in 1648. Later also became a judge and politician and served successive rulers until his death. Published his *Institutions of the Laws of Scotland* in 1681; often considered a trimmer.

Dalrymple, Sir David (c1665–1721) 1st Baronet of Hailes, brother of James,the master of Stair, and youngest (5th) son of James, the 1st Viscount Stair. His wife was the sister-in-law of Lady Milton's bro, Sir Francis Kinloch of Gilmerton. (Milton was app. Dalrymple's factor in 1721); solicitor general 1701–9. MP for Culross, 1698–1707, then Haddington Burghs from 1708 until his death. Lord Advocate from 1709 to 1711, when dismissed over his handling of the Jacobite medal incident [see below on Dundas of Arniston]. Reappointed 1714–1720. Dean of the Fculty of Advocates 1712–21; feuded with Lord Justice Clerk, Cockburn of Ormiston; reputed to have framed the Patronage Act. Agreed to be lenient with '15 rebels. This may have been why he reports he was ostracised in London in 1716. Dismissed 1720 but remained an auditor of Scots revenue until death in 1721.

Dalrymple, Sir James of Newhailes, Midlothian and Hailes, Haddington-shire (1692–1751). 1st s of Sir David. MP for the county 1722–34. Went bankrupt over the S Sea Bubble, but his son, Sir James, as Auditor of the Exchequer "kept up the rank of the family" acc. to Carlyle. Married Lady Christian Hamilton, a sister of Lord Binning and d of the Earl of Haddington.

Dalrymple, Sir Hew of North Berwick (1652–1737): 3rd son of James, 1st Viscount Stair. Lord President of the Ct. of Session. Commissioner for the Union.

Dalrymple, John (1648–1707). Became 2nd Viscount Stair in 1695, and 1st Earl of Stair in 1703.As Lord Justice Clerk was pro–William during 1688–9; became Lord Advocate (1689–92), and Joint Secretary of State (1690–95); was a commissioner for the Union.

Drummond, George (1687–1766): Lord Provost of Edinburgh; made Accountant–General of Excise in 1707 in recognition of his assistance in preparing valuation reports for use in the Union negotiations; app. A commissioner of customs 1715; took part with Argyll in the battle of Sherrifmuir; elected Edin. City Treasurer 1717, Dean of Guild 1722, Provost, for first of six times, in 1725; adhered to Argathelians, but was an erratic ally; helped raise volunteers to defend the city in the '45; frequent commissioner to the Assembly; joined the Robertson moderates in 1751; Carlyle said of him: "want of personal courage was not his defect. It was civil courage in which he failed; for all his life he had a great deference to his superiors" [*Autobiog*. 130]

Dundas, Robert of Arniston (d. 1726): Squadrone politician and 2nd Lord Arniston, eldest s of Sir James Dundas and Marion Boyd (d of Lord Boyd). [Robert's bros and sisters were: Mary, md to J. Home of Blackadder; Christian, md to Sir Chas Erskine of Alva; Katherine, md to Sir J. Dalrymple of Borthwick; + 3 half bros]; md Margaret, d of Sir Robert Sinclair of Stevenson; was abroad before Revolution and returned as a supporter of K William. MP for Midlothian 1689–1707; also made a Lord of Session 1689; his son, James, went into the law, and in 1711 was caught up in the Jacobite Medal controversy. [The Duchess of Gordon had presented a medal to the Faculty of Advocates and James spoke strongly in favour of receiving it. He then co-published a pamphlet about it, and this led to his prosecution for sedition, as well as the dismissal of the LA, Sir David Dalrymple who was replaced, for a 2nd time, by Sir James Stewart of Goodtrees. The case collapsed in 1712.] Succeeded by his 2nd son, Robert.

Dundas, Robert (1685–1753): Admitted advocate 1709. In 1717, (only 8 years after being called to the bar) he became Solicitor General, in place of Sir James Stewart of Goodtrees [s of the LA of the same name]. In 1720, became LA, succeeding Sir David Dalrymple. In 1721 became Dean of the Faculty. md Elizabeth, d of Robert Watson of Muirhouse in 1712. Married twice. 1st wife died in Jan 1734. md. later the same year to Anne, d of Sir William Gordon of Invergordon. Elected MP for Midlothian in 1722. Dismissed as LA in May 1725: [Roxburghe to Dundas, 4 June 1725: "the only reason that was ever given to me for your being dismissed was the part you had acted against Sir R. Walpole's scheme proposed in lieu of the Malt Tax"] Dundas returned to the Bar, while succeeded by Duncan Forbes of Culloden. Although not allied with Ilay, he decided to accept appointment as a Lord of Session on 10 June 1737, as Ld Arniston. Was made Lord President as compromise candidate by Pelham in 1748 (until 1754). Carlyle says he inclined to the Popular Party, but could not go along with their fixed opposition to patronage, and that he led the opposition to the Augmentation Scheme.

Erskine, Hon. James (Lord Grange) (1679–1754): son of the 5th. Earl of Mar. Lord of Session 1707–34 as Lord Grange. Lord Justice Clerk 1710–34; resigned his position as a Lord of Session in 1734 to re-enter Parliament and oppose Walpole; was returned for Clackmananshire 1734–41 and Stirling burghs 1741–47; Made his maiden speech on the Witches Bill and made a fool of himself: "the truth was, that the man had neither learning nor ability. He was no lawyer and he was a bad speaker. He had been raised on the shoulders of his bro., the E of Mar, in the end of the Queen's reign, but never distinguished himself." [Carlyle 11] Became Scottish secretary to the Prince of Wales; corresponded with Wodrow, and took part in GAs. "In the Assembly itself . . . he took the high-flying side that he might annoy govt., his appearances were but rare and unimpressive; but as he was understood to be a great plotter, he was supposed to reserve himself for some greater occasions" [Carlyle 10]; married Rachel, d. of Chiesly of Dalry (who shot Lord President Lockhart); she was intemperate and bibulous; eventually he had her abducted to the Outer Hebrides, with help from Lord Lovat; his exiled brother (because of his part in the '15) made Grange 's reputation always vulnerable by association; was leading heretor in Prestonpans.

Erskine, Ebenezer (1680–1754): celebrated preacher, minister of Portmoak from 1703 and joint founder of the Secession Church; bro. of Ralph; non–juror; pro-Marrow; in 1731 was called to Stirling 3rd charge; preached before the synod of Perth and Stirling against the 1732 Act anent *the method of planting vacant churches;* was rebuked by synod and ensuing Assembly; he and three colleagues were sentenced to be loosed from their charges; they formed the Associate Presbytery and were deposed 1740;

Erskine, Henry, 3rd Lord Cardross ((1650–1693): succeeded to title in 1671; fined and imprisoned during Restoration period; left for S. Carolina where he founded a settlement; returned to Europe and accompanied William of Orange to England in 1688; he had his estates returned to him in 1689.

Erskine, John (1675–1732): 6th E of Mar and bro of James. Cousin and friend of the Earl of Glencairn. Court Party member, which was led by Queensberry. He and the E of Loudoun were made Secretaries of State for Scotland in 1705, in succession to Annandale. Scots representative peer 1707–15. He used Sir David Nairne as his Under-secretary in London, and through him the Queen was kept informed of events in Scotland; ceased to be Secy. in February 1709. Queensberry succeeded until his death in July 1711, then Hamilton and Mar fought each other for the post, with Mar getting it through influence of Oxford in 1713 [HMC Mar and Kellie MSS, xxvi]. Lost office next year with Q's death, then after being snubbed by the new K, went off to join the '15. Died at Aix-la-chappelle in 1732. His father in law was Viscount Dupplin.

Erskine, Ralph (1685–1752): evangelical minister; bro. of Ebenezer; ord. to Dunfermline 2nd charge, 1711, trans to 1st charge 1716; non-juror; pro-Marrow; anti-Simson; opposed Overture *anent the method of planting vacant churches*; joined Associate Presbytery 1737 and was deposed 1740; most famous work: *Faith no fancy* [1745]

Fletcher, Andrew, Lord Milton (1692–1766): prominent lawyer and political agaent; nephew of the famous republican and opponent of the Union; admitted advocate 1717; app. a Lord of Session 1724; Lord Justice Clerk 1735; Keeper of the Signet 1746; presided at trial of Porteous 1736; was Ilay's chief agent and adviser in Scottish affairs.

Gillespie, Thomas (1708–74): evangelical minister and joint founder of the Relief Church; studied at the dissenting academy at Northampton; ord. 1741 in England, then came to the charge of Carnock in Fife; assisted at the Kilsyth Revival; was deposed in the wake of the Inverkeithingcase; the Presbytery of Relief was eventually formed in 1761.

Gowdie, John, (1682–1762), minister and EU principal; ordained to Earlston (Berwickshire) 1704; anti-*Marrow;* defended Simson before the Assembly; his moderate principles won him favour from the Argyll interest, who brought him to Edinburgh, Lady Yester's in 1730, then to West St. Giles (New North Kirk) in 1732. In 1733, he was elected Assembly moderator and used his casting vote at the Commission to depose Ebenezer Erskine and his supporters; elected professor of Divinity 1733; became Principal 1754; his lectures were thought to be dull and was generally regarded as having little academic ability.

Grant, William (1701–64): lawyer and churchman, MP Elgin burghs 1747–54; s of Sir Francis Grant, bro. of Archibald Grant of Monymusk; procurator and Principal Clerk of Assembly 1731–46; solicitor general for Scotland 1737–42; Lord Advocate 1746–54; judge of the Ct of Session as Lord Prestongrange 1754–64; Argathelian

Grant, Francis (c.1660–1726) lawyer and lord of Session; pamphleteer; pro-Union on grounds it would secure presbyterianism; moderate in outlook and argued for ecclesiastical pluralism so that where presbyterianism could not be established, as in England, then episcopacy should be allowed; believed that certain fundamentals in church matters, were fundamental and immutable, and that therefore Parliament was not absolute.

Hamilton, William (1669–1732): Divinity Professor; ordained to Cramond (Edinburgh) 1694; appointed 1709 prof. of Divinity at Edinburgh; believed in encouraging the Church away from the harshness of the past; after death of Carstares in 1715, leadership of the Church fell to Hamilton and William Mitchell; after Mitchell died in 1727 transferred allegiance from *Squadrone* to Argathelians; did not favour patronage but believed heritors had to be included; moderator 5 times; made principal in 1732.

Harley, Robert, 1st. Earl of Oxford and Earl Mortimer. (1661–1724). Lead the government as First Lord of the Treasury between 1711 and 1714, under Queen Anne. Credited with bringing the War of Spanish Succession to an end with the Treaty of Utrecht in 1713. Lost power with the accession of George I.

Hay, Thomas of Huntington (d.1755): adviser to Tweeddale during his administration 1742–6; became advocate 1725; app. keeper of the Signet 1742; became a lord of Session 1754 with the title Lord Huntington.

Hay, John, 4th Marquis of Tweeddale (d. 1762): *Squadrone* secretary of state; succeeded to title 1715; app. a Lord of Session 1721; representative peer 1722, 1727, 1742, 1747, 1752, 1761; secy. of state for Scotland 1742–6; married the d of Carteret 1748.

Henderson, Alexander (1583–1646): minister of Leachars, then Greyfriars, then St Giles, Edinburgh; initially favoured episcopacy then changed his mind; prominent in composing both Covenants; representative to Westminster Assembly; acknowledged as the leading and most able figure in the Church until his death.

Honyman, Andrew (1619–76): bishop of Orkney; minister at Ferryport-on-Craig, trans to St Andrews 2nd Charge in 1642, then 1st charge in 1662; initially a Covenanter but changed his mind; made bishop in 1664;

Hutcheson, Francis (1694–1746): professor of moral philosophy at Glasgow; b County Down; originally entered ministry, but turned to philosophy and became professor at Glasgow in 1729; has been called the "apostle of the Enlightenment;" lectured in English instead of traditional Latin and espoused a utilitarian view of virtue; along with the professor of divinity, William Leechman, he was reckoned to have done much to increase the good taste and liberality of the ministers in the west .

Jardine, Robert (d 1749): ord. to Cummertrees (Annan) 1713; trans. to Glencairn 1719;trans. to Lochmaben 1732; his son John became a minister of Edinburgh [see below]

Jardine, John (s of Robert) (1715–66): minister of Liberton from 1741; trans. to Edinburgh Lady Yester's 1750, then to Tron 2nd charge 1754; married the d. of George Drummond; joined the Robertson moderates and was an influential figure in the Church becoming Dean of the Chapel Royal in 1761 and Dean of the Thistle in 1763; a humorist like his father, he nonetheless caused trouble in 1755 by using his friends' *Edinburgh Review* to ridicule evangelicals like Boston; the magazine was closed after 2 issues.

Johnston, (Sir) Archibald, of Wariston (1611–63): advocate and joint author of the National Covenant; appointed clerk to GA in 1638; made a Lord of Session in 1641 and was a representative to the Westminster Assembly; a radical of the Protester faction, he reluctantly accepted office under Cromwell, for which he was later condemned and executed.

Loudoun, Hugh, 3rd Earl of (d. 1731): app. joint secy. of state 1705; Keeper of the Great Seal of Scotland; a commissioner for the Union; fought with Argyll at Sheriffmuir;

Melville, George, 1st Earl (d. 1707): involved in plot against James vii in 1685, for which his estates were forfeit; these were restored by William who made him an Earl and his High Commissioner to the Scots Parliament; appointed Keeper of the Privy Seal in 1691 and President of the Council in 1696.

Mitchell, William (1670–1727): minister Canongate, Old Kirk and St Giles', Edinburgh; moderator 5 times, he rose to become the leading man in the Kirk until his death; was also reputed to be very wealthy; anti-Marrow; anti-Simson.

Newcastle, Thomas Pelham-Holles, 1st Duke of (1693–1768), whig statesman, secretary of state under Walpole 1724–42 and under his brother, Henry Pelham 1743–54; was first minister 1754–56; formed a coalition ministry with William Pitt the Elder 1757–62.

Pelham, Henry (1695–1754): MP Seaford 1717–22 and Sussex 1722–54; treasurer of the chamber 1720–22; a lord of Treasury 1721–4; secy. at war 1724–30; paymaster general 1730–43; 1st lord of the Treasury and chancellor of the Exchequer 1743–54.

Robertson, William (1721–93): minister, historian and dominant figure in the Kirk in second half of 18th century; ord. to Gladsmuir 1744; led those who believed the Church's inferior courts should obey they superiors; having made his mark at the Assembly in a speech regarding the Torphichen case of 1751, he led the move to assert the Assembly's authority against recalcitrants in the settlement of Inverkeithing in 1752; trans. to Lady Yesters' then Old Greyfriars 1758; app. principal of EU 1752; displaced Patrick Cuming as dominant figure in the Kirk and was prominent man in the grouping known as the Moderates until withdrawing from public life in 1780.

Rule, Gilbert (c.1629–1701): minister and physician; imprisoned on Bass Rock during Restoration period; in 1690 was made principal of Edinburgh University; favoured moderation and tolerance of episcopal incumbents.

Sharp, James (1618–79): Archbishop of St Andrews; minister of Crail from 1649; sent to London in 1657 to safeguard the Kirk's privileges, but after Restoration was made Archbishop and Primate; led persecution of non-conformists; assassinated 1679

Smith, James (1680–1736), minister and Edinburgh University Principal, was tutor, to Dalrymples of Cousland, then Dundases of Arniston. The nexus with the Dundases assisted Smith's career until he deserted the *Squadrone* for Argathelians in 1730; ordained to Morham 1706; inducted to Cramond 1712; showed adherence to moderate principles, by publishing two *Dialogues* (1712, 1713) which refuted evangelical scruples about the Abjuration Oath; prominent in the Assembly's firm response to Auchterarder Creed, Marrow Controversy, second Simson case and John Glas. believed the Church's authority must outweigh individual conscience; twice moderator; assumed leading role in church affairs until his death.

Stewart, James (Sir) of Goodtrees (1635–1713): lawyer and apologist for the Covenanting cause; because of his writings, he had repeatedly to leave the country; appointed Lord Advocate in 1692; helped draw up the 1690 abolition of patronage and many of the Kirk's public statements.

Stirling, James (1631–c.1671); minister of Paisley, 2nd charge from 1654; deprived 1662; left for India where he died after an accident.

Tullideph, Thomas (d. 1777): university principal and ecclesiastical adviser to Tweeddale when secy. of state; ord. to Dron 1727; trans. to Markinch 1731; app. professor of Divinity at St Mary's, St Andrews 1734; trans. to St Leonard's church with principalship of St Leonard's college in conjunction 1739; principal of united colleges from 1747; moderator 1742.

Wallace, Robert (1696–1771): minister and adviser on church affairs to secy. of state Tweeddale; ord. to Moffat 1723; trans. to Edinburgh New Greyfriars 1733 then to West St Giles 1738; moderator 1743; espoused a liberality and the moderate views that were to be characteristic of the later Moderates, yet refused to read the Act concerning the murder of Porteous (1737) and tried, when Tweeddale's ecclesiastical manager, to avoid confrontation in the exercise of presentations; moderator 1743.

Walpole, Sir Robert. 1st Earl of Orford (1676–1745): whig statesman, sometimes referred to as Britain's first prime minister; secretary at war 1708–10; treasurer of the navy 1710–11; with accession of George I, became 1st lord of the Treasury and chancellor of the Exchequer; resigned along with his bro-in-law, Lord Townshend 1717; returned to office in 1721, maintaining power until 1742, when made Earl of Orford; fell out with Argyll in 1739.

Wishart, George (1703–85): minister St Cuthbert's, Edin, 1726–30, then succeeded his father at the Tron (1st charge) 1730–85; anti-patronage; app. Assembly Clerk 1746; moderator 1748; it was considered that his bro. led him astray in ecclesiastical affairs, but when William died in 1754, he came back to the moderate cause.

Wishart, William, jnr. (d 1753): became Principal of EU in 1737; minister of Glasgow Tron 1724–30; then Scots church in London for 7 years;

became principal of EU in 1737; New Greyfriars, Edin., 1739–44; Tron, (2nd charge) Edin. 1745–53; his enlightened teaching was supposed to have paved the way for Moderatism, but nonetheless opposed patronage; Carlyle said of him: "He had said some things rashly while the Augmentation scheme was going on, which betrayed contempt of the clergy; and as he was rich . . . his sayings gave still greater offence." [238]

Wishart. William (1660–1729): Principal of Edinburgh Univ.; suffered during Restoration period; ord. in 1688 at S. Leith, trans to Tron, Edinburgh in 1707; app. Principal in 1716; anti-Simson; moderator 5 times; s George followed him at the Tron while s William followed him as Principal.

Wodrow, Robert (1679–1734): minister of Eastwood and historian; his letters and *Analecta* give often detailed commentary on contemporary affairs; non-jurant and opposed patronage, but not opposed to the 1731 Assembly Overture on *the method of planting*.

[Sources: Romney Sedgwick, *The House of Commons, 1715–1754*, (HMSO: 1970); HMC Mar and Kellie MSS; HMC Portland MSS; *Autobiography of Dr Alexander Carlyle of Inveresk. 1722–1805*, (Edinburgh: 1910); *Selections from the Caldwell Papers*, 2 vols, Maitland Club Publications. (Glasgow: 1854); SRO Dundas of Arniston Papers RH4/15/2; James Erskine, Lord Grange, *Diary of a Senator of the College of Justice*, (Edinburgh:1843); Wodrow: *Correspondence*, 3 vols., ed Thos. McCrie, Wodrow Society, (Edinburgh: 1843); N.T. Phillipson and R. Mitchison, *Scotland in the Age of Improvement*, (EUP: 1970); J.B. Owen, *The Rise of the Pelhams*, (London: 1957); W. Marshall, *Historic Scenes in Perthshire*, (Edinburgh: 1880); Geoffrey Holmes, *British Politics in the age of Anne*, (Hambledon Continuum: 1987); James MacVeigh, *The Scottish Family History*, 3 vols., (Dumfries: 1891); *FES; ODNB; DSCHT.*]

Bibliography—Up to 1690

Manuscript Sources

Wodrow MS. NLS.

Primary Sources

Anon. "Concerning the people's interest in calling them pastoris": notes on calling of ministers addressed to Rev William Tweedie [of Slamanan, Linlithgow presbytery]. *Wodrow mss*. [NLS Wod.Fol.xxviii, 28]

A source book of Scottish history, eds. Dickinson, William Croft, and Donaldson, Gordon, vol. iii

"Answer to the paper of Mr Calderwood against the directory for election of ministers presented to the General Assembly." nd. *Wodrow mss*, NLS. Wod.Fol.xxix, 22.

The letters and journals of Robert Baillie, AM, principal of the university of Glasgow, 1637-62 ed. Laing, David, 3 vols, Edinburgh 1841

The historical works of Sir James Balfour of Denmylne and Kinnaird, Kt. and Bt.; Lord Lyon, king of Arms to Charles I and Charles II, ed., Haig, J., Edinburgh: 1824, 4 vols.

The Booke of the Universall Kirk of Scotland: wherein the headis and conclusionis devysit be the ministers and commissionaris of the particular kirks thereof, are specially expressed and contained. ed. Peterkin, Alexander. Edinburgh 1889. This text has been modernized and published as: *The Acts and Proceedings of the General Assemblies of the Church of Scotland 1560-1618*, ed. Shaw, Duncan, 3 vols., Scottish Record Society, Edinburgh: 2004

John Brown, *An apologetical relation of the particular sufferings of the faithful ministers and professors of the church of Scotland since August 1660* (n.p. 1665)

Burnet's history of his own time from the restoration of king Charles II to the treaty of peace at Utrecht, in the reign of Queen Anne. London: 1883

The diary of Alexander Brodie of Brodie, 1652-80 and of his son James Brodie of Brodie, 1680-85, Spalding Club, Aberdeen: 1863

David Calderwood's History of the kirk of Scotland, Wodrow Society, Edinburgh: 1845

Calendar of Scottish supplications to Rome 1428-1432, eds. Dunlop, Annie I. and Cowan, Ian B. (SHS. series 4, vii)

State papers and letters addressed to William Carstares, ed. McCormick, Joseph. Edinburgh: 1774

"Notes of debates and proceedings of the Assembly of divines and other commissioners at Westminster, February 1644 to January 1645, by George Gillespie, minister at

Edinburgh, from unpublished manuscripts," ed, Meek, David, from *The works of Mr George Gillespie in two volumes*, in *The presbyterian's armoury in three volumes*. Edinburgh: 1846

Extracts from the presbytery book of Strathbogie, 1631-54, Spalding Club, Aberdeen: 1843

The first Book of discipline, ed. Cameron, James K., Edinburgh 1972

Honeyman, Andrew, *A survey of the insolent and infamous libel entitled Naphtali, etc.* Edinburgh: 1668

Diary of Sir Archibald Johnston of Wariston, Scottish History Society, second series, vol. xviii, II; vol. xxxiv, III; Edinburgh 1919 & 1940

Kenyon, J.P., *The Stuart constitution, 1603-1688, documents and commentary.* Cambridge 1966

James Kirkton's history of the church of Scotland, 1660-1679, ed. Stewart, Ralph, Lampeter: 1992

John Knox's History of the Reformation in Scotland, ed. Dickinson, William Croft, Edinburgh 1949, 2 vols.

Letters and state papers during the reign of King James the sixth, Abbotsford Club, Edinburgh: 1838

Leven and Melville Papers, Bannatyne Club. lxxvii. Edinburgh: 1843

The diary of Mr John Lamont of Newton, from the year 1649 to the year 1671, Maitland Club Edinburgh: 1830

The whole works of the Rev John Lightfoot, D.D., ed., John Rogers, London: 1824, vol. xiii, "The journal of the proceedings of the assembly of divines, from January 1st, 1643 to December 31, 1644".

The records of the commissions of the general assemblies of the church of Scotland holden in Edinburgh the years 1648 and 1649, Mitchell, A.F., and Christie, J., (eds), Scottish History Society, vol. xxv, II, 1896; vol. lviii, III, 1909

Minutes of the sessions of the Westminster Assembly of divines, Mitchell, Alexander F., & Struthers, John (eds), Edinburgh: 1874

Records of the kirk of Scotland, containing the acts and proceedings of the general assemblies from the year 1638 downwards, ed., Peterkin, Alexander, Edinburgh: 1843

Park, Robert, *The rights and liberties of the church asserted and vidicated against the pretended right and usurpating of patronage.* Edinburgh: 1689

Register of the consultations of the ministers of Edinburgh and some other brethren of the minstry, ed., Stephen, W., Scottish History Society, third series, i & ii, Edinburgh: 1921 and 1930

Registers of the privy council of Scotland. Hume Brown, P., (ed.), 2nd series, i, (1625-7), Edinburgh: 1899; iv, (1630-2), Edinburgh: 1902; vi (1635-7), Edinburgh: 1905; vii (1638-43), Edinburgh: 1906.

John Row's History of the kirk of Scotland 1558-1639 Wodrow Society, Edinburgh: 1842

Selections from the records of the kirk session, presbytery and synod of Aberdeen, Spalding Club. Aberdeen: 1846

Selections from the minutes of the presbyteries of St Andrews and Cupar 1641-98, Abbotsford Club. Edinburgh: 1837

Spalding, John, *The history of the troubles and memorable transactions in Scotland and England from 1624 to 1645* Bannatyne Club, 25, Edinburgh: 1828, vol. I

James Stewart, and James Stirling, *Naphtali, or the wrestlings of the church of Scotland for the kingdom of Christ, contained in a true and short deduction thereof, from the beginning of the reformation of religion until the year 1667.* n.p. 1667, ed., Duncan, Henry, Kirkcudbright: 1845

Scottish diaries and memoirs, 1550-1746, ed. Fyfe, JG., Stirling: 1928

The second book of discipline, ed. Kirk, James, Edinburgh 1980

Wodrow, Robert, *The history of the sufferings of the Church of Scotland from the Restoration to the Revolution* ed., Burns, R., Glasgow: 1828

Printed Pamphlets

Anon., *Canons and constitutions ecclesiastical gathered and put in form for the government of the church of Scotland.* Aberdeen: 1636

Anon., *A memorial for His Highness the prince of Orange, in relation to the affairs of Scotland together with the address of the presbyterian party in that kingdom to His Highness and some observations on that address by two persons of quality.* London: 1689

Anon., *To his grace, his majesty's high commissioner and the the right honourable, the estates of parliament, the humble address of the presbyterian ministers and professors of the church of Scotland.* Edinburgh: n.d., prob. early 1690

Anon., *His highness the prince of Orange, his speech to the Scots lords and gentlemen, with their address, and his highness, his answer. With a true account of what passed at their meeting, in the council chamber at Whitehall 7 January 1689.* n.p. 1689-90

[Rule, Gilbert] *A true representation of presbyterian government wherein a short and clear account is given of the principles of them that owne it, the common objections against it answered and some other things opened that concern it in the present circumstances, by a friend of that interest.* Edinburgh: 1690

Alexander Shields, *A hind let loose or an historical representation of the testimonies of the church of Scotland for the interest of Christ.* (np. 1687)

Articles And Essays

Clarke, Tristram, "The Williamite episcopalians and the Glorious Revolution in Scotland," *RSCHS*, xxiv (1990)

Cowan, Ian B., "Some aspects of the appropriation of parish churches in medieval Scotland," *RSCHS*, vol. xiii, (1959).

Cowan, Ian B., "Patronage, provision and reservation, pre-Reformation appointments to Scottish benefices," in Cowan, Ian B., and Shaw, D. (eds), *The Renaissance and Reformation in Scotland*, (Edinburgh 1983), 75 ff.

Cowan, Ian B., "Church and society in post-Reformation Scotland," *RSCHS*, vol. 17, (1969-71)

Cowan, Ian B., "The Five Articles of Perth," in *Reformation and revolution, essays presented to the Very Rev. Hugh Watt.* Edinburgh: 1967

Donaldson, Gordon, "The rights of the Scottish crown in epsicopal vacancies," *Scottish Historical Review*, xlv (1966)

Dunlop, A.I., "The polity of the Scottish church, 1600-1637," *RSCHS*, xii, (1955-6)

W. Roland Foster, `A constant platt achieved: provision for the ministry, 1600-38' in *Reformation and revolution*

Glassey, Lionel, "William II and the Settlement of Religion in Scotland, 1688-1690," *RSCHS*, xxiii (1989)

Halliday, James, "The Club and the Revolution in Scotland 1689-90," *SHR*, xlv

Innes, George P., "Ecclesiastical patronage in Scotland in the 12th. and 13th. centuries," *RSCHS*, xii, part 1, (1954)

Innes, George P., `Ecclesiastical patronage....in Scotland in the later middle ages', *RSCHS*, xiii (1957-9)

Kirk, James,"The exercise of ecclesiastical patronage by the crown, 1560-1572," in Cowan, Ian B., and Shaw, D. (eds), *The Renaissance and Reformation in Scotland*, Edinburgh 1983.

Lee, Maurice, Jr., "James VI's government of Scotland after 1603," *SHR*, Vol. lv, 1, no 159, April 1976.

MacDonald, Alan R., "Ecclesiastical representation in parliament in post-Reformation Scotland: the two kingdoms theory in practice," *Journal of Ecclesastical History*, vol.l, 1, January 1999.

Raffe, Alasdair, "Presbyterians and Episcopalians: the formation of confessional cultures in Scotland 1660-1715." *English Historical Review* 53. (2010)

Smith, Peter M., "The advowson: the history and development of a most peculiar property" in *Ecclesiastical Law Journal*, 26 (2000)

Young, John R., "Scottish covenanting radicalism, the commission of the Kirk and the establishment of the parliamentary radical regime of 1648-1649," *RSCHS*, xxv, 3, (1995)

Reference Woks

Cameron, Nigel M. deS., *Dictionary of Scottish church history and theology*. Edinburgh: 1993.

Cowan, Ian B., *Parishes of medieval Scotland*, SRS. vol. 93, 1967

Duncan, John M., *Treatise on the parochial ecclesiastical law of Scotland*, Edinburgh: 1869

Dunlop, Alexander, *Parochial law*. Edinburgh: 1841

Elliot, Nenion, *Teinds or tithes and procedure in the court of teinds in Scotland*, Edinburgh: 1893

Morison, W.M., *Dictionary of decisions of the Court of Session*. Edinburgh: 1805

Oxford Dictionary of National Biography. Online: http://www.oxforddnb.com

Scannell, T.B., *Addis and Arnold's Catholic Dictionary*. London: 1928

James, viscount of Stair, *The institutions of the law of Scotland*, ed., Walker, David M., Edinurgh: 1981

Steuart, Walter, of Pardovan, "Collections and Observations Methodized, Concerning the Worship, Discipline and Government of the Church of Scotland," [1709], in *A Copious and Comprehensive Summary of the Laws and Regulations of the Church of Scotland from 1560-1850*. Aberdeen: 1850

Books

Brown, Keith M., *Kingdom or province? Scotland and the regal union, 1603-1715*, Basingstoke: 1992

Buckroyd, Julia, *Church and state in Scotland 1660-81*. Edinburgh: 1980

Burleigh, J. H. S., *A church history of Scotland*. London: 1960

Cheyne, A.C., *Studies in Scottish church history*. Edinburgh: 1999

Cormack, Alexander A., *Teinds and agriculture, an historical survey*. Oxford: 1930

Cowan, Ian B., *The Scottish Reformation*. London: 1982

Cowan, Ian B., *The Scottish Covenanters, 1660-88*, London: 1976

Cunningham, J., *Church History of Scotland*, Edinburgh: 1859

Davies, Godfrey, *The Early Stuarts 1603-1660*. Matrix: The Oxford History of England, 2nd. Edn. OUP: 1959

Dilworth, Mark, *Scottish monasteries in the late middle ages,* Edinburgh: 1995

Eighteenth century Scotland: new perspectives, Devine, TM., and Young, JR., eds., East Lothian: 1999

Donaldson, Gordon, *The Scottish Reformation*, Cambridge 1960

Douglas, J. D., *Light in the north, the story of the Scottish covenanters*. Exeter: 1964

Dow, F. D., *Cromwellian Scotland 1561-1660*, Edinburgh: 1979

Drummond, Andrew L., *The kirk and the continent*, Edinburgh: 1956

Fergusson, Charles, *The early history of Church patronage,* Edinburgh: 1833

Foster, W. Roland, *The church before the Covenants*, Edinburgh: 1975

Foster, W. Roland, *Bishop and presbytery, the church of Scotland 1661-88*. London: 1958

Forbes, William, *A treatise of church lands and tithes in two parts*. Edinburgh: 1703

Jacob, Violet, *The lairds of Dun*. London: 1931

Kirk, James, *Patterns of reform: continuity and change in the Reformation Kirk*, Edinburgh: 1989

McCall, Hardy Bertram, *The history and antiquities of the parish of Mid-Calder*. Edinburgh: 1894.

MacDonald, Alan R., *The Jacobean kirk, 1567-1625, sovereignty, polity and liturgy* Aldershot: 1998

Macinnes, Allan I., *Charles I and the making of the Covenanting movement 1625-1641*, Edinburgh: 1991

MacKay, EJG, *Memoir of Sir James Dalrymple, 1st Viscount Stair*, Edinburgh: 1873

Makey, W., *The church of the Covenant 1637-1651*, Edinburgh: 1979

Mason, Roger A. (ed.), *Scots and Britons, Scottish political thought and the union of 1603*, Cambridge: 1994

Mullen, David G., *Episcopacy in Scotland: the history of an idea*, Edinburgh: 1986

Paul, Robert S., *The Assembly of the Lord; politics and religion in the Westminster Assembly and the Grand Debate*. Edinburgh: 1985

Raffe, Alasdair, *The Culture of Controversy: Religious Arguments in Scotland, 1660–1714*, Studies in Modern British Religious History, vol. 28, Woodbridge: 2012.

Rendall, Jane, *The origins of the Scottish Enlightenment*. London: 1978

Riley, PWJ., *King William and the Scottish politicians*, Edinburgh: 1979

Robertson, John, (ed.), *A union for empire, political thought and the British union of 1707*, Cambridge: 1995

Shaw, Duncan, *The General Assemblies of the Church of Scotland, 1560-1600.* Edinburgh: 1964.

Shaw, Duncan, (ed.), *Reformation and Revolution, essays presented to the very Rev. Hugh Watt, DD.* Edinburgh: 1967

Stark, W.A., *The book of Kirkpatrick Durham.* Castle Douglas: 1903

Stevenson, David, *Union, revolution and religion in 17th-century Scotland.* Variorum Collected Studies Series, 570. Aldershot: 1997

Stevenson, David, *The Scottish revolution 1637-1644; the triumph of the Covenanters.* Newton Abbott: 1973

Stevenson, David, *King or Covenant? Voices from the civil war.* East Linton: 1996

Young, John R., *The Scottish parliament 1639-1661, a political and constitutional analysis,* Edinburgh: 1996

Unpublished Theses

Beisner, E. Calvin, "His Majesty's Advocate: Sir James Stewart of Goodtrees (1635–1713) and Covenanter resistance theory under the Restoration monarchy," PhD diss. St Andrews: 2003

R.G. MacPherson, "Francis Stewart, 5th. earl of Bothwell, c.1562-1612, lordship and politics in Jacobean Scotland." unpubl. PhD diss., Edinburgh: 1998.

BIBLIOGRAPHY—AFTER 1690

Manuscript Sources

BL., Newcastle MSS.

BL., Hardwicke Papers

Central Region Archives GD 189 2/..

Edinburgh City Archives, Edinburgh Town Council Minutes.

EUL., "The Private Diary of George Drummond." (1736-38), [DC.1.82/3],

EUL., Laing MSS, Papers of Robert Wallace

Floors Castle muniments, especially the period 1736 to 1742, WRH., TD87/9/1277 and TD86/44/402.

Hay Muniments at Duns Castle

NLS., MSS 3517, Lee Papers, Notebook on settlements,

NLS., Letters to Wodrow (1728-9), Quarto XVIII.

NLS., Lee MSS.

NLS., Saltoun MSS.

NLS., Yester MSS.

SRO CH8/184, "Instructions Given by undersubscribing Noblemen to their Commissioner" [1702]

SRO. GD 158/2519. Diary of Hugh, 3rd. Earl of Marchmont,

SRO Dundas of Arniston Papers RH4/15/2

SRO General Assembly Commission Registers CH1/3 onwards

SRO General Assembly Papers CH1/2/32; CH1/1/26; Ch1/2/78;

SRO Lanark Presbytery Minutes CH2/234/..

SRO Brechin Presbytery Minutes CH2/40/..

SRO Duns Presbytery Minutes CH2/113/..

SRO Aberdeen Presbytery Minutes CH2/1/..

SRO Chirnside Presbytery Minutes CH2/316/..

SRO Paisley Presbytery Minutes CH2/294/..

SRO Perth Presbytery Minutes CH2/299/..

SRO Edinburgh Presbytery Minutes CH2/121/..

SRO Synod of Glasgow and Ayr Minutes CH2/464/..

SRO Synod of Lothian Minutes CH2/252/..

SRO Miscellaneous MSS., CH8\195

SRO Breadalbane MSS., GD 112/39/267/

SRO Dalhousie MSS GD 14/352

SRO Mar and Kellie Papers, GD124\15\410

SRO State Papers, Scotland, (SP.54), Series II, No. 4, 1711-1712, [RH.2/4/300]; (SP.55).
    Vol.I, Sept.1713 - Sept.1714, [RH.2/4/390].

StAUL General Assembly Registers

Unpublished Memoranda

BL., Hardwicke MSS.35891, Bundle 78, unsigned memo: "Note Relative to Collusive Presentations in Scotland" [undated, presumed 1753-60]

Edinburgh City Archives, Miscellaneous MSS., "Memorial for the Magistrates, Council and Community of the City of Edinburgh - 1738".

SRO. GD157/1392. "A Short Memorandum relating to the Situation and Management of Church Affairs in Scotland at least so far as The King's Ministry or those employed by them seem to have been Concerned."

Primary Sources

The Autobiography of Dr Alexander Carlyle of Inveresk. 1722-1805. TN Foulis, Edinburgh: 1910.

"Clerical Corridors of Power: Extracts from Letters concerning Robert Wallace's involvement in Ecclesiastical politics, 1742-1743", N. Smith, *Notes and Queries*, Vol. 218, June 1973, 214-9.

"Extracts from the Records of the Burgh of Glasgow", J.D. Marwick, ed., Glasgow 1878

"Extracts from the Records of the Burgh of Edinburgh, 1589-1603," Scottish Burgh Records Society Edinburgh 1875

"Memorandum of the Present State of the Political Differences in the City of Edinburgh - July 1763", contained in *Selections from the Caldwell Papers*, Part II, Vol.I, Maitland Club Publications. Glasgow: 1854, 182-187.

"Records of Falkirk Parish", Vol.II, ed. Murray, G.I., Falkirk: 1888

"The Registers of the General Kirk-Session of Edinburgh", reprinted in *The Scottish Antiquary, or, Northern Notes and Queries*, vol.13. 1898; The original minute book is in: SRO., CH2\131\2.

Burnet, Gilbert, *History of his Own Time*, Reeves and Turner. London: 1883

Calamy, Edmund, *An Historical Account of my own Life*, 2 Vols., London: 1829

Cobbett, W. and Wright, J. eds., *The Parliamentary History of England*, London: 1806-1812

Maurice Cross, ed., *Selections from the Edinburgh Review* 6 vols, Edinburgh: 1835

Erskine, James, Lord Grange, *Diary of a Senator of the College of Justice*, Edinburgh: 1843

Extracts from the minute books of the Presbytery of Fordyce, contained in Cramond, W., *The Church and Churchyard of Rathven*, Banff: 1885

Hervy, Lord John, *Memoirs of the reign of King George II*, ed., R. Sedgwick, 3 Vols. London: 1931.

History and proceedings of the House of Commons from the Restoration to the present time, ix, na., London: 1741.

HMC Bute MSS

HMC., Portland MSS., 15th Report, Appendix, part IV, 1897. Also Vol. V and Vol. X

HMC. Portland MSS, vol.X

HMC., Mar and Kellie MSS., London: 1904

Jones, C., and Holmes, G.S., *The London Diaries of William Nicolson, 1702-18*, OUP: 1985.

Lauder, Sir John, of Fountainhall, *Historical Notices of Scotish Affairs*, The Bannatyne Club. 1848, Vol.I. 20 Novembris 1678. 205-215.

Leven and Melville Papers, Bannatyne Club, vol. 77, Edinburgh: 1843

Scotland's Ruine, Lockhart of Carnwath's memoirs of the Union, ed., Szechi, Daniel, Aberdeen: 1995

Letters of George Lockhart of Carnwath, 1698-1732, ed. Daniel Szechi, SHS., Edinburgh: 1989

Letters of Lord Balmerino to Harry Maule, 1710–1713, 1721–1722, ed. Jones, Clyve, Miscellany of the Scottish History Society, Vol. XII, Edinburgh: 1994. 99–168.

Marchmont, *A selection from the papers of the Earls of Marchmont*, ed., Rose, G., 3 vols. London: 1831.

McCormick, J., *State Papers and Letters addressed to William Carstares, to which is prefaced the Life of Mr. Carstares*, Edinburgh: 1774

Memoirs of the Life, Time, and Writings of Thomas Boston, AM, ed. Morrison, G.H., Edinburgh: 1899

Mitchell, Rev. William, *Diary of the Rev. William Mitchell, Minister at Edinburgh, 1717*, in Miscellany of the Spalding Club, Vol.I, Aberdeen: 1841

MSS of the House of Lords, Vol. IX

Origins of the 'Forty-Five and other papers relaying to that Rising, ed. Blaikie, W.B., SAP, Edinburgh: 1975

Peterkin, A., *Records of the Kirk of Scotland*, vol 1. Edinburgh: 1838

Roberts, P., ed., *Diary of Sir David Hamilton, 1709-1714*, OUP: 1975

The Coltness Collections, 1608-1840, Maitland Club, Glasgow: 1842

Wodrow, Robert, *Correspondence*, 3 vols., ed. Thomas McCrie, Wodrow Society, Edinburgh: 1843

Wodrow, Robert, *Analecta: or Materials for a History of Remarkable Providences*, 4 vols., Maitland Club, vol 60. 1842-3

Wodrow, Robert, *History of the Sufferings of the Church of Scotland*, 4 vols., Glasgow: 1830

Periodicals

Caledonian Mercury
Edinburgh Evening Courant
Scots Courant
Scots Magazine
The Patriot
Edinburgh Christian Instructor
The Scottish Chronicle (15 June 1906-16 November 1906)
The Thistle

Printed Pamphlets

Anon., *A True Representation of Presbyterian Government, wherein a short and clear Account is given of the Principles of them that owne it. The Common Objections against it answered, and some other things Opened that concern it in the Present Circumstances - by A Friend to that Interest.* Edinburgh:1690. (licensed, 18 April 1690.)

Anon., "A Candid Enquiry into the Constitution of the Church of Scotland in Relation to the Settlement of Ministers", in *Tracts Concerning Patronage*, W. Gray, Edinburgh: 1770

Anon., but possibly by Bishop John Sage, *An Account of the Late Establishment of Presbyterian Government by the Parliament of Scotland, Anno 1690, together with the Methods by which it was settled.* Jos Hindmarsh, London: 1693

Anon. (? John Hyndman, West Church, Edinburgh) "A just view of the constitution of the Church of Scotland, and of the proceedings of the last General Assembly in relation to the deposition of Mr Gillespie," of which, extracts quoted in *Scots Magazine*, xv, February 1753

Anon., *A letter from a friend in the city to a MP anent patronages*, Edinburgh: 1703

Anon., *A letter from a gentleman in Edinburgh to his friend in the country concerning the way and manner in which the Abjuration Oath was sworn by the ministers in the shire of Edinburgh*, Edinburgh: 1712

Anon., *A Letter from a gentleman in Edinburgh to his friend in the country*, Edinburgh: 1749

Anon., *A letter from the north in answer to another from a friend in the south, concerning Principal Chalmers, his call to Old Machar, and the conduct of the presbytery of Aberdeen and the people of Old Machar thereanent*, np. 1730

Anon., *A letter to a minister of the gospel, concerning the parish of Bathgate*, Edinburgh: 1720

Anon., *A Letter to a Scots Clergyman, lately ordained, Concerning his behaviour in the Judicatories of the Church*, Edinburgh: 1735

Anon., *A plea for the Church of Scotland against patronages, with reasons for relieving her from them and repealing the Act made in the reign of Queen Anne 1712 whereby patronages were restored, and full answers are made to all objections,* London: 1735

Anon., *A seasonable warning to all the lovers of Jesus Christ, members of the Church of Scotland, relative to the Act of Assembly 1732 anent planting vacant Churches, etc.,* np. c. 1732

Anon., *"A true and fair representation of the case concerning the settlement of Lochmaben with a gospel minister"* in a letter from a gentleman in Annandale to his friend at Edinburgh np. 1724

Anon., *A True Representation of Presbyterian Government wherein a short and clear Account is given of the Principles of them that owne it: the Common Objections against it Answered, and some other things opened that concern it in the Present Circumstances - by a Friend to that Interest.* Edinburgh: 1690. (licensed: 18 April 1690).

Anon., "A Collection of Important Acts of Parliament and Assembly connected with Patronage", Select Anti Patronage Library: 1841

Anon., *An account of the reasons of some people in Galloway, their meetings anent public grievances through enclosures,* np., 1724

Anon., *An Answer to the Patrons of the New Principle of the Presbytery's Right in opposition to all else...to elect pastors to vacant Congregations within their Bounds,* np. 1753

Anon., *A mutual negative in parish and presbytery in the election of a minister in opposition to episcopacy on the one hand, and independency on the other, instructed from both Books of Discipline by some member of the last General Assembly who protested against the Act anent the method of planting vacant churches,* Edinburgh: 1733

Anon., *A testimony to the doctrine, worship, government and discipline of the Church of Scotland . . . or reasons . . . for their protestation.* Edinburgh: 1734.

Anon., *A voice from the north or an answer to the voice from the south, written by the presbyterians of Scotland, to the dissenters in England - a poem.* Edinburgh: 1707

Anon., *Ancient and modern presbytery considered, being a true and candid representation of the principles and practices of the presbyterian clergy in Scotland with relation to their settlement of churches by popular elections. To which is added a brief answer to the most material objections in their late plea against patronages,* London: 1735

Anon., *Good news from Scotland: or the Abjuration and the Kirk of Scotland reconcil'd,* np. 1712

Anon., *Memorial concerning the Call of Ministers to Parochial charges: drawn up and published for general use but specially calculated for the city of Edinburgh, and therefore addressed to the Lord Provost, Magistrates, Counsellors and Elders who now are or shall at any time hereafter be in Office. - by a citizen and Native who is an elder and Heritor,* Edinburgh: 1736. (BL., 4175 aaa78)

Anon., *News from Galloway; or the poor man's plea against his landlord, in a letter to a friend,* np., c. 1724

Anon. *Remarks upon the representation made by the kirk of Scotland concerning patronages,* np. 1712

Anon., *The Progress and State of Patronage,* np. 1783

Anon., *The Lawfulness and Necessity of Ministers, their reading the Act of Parliament for bringing to justice the Murderes of Capt. John Porteous.* np. 1737

Anon., *Sound and solid reason against the presbyterian prints anent patronages whereby the pretended divine right of the popular election of pastors is perpetually barred*, np. 1703.

Anon., *The act, declaration and testimony of the Reformed Presbyterian church of Scotland*, np. 1761

Anon., *The nature of patronage and the duty of patrons, considered in three letters published in the Weekly Miscellany*, by Generosus, London: 1735

Begg, James, *History of the Act of Queen Anne 1711*, np., c.1840

Cockburn, John, [prob.], *An historical relation of the late general assembly held at Edinburgh from October 16 to November 13 1690, in a letter from a person in Edinburgh to his friend in London*. London: 1691

Crosbie, Andrew, *Thoughts of a layman concerning patronage and presentations*. Edinburgh: 1769

Currie, John, *Jus populi vindicatum*, Edinburgh: 1720

Currie, John, *Jus Populi Divinum, or, the People's Divine Right to Choose Their own Pastor*, Edinburgh: 1727

Currie, John, *A full vindication of the people's right to elect their own pastors*, Edinburgh: 1733

Dalrymple, Sir David, *An Account of Lay Patronages in Scotland and of the fatal differences they have occasioned betwixt the church and lay patrons; with observations on the arguments for Restoring them in 1711*, np. 1711

Defoe, Daniel, *Memoir of the Church of Scotland in Four Periods*, London: 1717

Erskine, Ebenezer, *The testimony and contendings of the Rev Mr Alexander Hamilton, one of the ministers of the gospel at Stirling, gagainst the violent settlement of Mr James Mackie in the parish of St Ninians*, Edinburgh: 1736.

Farquhar, J., Osborn, W., Melville, R., Bisset, J., (signatories), *A fuller and truer state of the case of the parish of Old Machar*, np., 1730

Farquhar, J., Osborn, W., Melville, R., Bisset, J., (signatories), *The state of the case of the parish of New Machar and Mr. Thomas Ray and the conduct of the presbytery of Aberdeen in relation to there*, np. 1730.

Gibb, Adam, *The present truth: a display of the Secession Testimony; in the three periods of the rise, state and maintenance of that Testimony*, Edinburgh: 1774

Gordon, James, *The state and duty of the Church of Scotland, especially with respect to the settlement of ministers set in a just light*, Edinburgh: 1732.

Grant, Sir Francis, *Reasons in Defence of the Standing Laws about the Right of Presentation in Patronages*, np.1703

Grant, William (later Lord Prestongrange), *Remarks on the state of the Church of Scotland with respect to Patronages, and with reference to a bill now depending before Parliament*, London: 1736.

Grant, William, *The case of the heritors, elders and other parishioners of Renfrew: their complaint to the General Assembly, 8 May 1730*, np. 1730

Hutcheson, Francis, *Considerations on Patronages addressed to the Gentlemen of Scotland*, Glasgow: 1735. reprinted 1774.

Logan, George, *A modest and humble enquiry concerning the right and power of electing and calling ministers to vacant churches*, Edinburgh: 1732.

Logan, George, *The public testimony of above 1600 Christian people against the overture of the General Assembly 1731 made more publick and set in its due light being a full confutation of their arguments adduced for the divine right of popular elections,* Edinburgh: 1733.

Lowe, Andrew, *A Vindication of the Church of Scotland from the Groundless Aspersions of Mr. William Dugud,* np. 1714

[George McKenzie, earl of Cromartie], *The Scottish Toleration truly stated in a letter to a peer* London: 1712

MacMillan, John, "Protestation, declinature and appeal, 24 September 1708," in *The covenants and the covenanters; covenants, sermons and documents of the covenanted reformation,* ed., James Kerr, Edinburgh: 1895

[Morer, Thomas, Sage, John, Munro, Alexander], *An account of the present persecution of the church in Scotland in several letters,* London: 1690

[Munro, Alexander], *An apology for the clergy of Scotland chiefly opposed to the censures, calumnies and accusations of a late presbyterian vindicator in a letter to a friend wherein his vanity, partiality and sophistry are modestly reproved,* London: 1692

Murray, Archibald, *The state of the case of the parish of Old Machar,* np. 1730

Murray, Archibald, *The case of Mr. Thomas Ray, minister of the gospel at New Machar,* np. 1730

Park, Robert, *The Rights and Liberties of the Church asserted and vindicated against the pretended right and usurpation of Patronage,* Edinburgh: 1689

"Philumen Scotsman," *Grange: or, the schemists on calling of ministers and presentations in Scotland,* i, *On calls,* Edinburgh: 1735.

[Rule, Gilbert], *A true representation of presbyterian government wherein a short and clear account is given of the principles of them that own it. The common objections answered and some other things opened that concern it in the present circumstances by a friend to that interest.* Edinburgh: 1690

[Sage, John], *An account of the late establishment of presbyterian government by the parliament of Scotland, anno 1690, together with the methods by which it was settled.* London: 1693.

Sage, John, *Fundamental Charter of Presbytery as it hath lately been established in the Kingdom of Scotland, Examin'd and Disprov'd,* London: 1695

[?Wallace, Robert], "Some Good Hints with respect to Patronages of Churches". [undated] E.U., Laing MSS., II, 620.29,

Willison, John, *A Fair and Impartial Testimony against the Defections of the National Church,* Edinburgh: 1744

Wright, William, *The negative discussed in two parts,* Glasgow: 1721.

Articles and Essays

Dodgshon, R.A., "Farming in Roxburghshire and Berwickshire on the eve of Improvement", *SHR.,* Vol.54. 1975

Dunlop, A.I., "The General Session: A Controversy of 1720," in *RSCHS,* Vol.13, 1957-59

Fagg, Jane B.,"'Complaints and clamours': the ministry of Adam Fergusson, 1700-1754," *RSCHS,* 1994, xxv, part 2,

Ferguson, W., "The Problems of the Kirk in the West Highlands and Islands in the 18th. Century", *RSCHS,* Vol. 17

Forrester, DM., "Adam Gib, the Anti-Burgher", *RSCHS,* vol.7, 1940, 141-154.

Foster, W. Roland, "A Constant Platt Achieved: Provision for the Ministry, 1600-1638" in, *Reformation and Revolution: Essays presented to the Very Rev Hugh Watt.* ed. Duncan Shaw. Edinburgh: 1967

Glassey, Lionel, "William II and the Settlement of Religion in Scotland, 1688-1690." *RSCHS*, Vol.XXIII, Pt.3, 1989.

Hannay, R.K. and Watson, G.P.H., "The Building of the Parliament House." in *The Book of the Old Edinburgh Club*, vol. XIII. 1924.

Jones, Clyve, "The Scheme Lords, the Neccessitous Lords, and the Scots Lords: The Earl of Oxford's Management and the 'Party of the Crown' in the House of Lords, 1711-1714", Article 5 in *Party and Management in Parliament, 1660-1784*, ed. Clyve Jones. LUP: 1984.

Landsman, Ned C., "Liberty, piety and patronage: the social context of contested clerical calls in eighteenth-century Glasgow," in *The Glasgow Enlightenment*, eds., Andrew Hook and RB. Sher, East Linton: 1995

"Lochmaben Council minutes," ed., J.B. Wilson in *The transactions of the Dumfries and Galloway Natural History and Antiquarian Society*, 3rd. series, lii, 1977

Maxwell, Thomas, "The Church union attempt at the General Assembly of 1692," in *Reformation and Revolution*, 212-57

Murdoch, Alexander, "The Importance of Being Edinburgh: Management and Opposition in Edinburgh Politics, 1746-1784", in *SHR*, Vol.LXII, 1: No.173: April 1983,

Raffe, Alasdair, "Episcopalian polemic, the London printing press and Anglo-Scottish divergence in the 1690s", *Journal of Scottish Historical Studies*, 26. 2006

Robertson, John, "An elusive sovereignty. The course of the Union debate in Scotland 1698-1707," in *A union for empire; political thought and the British union of 1707*, ed., John Robertson, Cambridge: 1995

Riley, PWJ., "The Formation of the Scottish Ministry of 1703", *SHR*, Vol.44.

Sefton, H.R., "Robert Wallace: An Early Moderate", *RSCHS.*, Vol. 16, 1966-68,

Sefton, H.R., "Lord Ilay and Patrick Cuming: A Study in Eighteenth-Century Ecclesiastical Management.", *RSCHS*, Vol.xix, 1977, 203-16,

Sher, R.B., "Moderates, Managers and Popular Politics in Mid-Eighteenth Century Edinburgh: The Drysdale 'Bustle' of the 1760s," in *New Perspectives on the Politics and Culture of Early Modern Scotland*, ed. J. Dwyer et al., John Donald: 1982

Sher, RB. and Murdoch, A., "Patronage and Party in the Church of Scotland, 1750-1800", in *Church, Politics and Society: Scotland 1408-1929*, ed. N. MacDougall, John Donald, Edinburgh: 1983

Simpson, J.M.,"Who Steered the Gravy Train?" in *Scotland in the Age of Improvement*, eds. N.T. Phillipson, and R. Mitchison, Edinburgh University Press, 1970.

Smith, Peter M., "The advowson: the history and development of a most peculiar property," in *Ecclesiastical Law Journal*, xxvi, 2000, 320-39.

Smith, T.B., "The union of 1707 as fundamental law," reprinted from *Public Law*, Summer 1957

Stephen, Jeffrey, "Defending the Revolution: The Church of Scotland and the Scottish Parliament, 1689-95", *SHR*, vol. 89, April 2010, 19-53

Szechi, D., "The Politics of 'Persecution': Scots Episcopalian Toleration and the Harley Ministry, 1710-12", article in *Toleration and Persecution, Studies in Church History*, W.J. Sheils, ed., vol.xxi, 1984.

Szechi, D., "Some Insights on the Scottish MPs and Peers Returned in the 1710 Election", *SHR.,*LX,1: No.169: April 1981

The Scottish Chronicle, series of articles entitled "A Ten Years' Conflict", 15 June 1906 - 16 November 1906;

Whyte, Ian, "Rural transformation and lowland society," in *Modern Scottish History 1707 to the present*, eds., A. Cooke, I. Donnachie, A. Macsween, C.A. Whatley, East Linton: 1998

Reference Works

An Introduction to Scottish Legal History, ed. G.C.H. Paton, Stair Society Publications, Book 20, Edinburgh: 1958

Baron David Hume's Lectures, 1786-1822, ed. G.C.H. Paton, Stair Society Publications, Vol.VI, Book 19, Edinburgh: 1958

Chamberlayne, John, *Present State of Great Britain*, London: 1755

Cobbett, W., *Parliamentary History of England*, London: 1806-12

Connell, John, *Treatise on the Law of Scotland Respecting Erection, etc. of Parishes*, Edinburgh: 1818

Dalrymple, Sir Hew, *Decisions of the Court of Session, 1698-1718*, Edinburgh: 1792

Dictionary of National Biography

Duncan, J.M., *Treatise on the Parochial and Ecclesiastical Law of Scotland"*, Edinburgh: 1869

Dundas, J., *Abridgement of the Acts of the General Assembly of the Church of Scotland, 1638-1720*, Edinburgh: 1721

Dunlop, Alex., *Parochial Law*, 3rd edn., Blackwood: 1841

Fergusson, Sir James, of Kilkerran, *The 16 Peers of Scotland, 1707-1959*, OUP: 1960

Foster, J., *Members of Parliament, Scotland, 1357-1882*, London: 1882

MacKenzie, Colin, *Notes relating to the Procedure in the Elections of the Representatives in the British Parliament of the Peers of Scotland*, Edinburgh: 1818

MacVeigh, James, *The Scottish Family History*, 3 vols., Dumfries: 1891

More, J.S., *Lectures on the Law of Scotland*, 2 vols., Edinburgh: 1864

Morren, N., *Annals of the General Assembly of the Church of Scotland, 1739-66*, 2 vols., Edinburgh: 1838-40

Omond, G.W.T., *The Lord Advocates of Scotland*, 2 vols. David Douglas. Edinburgh: 1883

Parliamentary Papers, "Report from the Select Committee on Church Patronage (Scotland), with the Minutes of Evidence", vol.v, 1834.

Ramsay, J., *Scotland and Scotsmen in the Eighteenth Century*, 2 vols. Edinburgh: 1888

Romney Sedgwick, *The House of Commons, 1715-1754*, 2 vols. HMSO: 1970

Scott, Hew, *Fasti Ecclesiae Scoticanae*, 7 vols., Edinburgh: 1915

Steuart, Walter, of Pardovan, "Collections and Observations Methodized, Concerning the Worship, Discipline and Government of the Church of Scotland", (c. 1709). Published in *A Copious and Comprehensive Summary of the Laws and Regulations of the Church of Scotland from 1560-1850*. G and R King, Aberdeen: 1850

Tytler, Alexander, *Decisions of the Court of Session*, Vol. III, 1738-1770, Creech, Edinburgh: 1778

Warrick, John, *The Moderators of the Church of Scotland, 1690-1740*, Edinburgh: 1913

Wilson, John, *Index to the Acts and Proceedings of the General Assembly of the Church of Scotland*, Blackwood, Edinburgh: 1863

Unpublished Theses

Clark, I.D.L.,"Moderatism and the Moderate Party in the Church of Scotland, 1752-1805," Cambridge Phd. Diss. 1964

Graham, R.M., "Ecclesiastical Discipline in the Church of Scotland, 1690-1730", Phd. diss. Glasgow 1964

Muirhead, A.T.N., "Religion, Politics and Society in Stirling during the Ministry of Ebenezer Erskine, 1731-54", Stirling University M.Litt. diss. 1983

Phillipson, N.T., "The Scots Whigs and the Reform of the Court of Session 1780-1830", Cambridge Phd. Diss. 1967

Pomeroy, Webb D., "John Willison of Dundee 1680-1750," PhD diss., Edinburgh, 1953

Scott R.H., "The Politics and Administration of Scotland, 1725-48", Edinburgh Phd. diss., 1982

Sefton, H.R., "The Early Development of Moderatism in the Church of Scotland", Glasgow Phd. diss. 1962

Shaw, J.S., "Civic Leadership and the Edinburgh Lawyers in Eighteenth Century Scotland," Stirling Phd. diss., 1979

Smith, Norah, "The literary career and achievement of Robert Wallace (1697-1771)," PhD diss. Edinburgh: 1973

Whitley, Laurence A.B., `The operation of lay patronage in the church of Scotland from the Act of 1712 until 1746, with particular reference to the presbyteries of Duns, Edinburgh and Brechin', PhD. diss. St Andrews 1993

Books

Allan, Archibald, *History of Channelkirk*, Edinburgh: 1900

Allan, David, *Scotland in the Eighteenth Century: Union and Enlightenment*, Pearson Education: 2002

Arnot, Hugo, *History of Edinburgh*, Edinburgh: 1788, Book II,

Atholl, John, 7th. Duke, *Chronicles of the Atholl and Tullibardine Families*, Edinburgh: 1908

Bain, Robert, *History of Ross*, Dingwall: 1899

Brown, JTT., *Cambuslang and its Ministers*, Glasgow: 1884

Brown, Calum, *The Social History of Religion in Scotland since 1730*, Methuen, London: 1987

Brown, John, *An historical account of the rise and progress of the Secession,* Edinburgh: 1775.

Buchan, J.W.. and Paton, H., *History of Peebleshire*, Glasgow: 1927

Burleigh, J.H.S., *A Church History of Scotland*, Edinburgh: 1960

Burnet, JB., *The Kirks of Cowie and Fetteresso*, 1933

Burns, Thomas, *The Benefice Lectures*, Edinburgh: 1905

Chitnis, A., *The Scottish Enlightenment*, London: 1976

Collins, G.N.M., *The Heritage of our Fathers*. Knox Press, Edinburgh: 1974

Cormack, A.A., *Teinds and Agriculture,- An Historical Survey*, Oxford University Press:1930

Cormack, AA., *Susan Carnegie, 1744-1821*, Aberdeen: 1966

Coutts, J., *History of Glasgow University*, Glasgow: 1909

Craig-Brown, T., *History of Selkirkshire or chronicles of Ettrick Forest*, Edinburgh: 1886

Cranna, John, *Fraserburgh: Past and Present*, Aberdeen: 1914

Cunningham, J., *Church History of Scotland*, Edinburgh:1859, vol 2.

Douglas, J.D., *Light in the north*, Exeter: 1964

Drummond, Andrew L., *The Kirk and the Continent*. Edinburgh 1956

Drummond, AL. and Bulloch, J, *The Scottish Church, 1688-1843*, St Andrew Press: 1973

Dunlop, AI., *William Carstares and the Kirk by Law Established*, St. Andrew Press Edinburgh: 1967

Eadie, J., "The Life and Times of the Rev William Wilson, AM.", contained in *Lives of Erskine, Wilson and Gillespie, Fathers of the U.P. Church*, by J. Harper, J. Eadie and W. Lindsay, Edinburgh: 1849

Emerson, R.L., *Professors, Patronage and Politics, The Aberdeen Universities in the Eighteenth Century*, Aberdeen University Press, 1992.

Ferguson, William, *Scotland, 1689 to the Present*, Oliver & Boyd: 1968

Foord, A.S., *His Majesty's Opposition*, London: 1975

Graham, H.G., *The Social Life of Scotland in the Eighteenth Century*, London: 1901

Handley, J.E., *Scottish Farming in the Eighteenth Century*, London: 1953

Herman, Arthur, *The Scottish enlightenment: The Scots' invention of the modern world*, Harper Perennial, London: 2006.

Hetherington, W.M. *History of the Church of Scotland*, Edinburgh: 1848

Jervise, A., *History and Traditions of the Land of the Lindsays*, Edinburgh:1882

Lachman, David C., *The Marrow controversy*, Edinburgh: 1988

Leneman, Leah, *Living in Atholl, 1685-1785*, Edinburgh University Press: 1986

Lindsay, Lord, *Lives of the Lindsays*, 2 vols. London: 1858

Lynch, Michael, *Edinburgh and the Reformation*, John Donald: 1981

MacGill, W., *Old Ross-shire and Scotland, as seen in the Tain and Balnagowan documents* Inverness: 1909

MacInnes, John, *The Evangelical Movement in the Highlands of Scotland, 1688-1800*, Aberdeen University Press: 1951

McIntosh, John R., *Church and theology in Enlightenment Scotland: The Popular Party, 1740-1800*, East Linton: 1998

MacKay, EJG., *Memoir of Sir James Dalrymple, 1st Viscount Stair*, Edmonston and Douglas, Edinburgh: 1873

Maitland, William, *History of Edinburgh*, Edinburgh: 1753.

Makey, Walter, *The Church of the Covenant. (1637-1651)*, John Donald: 1979

Mangles, J.L., *Troqueer Parish Church*, Dumfries: 1971

Marshall, Dorothy, *Eighteenth Century England*, Longman, London: 1962

Mathieson, W.L., *Scotland and the Union*, Glasgow: 1905

Mitchison, Rosalind, *Lordship to Patronage*, Arnold: 1983

Munro, A.M., *Memorials of the provosts of Aberdeen, 1272-1897*, Aberdeen: 1897

Murdoch, A., *The People Above: Politics and Administration in Mid-Eighteenth Century Scotland*, John Donald: 1980

Noble, John, *Religious Life in Ross*, ed. JK. Cameron and D. MacLean, Edinburgh: 1909

Owen, J.B., *The Rise of the Pelhams*, London: 1957

Patronage, Presbyterian Union and Home Work of the Church of Scotland: A Chronicle of the General Assembly of 1870. Wm. Blackwood, Edinburgh:1870

Paley R., and P. Seaward. *Honour, interest and power: an illustrated history of the House of Lords, 1660-1715.* Boydell Press: 2010

Phillipson, N.T. and Mitchison R., *Scotland in the Age of Improvement*, EUP: 1970

Riley, P.W.J., *The English Ministers and Scotland, 1707-1727*, London: 1964

Riley, P.W.J., *The Union of England and Scotland, A study in Anglo-Scottish politics of the eighteenth century*, MUP: 1978

Riley, P.W.J., *King William and the Scottish Politicians*, John Donald, Edinburgh: 1979

Robertson, William, *Proceedings Relating to the Peerage of Scotland*, Edinburgh: 1790

Roger, William, *The Feudal Forms of Scotland, Viewed Historically*, Constable, Edinburgh: 1857

Roughead, William, *The Trial of Captain Porteous*, Notable Scottish Trials Series, Wm. Hodge: 1909.

Roxburgh, K.B.E., *Thomas Gillespie and the origins of the Relief Church in 18th. Century Scotland*, Berne: 1999

Shaw, J.S., *The Management of Scottish Society, 1707-1764*, John Donald: 1983

Sher, R.B., *Church and University in the Scottish Enlightenment*, EUP: 1985

Smith, T.B., *British Justice: The Scottish Contribution*, London: 1961

Smith, John Guthrie, *The parish of Strathblane*, Glasgow: 1886

Smout, T.C., *A History of the Scottish People, 1560-1830*, Collins, London: 1969

Story, R.H., ed., *The Church of Scotland: Past and Present*, 5 vols., London: 1890.

Struthers, J., *History of Scotland from the Union to 1748*, 2 vols., 1827-8

Sunter, R.M., *Patronage and Politics in Scotland, 1707-1832*, John Donald: 1986.

Szechi, D., *Jacobitism and Tory Politics, 1710-1714*, John Donald 1984

Tait, J., *Border Church Life*, 2 Vols., np. 1911

Temple, William, *The Thanage of Fermartyn*, Wyllie, Aberdeen: 1894

Thomson, MA., *Secretaries of State, 1681-1782*, OUP: 1932

Wellwood, Henry Moncrieff, *Account of the Life and Writings of John Erskine*, Edinburgh: 1818

Whetstone, A.E., *Scottish County Government in the 18th. and 19th. Centuries.* Edinburgh 1981

Whitley, Elizabeth Y., *The Two Kingdoms*, Edinburgh: 1977

Williams, Basil, *Carteret and Newcastle, A contrast in contemporaries*, Frank Cass: 1966.

Williamson, A., *Glimpses of Peebles, or Forgotten Chapters in its History*, Selkirk: 1895

Wilson, John, *Dunning*, Crieff: 1906.

Wilson, J., *The Churches of Lochmaben*, Dumfries: 1971.

Subject/Name Index

Printed in Great Britain
by Amazon.co.uk, Ltd.,
Marston Gate.